Tax Law and Social Norms in Mandatory Palestine and Israel

This book describes how a social-norms model of taxation rose and fell in British-ruled Palestine and the State of Israel in the mid-twentieth century. Such a model, in which non-legal means were used to foster compliance, appeared in the tax system created by the Jewish community in 1940s Palestine, and was later adopted by the new Israeli state in the 1950s. It gradually disappeared in subsequent decades as law and its agents, lawyers and accountants, came to play a larger role in the process of taxation. By describing the historical interplay between formal and informal tools for creating compliance, *Tax Law and Social Norms in Mandatory Palestine and Israel* sheds new light on our understanding of the relationship between law and other methods of social control, and reveals the complex links between taxation and citizenship.

Assaf Likhovski is a professor of law and legal history at Tel Aviv University Faculty of Law. He is the author of *Law and Identity in Mandate Palestine* (2006), which was awarded the Yonathan Shapiro Best Book Award in Israel Studies.

See the Studies in Legal History series website at studiesinlegalhistory.org

STUDIES IN LEGAL HISTORY

Editors

Robert W. Gordon, *Taming the Past: Essays on Law and History and History in Law*

Paul Garfinkel, *Criminal Law in Liberal and Fascist Italy*

Michelle A. McKinley, *Fractional Freedoms: Slavery, Intimacy, and Legal Mobilization in Colonial Lima, 1600–1700*

Mitra Sharafi, *Law and Identity in Colonial South Asia: Parsi Legal Culture, 1772–1947*

Karen M. Tani, *States of Dependency: Welfare, Rights, and American Governance, 1935–1972*

Stefan Jurasinski, *The Old English Penitentials and Anglo- Saxon Law*

Felice Batlan, *Women and Justice for the Poor: A History of Legal Aid, 1863–1945*

Sophia Z. Lee, *The Workplace Constitution from the New Deal to the New Right*

Michael A. Livingston, *The Fascists and the Jews of Italy: Mussolini's Race Laws, 1938–1943*

Tax Law and Social Norms in Mandatory Palestine and Israel

ASSAF LIKHOVSKI

Tel Aviv University

CAMBRIDGE
UNIVERSITY PRESS

CAMBRIDGE
UNIVERSITY PRESS

University Printing House, Cambridge CB2 8BS, United Kingdom

One Liberty Plaza, 20th Floor, New York, NY 10006, USA

477 Williamstown Road, Port Melbourne, VIC 3207, Australia

4843/24, 2nd Floor, Ansari Road, Daryaganj, Delhi – 110002, India

79 Anson Road, #06-04/06, Singapore 079906

Cambridge University Press is part of the University of Cambridge.

It furthers the University's mission by disseminating knowledge in the pursuit of education, learning, and research at the highest international levels of excellence.

www.cambridge.org
Information on this title: www.cambridge.org/9781107176294
DOI: 10.1017/9781316816851

First published 2017

Printed in the United States of America by Sheridan Books, Inc.

A catalog record for this publication is available from the British Library.

Library of Congress Cataloging-in-Publication Data
Names: Likhovski, Assaf, author.
Title: Tax law and social norms in mandatory Palestine and Israel / Assaf Likhovski, Tel Aviv University.
Description: Cambridge, United Kingdom; New York, NY, USA: Cambridge University Press, 2017. | Series: Studies in legal history | Includes bibliographical references and index.
Identifiers: LCCN 2017003107 | ISBN 9781107176294 (hardback)
Subjects: LCSH: Taxation – Law and legislation – Israel – History – 20th century. | Taxation – Law and legislation – Palestine – History – 20th century. | Taxation – Israel – History – 20th century. | Taxation – Palestine – History – 20th century. | BISAC: HISTORY / Middle East / General.
Classification: LCC KMK2790.L55 2017 | DDC 343.569404–dc23
LC record available at https://lccn.loc.gov/2017003107

ISBN 978-1-107-17629-4 Hardback

In memory of my mother

Contents

Figures

Tables

Acknowledgments

Over the years it took me to write this book, I have been fortunate to be surrounded by many generous colleagues and friends at Tel Aviv University and beyond. For their advice, assistance, and feedback I thank: David Assaf, Steve Bank, Lior Ben-David, Yael Berda, Yishai Blank, Leora Bilsky, Michael Birnhack, Natan Brun, Tsilly Dagan, Linda Darling, Talia Diskin, David Duff, Arye Edrei, Mirit Eyal-Cohen, Judith Freedman, David Gliksberg, Dror Goldberg, Tom Green, Daphna Hacker, Adam Hofri-Winogradow, Sandy Kedar, Yanni Kotsonis, Roy Kreitner, Shai Lavi, Anat Leibler, Nomi Levenkron, Michael Livingston, Guy Lurie, Doreen Lustig, Yoram Margalioth, Avital Margalit, Ajay Mehrotra, Noga Morag-Levine, Amihai Radzyner, Anat Rosenberg, Avi Rubin, Lena Salaymeh, David Schorr, Ido Shahar, John Tiley, Chris Tomlins, Dennis Ventry, Steven Wilf, Ursula Wokoeck, Assaf Yaakov, Neta Ziv, and Eric Zolt.

I received many important comments on earlier drafts of the chapters of this book when I presented them at workshops, faculty seminars, and conferences at Bar-Ilan University, Ben-Gurion University, University of Cambridge, Haifa University, the Hebrew University, the Institute for Advanced Studies in Jerusalem, Monash University, Netanya College, NYU, Princeton University, Stanford University, Tel Aviv University, UBC, UCLA, and USC, as well as at conferences of the Association for Israel Studies, the American Society for Legal History, the Canadian Law and Society Association, the German Legal Historians Association, the Israel Economic Association, the Israeli Law and History Association, the Israeli Law and Society Association, the Israeli Political Science Association, and the Law and Society Association.

I owe a debt of gratitude to my research assistants at Tel Aviv University, Roii Ball, Rivka Brot, Katarzyna Czerwonogóra, Yoni Filc, Eden Lang, Danny Maggen, Omri Marian, Adar Ortal, Yael Plitman, Taghreed Qaadan, Aviram Shahal, Dan Wiesenfeld, and Amit Yariv. I am especially obliged to my current research assistant, Shani Schnitzer, who assisted me in preparing the manuscript for publication and did so with utmost efficiency, thoroughness, and intelligence. I would also like to thank the staff at the many libraries and archives I used, including Shir Issar, Batya Leshem, Fanny Mordechai, Gilad Natan, Irina Rozenfeld, Michal Tomer, Shimri Salomon, and Hila Zahavi, as well as Gila Haimovic and Adam Vital for their editorial assistance, and Shai Halevi for some of the photographs used in this book (Figures 2.1, 2.2, 4.2, 4.3, 5.1, 6.1, and 6.2). Special thanks are due to Amanda Dale and Lorainne Slipper for their excellent editorial work on the final version of the manuscript. For their financial support I would like to thank the David Berg Foundation Institute for Law and History at Tel Aviv University, the Cegla Center for Interdisciplinary Research of the Law at Tel Aviv University, the Israel Science Foundation (grants 510/04, 1609/07, and 337/10), the Marc Rich Foundation, and the Tel Aviv University Faculty of Law.

I am indebted to Bloomsbury Publishing Plc., the Cegla Center for Interdisciplinary Research of the Law, and John Wiley and Sons for their permission to use materials from the following articles in this book: "Formalism and Israeli Anti-Avoidance Doctrines in the 1950s and 1960s," published in *Studies in the History of Tax Law*, ed. John Tiley (Oxford: Hart, 2004), 1: 339–77; "'Training in Citizenship': Tax Compliance and Modernity," *Law and Social Inquiry* 32 (2007): 665–700, and "Is Tax Law Culturally Specific? Lessons from the History of Income Tax Law in Mandatory Palestine," *Theoretical Inquiries in Law* 11 (2010): 725–63. Figures 2.1, 2.2, 4.2, 4.3, 5.1, and 6.2 are published by permission of the Museum of Taxes, Jerusalem. Figure 3.1 is published by permission of the Nahum Gutman Museum of Art. Figure 3.2 is reproduced from the Haganah Historical Archives collection. Figure 4.1 is published by permission of the Israel Film Service. Figure 6.1 is published by permission of Nissan Bar-Dayan.

I follow in the footsteps of two pioneers of the study of Israeli tax history: Harold C. Wilkenfeld, who chronicled the birth of the Israeli tax system, and Avraham Mandel, the founder of the Museum of Taxes in Jerusalem. I am grateful to Mira Dror, Mandel's heir as the director of the Museum of Taxes, who keeps the flame of the Museum burning despite the odds, and who kindly provided advice and access to rare materials preserved there. Ron Harris, Pnina Lahav, Menny Mautner, Orit Rozin, and Yoram Shachar, my friends and colleagues, have been a constant source of inspiration and encouragement. I cannot imagine my intellectual journey as an Israeli legal historian without their generous presence and support.

Michael Lobban was an outstanding academic editor, and the book greatly benefited from his remarkable insights, wisdom, and advice. The two readers of my manuscript for Cambridge University Press wrote perceptive and detailed reviews containing many extremely valuable suggestions that greatly improved the book. I would also like to thank Sally Gordon and Holly Brewer who, together with Michael, are the coeditors of the Studies in Legal History series, and Lew Bateman, Deborah Gershenowitz, Kristina Deusch, Matt Sweeney, and the rest of the editorial team at Cambridge University Press, as well as Helen Flitton, the project manager of this book.

My greatest debt over the years has been to my family, to my late parents, Eliahu and Ruth Likhovski, to my sister Michal, and to my brother Edo, an endless source of optimism for me in this and many other tasks. My children, Yotam, Hagar, and Daniel, patiently endured my strange infatuation with tax history, and I love them for this and for everything else. Finally, I would like to thank my wife, Orly Erez-Likhovski. *She openeth her mouth with wisdom; and in her tongue is the law of kindness.*

Note on Transliteration

Commonly used Hebrew words are not transliterated (*Haaretz*, and not *ha-Arets*). I use ' for the Hebrew letter *'ayin*. I use ' for the Hebrew letter *alef* (in circumstances where its omission would be ambiguous). I use the letter h for the Hebrew letters *he* and *het*.

Abbreviations

ACAA	Association of Certified Accountants and Auditors
AG	Attorney General
AO	Assessing Officer
AOLE	Assessing Officer for Large Enterprises
CA	Civil Appeal
CO	Colonial Office
CrimA	Criminal Appeal
CrimC	Criminal Case
CSR	corporate social responsibility
CZA	Central Zionist Archives, Jerusalem
DK	*Divrey ha-Knesset*
DLBT	Director of Land Betterment Tax
Drayton	*The Laws of Palestine: In Force on the 31st Day of December, 1933*, ed. Robert Harry Drayton (London: Waterlow and Sons, 1934)
HA	Haganah Historical Archives, Tel Aviv
HCJ	High Court of Justice
HH	*Hatsa'ot Hok*
I£	Israeli pound
ICPAI	Institute of Certified Public Accountants in Israel
ISA	Israel State Archives, Jerusalem
ITA	Income Tax Appeal
JIA	Jabotinsky Institute Archive, Tel Aviv
JP	*Jerusalem Post*

KA	Knesset Archive, Jerusalem
LSI	*Laws of the State of Israel*
MK	Member of the Knesset
MT	Museum of Taxes, Jerusalem
NLI	National Library of Israel, Jerusalem
P£	Palestine pound
PCA	Privy Council Appeal
PG	*Palestine Gazette*
PD	*Piskey Din*
PDE	*Piskey Din Ezrahiyim*
PLR	*Palestine Law Reports*
PM	*Psakim Mehoziyim*
PP	*Palestine Post*
RH	*Ro'eh ha-Heshbon*
RK	*Ha-Riv'on le-Kalkalah*
RYM	*Ha-Riv'on ha-Yisre'eli le-Misim*
Sherut	*Sherut: Divrey 'Ovdim be-Sherutey ha-Misim*
SH	*Sefer ha-Hukim*
TNA	The National Archives, London
VAT	value-added taxation
YP	*Agaf Mas Hakhnasah: Yedi'on Pnimi*

Introduction: The Intimate Fiscal State

In 1905 the farmers of Be'er Tuvia, a small Jewish village in the southern part of Ottoman-ruled Palestine, wrote a letter in which they complained about the collection of the Ottoman produce tax, the tithe. The official rate of the tithe at the time was 12.63 percent. However, the actual rate paid by the farmers of Be'er Tuvia was between 30 and 50 percent. The tax was collected using a system of tax farming. A local Arab notable leased the right to collect the tax from the government. Although he was supposed to be under government supervision, he and his assistants, said the farmers, "do as they wish," and "steal as much as they desire of our grain, in addition to all that they eat during the threshing season, they, and their servants, and the servants of their servants, their horses and camels, a large locust-like camp." Complaints to the local authorities (who sat in Gaza) did not help, because "the government [officials] of Gaza are evil and corrupt."[1]

---

[1] Avraham 'Etz-Hadar, *Ilanot: Le-Toldot ha-Yishuv be-Erets Yisrael 1830–1920* (Tel Aviv: Dfus Niv, 1967), 216–18. On the date of this letter, see Imanu'el Hareuveni, *Leksikon Erets-Yisrael* (Tel Aviv: Yedioth Ahronoth, 1999), 75. The letter is discussed in Haim Gerber, *Ottoman Rule in Jerusalem, 1890–1914* (Berlin: Klaus Schwarz, 1985), 168–9. On the rate of the tithe in the late nineteenth century see George Young, *Corps de Droit Ottoman* (Oxford: Clarendon Press, 1905–06), 5:303; Israel State Archives (ISA), Record Group 2, M 132/8, Report of the Rural Taxation Machinery Committee, June 22, 1933, appendix I, 4; Martin Bunton, *Colonial Land Policies in Palestine, 1917–1936* (Oxford: Oxford University Press, 2007), 141.

The letter written by the farmers of Be'er Tuvia was not part of a legal process in the local Ottoman courts or administrative bodies. Nor did the complaint appear in a petition sent to the Ottoman sultan in Istanbul.[2] Instead, the farmers chose another addressee: Michal Leib Katz, a Hungarian Jew living in Palestine.[3] Katz was a subject of the Austro-Hungarian Empire, and as such he enjoyed the protection of the Austrian consul in Jerusalem. Such protection was part of the capitulation regime – grants of privileges made by the Ottoman Empire to citizens of various European countries.[4] The farmers of Be'er Tuvia asked Katz to become the formal owner of their land, hoping that his foreign nationality would enable him to defend them from the rapacious tax collectors, which indeed proved to be the case.

Notably, there were no lawyers or courts involved in resolving the farmers' tax dispute. In their distress, the farmers did not turn to a lawyer to represent them in court in their case against the tax collectors. This was a result of the fact that, in the tax system to which these farmers were subject, legal norms played only a minor role, and the professional agents using legal norms – lawyers – were almost totally absent.[5]

During the First World War, Palestine was occupied by the British, who continued to tax the farmers of Palestine with little resort to formal law, its agents, or institutions. Edwin Samuel, a young District Officer in British-ruled Palestine of the 1920s, recalled in his autobiography that his:

---

[2] On petitions to the sultan see Yuval Ben-Bassat, "In Search of Justice: Petitions Sent from Palestine to Istanbul from the 1870's Onwards," *Turcica* 41 (2009): 89–114; Yuval Ben-Bassat, *Petitioning the Sultan: Protests and Justice in Late Ottoman Palestine* (London: I. B. Tauris, 2013).

[3] On Katz see David Tidhar, *Entsiklopedyah le-Halutsey ha-Yishuv u-Vonav: Dmuyot u-Tmunot* (Tel Aviv: Sifriyat Rishonim, 1950), 4:1637–8.

[4] See generally, Maurits H. van den Boogert, *The Capitulations and the Ottoman Legal System: Qadis, Consuls and Beratlıs in the 18th Century* (Leiden: Brill, 2005), 7–9, 63–115.

[5] I use the term legal norms in the traditional positivist sense, referring to written norms created and enforced by formally authorized and centralized state institutions (legislature, the courts, the police). On professional lawyers in late Ottoman Palestine see Chapter 5, text to nn. 45–6.

most unpleasant task was trying to collect current taxes, and astronomic arrears, from heavily-indebted [Arab] peasants ... I tried to collect [these taxes] by fearsome threats in broken Arabic but on biblical models. "If you pay now what I ask, oh, my children, I shall be as dew upon your fields, as honey on your lips. But if you do *not*, then I shall come as a wolf in your sheep-fold by night and you shall be consumed as by fire on your threshing-floor." When I had got their eyes fairly popping out of their heads, I told them to scurry home and bring something on account.[6]

Over time, the mode of tax assessment and collection evident in both this story and that of the farmers of Be'er Tuvia gradually gave way, in British-ruled Palestine and later in the State of Israel, to a different kind of taxation system, one that relied more heavily on law and its professional agents. However, the rise in the use of legal norms in the process of taxation was not the only change that occurred. It was accompanied in the middle decades of the twentieth century by the use of "softer" means to ensure compliance, in the form of social norms, that is "social attitudes of approval and disapproval, specifying what ought to be done and what ought not to be done."[7] These norms were generated by the state as part of a broader attempt to induce taxpayers to provide information on their economic affairs and pay their tax without the threat of criminal sanctions, relying instead on loyalty, a sense of duty, and a feeling of individual and collective civic engagement, thus transforming taxpayers from disobedient subjects into cooperative citizens.

I call this kind of taxing regime *the intimate fiscal state*. This regime was "intimate" in that it gathered detailed information on the economic affairs of its taxpayers. It was also "intimate" because it sought to create a familylike, direct, and close relationship between itself and its

---

[6] Edwin Samuel, *A Lifetime in Jerusalem: The Memoirs of the Second Viscount Samuel* (London: Vallentine Mitchell, 1970), 73–4.

[7] See Cass R. Sunstein, "Social Norms and Social Roles," *Columbia Law Review* 96 (1996): 903–68, 914. There is a large literature on the differences and similarities between legal and social norms. See, e.g., Matthias Baier, ed., *Social and Legal Norms: Towards a Socio-legal Understanding of Normativity* (Farnham: Ashgate, 2013); Gillian K. Hadfield and Barry R. Weingast, "Law without the State: Legal Attributes and the Coordination of Decentralized Collective Punishment," *Journal of Law and Courts* 1 (2013): 3–34.

taxpayers as a way of ensuring tax compliance. In this book, I tell the story of the rise, and subsequent decline, of the intimate fiscal state. The story is told by analyzing the history of taxation in late-Ottoman and British-ruled Palestine, as well as in the State of Israel after its independence in 1948, focusing specifically on income taxation and its norms.

Twentieth-Century Law

The story of the rise and decline of the intimate fiscal state offers a unique vantage point from which to understand the nature of law in twentieth-century states.[8] What characterizes law in such states? One account, reflecting the nature of continental law at the beginning of the twentieth century, associated twentieth-century legal systems with formal–rational law.[9] Another view, mainly describing Western states in the nineteenth and twentieth centuries, emphasized the appearance of sublegal, diffuse types of power, notably scientific and administrative

---

[8] One can also talk about "modern" states, but modernity is a notoriously problematic concept to define. See, e.g., C. A. Bayly, *The Birth of the Modern World: 1780–1914* (Oxford: Blackwell, 2004), 9–12; Frederick Cooper, *Colonialism in Question: Theory, Knowledge, History* (Berkeley: University of California Press, 2005), 113–49; "AHR Roundtable: Historians and the Question of 'Modernity'," *American Historical Review* 116 (2011): 631–751. On modernity in the Middle East see, e.g., Timothy Mitchell, *Rule of Experts: Egypt, Techno-Politics, Modernity* (Berkeley: University of California Press, 2002), 247–8; Keith David Watenpaugh, *Being Modern in the Middle East: Revolution, Nationalism, Colonialism, and the Arab Middle Class* (Princeton: Princeton University Press, 2006); Huri İslamoğlu and Peter C. Perdue, eds., *Shared Histories of Modernity: China, India and the Ottoman Empire* (New Delhi: Routledge, 2009).

[9] A "formal–rational" system is one based on general, abstract norms, logically derived from a limited set of principles, arranged in a gapless code that is created and mechanically applied by a special class of professionally trained jurists. See Max Weber, *Economy and Society*, eds. Guenther Roth and Claus Wittich (New York: Bedminster, 1968), 2:654–8, 2:789–92, 2:809–16, 2:852–5, 2:880–95, 3:976–8. For a discussion and critique, see Alan Hunt, *The Sociological Movement in Law* (Philadelphia: Temple University Press, 1978); Antony T. Kronman, *Max Weber* (Stanford: Stanford University Press, 1983); Joyce S. Sterling and Wilbert E. Moore, "Weber's Analysis of Legal Rationalization: A Critique and Constructive Modification," *Sociological Forum* 2 (1987): 67–89, 75–6. On the early modern roots of such systems see Assaf Likhovski, "Protestantism and the Rationalization of English Law: A Variation on a Theme by Weber," *Law and Society Review* 33 (1999): 365–91.

techniques designed to efficiently control and discipline individuals and entire populations. These techniques were associated with institutions such as prisons, hospitals, and schools.[10] These new types of power, it was argued, partly replaced and partly augmented law.[11]

Taxation is an important aspect of state action, and the tax office, no less than the prison, hospital, or school, is an important site where the changing nature of states and societies can be observed. Sociologists, political scientists, historians, and scholars of accounting have therefore linked the study of taxation and its history to broader debates about the nature and transformation of various state forms during the twentieth century.[12] However, the history of tax *law* is not usually a major focus

[10] See Michel Foucault, *Madness and Civilization: A History of Insanity in the Age of Reason*, trans. Richard Howard (London: Routledge, 1989); Michel Foucault, *Discipline and Punish: The Birth of the Prison*, 2nd edn (New York: Vintage Books, 1995); Michel Foucault, *"Society Must Be Defended": Lectures at the Collège de France, 1975–1976*, eds. Mauro Bertani and Alessandro Fontana, trans. David Macey (New York: Picador, 1997); Michel Foucault, *Security, Territory, Population: Lectures at the Collège de France, 1977–1978*, ed. Michel Senellart, trans. Graham Burchell (Basingstoke: Palgrave Macmillan, 2009). For a specific discussion of the nature of law in post-1945 neoliberal states, see Michel Foucault, *The Birth of Biopolitics: Lectures at the Collège de France, 1978–1979*, ed. Michel Senellart, trans. Graham Burchell (Basingstoke: Palgrave Macmillan, 2010). Historians have often questioned the accuracy of the historical narrative found in Foucault's works, arguing, for example, that pre-nineteenth-century states also used many of the techniques that Foucault associates with the nineteenth and twentieth centuries. See, e.g., Pieter Spierenburg, *The Spectacle of Suffering: Executions and the Evolution of Repression* (Cambridge: Cambridge University Press, 1984); Laura Engelstein, "Combined Underdevelopment: Discipline and the Law in Imperial and Soviet Russia," *American Historical Review* 98 (1993): 338–53; Edward Higgs, *The Information State in England* (London: Palgrave Macmillan, 2004). See also James C. Scott, *Seeing Like a State: How Certain Schemes to Improve the Human Condition Have Failed* (New Haven: Yale University Press, 1998).

[11] Foucault's views on the exact relationship of law and newer types of power (the disciplines and bio-power) are unclear. See, e.g., Foucault, *"Society Must Be Defended,"* 243; Foucault, *The Birth of Biopolitics*, 312–13; Foucault *Security, Territory, Population*, 6–10. See generally, Alan Hunt and Gary Wickham, *Foucault and Law: Towards a Sociology of Law as Governance* (London: Pluto Press, 1994); Ben Golder and Peter Fitzpatrick, *Foucault's Law* (New York: Routledge, 2009); Ben Golder, ed., *Re-reading Foucault: On Law, Power and Rights* (Abingdon: Routledge, 2012).

[12] For surveys of recent trends in fiscal sociology and fiscal history see Isaac William Martin, Ajay K. Mehrotra, and Monica Prasad, eds., *The New Fiscal*

of such studies. Yet one cannot fully understand the history of taxation without taking into account the history of tax law. When and how did law, courts, and lawyers become involved in the process of taxation, and how did this involvement change over time? What other tools for extracting taxes from taxpayers did twentieth-century states use, and how did the use of these tools impact tax law? How were taxation and its law related to changing notions of civic identity and citizenship?

In this book, I answer these questions by analyzing the history of taxation and its law in a specific place and at a specific time, namely late-Ottoman and mandatory Palestine, and post-1948 Israel. The history of tax law in this specific locale shows that existing accounts of the transformation of law in the nineteenth and twentieth centuries are incomplete. In Palestine and Israel, law and its professional carriers – lawyers, of course, but also accountants – did indeed become more important over time, as the reliance of the state on law in the process of taxation grew. The rise of law was indeed accompanied by increasingly widespread use of scientific and administrative techniques designed to provide more information about taxpayers and ease the process of tax assessment and collection. However, there was another important aspect of the transformation in the use of law that accounts to date have ignored. At least in the Israeli case, the nation-state of the middle decades of the twentieth century also sought to tax its subjects by utilizing state-created social norms meant to generate community pressure on tax evaders, turning them into compliant citizens. The Israeli state understood itself as a community, modeled in some respects on pre-twentieth-century

Sociology: Taxation in Comparative and Historical Perspective (New York: Cambridge University Press, 2009); Margaret Lamb, "Taxation," in *The Routledge Companion to Accounting History*, eds. John Richard Edwards and Stephen P. Walker (Abingdon: Routledge, 2009), 579–97; Lynne Oats, ed., *Taxation: A Fieldwork Research Handbook* (Abingdon: Routledge, 2012). For a discussion of the pre-nineteenth-century period, including a typology of different types of states and their tax systems see Richard Bonney and W. M. Ormrod, "Introduction: Crises, Revolutions and Self-Sustained Growth: Towards a Conceptual Model of Change in Fiscal History" in *Crises, Revolutions and Self-Sustained Growth: Essays in European Fiscal History, 1130–1830*, eds. W. M. Ormrod, Margaret Bonney, and Richard Bonney (Stamford: Shaun Tyas, 1999), 4–8. See also Bartolomé Yun-Casalilla and Patrick K. O'Brien with Francisco Comín Comín, eds., *The Rise of Fiscal States: A Global History, 1500–1914* (Cambridge: Cambridge University Press, 2012).

communities.[13] As such, it attempted to augment the coercion already provided by state law with older, nonlegal, forms of community pressure. The result was the appearance of a specific type of taxing state, one that sought to create tax compliance based on a sense of duty, trust, and loyalty using social norms – an intimate fiscal state.

The attempt by the state to induce tax compliance using nonlegal means was largely abandoned after the 1960s, and was replaced by a reliance on professional intermediaries between the state and taxpayers speaking the language of law. However, in the process law itself was transformed. It became both more flexible (substantive rather than formal) and more intrusive (interested in taxpayers' states of mind), taking upon itself a role that social norms had taken in the past.

I provide a three-stage periodization scheme of the history of tax law and social norms in Ottoman and mandatory Palestine and post-1948 Israel.[14] Before the twentieth century, taxation in Palestine (and in many other tax systems) was characterized by a two-tier model in which a layer of intermediaries existed between the state and individual taxpayers. The state collecting the taxes was distant and did not interact in a continuous or systematic manner with individual taxpayers. Taxation required relatively little information-collection, assessment was often arbitrary, and force (or the threat of its use) was an important method of ensuring compliance. The state lacked the necessary local information for effective tax collection, and therefore often outsourced the assessment and collection process to tax farmers – that is, rural village communities, or urban ethnic communities, or individual tax farmers, such as the Arab notable about whom the farmers of Be'er Tuvia complained in 1905. There were no professional intermediaries using legal norms to mediate between taxpayers and the state. Although taxation during this period was sometimes related to notions of social inclusion and exclusion, the intimate link between taxation and citizenship that we see later did not yet exist.[15]

---

[13] See generally, Benedict Anderson, *Imagined Communities: Reflections on the Origin and Spread of Nationalism*, new edn (London: Verso, 2006).

[14] The three stages described are ideal types. In reality, the boundaries between the stages were not clearly demarcated, and the transition from one stage to the next was not a linear one.

[15] The description of taxation during the first stage is based on the general characteristics of Ottoman taxation, but many of these characteristics can be found elsewhere.

The two-tier model began to wane in the Ottoman Empire in the mid- and late nineteenth century with the rise of a reformed, centralized, and bureaucratic state.[16] The advent of British rule in Palestine in the first decades of the twentieth century (formally as a trustee of the League of Nations, but practically as a colonial power) accelerated this process.[17] However, the appearance of law and its agents initially had relatively little impact on the actual process of tax assessment and collection, and as we saw, the late Ottoman and British-colonial states often taxed their subjects with little regard to law and little resort to state courts.

Another important development that occurred with the growth in the power of the centralized state in the late Ottoman period was a weakening of the traditional separation between rulers and the ruled, leading to the rise of notions of citizenship rather than subjecthood.[18] The appearance of the nation-state (in our case, the birth of the State of Israel in 1948) accelerated this process. The nation-state flattened

---

See generally Charles Tilly, *Coercion, Capital and European States, AD 990–1992*, rev. edn (Cambridge, MA: Blackwell, 1992). On taxation and social exclusion/ inclusion in different places and eras see, e.g., David Nirenberg, *Communities of Violence: Persecution of Minorities in the Middle Ages* (Princeton: Princeton University Press, 1998), 21; Michael Kwass, *Privilege and the Politics of Taxation in Eighteenth-Century France: Liberté, Égalité, Fiscalité* (New York: Cambridge University Press, 2000); Yanni Kotsonis, *States of Obligation: Taxes and Citizenship in the Russian Empire and Early Soviet Republic* (Toronto: University of Toronto Press, 2014), 27–54; Lena Salaymeh, "Taxing Citizens: Socio-Legal Constructions of Late Antique Muslim Identity," *Islamic Law and Society* 23:4 (2016), 333–67.

[16] On the Ottoman state see, generally, Ergun Özbudun, "The Continuing Ottoman Legacy and the State Tradition in the Middle East," in *Imperial Legacy: The Ottoman Imprint on the Balkans and the Middle East*, ed. L. Carl Brown (New York: Columbia University Press, 1996), 133–57; Carter Vaughn Findley, "The Ottoman Administrative Legacy and the Modern Middle East," in Brown, ed., *Imperial Legacy*, 158–60.

[17] Palestine was not a British colony, but a territory granted to Britain by the League of Nations as part of the post–First World War mandate regime. However, in practice the British treated the territory in almost every respect as if it were a colony.

[18] On the separation of rulers and the ruled in the Ottoman Empire, see L. Carl Brown, "The Setting: An Introduction," in Brown, ed., *Imperial Legacy*, 1, 7. On the attempt to create a shared sense of Ottoman citizenship during the late Ottoman period, see Ariel Salzmann, "Citizens in Search of a State: The Limits of Political Participation in the Late Ottoman Empire," in *Extending Citizenship, Reconfiguring States*, eds. Michael Hanagan and Charles Tilly (Lanham: Rowman and Littlefield, 1999), 37–66; Michelle U. Campos, *Ottoman Brothers: Muslims, Christians and Jews in*

hierarchical social structures. Taxation now became individualized as the state gradually eliminated the use of local intermediaries between itself and individual taxpayers, and monopolized claims to revenue.[19] Tax norms were no longer local, customary, and negotiated. They became universal, formal, and standardized. The relationship between the state and individual taxpayers also changed. The nation-state sought to create a sustained relationship with individual taxpayers over time, and to shape the mindsets of these taxpayers to increase their compliance. The threat of the use of force, while still present, mostly receded into the background as new tools for governing – administrative technologies but also state-produced social norms – augmented the power of the law to enforce compliance. The hierarchical relationship between government and subjects implicit in the old tax assessment and collection process was transformed into a more equal interaction between individual citizens and "their" state. The nation-state, which represented itself as an enlarged community belonging to the people, could make claims on its subjects that the older empires could not, based on the intimate fiscal relationship that it created.

Early Twentieth-Century Palestine (Stanford: Stanford University Press, 2011), 3–7, 60–5; Julia Phillips Cohen, *Becoming Ottomans: Sephardi Jews and Imperial Citizenship in the Modern Era* (Oxford: Oxford University Press, 2014). On post-Ottoman notions of citizenship in mandatory Palestine and Israel, see Gershon Shafir and Yoav Peled, *Being Israeli: The Dynamics of Multiple Citizenship* (New York: Cambridge University Press, 2002). On citizenship in British territories see Niraja Gopal Jayal, *Citizenship and Its Discontents: An Indian History* (Cambridge, MA: Harvard University Press, 2013), 27–50. On the history of citizenship, see, generally, Peter Riesenberg, *Citizenship in the Western Tradition: Plato to Rousseau* (Chapel Hill: University of North Carolina Press, 1992); Quentin Skinner and Bo Stråth, eds., *States and Citizens: History, Theory, Prospects* (New York: Cambridge University Press, 2003).

[19] For a critical discussion of the beginning of this process in the late Ottoman Empire, see Huri İslamoğlu, "Towards a Political Economy of Legal and Administrative Constitutions of Individual Property," in *Constituting Modernity: Private Property in the East and West*, ed. Huri İslamoğlu (London: I. B. Tauris, 2004), 3, 5, 12; Huri İslamoğlu, "Politics of Administering Property: Law and Statistics in the Nineteenth-Century Ottoman Empire," in İslamoğlu, ed., *Constituting Modernity*, 276–319; Huri İslamoğlu, "Modernities Compared: State Transformations and Constitutions of Property in the Qing and Ottoman Empires," in İslamoğlu and Perdue, *Shared Histories*, 109–46. On the beginning of this process in early modern France, see Kwass, *Privilege and the Politics of Taxation in Eighteenth-Century France*, 51–3.

However, this intimate fiscal relationship between taxpayer and state did not last long. Social, political, cultural, and professional changes beginning in the late 1960s led to a return, in some sense, to a two-tier system. Professional intermediaries that had played a minimal role in pre-twentieth-century taxation now assumed a growing role, blunting the communal, civic engagement model of taxation typical of the mid-twentieth century.[20]

The role of these new intermediaries was different from that of tax farmers in the old empires. These professional agents served the tax-payers rather than the state. The fact that the law and its agents came to serve the tax-paying public in its attempts to reduce its tax burden, rather than serving the state, forced the state to change the nature of tax law to ensure continued compliance. Hence, tax law, or certain aspects of it, became substantive rather than formal, providing the government and the courts with new tools to deal with noncompliant taxpayers, and allowing them to intervene more freely in taxpayers' affairs in order to better tax them.

By describing the interplay between legal and social norms in the process of taxation, based on this three-stage periodization scheme, I seek to improve our understanding of the relationship between law and society. Rather than perpetuating the conventional story in which state law simply replaced community-based social norms during the nineteenth and twentieth centuries (or an equally incomplete story in which law was augmented in the nineteenth and twentieth centuries by the use of disciplinary techniques and scientific knowledge), I show how the mid-twentieth-century state attempted to turn itself into a large imagined community, using older, community-like techniques of social control to ensure tax compliance, and how this attempt gradually waned after the 1960s.

Existing Accounts

This book is not a history of types of taxes and their rates, of the politics of taxation, or of the technical aspects of tax law doctrines. Rather,

---

[20] For a somewhat similar argument about the changing role of experts in determining monetary policy in the twentieth century see Roy Kreitner, "The Jurisprudence of Global Money," *Theoretical Inquiries in Law* 11 (2010): 177–208.

it is a history of how the entity called "tax law" came into being in one specific historical context: twentieth-century Palestine and Israel. It shows how tax law competed with other forms of social control as a method of ensuring tax compliance, how the law prevailed, and how the nature of law changed following its victory. The story is told from a perspective that is mostly top-down, but I augment it with some bottom-up social and cultural history of tax morale and tax compliance. I am concerned with major events such as the introduction of income tax legislation in mandatory Palestine in 1941, but also with more mundane practices – the daily routines of tax assessment and collection.

There are a number of works that analyze specific aspects of the larger story explored in this book. Jacob Metzer's *The Divided Economy of Mandatory Palestine* includes an overview of some aspects of the development of the tax system of the country during the period of British rule.[21] Two surveys of Israeli taxation (by Avraham Mandel in 1968 and Avraham Mandel and Asher Arin in 1982) discuss changes in income taxation between the 1940s and the late 1970s, focusing mainly on rates and the revenue from the tax.[22] Harold C. Wilkenfeld, an American tax adviser to the Israeli government, wrote *Taxes and People in Israel* in 1973. This important book tells the story of the creation of a tax compliance culture in Israel of the 1950s and 1960s.[23] However, none of these works is comprehensive. Each focuses on some specific detail of the bigger story told here. In addition, these works are mostly based on published or secondary, rather than archival, sources. They are descriptive, and none of them attempts to use the history of taxation to gain a broader understanding of the change in the relative use of social and legal norms by the state, or the relationship of taxation to the construction of civic identity.

[21] Jacob Metzer, *The Divided Economy of Mandatory Palestine* (Cambridge: Cambridge University Press, 1998), 180–90.

[22] Avraham Mandel, ed., *Hitpat'hut ha-Misim be-Erets Yisrael: Skirah Historit* (Jerusalem: Muze'on le-Misim, 1968), 39–77. Avraham Mandel and Asher Arin, eds., *'Idkunim le-Sefer Hitpat'hut ha-Misim be-Erets Yisrael: Legabey ha-Shanim 1964–1978* (Jerusalem: Muze'on le-Misim, 1982), 45–61.

[23] Harold C. Wilkenfeld, *Taxes and People in Israel* (Cambridge, MA: Harvard University Press, 1973).

Histories of taxation in other jurisdictions also mostly ignore these topics. Tax history is dominated by macrohistories of taxation – works that analyze questions such as the introduction of new types of taxes, changes in the rates or incidence of these taxes or the politics of taxation.[24] A number of important histories of taxation paying some attention to tax *law* have appeared in recent years.[25] Some of these works focus on the internal history of tax law, rather than on the relationship between law and society. Other works in this category do take into account the relationship of law, politics, and society, but they mainly use a top-down approach that centers on actors such as politicians, bureaucrats, legislators, and judges, and on the legal norms they produced. They devote less attention to the ordinary daily interactions between taxpayers and the state, and to issues such as the relative use of legal and social norms in the process of creating a tax compliance culture.

The relative lack of interest in the legal history of taxation generally, and tax compliance in particular, is somewhat surprising, given the intense interest in the social science literature in tax compliance, tax morale, and the role of factors such as trust and political participation in the creation and transformation of tax regimes. Unfortunately,

[24] For a survey of the (American) historiography see W. Elliot Brownlee, *Federal Taxation in America: A Short History*, 2nd edn (Cambridge: Cambridge University Press, 2004).

[25] See, e.g., Peter Harris, *Income Tax in Common Law Jurisdictions: From the Origins to 1820* (Cambridge: Cambridge University Press, 2006); Steven A. Bank, Kirk J. Stark, and Joseph J. Thorndike, *War and Taxes* (Washington, DC: Urban Institute Press, 2008); Chantal Stebbings, *The Victorian Taxpayer and the Law: A Study in Constitutional Conflict* (Cambridge: Cambridge University Press, 2009); Michael Littlewood, *Taxation without Representation: The History of Hong Kong's Troublingly Successful Tax System* (Hong Kong: Hong Kong University Press, 2010); Steven A. Bank, *From Sword to Shield: The Transformation of the Corporate Income Tax, 1861 to Present* (New York: Oxford University Press, 2010); Steven A. Bank, *Anglo-American Corporate Taxation: Tracing the Common Roots of Divergent Approaches* (Cambridge: Cambridge University Press, 2011); Leigh A. Gardner, *Taxing Colonial Africa: The Political Economy of British Imperialism* (Oxford: Oxford University Press, 2012). A recent addition to this body of scholarship is Gautham Rao, *National Duties: Custom Houses and the Making of the American State* (Chicago: University of Chicago Press, 2016), which combines the economic and legal history of customs duties in the early American state with a business and social history of the actual enforcement of these duties.

the social science interest in these topics has not percolated through to tax historiography, and existing works on tax compliance, with some notable exceptions, analyze contemporary societies, failing to provide a dynamic examination of the historical processes that led to the formation of a given tax culture.[26]

There are a few studies that do link the history of taxation to the history of changing civic identities. Michael Kwass, for example, discussed the emergence of a notion of taxpayers as citizens in eighteenth-century France.[27] Ajay Mehrotra analyzed the rise in the United States of a new conception of fiscal citizenship in the late nineteenth and early twentieth centuries.[28] Marjorie Kornhauser and

---

[26] For surveys of the social science literature on tax compliance, see, e.g., Benno Torgler, *Tax Compliance and Tax Morale: A Theoretical and Empirical Analysis* (Cheltenham: Edward Elgar, 2007); Marjorie E. Kornhauser, "A Tax Morale Approach to Compliance: Recommendations for the IRS," *Florida Tax Review* 8 (2007): 599–640; Ken Devos, *Factors Influencing Individual Taxpayer Compliance Behaviour* (Dordrecht: Springer, 2014); Diana Onu and Lynne Oats, "The Role of Social Norms in Tax Compliance: Theoretical Overview and Practical Implications," *Journal of Tax Administration* 1 (2015): 113–37. See also Eric A. Posner, "Law and Social Norms: The Case of Tax Compliance," *Virginia Law Review* 86 (2000): 1781–819. On tax culture and its relationship to law, see, e.g., Ann Mumford, *Taxing Culture: Toward a Theory of Tax Collection Law* (Aldershot: Ashgate, 2002); Michael A. Livingston, "Law, Culture, and Anthropology: On the Hopes and Limits of Comparative Tax," *Canadian Journal of Law and Jurisprudence* 18 (2005): 119–34; Birger Nerré, "Tax Culture: A Basic Concept for Tax Politics," *Economic Analysis and Policy* 38 (2008): 153–67; Tsilly Dagan et al., eds., "Comparative Tax Law and Culture," special issue, *Theoretical Inquiries in Law* 11 (2010): 469–821. One important aspect of the history of tax compliance that has received some scholarly attention is the history of tax revolts. See, e.g., David T. Beito, *Taxpayers in Revolt: Tax Resistance during the Great Depression* (Chapel Hill: University of North Carolina Press, 1989); David F. Burg, *A World History of Tax Rebellions: An Encyclopedia of Tax Rebels, Revolts, and Riots from Antiquity to the Present* (New York: Routledge, 2004). Another important aspect is the history of the relationship between political rights, trust, and tax compliance. See Margaret Levi, *Of Rule and Revenue* (Berkeley: University of California Press, 1988); Martin Daunton, *Trusting Leviathan: The Politics of Taxation in Britain, 1799–1914* (New York: Cambridge University Press, 2001); Martin Daunton, *Just Taxes: The Politics of Taxation in Britain, 1914–1979* (Cambridge: Cambridge University Press, 2002).

[27] Kwass, *Privilege and the Politics of Taxation in Eighteenth-Century France.*

[28] Ajay K. Mehrotra, *Making the Modern American Fiscal State: Law, Politics, and the Rise of Progressive Taxation, 1877–1929* (New York: Cambridge University Press,

Carolyn Jones studied the formation of an American tax compliance culture during the mid-twentieth century.[29] Yanni Kotsonis examined the history of taxation in late imperial Russia and the early Soviet Union, to determine how taxation transformed the identity of both taxpayers and the state, turning Russians (at least urban ones) from subjects into citizens.[30] There have also been studies of the relationship between taxation, compliance, and citizenship in Germany and Argentina.[31]

Like the works just mentioned, this book reflects my belief that taxation is not only a revenue-raising tool or an incentive-providing mechanism, but also a method for social construction – a way to create a shared identity and common notions of citizenship and community.[32] However, I am also interested in the role of law and social norms in this process, unlike some of the aforementioned works that

2013). On fiscal citizenship see also Lawrence Zelenak, *Learning to Love Form 1040: Two Cheers for the Return-Based Mass Income Tax* (Chicago: University of Chicago Press, 2013); Ajay K. Mehrotra, "Reviving Fiscal Citizenship," *Michigan Law Review* 113 (2015): 943–72, 946.

[29] Marjorie E. Kornhauser, "Doing the Full Monty: Will Publicizing Tax Information Increase Compliance?" *Canadian Journal of Law and Jurisprudence* 18 (2005): 95–117; Marjorie E. Kornhauser, "Shaping Public Opinion and the Law in the 1930s: How a 'Common Man' Campaign Ended a Rich Man's Law," *Law and Contemporary Problems* 73 (2010): 123–47; Carolyn C. Jones, "Class Tax to Mass Tax: The Role of Propaganda in the Expansion of the Income Tax during World War II," *Buffalo Law Review* 37 (1988): 685–737; Carolyn C. Jones, "Mass-Based Income Taxation: Creating a Taxpaying Culture, 1940–1952," in *Funding the Modern American State, 1941–1995: The Rise and Fall of the Era of Easy Finance*, ed. W. Elliot Brownlee (Washington, DC: Woodrow Wilson Center Press, 1996), 107–47; Carolyn C. Jones, "Bonds, Voluntarism and Taxation," in *Studies in the History of Tax Law*, ed. John Tiley (Oxford: Hart, 2007), 2:427–42.

[30] Kotsonis, *States of Obligation*.

[31] Alexander Nützenadel and Christoph Strupp, eds., *Taxation, State, and Civil Society in Germany and the United States from the 18th to the 20th Century* (Baden-Baden: Nomos, 2007); Martin Nonhoff and Frieder Vogelmann, "Paying for Identity: The Formation of Differentiated Collectives through Taxes," http://ecpr.eu/filestore/paperproposal/52007b86-b202-4b1e-920d-fa284438dfd7.pdf; José Antonio Sánchez Román, *Taxation and Society in Twentieth-Century Argentina* (New York: Palgrave Macmillan, 2012).

[32] Assaf Likhovski, "'Training in Citizenship': Tax Compliance and Modernity," *Law and Social Inquiry* 32 (2007): 665–700.

pay relatively less attention to the role of tax *law* in the history of taxation and citizenship.[33]

Scope of Analysis

This book discusses the history of taxation and its law in Palestine/Israel from the late nineteenth century to 1985.[34] Some aspects of the history of late Ottoman, mandatory, and Israeli state and society were unique, or at least not universal. Similarly, some aspects of Israeli tax history were also unique. However, many features of this tax history were less particular and were similar to developments that also occurred in many other countries.[35] For example, the rise of notions of fiscal citizenship in Israel in the mid-twentieth century reflected important shifts that had occurred earlier in Europe and the United States, as

[33] For example, Ajay Mehrotra's pathbreaking book is based on an approach that sees law as the "language of state power," and expresses an interest in the role of "law, juridical institutions and legal processes" in the advancement of the notion of fiscal citizenship in the United States. See Mehrotra, *Making the Modern American Fiscal State*, 29–30. However, Mehrotra's interest in law is focused mainly on the role of *constitutional* law in hindering tax reform, on the enactment of tax legislation, and on the contribution of some elite government lawyers to tax policy debates. It does not discuss the changing role of law in inducing compliance, nor does it analyze the changing use of social norms in creating fiscal citizenship.

[34] The year 1985 was chosen as the date ending the period discussed in this book because the mid-1980s saw a number of important changes relevant to the topics discussed here. By the mid-1980s right-wing governments headed by the Likud Party had consolidated a series of political, social, and cultural changes in Israel that partly undermine the previous civic republican notion of Israeli citizenship. In the legal realm, the mid-1980s marked a new era characterized by the decline of legal formalism. In addition, in 1985 the era of hyperinflation in Israel ended. See generally Menachem Mautner, *Law and the Culture of Israel* (Oxford: Oxford University Press, 2011); Paul Rivlin, *The Israeli Economy from the Foundation of the State through the 21st Century* (New York: Cambridge University Press, 2011), 57.

[35] On the tension between the particular and the universal in writing comparative histories of states and taxation, see, generally, Richard Bonney, "Introduction" to *The Rise of the Fiscal State in Europe, c.1200–1815*, ed. Richard Bonney (Oxford: Oxford University Press, 1999), 1–3; Yun-Casalilla and O'Brien, *The Rise of Fiscal States*, 17–18. On Israeli society and politics in comparative perspective, see, e.g., Yoav Peled, *The Challenge of Ethnic Democracy: The State and Minority Groups in Israel, Poland and Northern Ireland* (New York: Routledge, 2014), 1–14, 93–142.

taxation came to be based on trust and semi-voluntary compliance.[36]
Likewise, the widespread reliance on the use of social norms to induce
compliance that appeared in the Jewish community in 1940s Palestine,
and later in the new Israeli state of the 1950s, was evident in other
mobilized twentieth-century societies, for example in the United States
during the First and Second World Wars.[37] Finally, some of the changes
evident in Israel, beginning in the late 1960s – such as the decline in the
reliance on nonlegal norms to induce compliance, or changing notions
of the proper relationship between citizens and their state – could also
be found in other countries, for example, the United States.[38]

While Israeli tax history is certainly not unique, it is, I believe, more
revealing than tax histories elsewhere. Unlike Western tax systems, in
which a tax compliance culture was created over the course of many
decades, in twentieth-century Palestine and Israel this process occurred

[36] See, generally, Mehrotra, *Making the Modern American Fiscal State*; Kotsonis, *States of Obligation*; Nicholas R. Parrillo, *Against the Profit Motive: The Salary Revolution in American Government, 1780–1940* (New Haven: Yale University Press, 2013), 183–220.

[37] Mobilized societies are ones in which economic and social resources are marshaled and controlled by the state using education and propaganda, and in which civil society organizations and substate communities are used by the state to further its goals. Totalitarian societies are mobilized, but democratic ones, especially during periods of crisis, may also be mobilized. On Israel see, e.g., Yoav Peled and Adi Ophir, eds., *Yisrael: Mi-Hevrah Meguyeset le-Hevrah Ezrahit?* (Tel Aviv: Ha-Kibbutz ha-Me'uhad, 2001); Orit Rozin, *A Home for All Jews: Citizenship, Rights, and National Identity in the New Israeli State*, trans. Haim Watzman (Waltham, MA: Brandeis University Press, 2016), 11; Anat Helman, *Becoming Israeli: National Ideals and Everyday Life in the 1950s* (Waltham, MA: Brandeis University Press, 2014), 68–85. On the United States see, e.g., Christopher Capozzola, *Uncle Sam Wants You: World War I and the Making of the Modern American Citizen* (New York: Oxford University Press, 2008); James T. Sparrow, *Warfare State: World War II Americans and the Age of Big Government* (New York: Oxford University Press, 2011). On the Soviet Union see, e.g., Alfred B. Evans Jr., "Civil Society in the Soviet Union?" in *Russian Civil Society: A Critical Assessment*, eds. Alfred B. Evans Jr., Laura A. Henry, and Lisa McIntosh Sundstrom (Armonk: M. E. Sharpe, 2006), 28–54. See generally William Kornhauser, *The Politics of Mass Society* (New York: Free Press, 1965); Robert Orr, "Reflections on Totalitarianism, Leading to Reflections on Two Ways of Theorizing," *Political Studies* 21 (1973): 481–9.

[38] On the decline of the civic republican view of taxation in the United States since the late 1960s, see Lawrence Zelenak, "The Great American Tax Novel," *Michigan Law Review* 110 (2012): 969–84, 977; Zelenak, *Learning to Love Form 1040*, 116–20.

relatively quickly. Here, different types of state structures replaced each other rapidly. A non-Western power, the Ottoman Empire, which ruled the country until the First World War, was replaced after the war by a Western power, the British Empire, and then, after 1948, by a mobilized nation-state committed to a quasi-socialist ideology: Israel.[39] This new state, however, has been transformed (beginning in the late 1960s and especially since the 1980s) into a neoliberal state. The society that ultimately emerged in this territory was thus in a continual state of flux. Ethnic conflict, postcolonial partition, constant wars, and large waves of immigration all rapidly shaped and reshaped Israeli society and its identity, transforming a collection of distinct religious communities that had characterized Palestine in the late Ottoman period into a Jewish-dominated nation-state in the mid-twentieth century, later moving toward an Americanized multicultural society in the late twentieth and early twenty-first century.

The political, military, and economic fluidity of this state and its society meant that the problems faced by Israeli tax collectors were more challenging, and their responses to these problems more visible than in other, more stable societies. Israeli tax history thus provides a sequence of swift changes between different state models (imperial, colonial, mobilized nation-state, and neoliberal state) that reveal developments obscured elsewhere.[40]

In this book I focus on the relationship between civic identity and income taxation. Generally speaking, the three most important classes of taxes that states now use to raise revenue are taxes on property, on transactions (for example, customs duties or excise taxes), and on income. Each class of taxes poses specific types of administrative

---

[39] For a critical perspective on Israeli socialism see Zeev Sternhell, *The Founding Myths of Israel: Nationalism, Socialism, and the Making of the Jewish State*, trans. David Maisel (Princeton: Princeton University Press, 1999).

[40] For other works that focus on the relationship between taxation and state models, albeit from different theoretical approach, see, e.g., Carolyn Webber and Aaron Wildavsky, *A History of Taxation and Expenditure in the Western World* (New York: Simon and Schuster, 1986); Sven Steinmo, *Taxation and Democracy: Swedish, British, and American Approaches to Financing the Modern State* (New Haven: Yale University Press, 1996); Kimberly J. Morgan and Monica Prasad, "The Origins of Tax Systems: A French-American Comparison," *American Journal of Sociology* 114 (2009): 1350–94.

and technical challenges. Property taxation (on land) requires survey-
ing abilities. Customs duties call for efficient border control. Income
taxation demands the ability to ensure continuous surveillance of each
taxpayer's economic activity.[41] Some aspects of the intrusive system
of information-gathering that the taxation of income entails existed
before the introduction of the income tax. However, this type of taxation greatly increased the volume of information collected by the state.
Unsurprisingly, this led to friction between the state and taxpayers. One
way to overcome this problem is to use third parties as collection agents
of the state (for example, employers withholding the tax on the income
of employees).[42] However, such third parties also sometimes have an
incentive to misreport the tax due, if they can share the tax saved with
the taxpayer. Another solution to the problem is to encourage taxpayers to identify with the state and thus self-report their income, complying with taxation out of a sense of internal conviction rather than as a
result of external force. Income taxation thus required a new relationship between the state and its subjects, one of self-compliance.[43]

I am interested in the history of the emergence, and the subsequent
decline, of this new type of relationship, rather than, for example, the
history of new technological methods of controlling borders or of sur-
veying land for tax purposes. Income tax, at least in the Israeli context,
also produced the greatest volume of litigation in the courts in the period
under study, thus making it the most interesting tax from a legal history
point of view.[44] The book will therefore focus primarily on income tax,
although it will also briefly mention some other types of taxes, such as
value-added taxation. The discussion of income taxation will mainly
center on individual taxpayers rather than on the taxation of the income
of other entities such as cooperatives or business corporations, again to
illuminate the relationship between the state and civic identity.[45]

---

[41] See, e.g., Tilly, *Coercion, Capital and European States*, 87–8.
[42] For such provisions in the case of mandatory Palestine and Israel see Chapter 2, text
to n. 82 and Chapter 6, text to n. 50.
[43] See, e.g., Lawrence W. Kenny and Stanley L. Winer, "Tax Systems in the World: An
Empirical Investigation into the Importance of Tax Bases, Administration Costs, Scale
and Political Regime," *International Tax and Public Finance* 13 (2006): 181–215, 209.
[44] See Wilkenfeld, *Taxes and People in Israel*, 177.
[45] During the mandatory period and the first years after Israeli independence in 1948
the income of business corporations was taxed by two separate laws, by the Income

Taxation is a civic duty. There are other civic duties (some of them similar to taxation). For example, compulsory army service can be viewed as a form of corvée, a tax (in-kind) on labor. Compulsory army service forms a major part of the Israeli civic identity. Indeed, in some respects it plays a bigger role in the formation of this identity than the payment of taxes.[46] However, to keep this book within reasonable bounds, army service (as well as other topics related to taxation, such as the use of public debt) will not be explored here.

My interest in civic identity also determines the attention paid in the book to various ethnic or social groups. In Chapters 1 and 2, the Jewish and the Arab communities of Palestine receive equal attention.[47]

Tax Ordinance and by the War Revenue (Company Profits Tax) Ordinance, 1945 (and later by the Company Profits Tax Ordinance, 1947). In 1953 the provisions of the Company Profits Tax Ordinance, 1947 were incorporated into the Income Tax Ordinance. In 1992 the formal distinction between an "income tax" and "company tax" paid on the income of corporations was abolished and, since then, corporations only pay a single flat rate tax on their income. See Income Tax Ordinance (New Version), 1961, sec. 126. For a discussion of the history of the taxation of the income of corporations in Israel see Yosef Stern, *Mas Hakhnasah: Le-Halakhah ule-Ma'aseh* (Tel Aviv: Yavneh, 1949), 79; Arye Lapidoth, *'Ekronot Mas Hakhnasah ve-Mas Rivhey Hon* (Jerusalem: Muze'on le-Misim, 1970), 177–8; Amnon Rafael and Shlomi Lazar, *Mas Hakhnasah*, 2nd edn (Tel Aviv: Ronen, 2014), 2:197–8n613, 2:204–5n641.

[46] See, e.g., Sara Helman, "Militarism and the Construction of Community," *Journal of Political and Military Sociology* 25 (1997): 305–32.

[47] Like other aspects of the Arab–Jewish conflict in Palestine and Israel, the terms used to designate the non-Jewish Arabic-speaking population of late Ottoman and mandatory Palestine and Israel are fraught with debate, partly because of their historical contingency and constructedness and partly because of their political implications. In this book I will use the terms Arabs and then Arab-Israelis (in the post-1948 period). I do so for clarity's sake and because most of this book deals with the period before the 1970s, a period when these terms were deemed unproblematic. On the many terms used to designate this population see, e.g., Ilan Peleg and Dov Waxman, *Israel's Palestinians: The Conflict Within* (Cambridge: Cambridge University Press, 2011), 2–3, 26–9. One can also note here other historiographical debates, such as the debate about the relationship of Zionism and European colonialism, or the debate on whether the economic history of the two major communities in mandatory Palestine can be told separately. See, e.g., Shafir and Peled, *Being Israeli*, 1–33; Jacob Metzer, "Jews in Mandatory Palestine and Additional Phenomena of Atypical Settler Colonization in Modern Time," in *Settler Economies in World History*, eds. Christopher Lloyd, Jacob Metzer, and Richard Sutch (Leiden: Brill, 2013), 169–202 (on Zionism and

However, the focus of the discussion then shifts to the Jewish population and, within the Jewish population, to Zionist Jews rather than small subcommunities within the larger Jewish population (such as ultraorthodox non-Zionist Jews). This emphasis on Zionist Jews stems primarily from the fact that a major theme of this book is the way income taxation created a new type of taxpayer, one that was a citizen rather than a subject. While the Jews of mandatory Palestine were transformed from colonial subjects into citizens after Israeli independence in 1948, the Arabs of Israel remained, in many respects, semicitizens.[48] As such, they were less central to the story I tell here, a story of the Israeli state's efforts to construct a new type of taxpayer, although, as we shall see in Chapter 4, there were attempts in the 1950s to turn Israeli Arabs, like Israeli Jews, into fully-fledged compliant taxpayers.

The shift in attention also reflects the changing demographic weight of Jews and Arabs over time. The composition of the population of late Ottoman and mandatory Palestine and post-1948 Israel was not stable. It changed rapidly because of natural growth, immigration, and the results of the 1948 war, during which a large proportion of the Arab population of the territory that became Israel fled or was expelled. In Israel of the 1950s, for example, the Arab population comprised only about 10 percent of the country's population.[49] The relative amount of income tax collected from Arab taxpayers was even smaller than their relative population size. This was partly due to noncompliance, discussed in Chapter 4, and partly because the income tax was (indeed, still is) progressive, and therefore mainly targeted the urban, capitalist, and relatively wealthy

colonialism); Metzer, *The Divided Economy of Mandatory Palestine*; Sherene Seikaly, *Men of Capital: Scarcity and Economy in Mandate Palestine* (Stanford: Stanford University Press, 2016), 8–9 (on the economic history of mandatory Palestine). These debates are less relevant to the specific perspective used in this book.

[48] On semicitizenship see generally, Elizabeth F. Cohen, *Semi-Citizenship in Democratic Politics* (Cambridge: Cambridge University Press, 2009).

[49] On the size of the Arab population of Israel in the 1950s, see Shafir and Peled, *Being Israeli*, 110. Ultraorthodox Jews comprised only about 5 percent of the population at the time (based on the number of members of parliament belonging to ultraorthodox parties in the Israeli parliament in the 1950s). See Knesset, "Knesset Election Results," http://main.knesset.gov.il/mk/elections/Pages/default.aspx (in Hebrew).

sector of the economy, dominated (although not exclusively) by Jews, certainly after 1948.[50]

In 1967 Israel greatly expanded its territory and began ruling subject populations in a number of occupied territories such as Sinai, Gaza, and the West Bank for extended periods of time. The history of the taxation of these occupied territories is a fascinating topic in itself. However, given my focus on the relationship of civic identity-construction and taxation, an analysis of the history of Israeli taxation in the territories occupied by Israel after 1967 remains beyond the scope of this study.[51]

---

[50] See, for example, *Din ve-Heshbon Rishon 'al Hakhnasot ha-Medinah la-Shanim 1948/9–1954/5* (Jerusalem: Ha-Madpis ha-Memshalti, May 1956), 119, 131–2, comparing the number of taxpayers and the revenue raised in the Jewish and non-Jewish sectors. Such data later disappeared from government reports. Today there is a common perception that income tax compliance rates are lower in the Arab and ultraorthodox sectors of Israeli society. See, e.g., Eli Zipori, "Ha-Emet ha-Matridah," *Globes*, October 9, 2015, at 2–3. Part of this perception may be due to the fact that currently only the wealthiest five deciles of the Israeli population pay any income tax. Tax credits reduce the tax liability of the first five income deciles, in which the Arabs (and ultraorthodox Jews) are overrepresented, to zero. See OECD, *OECD Reviews of Labour Markets and Social Policies: Israel* (Paris: OECD Publishing, 2010), 16, 58–9; Minhal Hakhnasot ha-Medinah, *Dokh Shnati 2011–2012*, 109, http://mof.gov.il/ChiefEcon/StateRevenues/StateRevenuesReport/Pages/Report_2011-2012.aspx (in Hebrew). For discussions of contemporary tax compliance in the ultraorthodox and Arab sectors in Israel, dealing with income tax as well as other taxes, see Shahar Ilan, *Haredim Ba'am: Ha-Taktsivim, ha-Hishtamtut ve-Remisat ha-Hok* (Jerusalem: Keter, 2000), 283–98 (discussing tax compliance in the ultraorthodox community); Tal Shahor, "Hakhnasot me-Arnonah shel ha-Rashuyot ha-Mekomiyot be-Yisrael: Hashva'ah beyn Rashuyot Mekomiyot Yehudiyot ve-'Arviyot," *RK* 55 (2008): 7–33; Ziad Abou Habla, "Lo Meshalmim Arnonah, ve-Zehu," *RH*, n.s., 28 (2011): 98–104; Rafiq Haj, "Ha-He'anut le-Tashlum Misim 'Ironiyim ba-Hevrah ha-'Arvit be-Yisrael ke-Mikreh Bohan shel ha-Hishtatfut bi-Fe'ulah Kolektivit," in *Ha-Shilton ha-Mekomi ba-Hevrah ha-Falastinit be-Yisrael*, eds. Yousef Jabareen and Mohanad Mustafa (Haifa: Pardes, 2013), 283–323 (discussing the collection of municipal property taxes in Arab localities in Israel).

[51] Preliminary discussions can be found in Sidney J. Baxendale, "Taxation of Income in Israel and the West Bank: A Comparative Study," *Journal of Palestine Studies* 18 (1989): 134–41; Aharon Yoran, "Forty Years of Tax Law in Israel," *Israel Law Review* 24 (1990): 738–85, 769–73. See also Hadara Lazar, *Ma'arekhet ha-Misuy ba-Gadah ha-Ma'aravit uvi-Retsu'at 'Azah ke-Makhshir le-Akhifat ha-Shilton bi-Tkufat ha-Hitkomemut* (Jerusalem: B'tselem, 1990).

The book is divided into three parts. The first – the rise of income taxation – begins with a discussion of taxation in Jewish communities in the Diaspora, taxation in the Ottoman Empire before the twentieth century and taxation in late-Ottoman and mandatory Palestine before the 1940s, setting the stage for the story told in the rest of the book. I then analyze the process by which income taxation was introduced in Palestine in the 1930s and 1940s. The second part – the ascendancy of social norms – discusses the voluntary tax system established by the Jewish community in 1940s Palestine, and the Israeli tax system of the 1950s – a system that was influenced by the voluntary system of the 1940s. The third and final part – the transformation of Israeli taxation and its law – discusses the decline of the Israeli intimate fiscal state, charting the gradual rise of tax professionals in mandatory Palestine and Israel, and describing changes that occurred in Israeli taxation and Israeli tax law beginning in the late 1960s. Finally, in the Epilogue I show how the interest in using social norms to induce tax compliance has recently reemerged, on a global rather than a national scale, as a way of dealing with noncompliance by multinational corporations. I then briefly mention some of the lessons that the story told in this book contains.

PART I

THE RISE OF INCOME TAXATION

Before the Income Tax: Jewish, Ottoman, and Early Mandatory Taxation

In this chapter I examine three tax (and tax law) systems relevant to the story told in this book: the tax systems of Jewish communities in the Diaspora;[1] the tax system of the Ottoman Empire, focusing especially on the period following the Ottoman reforms of the nineteenth century; and the tax system of mandatory Palestine during the first two-and-a-half decades of British rule (1917–41), before income taxation was introduced.[2]

Jewish Taxation in the Diaspora

The history of Jewish tax law begins with the Bible, in which one can find some references – albeit superficial – to various types of taxes such as forced-labor duties, poll taxes, and tithes. The Mishnaic and

---

[1] I discuss Jewish communal taxation because it provides an example of a tax system in which community-based social norms, rather than legal norms, were the main method of ensuring compliance. Jewish communal taxation is also interesting because it served as one of the sources that inspired the voluntary tax system established by the Jewish community in Palestine during the last decade of British rule, a system that will be analyzed in detail in Chapter 3.

[2] Given the extensive scope, both in time and in space, of this chapter, it is obvious that the description provided here is incomplete. However, my purpose is not to provide a comprehensive description, but to establish the baseline for the story that I tell in the following chapters, highlighting a few general characteristics of pre-twentieth-century tax systems, and focusing specifically on the limited role that legal norms played in the process of taxation in Palestine before the mid-twentieth century.

Talmudic literature also contained a number of discussions on tax matters, but here, too, the deliberation was rather underdeveloped. Most of the Talmudic discussion dealt with specific rules relevant to foreign taxation imposed by the Roman Empire on Jews in Palestine, and by the Sasanian Empire on Jews in Mesopotamia.[3] However, the Talmud does contain several rules that were used by later generations to justify adherence to the tax law of the gentile state. Among these is the rule regarding the authority of the gentile state to impose taxes on the Jews: "the law of the state [or land] is law" (in Aramaic, *dina de-malkhuta dina*), which is found several times in the Talmud and was used, among other things, to justify the prohibition of deceiving (or concealing assets from) gentile tax collectors.[4] Additional Talmudic rules were used to justify the right of Jewish communities to create their own tax laws. For example, tractate Bava Batra states that "the townspeople are at liberty to fix weights and measures, prices, and wages, and to inflict penalties for the infringement of their rules."[5]

During Late Antiquity and the early medieval periods, the Jewish communities of the Diaspora generally followed rules established by the Talmudic academies of Palestine and Babylonia. However, the power of these academies gradually waned, and by the eleventh century individual Jewish communities in the Diaspora became more independent. This led to the growth of community-specific tax regulations

[3] On biblical taxation, see, e.g., Joshua Bar-Droma, *Ha-Mediniyut ha-Finansit shel Medinat Yehudah bi-Yemey ha-Bayit ha-Rishon veha-Sheni* (Jerusalem: Muze'on le-Misim, 1967); Menachem Elon, ed., *The Principles of Jewish Law* (Jerusalem: Encyclopaedia Judaica, 1975), 663; Robert A. Oden Jr., "Taxation in Biblical Israel," *Journal of Religious Ethics* 12 (1984): 162–81; Adam S. Chodorow, "Biblical Tax Systems and the Case for Progressive Taxation," *Journal of Law and Religion* 23 (2008): 51–96. On postbiblical taxation, see Elon, *The Principles of Jewish Law*, 665–6.

[4] Babylonian Talmud, Bava Kama, 113A; Babylonian Talmud, Nedarim, 28A. See also Elon, *The Principles of Jewish Law*, 667; Shmuel Shilo, *Dina de-Malkhutah Dina* (Jerusalem: Defus Akademi, 1974).

[5] Babylonian Talmud, Bava Batra, 8B. For the use of this provision to justify community autonomy in tax matters, see, e.g., Jacob Bazak, *Hilkhot Misim ba-Mekorot ha-'Ivriyim* (Jerusalem: Muze'on le-Misim, 1964), 73–5; Elon, *The Principles of Jewish Law*, 667; Arye L. Feldman, "Tshuvot Hakhmey Bartselonah ve-Kataluniyah be-'Inyan Misim ve-Arnoniyot ve-Dina de-Malkhuta Dina," *Gnuzot: Kovets-'Et li-Gnuzot Rishonim* 1 (1984): 67–98, 69.

covering both taxation by the community for internal purposes and taxation on behalf of gentile governments. One major reason for this growth was the practice, common in medieval states, of levying taxes indirectly, using local organizations and communities to gather taxes collectively on behalf of the state.[6] For example, in early–modern Poland the collection of taxes was farmed out to Jewish communities. They were responsible for collecting a fixed sum that was then transferred to the state treasury. Collective responsibility survived, in some cases, into the nineteenth and even twentieth centuries. For example, in eighteenth- and early nineteenth-century Russia, the Jewish community (*kahal*), in which every individual Jew was registered, collectively guaranteed the payment of the poll tax by its members.[7]

Because taxation was not a major topic of Mishnaic or Talmudic literature, and because tax rules were created by specific Jewish communities, no universal Jewish tax law was established. Instead, Jewish tax law was local and dynamic, responding to the economic conditions in each specific community at any given time.[8] Indeed, the traditional norm-makers of Jewish law, the rabbis, had relatively little say in creating and applying tax rules. When rabbis were asked about tax matters, they often stated that such affairs were not to be decided by the universal rules of Jewish law (*halakhah*) but by local community customs

[6] Bazak, *Hilkhot Misim*, 13–15; Elon, *The Principles of Jewish Law*, 666–8; Joseph Marcus, *Social and Political History of the Jews in Poland, 1919–1939* (Berlin: Mouton Publishers, 1983), 8–10; Aharon Frenkel and Yosef Rachman, "Ha-Yahas le-Ha'alamot Mas ba-Mishpat ha-'Ivri," *Magal: Hidushey Torah u-Ma'amarim* 11 (1995): 237–96, 259; Dov Levin, *The Litvaks: A Short History of the Jews of Lithuania* (Jerusalem: Yad Vashem, 2000), 53–8; Yehuda Altshuler, "Hitpat'hutam u-Mashma'utam shel Misey ha-Kahal be-Ashkenaz me-Reshit ha-Hityashvut ve-'Ad la-Magefah ha-Sh'horah" (Ph.D. diss., Bar-Ilan University, 2009). On premodern collective tax liability, see generally Michael Kwass, *Privilege and the Politics of Taxation in Eighteenth-Century France: Liberté, Égalité, Fiscalité* (New York: Cambridge University Press, 2000), 48–9; Yanni Kotsonis, *States of Obligation: Taxes and Citizenship in the Russian Empire and Early Soviet Republic* (Toronto: University of Toronto Press, 2014), 237–56.
[7] Avraham Mandel, "Pakim Historiyim 'al Hayey ha-Yehudim u-Misuyam ba-Nekhar" *RYM* 14 (1985): 308–14; Avraham Wein, "Ha-Irgun ha-Otonomi shel Yehudey Polin: Mi-Kehilah Masortit le-Va'ad Dati," in *Kiyum va-Shever: Yehudey Polin le-Doroteyhem*, eds. Israel Bartal and Israel Gutman (Jerusalem: Merkaz Zalman Shazar, 1997), 1: 49–50.
[8] Bazak, *Hilkhot Misim*, 16–19.

and regulations (whose validity the *halakhah* recognized, incorporating them as local norms). These customs and regulations were viewed as valid even when they were contrary to universal *halakhic* rules, the justification being that they involved matters of money (*diney mamon*) and that in such matters the *halakhah* was dispositive rather than binding. For example, in the thirteenth century, when Rabbi Meir of Rothenburg was asked to rule on a tax-related question, he voiced surprise at being asked to decide on such a concern, explaining that tax rules were a matter for community regulations, customs, and the law of state.[9] Similar sentiments were expressed by the sixteenth-century rabbi Benyamin Ze'ev of Arta, who said that "a custom of the town residents [in tax matters] overrides [a decision of] a court of Talmudic scholars, even though [the decision] relied on Scripture, and not merely the custom of scholars but also the custom of ass drivers is to be relied upon."[10] The rabbis were viewed as nonexperts in tax affairs and were therefore sometimes explicitly asked by those addressing questions to them to also consult nonrabbinical experts.[11]

Because rabbinical authorities had little say in these matters, universal *halakhic* rules were only used in cases where there were no local community customs or regulations, or when there was no existing gentile state law.[12] However, *halakhic* scholars were not totally absent from tax discussions and did indeed, on occasion, concede to requests to rule on tax matters. The *responsa* literature therefore contained discussions of the complex body of rules that had developed in Jewish communities to deal

---

[9] Bazak, *Hilkhot Misim*, 81; Elon, *The Principles of Jewish Law*, 666–9.

[10] Elon, *The Principles of Jewish Law*, 669.

[11] Bazak, *Hilkhot Misim*, 81–5; Simcha Meron, "Mekorot ha-Mishpat le-Diney Misim etsel Hamishah mi-Poskey Ashkenaz," *Diney Yisrael* 3 (1972): 61–70, 62, 65, 69–70; Meir Hildesheimer, "Misim ve-Tashlumehem be-Yahadut Ashkenaz ba-Me'ah ha-17 'al-Pi Sifrut ha-She'elot veha-Tshuvot," *Sinai* 73 (1973): 263–83, 266; Chaim Schenberger, "Sugyot bi-T'hum ha-Misim ba-Halakhah," *RYM* 14 (1984): 205, 207–8; Frenkel and Rachman, "Ha-Yahas," 256.

[12] Bazak, *Hilkhot Misim*, 88. On state law as a source of Jewish tax norms, see Meron, "Mekorot ha-Mishpat," 67–8. On disregarding Jewish law in tax assessment procedures, see Aryeh Shmuelevitz, *The Jews of the Ottoman Empire in the Late Fifteenth and the Sixteenth Centuries: Administrative, Economic, Legal and Social Relations as Reflected in the Responsa* (Leiden: Brill, 1984), 112–13. On the various links that *did* exist between tax law and the *halakhah*, see generally Elon, *The Principles of Jewish Law*, 670–1.

with tax matters.[13] There were even a few *halakhic* compilations entirely devoted to tax matters written between the eleventh and nineteenth centuries.[14] The largest of these compilations was a sixteenth-century book, *Masa Melekh*, written by Joseph Ben-Isaac Ibn-Ezra, a Salonika scholar. The book was divided into seven chapters dealing with *halakhic* rules and community customs on such issues as the determination of residency in a given community for tax purposes, external state and internal community tax exemptions, the nature of property taxes, and the process of determining the applicable tax rules and customs in a given tax dispute.[15]

The types of taxes imposed by, and on, Jewish communities varied from locality to locality. Often, property taxation was used. There were also some indirect taxes, usually (but not always) imposed on products and activities governed by Jewish religious rules (such as kosher food, wine, candles, or tombstones). For example, a major tax imposed on the Jewish communities in Russia was the *korobka*, which was a sales tax on kosher meat and various other types of kosher food as well as on wood, tobacco, candles, the use of bathhouses, and on weddings, divorces, and burials.[16] Similar taxes on kosher meat existed in Jewish communities in the Ottoman Empire. These indirect taxes

---

[13] Elon, *The Principles of Jewish Law*, 670–1. When and why were the rabbis asked to rule on tax-related matters? This is a question that is difficult to answer. The existing secondary literature does not provide a definite answer (and in any event, circumstances changed from one period to another, and from one region to another). A general description of the *responsa* literature and its history is found in Menachem Elon, *Jewish Law: History, Sources, Principles – Ha-Mishpat ha-Ivri*, trans. Bernard Auerbach and Melvin J. Sykes (Philadelphia: Jewish Publication Society, 1994), 3:1453–528. For an overview of the process involved in the writing of the *responsa*, see Elon, *Jewish Law: History, Sources, Principles*, 1501–12.

[14] Five such compilations were produced between the Middle Ages and the nineteenth century: two short medieval compilations written in eleventh-century France and fourteenth-century Germany, a large compilation produced in sixteenth-century Salonika, and two nineteenth-century compilations, also from the Ottoman Empire. See Bazak, *Hilkhot Misim*, 15–6; Elon, *The Principles of Jewish Law*, 699–700. Given such a meagre crop, it is not surprising that no substantial body of *halakhic* tax rules emerged.

[15] See Joseph Ben-Isaac Ibn-Ezra, *Masa Melekh: Diney Misim u-Minhagim*, ed. Yaakov Shmuel Spiegel (Jerusalem: Yad ha-Rav Nisim, 1988/89).

[16] Mandel, "Pakim," 308–14; Levin, *The Litvaks*, 57; Wein, "Ha-Irgun," 49, 50; Isaac Levitats, *The Jewish Community in Russia, 1772–1844* (New York: Columbia University Press, 1943), 46–57, 222–30.

came to play a larger role in the eighteenth and nineteenth centuries as wealthier taxpayers found ways of avoiding direct property taxation, thus passing the tax burden on to the poorer members of the community.[17] In addition to property taxation and various indirect taxes, sometimes an income tax was imposed on Jews by the gentile state, as was the case, for example, in Renaissance Italy.[18]

The money collected by the community was used to pay the gentile state and to finance the religious, educational, and social needs of the Jewish community. In medieval Egypt, for example, the money collected by the community was used to maintain religious students, both locally and also in the major centers of Jewish learning in the Middle East at the time (Jerusalem and Baghdad). It also supported the needy (again, both locally and in other communities), provided medical care and burial services, and was used to remunerate various community officials (judges, beadles, schoolteachers of poor and orphaned children, and so forth).[19] In early–modern Poland, tax revenues were used to fund synagogues and other religious institutions and services, the internal Jewish legal system, Jewish education, medical and social assistance for community members, and the salaries of all the officials involved in these activities. In the Polish town of Poznań in the seventeenth century, for example, tax revenues were used to pay the salaries of the rabbi, other religious officials (preachers, cantors, sextons), lobbyists, doctors, midwives, and gentile and Jewish guards.[20]

---

[17] Bazak, *Hilkhot Misim*, 23, 40, 44; Mandel, "Pakim," 316–17; Jacob Barnai, "Takanot Yerushalayim ba-Me'ah ha-Shmoneh-'Esreh ke-Makor le-Hakarat ha-Hevrah, ha-Kalkalah veha-Pe'ilut ha-Yom-Yomit shel ha-Kehilah ha-Yehudit," in *Prakim be-Toldot Yerushalayim be-Reshit ha-Tkufah ha-'Othmanit*, ed. Amnon Cohen (Jerusalem: Yad Izhak Ben-Zvi, 1979), 271, 299, 300; Nechama Grunhaus, "Nohal Ma'asi u-Basis Hilkhati le-Gviyat Mas ha-Kniyah bi-Kehilat Izmir," *Pe'amim* 116 (2008): 79–116; Minna Rozen, "Litrat ha-Basar: Sahar ha-Basar veha-Ma'avakim ha-Hevratiyim be-Istanbul ha-Yehudit, 1700–1918," *Pe'amim* 105–6 (2006): 83–126, 122–3.

[18] Kenneth R. Stow, *Taxation, Community and State: The Jews and the Fiscal Foundations of the Early Modern Papal State* (Stuttgart: Anton Hiersemann, 1982), 2.

[19] See S. D. Goitein, *A Mediterranean Society: The Jewish Communities of the Arab World as Portrayed in the Documents of the Cairo Geniza*, vol. 2, *The Community* (Berkeley: University of California Press, 1971), 91–143.

[20] Moshe Rosman, *Polin: Prakim be-Toldot Yehudey Mizrah Eropah ve-Tarbutam* (Tel Aviv: Ha-Universitah ha-Ptuhah, 1994), 3-4:55–6, 3-4:99, 3-4:105, 3-4:109–13; Levitats, *The Jewish Community in Russia*, 226.

How much was collected by the Jewish community to pay the gentile state and how much was used to finance internal activities? It is impossible to give a generalized answer to this question because the proportion varied from one community to the next, and because in many cases the data are missing. However, as an example one can note that in early nineteenth-century Russia the amounts collected for external and internal purposes were more or less equal. In Russia, Jews paid a number of state taxes, the most important of which was a state poll tax (collected by the community from individual members and then transferred to the state). In the 1830s the annual revenue from this tax amounted to about one million rubles. Russian Jews also paid indirect taxes used for internal communal needs. Again in the 1830s, such levies collected by Russian Jewish communities also amounted to about one million rubles.[21]

Tax rules were often determined democratically by majority vote among the entire community.[22] Taxpayers were sometimes required to declare their property every few years, the declarations being based on their own records (*hoda'ah*). Sometimes property was assessed by special assessors appointed by the community.[23] Collectors often belonged to the wealthier families, and in some cases they were selected by lottery.[24] When assessments were used, members of the community could appeal their assessment to special tribunals and sometimes to *halakhic* scholars. However, despite the existence of such tribunals, the final amount of tax due was often based on negotiations between the taxpayer and the collector rather than on rigid rules.[25]

Various means were used to ensure tax compliance. A common enforcement mechanism was the ban (*herem*) – a form of excommunication and social ostracism. The ban was effective not because of the threat of violence, but because it relied on social solidarity. When enforced, it meant the isolation of taxpayers from their community, effectively leading to civil death. The different sanctions associated with

[21] Levitats, *The Jewish Community in Russia*, 46, 52, 56.
[22] Azriel Shochat, "'Inyeney Misim ve-Hanhagot Tsibur bi-Kehilot Yavan ba-Me'ah ha-16," *Sfunot* 11 (1971/77): 299–339, 321–2.
[23] Bazak, *Hilkhot Misim*, 44; Elon, *The Principles of Jewish Law*, 685–6, 688; Altshuler, "Hitpat'hutam," 107.
[24] Bazak, *Hilkhot Misim*, 51–5.
[25] Bazak, *Hilkhot Misim*, 27, 29, 56; Elon, *The Principles of Jewish Law*, 690.

this form of excommunication included a prohibition on visiting, eating with, or drinking with the excommunicated person. His sons would not be circumcised and would be expelled from school. His wife would be expelled from the synagogue. Such persons would not be buried in a Jewish cemetery, and they were treated as non-Jews for ritual purposes.[26]

The threat of excommunication often accompanied newly enacted tax regulations. When these were created by a Jewish community, sometimes the entire community gathered in the synagogue to hear the regulations read out by the cantor before the open ark or while holding a Torah scroll. A ritual horn (*shofar*) was blown, and those present held candles, which were symbolically extinguished after the regulations were declared. Severe biblical curses were invoked on all who should fail to comply.[27]

An example of such a threat of excommunication can be found in a regulation enacted in 1580 by the Council of the Four Lands (*Va'ad Arba' Aratsot*), the main body of Polish Jews responsible for collecting taxes from Jewish communities between the sixteenth and eighteenth centuries, and for delivering the money to the gentile Polish authorities. This regulation – which sought to prohibit individual Jews from serving as tax farmers for the Polish state – stated that, should any Jew become a tax farmer:

> he would be banned in this world and the afterlife. He would be segregated from the rest of the Jewish [community], his bread would be considered [non-kosher] gentile bread, his wine would be considered [non-kosher] gentile wine, his slaughter would be considered [non-kosher] gentile slaughter, his sexual intercourse would be considered prostitution, and he would be given [an improper] donkey's burial. No rabbi will perform his marriage ceremony, or that of his sons or daughters, and no person will be married to him. He would be cursed by all the biblical curses including those curses that Elisha cursed [his servant] Gehazi [that is, leprosy], until he recanted and obeyed [this regulation].[28]

---

[26] On the *herem*, see generally Elon, *The Principles of Jewish Law*, 539–44; Simha Goldin, *Ha-Yihud veha-Yahad: Hidat Hisardutan shel ha-Kvutsot ha-Yehudiyot bi-Yemey ha-Beynayim* (Tel Aviv: Ha-Kibbutz ha-Me'uhad, 1997), 67–74.

[27] Elon, *The Principles of Jewish Law*, 544, 688; Grunhaus, "Nohal Ma'asi," 84. Altshuler, "Hitpat'hutam," 121–3.

[28] Israel Halperin, ed., *Pinkas Va'ad Arba' Aratsot* (Jerusalem: Mosad Bialik, 1945), 1.

Unsurprisingly, fear of such bans was strong. There were instances of community members paying taxes they did not even owe, just to avoid inadvertent activation of the ban. Individual oaths were also imposed when the tax collectors suspected false declarations or when a taxpayer claimed his assessment was excessive. Again, fear of such oaths was widespread – due to the inherent threat of heavenly retribution – and taxpayers were often willing to pay more, simply to avoid taking them.[29]

Religious sanctions were sometime accompanied by moral persuasion – rabbis urging their followers to comply by equating tax evasion with sinful theft, since evasion was a form of stealing from the public (*gezel ha-rabbim*). Rabbinical exhortations were directed not only at evaders but also at community leaders (even those who paid their own taxes) if they failed to encourage others to comply.[30]

Apart from using religious means, Jewish communities also relied on more earthly tools to ensure compliance, including the threat of imprisonment. Originally, Jewish law rejected the use of imprisonment in cases of nonpayment of debt (whether private or public). However, beginning in the Middle Ages Jewish communities used imprisonment as a way to enforce payment of taxes. For example, in Eastern Europe the regulations of many communities created a comprehensive procedure for dealing with evaders: if a tax debt remained unpaid for three days, the evader was declared "obdurate." Then a ban was imposed on him, and if, after a specified period of time, he had not paid the debt, he would be imprisoned.[31] Other means, similar in their severity to imprisonment, were also utilized. For example, in early–modern Lithuania beatings and public stocks were used.[32] It is interesting to note that, side by side with these systems of community-based taxation, a concurrent system of what might be called "voluntary" income taxation emerged in the Jewish Diaspora. This system, which had its roots in the Bible, was based on the practice of separating out a tithe (10 percent) from one's monetary income (*ma'aser kesafim*) and

[29] Bazak, *Hilkhot Misim*, 45–7.
[30] Elon, *The Principles of Jewish Law*, 698–9.
[31] Grunhaus, "Nohal Ma'asi," 83–4; Altshuler, "Hitpat'hutam," 123–7. On the use of imprisonment to collect tax debts, see also Elon, *The Principles of Jewish Law*, 697–8.
[32] Levin, *The Litvaks*, 57. On sanctions in other places, see Yehoshua Avraham Yehudah, *Sefer 'Avodat Masa: Saloniki 1846* (Salonika: Saadi ha-Levi Ashkenazi, 1846; repr., Jerusalem: Muze'on le-Misim, 1964).

distributing it to the poor. In effect, this was an individual voluntary income tax, offered up out of a sense of religious duty or charity rather than external enforcement. A sophisticated set of norms dealing with various legal issues involved in observing this religious duty was developed in the rabbinical literature.[33]

The tax system described throughout the previous pages was based on internal Jewish community autonomy and on the external collective responsibility of Jewish communities toward the state for the payment of taxes. In the nineteenth century this system began to wane. With the rise of the centralized state, the power of autonomous Jewish communities weakened, first in Europe and later in the Islamic world.[34] However, in some places, such as Yemen, Jewish tax autonomy existed even later. Here the *jizya*, the Islamic poll tax imposed on non-Muslims, was still collected by the Jewish community on behalf of the state in the early decades of the twentieth century.[35]

Ottoman Taxation

Jewish community taxation declined in the eighteenth and nineteenth centuries. More important in shaping the history of taxation in twentieth-century Palestine and Israel were the governmental tax systems of the late Ottoman and British-colonial periods.[36]

[33] Mark R. Cohen, *Poverty and Charity in the Jewish Community of Medieval Egypt* (Princeton: Princeton University Press, 2005), 2–8. See also Adam S. Chodorow, "Maaser Kesafim and the Development of Tax Law," *Florida Tax Review* 8 (2007): 153–208, 155, 161–4.

[34] For a general history of Jewish autonomy and its decline, see, e.g., Yisrael Bartal, ed., *Kehal Yisrael: Ha-Shilton ha-'Atsmi ha-Yehudi le-Dorotav*, vol. 3, *Ha-'Et ha-Hadashah* (Jerusalem: Merkaz Zalman Shazar, 2004). On Jewish autonomy in the Ottoman Empire, see also Benajamin Braude and Bernard Lewis, eds., *Christians and Jews in the Ottoman Empire* (New York: Holmes and Meier, 1982).

[35] David Tal, "*Al-Jizya*: Mas ha-Hasut shel Yehudey Teyman," *RYM* 15 (1986): 221–5.

[36] There is a large literature on the history of Ottoman taxation; see, e.g., Metin M. Coşgel, "Efficiency and Continuity in Public Finance: The Ottoman System of Taxation," *International Journal of Middle East Studies* 37 (2005): 567–86. For general surveys of the history of Ottoman law, see, e.g., Ruth Miller, "The Legal History of the Ottoman Empire," *History Compass* 6 (2008): 286–96; Avi Rubin, "Ottoman Judicial Change in the Age of Modernity: A Reappraisal," *History Compass* 7 (2009): 119–40.

Pre-nineteenth-century Ottoman taxation was based on a mixture of Islamic taxes and taxes based on local customary traditions that the Ottoman Empire had inherited from previous rulers of its territories, with some additions based on Ottoman regulations. The system prevalent in the territory that later became mandatory Palestine included personal taxes levied on people or households, such as the poll tax (*jizya* in Arabic, *cizye* in Turkish) imposed on non-Muslims, various excise taxes and market fees collected from the urban population, and, finally, rural production taxes such as the tithe (*öşür*, also spelled *osher* or *usher*), a tax levied on gross agricultural yield and paid in kind, and an animal tax (*ağnam resmi*) on some types of farm animals.[37]

While there were only a few basic types of taxes, their names and rates changed from region to region and sometimes even from village to village.[38] Many of these taxes were based on local custom rather than universal Islamic law, thus giving the Ottomans flexibility in shaping their tax system. However, like any other rulers, they were not totally free to impose any taxes they wished, due to the resistance of both taxpayers and other groups with vested interests in existing taxes. The ultimate shape of the Ottoman tax system and its regional variations were thus determined partly by history, partly by the outcome of interest group pressure, and partly by considerations of administrative efficiency.[39]

---

[37] See, e.g., Stanford J. Shaw, "The Nineteenth-Century Ottoman Tax Reforms and Revenue System," *International Journal of Middle East Studies* 6 (1975): 421–59; Halil İnalcık with Donald Quataert, *An Economic and Social History of the Ottoman Empire, 1300–1914* (New York: Cambridge University Press, 1994), 1:55–75; Linda T. Darling, *Revenue-Raising and Legitimacy: Tax Collection and Finance Administration in the Ottoman Empire, 1560–1660* (Leiden: Brill, 1996), 26; M. Şükrü Hanioğlu, *A Brief History of the Late Ottoman Empire* (Princeton: Princeton University Press, 2008), 9; Şevket Pamuk, "The Evolution of Fiscal Institutions in the Ottoman Empire," in *The Rise of Fiscal States: A Global History, 1500–1914*, eds. Bartolomé Yun-Casalilla and Patrick K. O'Brien with Francisco Comín Comín (Cambridge: Cambridge University Press, 2012), 304–31.

[38] See, e.g., Amy Singer, *Palestinian Peasants and Ottoman Officials: Rural Administration around Sixteenth-Century Jerusalem* (Cambridge: Cambridge University Press, 1994), 46; Metin M. Coşgel, "Taxes, Efficiency, and Redistribution: Discriminatory Taxation of Villages in Ottoman Palestine, Southern Syria, and Transjordan in the Sixteenth Century," *Explorations in Economic History* 43 (2006): 332–56, 338–40.

[39] Coşgel, "Efficiency and Continuity in Public Finance," 577–83.

Tax collection methods also varied. For example, the taxation of revenues from land was initially often based on a quasi-feudal division of territories between cavalrymen who owed a duty of military service to the
Empire (*sipahis*). Gradually, however, this system was partially replaced
in the sixteenth and seventeenth centuries by a system based on tax farming. Now the right to collect tax revenues was auctioned by the state to
local notables, who would then collect the tax revenue of given localities
for a specific period of time.[40] These tax farmers sometimes sought to
extract as much as they could from the peasants above and beyond what
it was legitimate to demand, and the peasants, in turn, did everything
they could to evade taxation.[41]

In the assessment and collection process within a given region, the
Ottomans relied on detailed regional tax registers (*tahrir defterleri*).
These registers were accompanied by collections of edicts or "codes"
(*kanunnames*) that cataloged rules about the taxes imposed in a
specific region and their rates. Unlike contemporary tax codes, the
kanunnames could not be used by taxpayers to challenge a tax assessment in a court of law. Instead, they were created solely for the use
of Ottoman administrators.[42] Another difference between these codes
and those we use today was that the rules contained in them were
often neither universal nor standardized. Rather, they were local and
particular, representing the outcome of a continuous process of negotiation and renegotiation between the government and local interest

[40] Darling, *Revenue-Raising and Legitimacy*, 119–60; Huri İslamoğlu, "Politics of
Administering Property: Law and Statistics in the Nineteenth-Century Ottoman
Empire," in *Constituting Modernity: Private Property in the East and West*, ed.
Huri İslamoğlu (London: I. B. Tauris, 2004), 276–319, 283–4; Metin M. Coşgel,
"The Political Economy of Law and Economic Development in Islamic History,"
in *Law and Long-Term Economic Change*, eds. Jan Luiten van Zanden and Debin
Ma (Stanford: Stanford University Press, 2011), 158, 159, 166–7. See also Metin
M. Coşgel and Thomas J. Miceli, "Tax Collection in History," *Public Finance Review*
37 (2009): 399–420.

[41] Roger Owen, *The Middle East in the World Economy 1800–1914*, rev. edn
(London: I. B. Tauris, 1993), 10–21, 36–7.

[42] Halil İnalcik, "Kanunname," in *Encyclopedia of Islam*, new edn (Leiden: Brill, 1978),
4:562–6; Douglas A. Howard, "Historical Scholarship and the Classical Ottoman
Kanunnames," *Archivum Ottomanicum* 14 (1995/96): 79–109, 81; Metin M. Coşgel,
"Ottoman Tax Registers (*Tahrir Defterleri*)," *Historical Methods* 37 (2004): 87–100;
İslamoğlu, "Politics," 569–70.

groups.[43] Even where more universal rules existed, for example in the case of taxes whose origin was Islamic rather than customary local traditions (such as the *cizye*), the assessment and collection process itself varied from locality to locality, and was based on special arrangements between the government, tax collectors, and taxpayers.[44] In a similar way, Ottoman tax appeals did not resemble those of today. Taxpayers who believed they were being overtaxed could petition the sultan. However, because of the relative lack of efficient means of communication, the intervention of the central government in local affairs was limited. Such intervention, when it did occur, was founded on the idea of the ruler as a font of "justice," rather than on a concept of taxation based on legal norms found in specific public acts of legislation.[45]

A further interesting aspect of pre-nineteenth-century Ottoman taxation was the fact that tax liability was often collective rather than individual. Hence, the recording units of Ottoman tax registers covering rural taxation were entire villages rather than individuals, and the payment of some taxes was seen as the collective responsibility of the village, to be divided among the various households on the basis of internal negotiation.[46] Even "urban" taxes such as the *cizye* were sometimes imposed on the community rather than on individuals. While Ottoman authorities did possess detailed information about

---

[43] See, e.g., İslamoğlu, "Politics of Administering Property," 282–5, 308; Huri İslamoğlu and Peter C. Perdue, "Introduction," in *Shared Histories of Modernity: China, India and the Ottoman Empire*, eds. Huri İslamoğlu and Peter C. Perdue (New Delhi: Routledge, 2009), 7–9; Dina Rizk Khoury, "Administrative Practice between Religious Law and State Law on the Eastern Frontiers of the Ottoman Empire," in İslamoğlu and Perdue, *Shared Histories*, 46–7.

[44] Shmuelevitz, *The Jews of the Ottoman Empire*, 81, 85.

[45] See Darling, *Revenue-Raising and Legitimacy*, 248–80; Haim Gerber, *Ottoman Rule in Jerusalem, 1890–1914* (Berlin: Klaus Schwarz, 1985),122–3; Khoury, "Administrative Practice between Religious Law and State Law," 49; Avi Rubin, *Ottoman Nizamiye Courts: Law and Modernity* (New York: Palgrave Macmillan, 2011), 83; Yuval Ben-Bassat, *Petitioning the Sultan: Protests and Justice in Late Ottoman Palestine* (London: I. B. Tauris, 2013); Linda T. Darling, *A History of Social Justice and Political Power in the Middle East: The Circle of Justice from Mesopotamia to Globalization* (New York: Routledge, 2013), 143–4.

[46] Darling, *Revenue-Raising and Legitimacy*, 29–35; İslamoğlu, "Politics of Administering Property," 297.

individual non-Muslims, they sometimes simply imposed the tax on a given religious community collectively, expecting it to collect the money from its individual members. Such was the case, for example, in eighteenth-century Palestine.[47]

Beginning in the middle of the nineteenth century, the Ottoman Empire embarked on a process of reforms (*tanzimat*) in an attempt to create a more centralized and bureaucratic state based on universal law rather than on particularistic and local accommodations and settlements.[48] This process was accompanied by many institutional and cultural changes, manifested in diverse ways. For example, before the reforms there were no official records of Ottoman legislation in printed form that the public could consult. It was only in 1866 that an official collection of such legislation was printed, and only in 1871 that a law was enacted requiring the publication of new laws in newspapers as a condition of their validity. These requirements, of course, reflected a new notion of the "proper way" to create public knowledge of legal rules.[49] This new approach to the promulgation of legislation was accompanied by additional changes. The nineteenth-century Ottoman Empire established a new court system, giving rise to the appearance of professional attorneys. Some scholars have also argued that these changes were accompanied by a shift in the legitimizing image of the state – from the state as a provider of justice because it was governed by a just ruler, to the state as a provider of justice because it was based on formal, general, and uniform norms dispensed by bureaucrats. Ultimately, in the late nineteenth and early twentieth centuries an Ottoman imperial citizenship project also emerged – the

---

[47] Uriel Heyd, "Yehudey Erets Yisrael be-Sof ha-Me'ah ha-17 'al-Pi Pinkasim Turkiyim shel Mas ha-Gulgolet," *Yerushalayim: Riv'on le-Heker Yerushaliyim ve-Toldotehah* 4 (1952/53): 173–84; Barnai, "Takanot," 280–1. This continued earlier practices. See Moshe Gil, "Ha-Misim be-Erets Yisrael bi-Tkufat ha-Kibush ha-Muslemi ha-Rishonah (634–1099)," *Zion* 45 (1980): 268–85, 270.

[48] See generally İslamoğlu, *Constituting Modernity*; İslamoğlu and Perdue, "Introduction" to *Shared Histories*, 1–20.

[49] See George Young, *Corps de Droit Ottoman* (Oxford: Clarendon Press, 1905–06), 1:xiii–xv; Eliezer Malchi, *Toldot ha-Mishpat be-Erets Yisrael: Mavo Histori la-Mishpat bi-Medinat Yisrael* (Tel Aviv: Dinim, 1953), 70–1; Brinkley Messick, *The Calligraphic State: Textual Domination and History in a Muslim Society* (Berkeley: University of California Press, 1996), 56.

attempt to create a shared Ottoman collective identity that would transform Ottoman subjects into Ottoman citizens.[50]

One major aspect of the wider nineteenth-century reform process was the overhaul of the Ottoman taxation system. As part of this overhaul, some taxes were modified and others abolished altogether. In the cities, market and urban excise taxes were replaced by a new profits tax (*temettu*), a forerunner of income taxation, which was imposed on the profits of certain classes of taxpayers (urban merchants, artisans, and industrialists) and later also on salaries and wages, based on presumed rather than actual income. The poll tax on non-Muslims, the *cizye*, was at first replaced by a military service tax on non-Muslims (that is, a tax that took account of the fact that they were exempt from military service). This tax would subsequently be abolished in 1909. Additional new taxes included a stamp tax imposed on all government and commercial documents. New local institutions established during the reform period (municipal councils) were financed by municipal taxes and a variety of fees.[51]

---

[50] See David Kushner, "Ha-Dor ha-Aharon le-Shilton ha-'Othmanim be-Erets Yisrael, 1882–1914," in *Toldot ha-Yishuv ha-Yehudi be-Erets Yisrael me-Az ha-'Aliyah ha-Rishonah: Ha-Tkufah ha-'Othmanit*, ed. Israel Kolatt (Jerusalem: Mosad Bialik, 1989/90), 1, 3–4; Carter Vaughn Findley, "The Ottoman Administrative Legacy and the Modern Middle East," in *Imperial Legacy: The Ottoman Imprint on the Balkans and the Middle East*, ed. L. Carl Brown (New York: Columbia University Press, 1996), 158, 168–70; Iris Agmon, *Family and Court: Legal Culture and Modernity in Late Ottoman Palestine* (Syracuse, NY: Syracuse University Press, 2006), 175–6; Huri İslamoğlu, "Modernities Compared: State Transformations and Constitutions of Property in the Qing and Ottoman Empires," in İslamoğlu and Perdue, *Shared Histories*, 109–46, 139; Rubin, *Ottoman Nizamiye Courts*; Michelle U. Campos, "Making Citizens, Contesting Citizenship in Late Ottoman Palestine," in *Late Ottoman Palestine: The Period of Young Turk Rule*, eds. Yuval Ben-Bassat and Eyal Ginio (London: I. B. Tauris, 2011), 17–33; Michelle U. Campos, *Ottoman Brothers: Muslims, Christians and Jews in Early Twentieth-Century Palestine* (Stanford: Stanford University Press, 2011), 3–7, 60–5.

[51] A. Granovsky, *The Fiscal System of Palestine* (Jerusalem: Palestine and Near East Publications, 1935), 302–3; Shaw, "The Nineteenth-Century Ottoman Tax Reforms and Revenue System," 421–5, 428, 429–32, 434–8; Kushner, "Ha-Dor," 23, 26–30. On the *temettu*, see also TNA: FO 198/86, *Nouvelle Loi du Temettu* ... (Constantinople: Levant Herald, 1908). Tax reforms were based on an income survey carried out in order to formulate tax policy. See generally Kayoko Hayashi and Mahir Aydin, eds., *The Ottoman State and Societies in Change: A Study of the Nineteenth Century Temettuat Registers* (London: Kegan Paul, 2004).

One particularly important aspect of the nineteenth-century Ottoman tax reforms was the attempt to create a land registration system designed to provide information on each plot of land and its owner. Such a system was to serve as the basis for a new property tax – the land and buildings tax (*arazi ve müsakkafat vergisi* or *werko*). This was a tax on cultivated land as well as urban land and buildings, which was collected by government officials rather than by tax farmers.[52] However, while a land registry was set up, it was not based on cadastral maps that would have provided definitive information about the exact boundaries of plots of land; rather, it drew on unreliable verbal descriptions.[53]

Some old Ottoman taxes were retained, but even those taxes were simplified, and the particularistic, negotiated tax settlements that characterized their implementation were now replaced, at least in theory, with standardized and universalized assessment and collection processes based on legal norms. For example, the government enacted a tithe law that created formal rules for the assessment and collection of the tithe. The rate of the tithe, which had previously varied from locality to locality, was now set at 10 percent of the gross yield (in kind). It later changed several times, reaching a rate of 12.63 percent in the first decade of the twentieth century in all regions of the Empire in which the tithe was in force. The process of auctioning tithe revenues to tax farmers was formalized, and safeguards were established to prevent its abuse. A legal right to appeal to the district's administrative council (*meclis i-idare*) regarding the assessment and collection process of the tithe was created.[54] Individual rather than collective liability became

---

[52] M. F. Abcarius, "The Fiscal System," in *Economic Organization of Palestine*, ed. Saʿid B. Himadeh (Beirut: American Press, 1938), 505–56, 508; Shaw, "The Nineteenth-Century Ottoman Tax Reforms and Revenue System," 426–8; İslamoğlu, "Politics of Administering Property," 276, 294.

[53] İslamoğlu, "Politics of Administering Property," 305–8.

[54] Young, *Corps de Droit Ottoman*, 5:302–41; Shlomo Yellin trans., *Sefer ha-Hukim le-Maʿaser Pri ha-Adamah ha-Nahug be-Artsot Turkiyah* (Jerusalem: Lunz, 1904/05), 3–4. See also Gabriel Baer, *Mavo le-Toldot ha-Yahasim ha-Agrariyim ba-Mizrah ha-Tikhon, 1800–1970* (Tel Aviv: Ha-Kibbutz ha-Meʾuhad, 1971/72), 28; Moshe Maʿoz, *Ottoman Reform in Syria and Palestine, 1840–1861: The Impact of the Tanzimat on Politics and Society* (Oxford: Clarendon Press, 1968), 78; İslamoğlu, "Politics of Administering Property," 302; Coşgel, "Taxes, Efficiency and Redistribution," 340; Hanioğlu, *A Brief History of the Late Ottoman Empire*, 89–90.

(at least formally) the basis of taxation, and was now enshrined in legislation and in the new Ottoman tax registers. Individualism was also reflected in the creation of the land registration system, which led to the appearance of private property rights and enabled individual property taxation.[55]

The tax collection process was also changed. Beginning in 1839, the state attempted to collect taxes such as the tithe via salaried state agents (*muhassils*) instead of tax farmers. However, in this specific case the reform attempts failed. Government officials lacked the local knowledge that tax farmers had. The state was therefore forced to reinstate the traditional tax-farming system in 1842. Later attempts, in 1856 and in 1910, to abolish the use of tax farming in the collection of the tithe also failed, and ultimately the farming of the tithe, albeit in a modified and supervised form, remained in force until the demise of the Empire. However, use was made of state officials rather than tax farmers in the collection of other taxes such as the animal tax, the poll tax, or customs duties.[56]

The reforms made to the nineteenth-century Ottoman tax system led to impressive growth in the amount of revenue collected by the state.[57] Yet the Ottoman system retained some pre-reform characteristics. The reformed Ottoman tax system relied on formal tax legislation enacted by the state and visible to the public. However, to a large extent taxes such as the Ottoman tithe were still based on local traditions, and the Ottoman tithe legislation therefore contained explicit provisions allowing for negotiations between the tax farmer and the taxpayer, rather than relying on fixed, formal rules.[58] One must also

[55] İslamoğlu, "Politics of Administering Property," 297, 302. On individual liability for the tithe, see Young, *Corps de Droit Ottoman*, 5:324; Yellin, *Sefer ha-Hukim*, 24–5.

[56] Avraham Mandel, ed., *Hitpat'hut ha-Misim be-Erets Yisrael: Skirah Historit* (Jerusalem: Muze'on le-Misim, 1968), 106; Baer, *Mavo*, 29; Shaw, "The Nineteenth-Century Ottoman Tax Reforms and Revenue System," 422–5, 428, 429–30, 445; Gerber, *Ottoman Rule*, 160–1, 229; Kushner, "Ha-Dor," 27–9; İslamoğlu, "Politics of Administering Property," 303.

[57] See, e.g., Eugene L. Rogan, *Frontiers of the State in the Late Ottoman Empire: Transjordan, 1850–1921* (Cambridge: Cambridge University Press, 2002), 82–3; İslamoğlu, "Politics of Administering Property," 308–10; Şevket Pamuk and K. Kivanç Karaman, "Ottoman State Finances in European Perspective, 1500–1914," *Journal of Economic History* 70 (2010): 593–629.

[58] Young, *Corps de Droit Ottoman*, 5:328–9. See also Yellin, "Ha-Tarifname Numer Alef," in *Sefer ha-Hukim*, 3. It should be noted that reliance on local knowledge,

remember that there was sometimes a discrepancy between the formal rules of taxation and how they were implemented in practice, both at the center of the Empire and certainly in faraway locations such as Ottoman Palestine, to which I will now turn.

The tax bases, collection methods, and even the interaction between taxpayers and tax collectors typical of nineteenth-century Palestine often echoed traditions that had existed in that territory for more than a millennium. Traditionally, even before Ottoman rule, which began in the sixteenth century, taxation in Palestine was based on local customs. Liability for the tax was collective rather than individual, and collection was indirect, the state relying on local dignitaries to perform this task. The use of local intermediaries to administer the collection process was especially evident in the case of rural taxes, which were mostly based on the taxation of produce, although certain peasant populations also paid a poll tax and were required to provide labor services, gifts on special occasions, and a number of other services such as quartering soldiers.[59]

Palestine became part of the Ottoman Empire in the sixteenth century. In the eighteenth century the relationship between the Ottoman center and the eastern provinces of the Ottoman Empire changed, as more power was given to local elites.[60] As a result, central government had little direct interaction with its subjects. In some senses, the Ottomans governed, in the words of historian Beshara Doumani, "from afar," resorting to force to induce compliance with their rule. Thus, every year the Ottoman governor of the Damascus province

widespread discretion, and relative flexibility also characterized other, seemingly more "advanced," nineteenth-century tax systems, such as the English tax system. See, e.g., Chantal Stebbings, "The General Commissioners of the Income Tax: Assessors or Adjudicators?" *British Tax Review*, 1993, 52–64, 52–3; Chantal Stebbings, "Popular Perceptions of Income Tax Law in the Nineteenth Century: A Local Tax Rebellion," *Journal of Legal History* 22 (2001): 45–71, 51.

59 On pre-Ottoman taxation in Palestine, see, e.g., Yehoshua Frenkel, "Mavo le-Toldot ha-Yahasim ha-Agrarim be-Erets Yisrael ba-Tkufah ha-Mamlukit: Hagdarot Mishpatiyot shel Mekarke'in, Misim ve-'Ikarim," *Ofakim be-Geografiyah* 44–45 (1996): 97–113.

60 See Ehud R. Toledano, "The Emergence of Ottoman-Local Elites (1700–1900): A Framework for Research," in *Middle Eastern Politics and Ideas: A History from Within*, eds. Ilan Pappé and Moshe Ma'oz (London: I. B. Tauris, 1997), 145–62.

would tour the rural areas with a contingent of troops to remind the inhabitants of their fiscal duties.[61]

In the nineteenth century this pattern of rule changed. Between 1831 and 1840, under Egyptian occupation, the Egyptian rulers changed the administrative system of Palestine, including its tax system. As one nineteenth-century source observed, "the Egyptian system of extortion was more permanent, general, systematic and extensive" than the previous Ottoman system, partly because it used soldiers to collect taxes directly. The system was also described as "more impoverishing and irresistible," which, predictably, caused local resentment and popular uprisings.[62]

Ottoman rule in Palestine was restored in 1840. The return of the Ottomans was accompanied by yet further changes in the tax system. The traditional rural produce tax (the tithe) and the animal tax were augmented by the new profits tax (*temettu*) and a new tax on property (*werko*), which was levied on land and buildings at a rate that varied between 0.4 percent and 1.128 percent of the capital value of the property (at certain points in time during the late Ottoman era, the tax was based on the expected annual rental value).[63] In addition to the property tax, a few other direct taxes existed (for example on fishing and on owners of means of transport). Indirect taxes included sales taxes on some mass-consumption items (salt, tobacco, and alcohol) and customs duties. Finally, there was a stamp duty, a fee on land transactions, and various municipal

---

[61] See generally, Ma'oz, *Ottoman Reform*, 4–11; Amnon Cohen, *Palestine in the 18th Century: Patterns of Government and Administration* (Jerusalem: Magnes, 1973), 204–69; Amnon Cohen and Bernard Lewis, *Population and Revenue in the Towns of Palestine in the Sixteenth Century* (Princeton: Princeton University Press, 1978), 42–75; Singer, *Palestinian Peasants*, 46–63; Beshara Doumani, *Rediscovering Palestine: Merchants and Peasants in Jabal Nablus, 1700–1900* (Berkeley: University of California Press, 1995), 18–19; Baruch Kimmerling and Joel S. Migdal, *The Palestinian People: A History* (Cambridge, MA: Harvard University Press, 2003), 13–21; Rogan, *Frontiers of the State*, 41–3.

[62] Richard Robert Madden, *The Turkish Empire: In Its Relations with Christianity and Civilization* (London: T. Cautley Newby, 1862), 47. See also Ma'oz, *Ottoman Reform*, 12–17.

[63] Granovsky, *The Fiscal System of Palestine*, 209–11; Mandel, *Hitpat'hut*, 107–9, 142; Gerber, *Ottoman Rule*, 204–6.

Table 1.1 Government revenues from two Ottoman districts in Palestine of
the 1870s[a]

	Revenues of the District of Jerusalem for the fiscal year 1871/72		Revenues of the District of Acre for the fiscal year 1876/77	
	Piasters	%	Piasters	%
Produce tax (*usher*)	3,627,500	35	4,612,938	59
Animal tax	–	–	456,877	6
Land and building tax	3,549,151	34	2,038,247	26
Military service tax	145,564	2	159,185	2
Other taxes	2,997,559	29	547,641	7
Total	10,319,774	100	7,814,888	100

Note:

[a] Data taken from Alexander Schölch, *Palestine in Transformation, 1856–1882:
Studies in Social, Economic and Political Development*, trans. William C. Young
and Michael C. Gerrity (Washington, DC: Institute for Palestine Studies, 1993),
255, 259. Schölch notes that "the information regarding revenues represents
only a fraction of what was actually squeezed out of the population."

taxes and fees.[64] However, the tithe (*usher*) remained the major
source of revenue (see Table 1.1).

Much of the revenue collected was not spent in the district in which
it was collected in Palestine, but was transferred to the provincial
capital, Damascus (and later Beirut), or to the capital of the Empire,
Istanbul. In the case of the district of Acre, in the 1870s only about
10–15 percent of the money collected in the district was spent there.
Most of the money spent in the district went to the administrative
urban centers, and only a very small amount was used to pay for public goods such as infrastructure that benefited the peasants who bore
the brunt of the tax burden.[65]

As we have seen, the Ottomans attempted to abolish tax farming
of the tithe in the 1840s and 1850s, seeking to replace it with direct

[64] Granovsky, *The Fiscal System of Palestine*, 23, 65, 84, 91, 119, 127, 171, 204, 234,
244, 252; Mandel, *Hitpat'hut*, 1.

[65] Alexander Schölch, *Palestine in Transformation, 1856–1882: Studies in Social,
Economic and Political Development*, trans. William C. Young and Michael C.
Gerrity (Washington, DC: Institute for Palestine Studies, 1993), 259–60.

collection of taxes, but tax farming proved resistant to change. Tax farmers were widely used in Palestine, taxing peasants but retaining much of the proceeds for themselves. Tax farmers sometimes used coercion, such as fines and corporal punishment, to extract revenue from peasants (often at a much higher rate than the official one). As a result of these methods, in the 1840s and 1850s the Ottomans generated less than half of the revenue that the Egyptians had been able to raise in Palestine when they ruled the country in the 1830s. An additional reason for the relative decline in revenues compared to the period of Egyptian rule was the fact that the work of tax farmers was now supervised by newly created local councils manned by local notables. The local councils favored the tax farmers, who were often the relatives of the notables, at the expense of the distant state. In the mountainous areas of Palestine, where government rule was weaker, local chieftains were given the power to collect taxes. In some remote areas, local autonomy was preserved to such a degree that the Ottomans could raise no taxes at all. Indeed, on Palestine's eastern frontier, in Transjordan, rather than collecting money from the local population, it was the government itself that paid an annual fee – protection money – to local Bedouin chiefs to prevent them from raiding the important hajj pilgrim caravan that passed through Transjordan on its way from Damascus to Mecca.[66]

After 1860, the central Ottoman government came to function in a more rigorous and bureaucratic way. Its power and efficiency grew, and it increased its direct contact with – and hold over – the population of Palestine. Local governors, who had enjoyed broad autonomy in the pre-reform period, became obedient servants of the Ottoman center. Gradually, even the Bedouins in the remote southern and eastern frontiers of the country, the Negev desert in the south and Transjordan in the east, began to pay their taxes, and tax revenues grew accordingly. The selection of tax farmers and the methods they used in the collection process were now regulated by legal rules and supervised by government officials.[67] The use of force to extract taxation was

[66] Ma'oz, *Ottoman Reform*, 72–3, 78–81, 93, 98, 118–19, 128, 132–3, 158–9.
[67] Gerber, *Ottoman Rule*, 15–27, 96, 103, 123, 160, 166–7, 176, 230, 250; Haim Gerber, "A New Look at the Tanzimat: The Case of the Province of Jerusalem," in *Palestine in the Late Ottoman Period: Political, Social, and Economic Transformation*, ed. David Kushner (Jerusalem: Yad Izhak Ben-Zvi, 1986), 30, 37; Kushner, "Ha-Dor,"

now curtailed and in some regions of Palestine tax farming of the tithe was even replaced by a system in which the tax was raised by the villagers themselves (self-farming) or by using salaried government officials. However, tax farming did not completely disappear, and in some regions tax farmers were still able to extract from the peasants far more of their harvest than the formal rules stipulated.[68]

Another aspect of earlier tax practices that did not entirely disappear was the collective liability for taxation in the villages. The Ottoman bureaucratic reforms of the nineteenth century set in motion a process of individuation, designed to create individual responsibility to the state. This process was assisted by such devices as the census and the land code of 1858, but collective village liability for the payment of the tithe nevertheless existed until the end of the Empire. In addition, negotiated settlements, as well as arbitrary assessments based on threats and violence, sometimes still occurred.[69]

It should also be noted that, while some aspects of tax collection were now regulated by legal rules, the application of these rules was not decided by legal institutions. For example, peasants disputing the amount of tithe they were asked to pay now had the right to appeal their assessments. However, these appeals were to be adjudicated not by courts but by local administrative councils established during the period of Ottoman reforms and manned by local notables as well as Ottoman officials. The function of such councils may have resembled the "bureaucratic adjudication" that characterized other nineteenth-century tax systems such as the English system.[70] It is unclear to what

---

25, 29–30; Rogan, *Frontiers of the State*, 12–3, 84–5, 92–3; Yasemin Avci, "The Application of *Tanzimat* in the Desert: The Bedouins and the Creation of a New Town in Southern Palestine (1860–1914)," *Middle Eastern Studies* 45 (2009): 969–83, 973; Young, *Corps de Droit Ottoman*, 312–23.

[68] Gerber, *Ottoman Rule*, 110, 160–77, 171–4, 254–5.

[69] Granovsky, *The Fiscal System of Palestine*, 155; Gabriel Baer, *Ha-Mukhtar ha-Kafri be-Erets Yisrael: Toldot Ma'amado ve-Tafkidav* (Jerusalem: Magnes, 1978), 29–33; Gerber, *Ottoman Rule*, 119–20, 168–9, 171–4, 230, 259; Rogan, *Frontiers of the State*, 13. For a critical discussion of the land code of 1858, as well as the census, tax surveys, and other administration tools used by the Ottomans, see İslamoğlu, "Modernities Compared," 109.

[70] See Chantal Stebbings, "The Origins of the Application of *Certiorari* to the General Commissioners of Income Tax," *British Tax Review*, 1997, 119–30,

extent these bodies adjudicated disputes based on formal rules, and whether, given their composition, they served as an objective forum for redress against tax farmers.[71]

Another avenue for redress in tax matters was found in petitions to the Ottoman sultan. Petitions to the sultan were a traditional method of redress that had existed for centuries, but the technological changes that Palestine and other parts of the Empire witnessed in the nineteenth century (especially the introduction of post offices and telegraph lines between Palestine and Istanbul) led to unprecedented growth in their use from the 1870s onward. Petitioners often employed the services of professional petition-writers (*arzuhalcis*). These were literate scribes with knowledge of Turkish, the official language of the bureaucracy. The petitions, often equitable in their nature, were directed to the grand vizier (the Ottoman equivalent of a prime minister) in Istanbul. A major topic of these petitions centered on complaints related to tax assessment and collection.[72] Petitioners often protested against the corruption and misconduct of government officials in tax matters, and about the enforcement of new tax laws and policies, relying on long-standing local rights and precedents that the central Ottoman government was keen to abolish in its drive to standardize taxation.[73] In this

---

126; Chantal Stebbings, "Bureaucratic Adjudication: The Internal Appeals of the Inland Revenue," in *Judges and Judging in the History of the Common Law and Civil Law from Antiquity to Modern Times*, eds. Paul Brand and Joshua Getzler (Cambridge: Cambridge University Press, 2012), 157–74, 158–9.

[71] See Yair Sagy, "Le-Ma'an ha-Tsedek? 'Al Hakamato shel Beyt ha-Mishpat ha-Gavohah le-Tsedek," *'Iyune Mishpat* 28 (2004): 225–98, 237–8. Beginning in the 1870s, appeals could also be made to the Ottoman *Nizamiye* courts. However, the use of these courts was expensive, partly because of the need to use professional attorneys versed in formal procedural rules. See Rubin, *Ottoman Nizamiye Courts*, 106; Avi Rubin, "From Legal Representation to Advocacy: Attorneys and Clients in the Ottoman *Nizamiye* Courts," *International Journal of Middle East Studies* 44 (2012): 111–27, 120.

[72] Yuval Ben-Bassat, "In Search of Justice: Petitions Sent from Palestine to Istanbul from the 1870's Onwards," *Turcica* 41 (2009): 89–114, 89–101; Yuval Ben-Bassat and Fruma Zachs, "Correspondence Manuals in Nineteenth-Century Greater Syria: Between the *Arzuhalci* and the Advent of Popular Letter Writing," *Turkish Historical Review* 4 (2013): 1–25, 8–11; Ben-Bassat, *Petitioning the Sultan*, 50–4, 152. For a comparison of *arzuhalcis* and lawyers, see Rubin, "From Legal Representation to Advocacy," 115.

[73] Ben-Bassat, "In Search of Justice," 101–2, 109; Ben-Bassat, *Petitioning the Sultan*, 120–2.

sense, the process of petitioning differed from contemporary tax adjudication based on legal norms, and was closer to an equity-like process (in the nontechnical sense), relying on ad hoc sultanic justice and striving to maintain local customary privileges that conflicted with law.[74]

Finally, it should be noted that, in some cases, no formal appeal mechanism existed. Thus, for example, the Ottoman property tax, created in the late nineteenth century, included no provisions for allowing objections to initial assessments. This may not have been as problematic as it seems because, in places where Ottoman rule was weak (such as in the southern and eastern desert parts of Palestine, dominated by nomadic or seminomadic Bedouin tribes), the Ottomans were, in any event, unable to assess property in the way required by the legislation. Instead, they resorted to a fixed commuted property tax (*werko maqtu‘*), similar, in fact, to a poll tax, that was imposed collectively on the Bedouin tribes and apportioned among the tribesmen by the Bedouin sheikhs rather than by the government.[75]

One can conclude that the reformed Ottoman tax system of the nineteenth century, especially the most important rural tax – the tithe, was in many respects different from contemporary tax systems, mainly because of the use of tax farming. While the tithe was supposedly regulated by law, it seems that the provisions of the law were often not enforced in certain areas, at least if we are to believe European accounts. German nineteenth-century sources reported that in central Palestine the amount of tithe collected rarely averaged "under one third of the whole crops, instead of the legal tenth."[76] This was also the British colonial view. According to British reports from the mandatory period, during Ottoman times taxes such as the tithe were open to "great abuse," and "the rich man rarely, if ever, paid his fair share," while the poor were overcharged.[77] Thus, a British committee

---

[74] See Ben-Bassat, *Petitioning the Sultan*, 139, 150–3.

[75] ISA, Record Group 2, M 132/8, Report of the Rural Taxation Machinery Committee, June 22, 1933, 4–6. In other areas appeals of property assessments did exist. Gerber's description of land surveys in the province of Jerusalem in the late Ottoman period mentions appeals to a "survey group for correction," and then to the administrative council of the province. See Gerber, *Ottoman Rule*, 205.

[76] See Schölch, *Palestine in Transformation*, 254.

[77] Palestine Royal Commission, *Report* (London: HMSO, 1937), 150–1. For a somewhat similar view, see Kenneth W. Stein, *The Land Question in Palestine, 1917–1939*

established in 1922 to examine the assessment and collection of the tithe argued that "the tithe collected [in Ottoman times] was generally in excess of the regular tax. Breaches committed by the contractors [tax farmers] were never looked into by the Government officials, who favoured the contractors in every case ... [and] the average tax collected by the contractor amounted to not less than from 18 percent to 20 percent of the produce ... in contravention to the Law."[78]

Abraham Granovsky, a Jewish economist in mandatory Palestine, whose book on the tax system of Palestine provided the most comprehensive survey of the subject published in the 1930s, expressed a similar view: "of all the antiquated institutions which the British administration inherited from the Ottoman régime and which hampered the economic progress of the country," he said, "the Osher [öşür – tithe] was probably the worst ... [the official rate] was always exceeded. In practice peasants paid 20 percent or 30 percent and sometimes as much as 40 percent [of their produce]" and, he continued, "all the legal regulations for supervising the assessments remained a dead letter. In point of fact, the peasants were at the mercy of the tax farmers and the assessors."[79]

However, it is possible to find descriptions to the contrary. For example, in an interview conducted in 1905, Haim Kalvarisky, the representative of the Jewish Colonization Association in the northern part of the country, the Galilee, stated that the farmers in the Jewish colonies there paid no more than the law required.[80] One of the leading scholars of late Ottoman Palestine, Haim Gerber, echoes this view. In his book on the administration of the region of Jerusalem in the late Ottoman era, Gerber noted that, by the beginning of the twentieth

---

(Chapel Hill: University of North Carolina Press, 1984), 16–17. For a general discussion of the problems associated with the use of British accounts as a source for the study of Ottoman legal history, see, e.g., Assaf Likhovski, *Law and Identity in Mandate Palestine* (Chapel Hill: University of North Carolina Press, 2006), 54–5; Avi Rubin, "British Perceptions of Ottoman Judicial Reform in the Late Nineteenth Century: Some Preliminary Insights," *Law and Social Inquiry* 37 (2012): 991–1012.

[78] Report of the Tithe Commission, Palestine, sec. 17, reprinted in Martin Bunton, ed., *Land Legislation in Mandate Palestine* (Cambridge: Cambridge Archive Editions, 2009), 5:357, 5:376.

[79] Granovsky, *The Fiscal System of Palestine*, 151–2, 153.

[80] "'Inyeney ha-Yishuv," *Hashkafah*, July 14, 1905, at 1.

century, tax farming in the Jerusalem region was more of "an orderly bureaucratic process than the wild 'catch as catch can'" of the pre-reform period, and that "statistically speaking, the tithe paid by the peasants in large areas of Palestine at the beginning of the twentieth century was the legal 12 percent."[81]

Early Mandatory Taxation

The British rulers of Palestine inherited a tax system in which the main direct tax was the tithe.[82] The British, more than the Ottomans, were viewed by their subjects as distant rulers unconnected to the local population, and they therefore lacked the political legitimacy that the Ottoman Empire had enjoyed.[83] This relative lack of legitimacy meant that the British were more constrained in their attempts to reform the local tax system than the Ottomans had been. In addition, during the

---

[81] Gerber, *Ottoman Rule*, 230.

[82] On the mandatory tax system, see generally Granovsky, *The Fiscal System of Palestine*; Arye Lapidoth, *Evasion and Avoidance of Income Tax: A Comparative Study of English Law and Israeli Law* (Jerusalem: Museum of Taxes, 1966), 16–25; Arye Lapidoth, "Trends in the Income Tax Legislation of Israel," in *Studies in Israel Legislative Problems*, eds. Gad Tedeschi and Uri Yadin (Jerusalem: Magnes Press, 1966), 325–41; Amotz Morag, *Mimun ha-Memshalah be-Yisrael: Hitpat'huyot u-Ve'ayot* (Jerusalem: Magnes, 1967), 1–28; Harold C. Wilkenfeld, *Taxes and People in Israel* (Cambridge, MA: Harvard University Press, 1973), 16–42; Aharon Yoran, "Forty Years of Tax Law in Israel," *Israel Law Review* 24 (1990): 738–85; Barbara J. Smith, *The Roots of Separatism in Palestine: British Economic Policy 1920–1929* (London: I. B. Tauris, 1993), 40–6; Jacob Metzer, *The Divided Economy of Mandatory Palestine* (Cambridge: Cambridge University Press, 1998), 180–90; Martin Bunton, *Colonial Land Policies in Palestine, 1917–1936* (Oxford: Oxford University Press, 2007), 132–70.

[83] See Ilana Feldman, *Governing Gaza: Bureaucracy, Authority, and the Work of Rule, 1917–1967* (Durham, NC: Duke University Press, 2008), 15. On British rule in Palestine, see generally Bernard Wasserstein, *The British in Palestine: The Mandatory Government and Arab-Jewish Conflict, 1917–1929*, 2nd edn (Oxford: Blackwell, 1991); Jacob Reuveny, *Mimshal ha-Mandat be-Erets Yisrael, 1920–1948: Nitu'ah Histori Medini* (Ramat-Gan: Bar-Ilan University Press, 1993). On the mandatory legal system see Likhovski, *Law and Identity in Mandate Palestine*. On the relationship of political legitimacy and revenue-raising in the colonial context, see, e.g., Ewout Frankema, "Raising Revenue in the British Empire, 1870–1940: How 'Extractive' Were Colonial Taxes?" *Journal of Global History* 5 (2010): 447–77, 451.

period of British rule, tensions between the Arabs and Jews of Palestine grew. The hostility between these two major sectors of the population meant that every new tax measure was viewed through the prism of its impact on each sector. Thus the Arabs opposed a capital gains tax (because many in the Arab elite sold land to the Jews and were thus liable to be taxed). Arabs also opposed custom duties, which were seen as protecting the nascent Jewish industry in Palestine, and estate taxation. Jews, on the other hand, opposed the income tax, which was viewed as targeting mainly the urban sector (the Jewish population was mostly urban).[84]

However, while the specific political and social conditions in Palestine were somewhat unique, the general trajectory of the development of its tax system during the period of British rule reflected a process that unfolded in many other places at the same time – the decline of traditional agricultural produce taxes, the rise in the importance of indirect taxation, especially customs duties, which had become the main source of government revenue in Palestine by the 1930s, and later (in Palestine's case, in the 1940s) the appearance of a new form of direct taxation – income tax (see Table 1.2).[85]

The British first occupied the south of Palestine in 1917 and then the north of the country in 1918. In early 1918 the British military government of the territory reinstated the taxes that had been in force in Palestine before the Ottoman Empire entered the war. In rural areas, the British reinstituted the tithe, the animal tax, and the land tax (*werko*). In urban areas, taxes included the *werko* as well as municipal taxes and fees. In addition, indirect taxes, such as customs duties, were also reimposed. One tax that was not carried over from the Ottoman

[84] Morag, *Mimun*, 1–6; Mandel, *Hitpat'hut*, 1–3, 107; Smith, *The Roots of Separatism in Palestine*, 38. On British fiscal conservatism, see Reuveny, *Mimshal ha-Mandat*, 77.

[85] Nachum Gross, "Ha-Medinyut ha-Kalkalit shel Memshelet Erets-Yisrael bi-Tkufat ha-Mandat" in *Lo 'Al ha-Ru'ah Levadah: 'Iyunim ba-Historiyah ha-Kalkalit shel Erets Yisrael ba-'Et ha-Hadashah* (Jerusalem: Yad Izhak Ben-Zvi, 1999), 172–227, 181; Bunton, *Colonial Land Policies in Palestine*, 141. For similar developments elsewhere, see, e.g., Neil Charlesworth, "The Problem of Government Finance in British India: Taxation, Borrowing and the Allocation of Resources in the Inter-war Period," *Modern Asian Studies* 19 (1985): 521–48; Anne Booth, "Night Watchman, Extractive, or Developmental States? Some Evidence from Late Colonial South-East Asia," *Economic History Review* 60 (2007): 241–66, 245.

Table 1.2 Government of Palestine revenues for the fiscal years 1922/23 and 1945/46

Fiscal year	1922/23		1945/46	
	P£	%	P£	%
Produce tax (*usher*)	208,000	16	9,000	0
Animal tax	41,000	3	207,000	1
Rural and urban property taxes and house tax	137,000	11	1,130,000	8
Income tax	0	0	3,117,000	21
Direct taxes (total)	386,000	30	1,346,000	30
Customs	610,000	48	4,985,000	34
Excise	43,000	4	2,063,000	14
Indirect taxes (total)	653,000	52	7,048,000	48
Stamp duty	50,000	4	317,000	2
Fees and licenses	181,000	14	2,929,000	20
Other taxes and fees (total)	231,000	18	3,246,000	22
Total	1,270,000	100	14,757,000	100

period was the profits tax, the *temettu,* that taxed the profits of urban artisans and merchants. This Ottoman tax was abolished by the British soon after the occupation of the country, thus tilting the balance of the tax burden in favor of the urban sector, at least until the 1940s.[86]

[86] Abcarius, "The Fiscal System," 556; "Income Tax," *PP*, April 3, 1941, at 4; Report of Committee on the Economic Condition of the Agriculturalists and the Fiscal Measures of Government in Relation Thereto, sec. 76, reprinted in Bunton, *Land Legislation in Mandate Palestine*, 6:87, 6:176–8. See also Bunton, *Colonial Land Policies in Palestine*, 133–5, 140, 148–9. The Jewish population in Palestine was mostly urban and the Arab population was mostly rural. This also determined the relative share of each sector of the population in different types of income. For example, in 1944, the Arabs earned 70% of the income derived from agriculture while the Jews earned 88% of the income derived from industry, and 70% of the income derived from commerce and finance. See P. J. Loftus, *National Income of Palestine, 1944* ([Jerusalem]: Government Printer, 1946). On the ethnic incidence of various types of taxes in mandatory Palestine, see generally Jacob Metzer, "Fiscal Incidence and Resource Transfer between Jews and Arabs in Mandatory Palestine," *Research in Economic History* 7 (1982): 87–132.

While the British at first retained most of the Ottoman taxes, they did initiate some reforms that economic historian Nachum Gross characterized as an attempt to "Europeanize" the tax administration of Palestine. Thus, in 1919 they abolished the use of tax farmers in the collection of the tithe. Instead, assessment was now performed by salaried government estimators. In Ottoman times, the tithe was often collected in kind. Now it was paid in cash to a government official – the village headman (*mukhtar*) – based on a redemption price fixed according to the market value of the crop. Villages' collective responsibility for the tax was formally abolished in 1922. Both the crop assessment and the redemption price of the crop were now subject to appeal to the district governor or to a special commission. In 1922 the British, apparently in an effort to combat the practice of peasants hiding their crops, passed the Tithe Law Amendment Ordinance, imposing penalties for such concealment. An additional reform of the tithe occurred in 1925 when the rate was lowered from 12.63 percent to 10 percent.

However, despite the changes brought about by the British administration, vestiges of the Ottoman tax assessment and collection system remained. First, tax farming did not entirely disappear. In addition to a fixed salary, the village headman received a certain percentage commission on the tax he collected (2 percent and later 5 percent), turning him into a quasi-tax farmer.[87]

A second example of continuity between Ottoman and British tax practices was the lack of involvement of lawyers in the assessment and collection process, this being carried out instead by local

---

[87] Report of the Tithe Commission – Palestine, secs. 19–26, 37, reprinted in Bunton, *Land Legislation in Mandate Palestine*, 5:378–85, 5:394–5; ISA, Record Group 2, M 132/8, Report of the Rural Taxation Machinery Committee, June 22, 1933, 20–4; Granovsky, *The Fiscal System of Palestine*, 145–57; Palestine Royal Commission, *Report* (London: HMSO, 1937), 156; Abcarius, "The Fiscal System," 505, 507–10, 516; Baer, *Ha-Mukhtar*, 29–33; Stein, *The Land Question in Palestine*, 17; Reuveny, *Mimshal ha-Mandat*, 80; Smith, *The Roots of Separatism in Palestine*, 40–1; Gross, "Ha-Medinyut," 172, 180; Bunton, *Colonial Land Policies in Palestine*, 165–6. The tithe was levied on the gross yield. The tax on the net return was actually 35 percent. Abcarius, "The Fiscal System," 516; Mandel, *Hitpat'hut*, 109, 114–17. While tax farming of the tithe was officially abolished, it seems that the use of tax farming did not completely disappear, at least not in the case of municipal taxation in the more backward parts of the country. See Feldman, *Governing Gaza*, 247, n. 91.

administrators. Appeals were referred to the British district commissioners, and lawyers and courts were not directly involved in the appeals process.[88]

Third, some aspects of collective tax collection remained. The British sought to create individualized property rights that would enable a direct relationship between the colonial government and individual taxpayers. This policy was based on an ideology (also manifested in the nineteenth-century Ottoman land reform) that sought to further the notions of private property and individualism. It was also the result of a belief that individualizing private property would enable a more efficient taxation of revenues from land because it would make potential taxpayers more readily identifiable to the state.[89] However, this desire for reform encountered an older property system that existed in Palestine's villages even during the mandatory era, a customary system of joint property called *musha'* in which land was held in common by a group of people – members of a few villages, a single village, or a single kinship group – and was redistributed among the members of the group every few years.[90] Considerations of administrative efficiency

---

[88] This was not unique. The process of taxation in Palestine during the first two-and-a-half decades of British rule was similar to the way the British taxed themselves and their Empire in the nineteenth century and early twentieth century: Tax assessment (and tax appeals) were considered an administrative matter, and law and lawyers did not play a major role in this process. On the UK system, see V. Grout and B. Sabine, "The First Hundred Years of Tax Cases," *British Tax Review*, 1975, 75–83; R. Cocks, "Victorian Barristers, Judges and Taxation: A Study in the Expansion of Legal Work," in *Law, Economy and Society, 1750–1914: Essays in the History of English Law*, eds. G. R. Rubin and D. Sugarman (Abingdon: Professional Books, 1984), 445, 446; Chantal Stebbings, "Income Tax Tribunals: Their Influence and Place in the Victorian Legal System," in *Studies in the History of Tax Law*, ed. John Tiley (Oxford: Hart, 2004), 57–79; Chantal Stebbings, *The Victorian Taxpayer and the Law: A Study in Constitutional Conflict* (Cambridge: Cambridge University Press, 2009); Stebbings, "Bureaucratic Adjudication," 171. On nineteenth-century India, see V. K. R. V. Rao, *Taxation of Income in India* (Calcutta: Longmans, 1931), 13–4, 29; C. L. Jenkins, "1860: India's First Income Tax," *British Tax Review*, 2012, 87–116, 107, 110–11.

[89] Bunton, *Colonial Land Policies in Palestine*, 8, 19–20.

[90] On the *musha'*, see, e.g., Scott Atran, "Le masha'a et la question foncière en Palestine, 1858–1948," *Annales. Économies, Sociétés, Civilisations* 42 (1987): 1361–89; Amos Nadan, *The Palestinian Peasant Economy under the Mandate: A Story of Colonial Bungling* (Cambridge, MA: Harvard Center for Middle Eastern Studies, 2006), 261–90.

forced the British to rely on this customary property system, and they therefore turned to village headmen and notables to assess and collect rural taxes, creating a system of taxation that, in practice, was governed by customary norms enforced collectively rather than by legal norms applied individually.[91]

Village headmen collected the tithe on behalf of their villages, dividing the burden among individual farmers. This was true both for villages in which land was held collectively and was periodically redistributed among villagers, and also for villages in which land was held by individual farmers. As a British tithe reform committee noted in 1922, the village headmen and elders were "made responsible for the tithes of the community by means of securing their signatures on a promissory note," contrary to the principle that the "tax was due from individuals and not from the community as a whole." Records of the payments of individual farmers or landowners were not kept. In each village, the village headman was required to post a notice of the tithe due from each farmer, but "although instructions [had] frequently been issued to this effect, in practice it [was] not often done." Even if it had been done, it would not have provided a real safeguard against the abuse of individual farmers by the headman because the majority of the farmers "were unable to read." In the case of taxpayers who refused to pay, the headman, not the individual taxpayer, was held liable and was sued by the government, based on the promissory note he had signed. Thus, just as in Ottoman times, there was no direct link between government and individual taxpayers, a link that would have enabled individual taxpayers to rely on their legal rights in tax disputes.[92] The reliance on village headmen was an administratively efficient way of assessing and collecting the tithe, but it also meant that the system was very inaccurate. Guesswork, error, lack of standardized weights and measures, the illiteracy and ignorance of many headmen, and outright corruption all led to large discrepancies in the actual rate of the taxes collected.[93]

---

[91] Bunton, *Colonial Land Policies in Palestine*, 169–70.

[92] See Report of the Tithe Commission – Palestine, secs. 24, 36, 38, 58, reprinted in Bunton, *Land Legislation in Mandate Palestine*, 5:381, 5:393–6, 5:424–6. See also Bunton, *Colonial Land Policies in Palestine*, 164–9.

[93] Bunton, *Colonial Land Policies in Palestine*, 143–5, 162–9.

A fourth manifestation of continuity between the Ottoman and British approaches to taxation was the fact that discretion and negotiations did not entirely disappear. On the one hand, some observers argued that the British strictly applied the letter of Ottoman law. Isaac Rokach, director of the largest Jewish orange-producing company in Palestine, recalled (in a story whose authenticity is difficult to ascertain) that British application of Ottoman law led to many complaints. A committee was appointed by the British to investigate the matter. When questioned on why there was such resentment toward a tax that the British had inherited from the Turks, one of the Arab witnesses before the committee answered that "the tithe was an age old Ottoman law, but this law was implemented *à la turca*. You English implement it *à l'anglaise* ... An Ottoman law implemented by an Ottoman sword is fine, but no one can withstand an Ottoman law implemented by a British sword."[94]

On the other hand, it would also be wrong to assume that the British always followed the letter of the law. Sometimes, the British applied the law less strictly as a policy matter, taking into account economic hardships. Thus, for example, the actual rate of the animal tax varied from village to village, depending on the hardships each village was experiencing. The rate of the tithe also changed, especially in the 1930s when a series of poor harvests ultimately forced the British to enact a law to commute and remit large amounts of the tithe.[95] In addition, there was no central tax office ensuring a standardized assessment and collection process. Instead, as we have seen, the tithe was assessed and collected locally by village headmen. The lack of any

---

[94] Isaac Rokach, *Pardesim Mesaprim* (Ramat-Gan: Masadah, 1970), 133–4. See also Ylana N. Miller, *Government and Society in Rural Palestine, 1920–1948* (Austin: University of Texas Press, 1985), 71–2. Rokach may have overstated the Ottoman disdain for the rule of law, both before and after Ottoman reforms in the nineteenth century.

[95] Palestine Royal Commission, *Report* (London: HMSO, 1937), 168; Roza I. M. El-Eini, "Government Fiscal Policy in Mandatory Palestine in the 1930s," *Middle Eastern Studies* 33 (1997): 570–96, 583, 584. One can sometimes find examples of British officials expressing such attitudes. For example, the first high commissioner, Herbert Samuel, said in a letter written in 1921 that "*[n]e pas trop gouverner* is a good maxim, particularly in an eastern country and above all in the early years of the regime." See Zeina B. Ghandour, *A Discourse on Domination in Mandate Palestine: Imperialism, Property and Insurgency* (Abingdon: Routledge, 2010), 54.

centralized supervisory authority led to a reality in which there was "a wide variety of internal regulations and practices between district and district and even between subdistricts of the same district." Variations also existed in individual assessments in the same locality because of the guesswork involved in estimating the amount of grain produced. This guesswork, of course, created opportunities for "corruption and oppression," making the tithe, in the words of one British district commissioner in the 1920s, "grossly immoral."[96]

Diversity was also a product of ethnic difference. Sometimes "the special conditions prevalent in Jewish colonies" led to "Jewish commissions being appointed" to assess produce in Jewish villages. This, explained a British report, was a result of the fact that "the more advanced agriculturalists, who in general [were] mostly Jews" used modern threshing machinery. This meant the ordinary procedure of assessment (counting sheaves of grain on the threshing floor) could not be followed, and instead resort had to be made to the registers of the local village council.[97]

Another British report explained that "tithes on crops in Arab villages were assessed by estimators hazarding a guess that heaps of sheaves placed on threshing floors contained so many camel or donkey loads of sheaves," and that inexperience, carelessness, and "biases" in such processes of estimation led to inaccurate assessments. In Jewish villages, on the other hand, "where threshing machines were used," the estimator "attended the threshing and weighed the grain itself. [Thus] while Arab cultivators' crops were only approximately estimated, those of Jewish cultivators were usually correctly assessed."[98]

In 1927 the tithe was reformed. Instead of annual assessments that delayed the marketing of the produce until the annual yield was assessed, the tithe was commuted. Villages were now required to pay

---

[96] ISA, Record Group 2, M 132/8, Report of the Rural Taxation Machinery Committee, June 22, 1933, 42–4; Sir Ernest M. Dowson, Notes on the Abolition of the Tithe and the Establishment of Land Tax in Palestine, April 1928, secs. 3–4, 7, reprinted in Bunton, *Land Legislation in Mandate Palestine*, 6:12, 6:20–2, 6:23–6. See also Bunton, *Colonial Land Policies in Palestine*, 160.

[97] Report of the Tithe Commission – Palestine, sec. 70, reprinted in Bunton, *Land Legislation in Mandate Palestine*, 5:433–5.

[98] A. Abramson, Proposal to Substitute a Land Tax for the Present Werko and Tithe, March 5, 1928, reprinted in Bunton, *Land Legislation in Mandate Palestine*, 6:55–61.

a sum based on the average aggregate amount they had paid in the previous four years. The tax was imposed on each village and, once again, was apportioned among the farmers using local knowledge. Assessment committees that included the village headman and notables distributed the burden among the villagers. Assessments could be appealed to a "revising" committee and later to the district commissioner, whose decision was final. The reform was gradually applied to all areas of Palestine except the Bedouin areas of Beersheba.[99]

The reform of the tithe in 1927 failed to stem the decline of this tax as an important source of revenue. One reason for this decline was economic. In the late 1920s and early 1930s, the peasants of Palestine experienced a series of disasters including droughts, the 1929 world depression, and poor harvests, thus severing the link between the commuted tithe and the actual return that farmers received from the soil. Another reason was political. In 1929 the country experienced widespread riots, with Arabs pitted against Jews. The government believed these riots were partly caused by the migration of Arab villagers to the cities of Palestine, and that one way to discourage such migration was to ease the burden of rural taxation. The government therefore decided to remit much of the tax due from farmers in the period between 1930 and 1935, lowering the amount demanded by one third in 1930, by another 20 percent in 1931, and, in some areas, by larger amounts. In 1935 the tithe was abolished in most of Palestine. As a consequence of all these changes, there was a sharp decline in the contribution of the tithe to the revenue of the government. While in 1922 the tithe (together with the animal tax) constituted almost 20 percent of government revenues, by 1935 the commuted tithe and the animal tax were jointly producing only about 3 percent of the total revenue of the government, and by the 1940s the contribution of the tithe had shrunk to 0.1 percent.[100]

[99] Commutation of Tithes Ordinance, 1927, PG, 16 October 1927, at 712–16; ISA, Record Group 2, M 132/8, Report of the Rural Taxation Machinery Committee, June 22, 1933, 20–4; Frederic M. Goadby and Moses J. Doukhan, *The Land Law of Palestine* (Tel Aviv: Shoshany, 1935), 359–63; Mandel, *Hitpat'hut*, 116–17; Stein, *The Land Question in Palestine*, 18; Bunton, *Colonial Land Policies in Palestine*, 145–50, 164–5.

[100] Sir John Hope Simpson, *Palestine: Report on Immigration, Land Settlement and Development* (London: HMSO, 1930), 70–3; ISA, Record Group 2, M 132/8, Report

Another major reform of the Ottoman tax system carried out by the British centered on the land tax (*werko*). This tax was based on assessments of the capital value of the land from the 1890s, augmented over time by arbitrary increases unrelated to the real increase in the value of the land. The replacement of the Ottoman land tax by a new tax based on the expected annual rental value of the land had already been suggested in the early 1920s.[101] In the late 1920s and early 1930s, as the importance of the tithe as a source of revenue declined, the *werko* was also gradually abolished. In urban areas, the *werko* was replaced in 1928 by an urban property tax. The new tax taxed the net annual value of buildings and land. This value was determined by assessment committees based on actual or estimated rental value. In 1935 the British enacted the Rural Property Tax Ordinance that was meant to replace the Ottoman tithe and *werko* in most rural areas.[102]

Collection of the new taxes in rural areas was collective rather than individual. The lands of each village were valued based on the type of produce grown and the expected annual yield. Committees manned by the villagers were then established to allocate the tax burden among all the farmers of the village. Their decisions were subject to appeal to the district commissioner. Taxes would be collected by government tax collectors, assisted by the village headman. The rural and urban property taxes in 1937–38 together yielded about 8 percent of the revenue of the government; and, together with the animal tax, all direct taxes in Palestine in this period yielded a meager 8.6 percent of government

of the Rural Taxation Machinery Committee, June 22, 1933, 25, 33–4, 40; Palestine Royal Commission, *Report* (London: HMSO, 1937), 168. The tithe was retained in both the Beersheba and the Hula areas. See ISA, Record Group 2, M 132/8, Chief Secretary Circular, March 17, 1943; Abcarius, "The Fiscal System," 516–19; Morag, *Mimun*, 8–11; Mandel, *Hitpat'hut*, 2, 117; Stein, *The Land Question in Palestine*, 18; Smith, *The Roots of Separatism in Palestine*, 40; Gross, "Ha-Medinyut," 180–1; Metzer, *The Divided Economy of Mandatory Palestine*, 182; Nadan, *The Palestinian Peasant Economy*, xxxv, 28–31, 40, 339; Bunton, *Colonial Land Policies in Palestine*, 141.

[101] Report of the Tithe Commission, Palestine, sec. 78, reprinted in Bunton, *Land Legislation in Mandate Palestine*, 5:443. See also Sir E. Dowson, Notes on the Abolition of the Tithe and the Establishment of a Land Tax in Palestine, April 1928, reprinted in Bunton, *Land Legislation in Mandate Palestine*, 6:11.

[102] Palestine Royal Commission, *Report* (London: HMSO, 1937), 127, 168, 224; Bunton, *Colonial Land Policies in Palestine*, 140–1, 150–5.

revenues, compared to almost 50 percent provided by customs and excise duties.[103]

Conclusion

One major characteristic common to all the systems described in this chapter was the absence, or relative absence, of universal, standard, individualized legal norms, and the relative absence of the carriers of such norms – that is, lawyers – from the taxation process. During the three decades of British rule in Palestine, the country underwent massive changes. As the economy of Palestine was partly transformed from an agricultural to an industrial economy, and as the population became more urban and literate, the tax system of the country changed accordingly. The tithe was first commuted and later almost totally abolished. Ottoman land taxation was also reformed and replaced by property taxes. However, the introduction of income taxation, which changed the nature of the relationship between taxation and law, had to wait until the 1940s, the last decade of British rule in Palestine. The process by which income taxation and its law arrived in Palestine is the subject of the next chapter.

---

[103] ISA, Record Group 2, M 132/8, Duties and Remuneration of Mukhtars in Rural Areas, June 14, 1935; Abcarius, "The Fiscal System," 517, 519–25, 527–9, 531; Bunton, *Colonial Land Policies in Palestine*, 166.

2

The Introduction of Income Taxation in Mandatory Palestine

In the early 1930s British officials in Palestine and in the Colonial Office in London began to seriously contemplate the introduction of income taxation in Palestine. In 1934 the Colonial Office sent John Francis Huntington, a tax expert, to the country. Following his visit, Huntington came to the conclusion that Palestine was not ready for such a tax. One of the reasons he gave concerned the difference between Britain and Palestine in the visibility of wealth. "In Palestine," he observed, "the style of life of quite wealthy persons bears, to Western ideas, little relation to their income ... I was told on good authority that the richest Arab in Haifa lives in a style of penury and that a Jew of the same city, reputed to be a millionaire, lives in a third-rate hotel." Huntington then quoted from a novel by German-Jewish author Arnold Zweig, in which it was said that "men who own whole districts of Jerusalem live unobtrusively among ancient gardens, whose existence behind high walls is more surmised than seen. And sheikhs, who may be observed buying costly carpets ... look as though they did not possess five pounds ... but in the end they produce thick bundles of notes from their pockets or from their broad girdles."[1]

Income taxation was finally imposed in Palestine at the beginning of the Second World War. The first reports of British officials administering the tax read like the reports of tropical explorers venturing into uncharted territory. In the District of Jerusalem, collection

[1] TNA: CO 733/261, J. F. Huntington, [Report], 12.

was entrusted to a team headed by J. G. T. Sheringham, a British cadet officer whose training was in theology and classics.[2] Just as Huntington had warned in 1934, this officer found that his British commonsense notions of wealth and its visible manifestations could not be relied on in assessing the income of his unfamiliar subjects: "Some of the wealthiest men in Jerusalem," he reported, "seem to be obscure ultra-orthodox Oriental or Ashkenazi Jews. ... [T]wo ultra-orthodox Ashkenazis made P£ [Palestine pounds] 6,299 and P£7,179 out of houses and money-lending; both of them prefer to walk rather than bear the expense of a bus fare, and the richer lives in a house worth P£46 a year. Their returns, though prepared by a 'reliable' auditor, were increased by P£1,600 and P£1,900 respectively."[3] The cafés

---

[2] Sheringham studied oriental languages at Trinity College, Dublin, and then pursued postgraduate studies at the universities of Oxford, Cambridge, and Berlin. He was ordained as a minister, but then moved to Palestine and served as an official of the mandatory government between 1939 and 1948. A government report noted that "despite the fact that Mr. Sheringham's previous training had been theological and classical rather than financial, and his only knowledge to begin with was the study of a text-book, he quickly grasped the rudiments of balance sheets ... and proved most successful." See ISA, Record Group 16, M-1379/24, Annual Progress Reports 1942–1945, Jerusalem District: Revenue Report for the Financial Year Ended March 31, 1942, at 2. See also Arye Halfin, ed., *Vatikey Mas Hakhnasah Mesaprim* (Jerusalem: Government Printer, 1971), 5, 8, 29 (a copy of this book can be found in the Museum of Taxes, Jerusalem); J. F. Barfoot and G. G. Evans, "Obituaries: John Guy Tempest Sheringham," *Montgomeryshire Collections* 84 (1996): 155. On the education and training of British colonial officials generally see Robert Heussler, *Yesterday's Rulers: The Making of the British Colonial Service* (Syracuse, NY: Syracuse University Press, 1963), 82–129. See also Phiroze Vasunia, *The Classics and Colonial India* (Oxford: Oxford University Press, 2013), 193–230 (on the training of Indian colonial officials). On the training of government officials in Palestine immediately after the British conquest, see Bernard Wasserstein, *The British in Palestine: The Mandatory Government and Arab-Jewish Conflict, 1917–1929*, 2nd edn (Oxford: Blackwell, 1991), 19–20. On the lack of formal economic training of senior mandatory economic officials during the last years of British rule, see Jacob Reuveny, *Mimshal ha-Mandat be-Erets Yisrael, 1920–1948: Nitu'ah Histori Medini* (Ramat-Gan: Bar-Ilan University Press, 1993), 65 n. 3.

[3] ISA, Record Group 16, M-1379/24, Annual Progress Reports 1942–1945, Jerusalem District: Revenue Report for the Financial Year Ended March 31, 1942, at 4–5. The Palestine pound was the official currency of mandatory Palestine from 1927 to 1948. Each Palestine pound was divided into 1,000 mils. It was pegged to the pound sterling. In August 1948, three months after Israeli independence, the Palestine pound

of Jerusalem presented similar challenges: "The highest income of all [in this sector]," Sheringham's report continued, "was from a café not at all fashionable, frequented mainly by NCOs [non-commissioned officers] and belonging to an Armenian [whose income was] P£3,377. One small café, which according to all appearances would not have yielded a chargeable income at all, brought P£869 to each of two partners; we have a suspicion that there, we may be living on certain illicit profits!" The report then added, as if this proved the point, that "this café is frequented by Australians."[4]

The wealthy beggars of Haifa, the shady café owners of Jerusalem, and the challenges that both groups posed to the British officials who were supposed to tax them are the subject of this chapter, which analyzes British attempts to transplant income taxation to Palestine. The transplantation of income tax legislation marked an important milestone in the history of Palestine's tax system and its law. The Income Tax Ordinance, enacted there in 1941, was an attempt to tax in an individualized and standardized way, creating taxpayers whose economic life would be totally visible to the authorities.

However, the reception of this new mode of taxation was neither smooth nor simple. Different actors involved in the process of transplantation pulled the new legislation in different directions. The complexity of income taxation, compared to other types of taxes, naturally raised many legal questions, thus opening a space for the specialized knowledge of lawyers and accountants – new professional groups that gradually emerged during the period of British rule in Palestine. These professionals sought a new role for themselves as tax experts who would be able to assist both the government and taxpayers in the application of the new income tax, based on their unique technical knowledge.

---

was replaced by the Israel pound. See Robert David Ottensooser, *The Palestine Pound and the Israel Pound: Transition from a Colonial to an Independent Currency* (Geneva: E. Droz, 1955), 34–43, 110.

[4] Ibid., 5. Australian soldiers were stationed in Palestine during the Second World War, and they earned certain notoriety among the local population. See Assaf Likhovski, *Law and Identity in Mandate Palestine* (Chapel Hill: University of North Carolina Press, 2006), 207–9. What exactly the Australians were doing in the café is difficult to know. However, cafés were one of the major sites linked to prostitution in mandatory Palestine. See generally Deborah S. Bernstein, *Nashim ba-Shulayim: Migdar ve-Leumiyut be-Tel Aviv ha-Mandatorit* (Jerusalem: Yad Izhak Ben-Zvi, 2008).

Other actors involved in the application of the Income Tax Ordinance did not share the lawyers' and accountants' approach. In the early stages of the process of legislation, local taxpayers and administrators sought to prevent the taxation of income by pointing to differences between Britain and Palestine that, they argued, prevented the reception of British income tax law. Once the Income Tax Ordinance was enacted, tax administrators, aware of widespread tax evasion that made the application of the letter of the income tax law difficult to achieve, sought to informally adapt the Palestine Income Tax Ordinance to local conditions. This meant applying the ordinance in a haphazard way, overlooking instances of tax evasion, and using official discretion to change some of the provisions of the ordinance. A gap thus opened between the professionals' approach, which ignored local conditions in applying the law, and the taxpayers' and administrators' approach, which sought to use discretion and local knowledge to circumvent the letter of the law and adapt the law to the actual conditions of local society. The introduction of income taxation to Palestine was therefore not a simple linear process marking the progress of the country's tax system to a more advanced stage dominated by law, but a complex process in which certain aspects typical of tax administration in Palestine in previous decades were retained.

1923–1939: Rejecting Income Taxation

The first indication of interest in the taxation of income in Palestine can be traced back to 1923 when Herbert Samuel, the British high commissioner of Palestine, appointed a commission to consider the desirability of reintroducing the Ottoman profits tax on merchants and artisans (*temettu*) in Palestine.[5] This tax had been abolished following the British conquest of the country, and its reimposition was contemplated in 1923 because the British believed that the rural population was paying more than its fair share of taxes, while urban merchants and professionals were lightly taxed. Samuel consulted the Colonial Office in London, seeking information about similar taxes in the British Empire. In response, the Colonial Office informed him that in 1922 it had convened an

---

[5] TNA: CO 765/1, Taxation Inquiry Appointees, June 15, 1923. See also "Mas Hakhnasah be-Erets Yisrael," *Davar*, November 6, 1939, at 2.

Imperial Interdepartmental Committee on Income Taxation, and that the Committee had created a Model Income Tax Ordinance for British colonies (a copy of which, apparently, was not sent to Palestine), adding a word of caution about income taxation. Because of the difficulties in assessing income, said the Colonial Office, income tax in colonies "tends to resolve itself into little more than a tax on Government officials, as being the only class whose income is readily ascertainable."[6] In light of the report's conclusions, Samuel dropped the matter.

While sporadic mentions of the income tax can be found in documents from the late 1920s, the idea of introducing income taxation in Palestine was seriously reconsidered only following the 1929 riots.[7] The riots led to the establishment of a committee composed of William Johnson, the deputy treasurer of Palestine, and Robert Crosbie, the assistant southern district commissioner, who suggested that income tax be introduced in Palestine, again as a way of alleviating the tax burden on Arab peasants who, it was claimed, were relatively heavily taxed compared to the urban population.[8]

---

[6] TNA: CO 733/51, Thomas to Samuel, January 28, 1924; TNA: CO 733/225, Minutes, July 21, 1932; "Income Tax," *PP*, April 3, 1941, at 4. See also A. Granovsky, *The Fiscal System of Palestine* (Jerusalem: Palestine and Near East Publications, 1935), 119, 209, 302–3; Great Britain, *Report of the Inter-Departmental Committee on Income Tax in the Colonies Not Possessing Responsible Government* (London: HMSO, 1922). For an early comparative survey of income tax legislation in the British Empire and its sources, see G. Eichelgrün, "Income-Tax in British Colonies," *Economic Journal* 58 (1948): 128–32. For a discussion of British-colonial income taxation, see Peter Harris, *Income Tax in Common Law Jurisdictions: From the Origins to 1820* (Cambridge: Cambridge University Press, 2006); Judith Freedman, ed., "The Legacy of UK Taxation," special issue, *British Tax Review*, 2008, 197–306. On the transfer of tax policy between jurisdictions, see generally Holger Nehring and Florian Schui, eds., *Global Debates about Taxation* (Basingstoke: Palgrave Macmillan, 2007); Martin Daunton, *State and Market in Victorian Britain: War, Welfare and Capitalism* (Woodbridge: Boydell Press, 2008), 128–46. On income taxation in India, see, e.g., Ritu Birla, *Stages of Capital: Law, Culture, and Market Governance in Late Colonial India* (Durham, NC: Duke University Press, 2009), 53–60.

[7] See, e.g., TNA: CO 814/23, Minutes of the Executive Council of the Government of Palestine, 183rd Meeting, June 27, 1927.

[8] Government of Palestine, *Report of a Committee on the Economic Conditions of Agriculturalists in Palestine and the Fiscal Measures of Government in Relation Thereto* (Jerusalem: Greek Conv. Press, 1930), 49, 56; Granovsky, *The Fiscal System of Palestine*, 305.

In June 1932 the government's Standing Committee on Trade and Industry was instructed to examine the problem of introducing income taxation in Palestine.[9] The renewed interest was again motivated by the desire to distribute the tax burden more equitably between the rural and urban sectors, and implicitly between (mostly rural) Arabs and (mostly urban) Jews. Another concern, raised perhaps by the economic crisis of the early 1930s, was that the revenue from customs duties might decrease in the future and that machinery for taxing income should therefore be put in place while Palestine enjoyed a period of relative prosperity, so that it could be used in the future to replace other sources of revenue.[10]

Palestine was not the first British territory in the Middle East to introduce the income tax. In 1927 it was imposed in Iraq, where it mostly targeted British individuals and firms.[11] Income taxation was also introduced in Transjordan in 1933.[12] There, too, the tax was actually imposed only on a small group of salaried employees, with exemptions provided for many occupations (including workers in religious and charitable organizations, "servants and employees carrying on agricultural work," and midwives).[13]

Unlike in Iraq and Transjordan, where the tax encountered little opposition from the local population, in Palestine the introduction of income taxation met with fierce resistance in some quarters. While initially there was some Arab opposition to the tax, most Arab politicians and businessmen ultimately came to support it, provided it would be used to replace other taxes, such as the tithe and customs duties that were seen as pro-Jewish.[14] The initial Jewish reaction, at least among

---

[9] "Sir Arthur Wauchope's Policy," *PP*, December 14, 1932, at 5; TNA: CO 733/ 260, Extract from Daily News Bulletin No. 36, February 10, 1934; "Income Tax Scheme: No Change in Jewish Attitude," *PP*, February 16, 1934, at 8; "Income Tax," *PP*, April 3, 1941, at 4.

[10] TNA: CO 733/225, Wauchope to Colonial Office, December 22, 1932; TNA: CO 733/261, Wauchope to Cunliffe-Lister, June 14, 1934.

[11] See TNA: CO 733/260, Minutes, Vernon, April 30, 1934; TNA: CO 730/121/6 Extract from *[Baghdad] Times* of May 30, 1927.

[12] "Income Tax in Trans-Jordan," *PP*, March 21, 1933, at 2; Granovsky, *The Fiscal System of Palestine*, 324.

[13] "Old Story Across the Jordan: Income Tax in Force since 1933," *PP*, April 29, 1941, at 3.

[14] The tithe was seen as pro-Jewish because it was mainly paid by Arab peasants. High customs rates were seen as pro-Jewish because they were perceived as a way

many in the politically dominant Jewish labor movement, was quite favorable despite the perceived adverse impact income taxation would have on the Jewish sector.[15] However, middle-class Jews opposed income taxation vehemently.[16] Muted opposition to the tax was probably also widespread among the British officials in the country, who, like the Jews of Palestine, saw themselves as one of the major targets of the tax.[17]

An article by Arthur Ruppin, a leading Zionist sociologist and economist, summarized the main arguments of the Jewish opponents

of protecting nascent Jewish industries from foreign competition. On Arab support for the income tax, see, for example, "Haifa Arabs Favour Low Income Tax," *PP*, February 25, 1934, at 5. On the argument that income tax should replace customs, see "Syrian Transport to Palestine Growing," *PP*, June 12, 1939, at 6. On Arab opponents of the income tax, see, for example, "More About Income Tax: View of Arab Opponents," *PP*, December 5, 1932, at 5; "Merchants and Proposed Income Tax," *PP*, February 15, 1934, at 5; "Proposed Election Boycott: Deprecated by Gaza Mayor," *PP*, February 16, 1934, at 8.

[15] See, e.g., Haim Arlosoroff, "Mi-Reshimot ha-Hodesh," *Ahdut ha-ʿAvodah* 1 (1930): 461–73, 470–1; "Ha-Vikuʾah ʿal Mas ha-Hakhnasah ba-Vaʿad ha-Leumi," *Davar*, November 16, 1932, at 1; "Le-Diyun be-ʿInyan Mas Hakhnasah," *Davar*, November 18, 1932, at 2; S. Sambursky, *Histadrut ha-ʿOvdim u-Mas ha-Hakhnasah: Mihtav Galuy le-Tsirey Veʿidat ha-Histadrut ha-Reviʿit* (Jerusalem: Dfus Weiss, 1933) (a copy of this pamphlet can be found in the National Library of Israel (NLI), Jerusalem). For an earlier declaration of support for progressive income taxation by the Jewish labor movement, see "Hahlatot ha-Veʿidah ha-Shlishit shel Histadrut ha-ʿOvdim ha-ʿIvriyim ha-Klalit be-Erets Yisrael," *Davar*, August 26, 1927, at 9. On the Jewish labor movement, socialist policies and taxation, see also Zeev Sternhell, *The Founding Myths of Israel: Nationalism, Socialism, and the Making of the Jewish State*, trans. David Maisel (Princeton: Princeton University Press, 1999), 6.

[16] On the Jewish Manufacturers' Association campaign against the tax, see Omri Metzer, "Ha-Politikah shel Hitʾahdut Baʿaley ha-Taʿasiyah bi-Shnot ha-Shloshim: Ha-Maʾamatsim li-vlimat Mas ha-Hakhnasah vele-ʿIdud Totseret ha-Arets," *ʿIyunim bi-Tkumat Yisrael* 22 (2012): 290–324. On settler resistance to income taxation in other parts of the British Empire, see Barbara Bush and Josephine Maltby, "Taxation in West Africa: Transforming the Colonial Subject into the 'Governable Person'," *Critical Perspectives on Accounting* 15 (2004), 5–34, 12; Michael Littlewood, *Taxation without Representation: The History of Hong Kong's Troublingly Successful Tax System* (Hong Kong: Hong Kong University Press, 2010), 33–6; Ern Chen Loo and Margaret McKerchar, "The Impact of British Colonial Rule on the Malaysian Income Tax System," *eJournal of Tax Research* 12 (2014): 238–52, 245–6.

[17] See, e.g., Mustard and Cress [P. E. F. Cressall], *Palestine Parodies: Being the Holy Land in Verse and Worse* (Tel Aviv: Azriel Press, printed for private circulation, 1938), 1, 102–6, 139–40 (a copy of this book can be found in the NLI).

of the tax. First, Ruppin explained, the tax morale and "economic maturity" of the native (that is, Arab) inhabitants of Palestine would not allow the introduction of the income tax. Second, racial animosity (between Jews and Arabs) meant that taxpayers of one nation would suspect the impartiality of officials of the other nation. Third, historically, income taxation had been introduced at times of budgetary deficit, but Palestine enjoyed a budget surplus at that time. Fourth, the main reason given for the introduction of the tax – the supposedly heavy tax burden on Arab peasants (who were paying the tithe and the land tax) – was simply erroneous. The tax burden on peasants was minimal (averaging, according to Ruppin, P£2 annually per family). Fifth, the income tax was expensive to administer, and experience in Iraq (the only other post-Ottoman country in which it was introduced at the time Ruppin was writing) showed that its yield was small (1.4 percent of the Iraqi revenue, even with a relatively low rate of exemption). Sixth, the Jews, who accounted for just 17 percent of the population at the time, already paid 40 percent of all taxes, and the income tax, which was mainly a tax on urban incomes, would further increase their share (since 75 percent of the Jews lived in urban areas, compared to only 30 percent of the Arabs). Finally, Ruppin said, the tax would deter foreign Jews from investing in Palestine. He therefore concluded that "the income tax, a product of long evolutionary process in Western countries, if mechanically transplanted into the backward conditions of Palestine, can do little good to state finance but may inflict serious harm on the country's economic fabric."[18]

In December 1932 the National Council of Jews in Palestine (Ha-Va'ad ha-Le'umi), one of the major political organizations of the Jewish community in Palestine, adopted an official resolution opposing the taxation of income, repeating Ruppin's first argument, that "the cultural level and economic situation of large sections of the country's inhabitants prevent a fair registration of their income, giving

---

[18] Arthur Ruppin, "Income Tax in Palestine: A Premature and Ill-Advised Project – A Serious Menace to Development," *Palestine and Near East Economic Magazine* 18–19 (1932): 443–6. Similar arguments were made by other Jewish opponents of the tax. See, e.g., TNA: CO 733/225, Dizengoff to Chancellor, November 20, 1932; TNA: CO 733/225, Note on Discussion on the Introduction of Income Tax in Palestine between the Acting Treasurer and the Jewish Agency, July 4, 1932; Granovsky, *The Fiscal System of Palestine*, 283–300, 305–16.

rise to the danger that instead of a fair distribution of taxes, an income tax will lead to an additional burden on those sections which either do not desire or are unable to conceal their income."[19] Other opponents of the tax echoed this argument. The income tax, it was claimed, was only appropriate in highly developed countries such as England. In underdeveloped countries such as Palestine, it would be as unnatural as a tax on "goats and camels" in England.[20]

While the debate on the taxation of income raged, the lawyers of the Colonial Office and the government of Palestine were busy drafting Palestine's Income Tax Ordinance. Their draft was based on the Model Colonial Income Tax Ordinance of 1922. Little attempt was made by the drafters either in London or Jerusalem to adapt the Model Ordinance to local conditions. This was perhaps partly the result of the recommendation of the Interdepartmental Committee that said in its report that the "uniformity of legislation should be aimed at as far as possible."[21]

While the draft ordinance was being prepared, a tax expert was sent to Palestine to examine local attitudes, interests, and circumstances. The official sent to Palestine was the aforementioned Board of Inland Revenue expert John Francis Huntington. Huntington arrived in Palestine in February 1934 to head a committee that also included three local officials. The committee heard evidence in March and April of 1934. Witnesses included members of local chambers of commerce, as well as representatives of major industries and the professions. Perhaps not surprisingly, workers and peasants, who were an indirect but important interest group, were not invited to give evidence.[22]

Huntington submitted his report in May 1934, concluding that income taxation should not be imposed in Palestine. He began his

[19] TNA: CO 733/260, Extract from Daily News Bulletin No. 36, February 10, 1934.

[20] "Income Tax – Why It Should Not Be Introduced," *PP*, April 26, 1934, at 19.

[21] *Report of the Inter-Departmental Committee on Income Tax*, 5. See also G. Eichelgrün, *Palestine Income Tax Guide* (Haifa: Paltax, 1945), 2. On the changes made in the Model Ordinance, see Assaf Likhovski, "Is Tax Law Culturally Specific? Lessons from the History of Income Tax Law in Mandatory Palestine," *Theoretical Inquiries in Law* 11 (2010): 725–63, 738–40.

[22] "A Low Income Tax Considered: Visiting Expert to Hear Local Evidence," *PP*, February 11, 1934, at 1. In total, the committee heard eighty-one witnesses, thirty-one of whom were Jews, and the rest coming from the Muslim, Christian-Arab and Christian-European communities in roughly equal numbers. See TNA: CO 733/261, Huntington, [Report], 35.

report by noting that while Muslim-Arabs favored the imposition of an income tax, everyone else (Christian-Arabs, Jews, and Christian-Europeans) opposed it. The argument made by the Muslims was that peasants and rural and urban landowners were unduly burdened by the existing system of taxation, while banks, corporations, merchants, and professionals contributed less than their fair share.[23] Huntington did not take this argument seriously. In his report, he suggested that the reasons for Muslim support of the tax were different. One reason, he said, was that the opposition of the Jews to the tax was, in itself, a sufficient reason for the Muslims to support it, but it was also due to the fact that "Arab standards ... both of truthfulness and of bookkeeping" ensured they would be able to evade the tax.[24]

Huntington's rejection of income taxation was based on three major arguments. First, taxation of income should target taxpayers' "ability" to pay by reference to their income, but in a country in which there were different cultural conceptions of what constituted a proper standard of living, the taxpayer's income could not provide an accurate measure of their ability to pay. Palestine, said Huntington, was a country of "strangely assorted standards of life," and monetary income could not "furnish a fair test of 'real' ability in a country in which the most widely different cultures and standards of life are found side by side." In Palestine, an income of £500 per annum provided a high standard of living for Arabs, but "for a European ... and for many Jews," such an income meant "bare livelihood," both because much of the income would be spent on rent and also because "many of the more numerous things which [the European's and the Jew's] culture and standard of living have made necessary to him are heavily taxed already." Living costs, Huntington concluded, "vary according to race and creed, of necessity and not of choice, in a way inconceivable in occidental countries."[25] Huntington added that:

> there were such vast differences in the standard of living and morality
> of various sections of the community, that an identical rate of tax on a
> given income would be burdensome on some classes and comparatively
> light for other sections assessed at that rate, e.g. a Government official

[23] TNA: CO 733/261, Huntington, [Report], 36.
[24] Ibid., 8.
[25] Ibid., 18, 23.

earning £1,000 a year is a comparatively poor man and a merchant in the Souk earning £1,000 a year is definitely a rich man.[26]

Huntington's second argument focused on the willingness of taxpayers in Palestine to pay the tax. Huntington emphasized that taxing income was dependent on what taxpayers chose to tell the authorities about themselves. The remedy for tax evasion in Britain was estimated assessments, but such assessments could be used effectively only on a small scale, where relatively few taxpayers evaded taxation. In Palestine, income taxation faced strong opposition from the Jews ("the most important section of the people to be taxed"), many of them "of high intelligence and all of them of a different race." Income tax could not be introduced without the consent and cooperation of those being taxed.[27]

Finally, Huntington turned to the difference between accountants in Britain and Palestine. In Palestine, he noted, 90 percent of the population (Arabs, but also Jews and "Europeans") did not keep books.[28] In Britain, the Inland Revenue could turn to accountants to prepare reasonably accurate statements when a taxpayer's books were inaccurate. But in Palestine, an accountant would "put his name to anything," because accountants were of poor standing and low quality, unregulated by any professional body, and lacking a spirit of independence toward their clients.[29] This problem, he said, was augmented by the "the engrained habits of bribery in an oriental country."[30] In support of his argument, Huntington also referred to the British experience in Iraq and Nyasaland. This experience showed that the imposition of an income tax by a colonial government yielded little revenue. It also showed that, over time, this revenue declined rather than increased.[31]

Based on Huntington's report, Arthur Wauchope, the high commissioner for Palestine, reached the conclusion that introducing an income tax in Palestine would be impractical. This conclusion was mainly based on the argument that there was a lack of taxpayer consent. Both

[26] Ibid., 40.
[27] Ibid., 13–14.
[28] Ibid., 13.
[29] Ibid., 14.
[30] Ibid., 20, 42.
[31] Ibid., 17–18.

Jews and Arabs, said Wauchope, regarded the government as foreign and would therefore "feel no sense of moral obligation" to pay the tax. This, the argument continued, meant that the collection of the tax would be disproportionately costly.[32] In an internal Colonial Office memo the argument was put more bluntly: income taxation should not be imposed because of the "disloyalty and dishonesty of both races [Arabs and Jews]."[33]

Huntington's report and the high commissioner's decision received a mixed reception at the Colonial Office in London. Some at the Colonial Office greeted the report with approval. The relative importance of direct and indirect taxation, said one official, "is a kind of rough index as to the general soundness of the system of taxation in any advanced community," but there was no point in "attempting to force up the index, as it were, corresponding to an advanced position, if the facts are that the country is still very primitive."[34]

However, other Colonial Office officials were not convinced.[35] One official, Roland V. Vernon, who had previously served in Iraq, noted that opposition to the tax was not unique to Palestine. "I believe," he said, "that the Baghdadi Jew is the greatest living expert in the production of fictitious accounts and that he ["the Jew"] has a high reputation for this in Manchester [too]. No doubt the Palestine Jew will have some similar qualifications and I should be surprised if the Palestine Arabs and Christians are behind him in this respect" (to which another official responded that "the Indian in Africa is not bad at it [either]"). However, the fact that Jews and Arabs would cheat, added Vernon, could not serve as a real objection to the introduction of the tax because, "if you are ever going to introduce income tax in Palestine you will have to face this difficulty," and the sooner it was done the better.[36] Another official noted that the arguments against income tax were the same ones that had always been advanced "whenever and wherever" such a tax had been first proposed, and that as

[32] TNA: CO 733/261, Wauchope to Cunliffe-Lister, June 14, 1934.
[33] TNA: CO 733/427/12, Minutes, Downie, May 6, 1940 (summarizing the arguments against the imposition of the tax in 1934).
[34] TNA: CO 733/260, Minutes, July 13, 1934.
[35] TNA: CO 733/261, Minutes, July 16, 1934.
[36] TNA: CO 733/261, Minutes, July 17, 1934.

long as the tax was introduced "upon scientific principles," it "[would] not be a failure."[37]

Ultimately, however, the Colonial Office decided to approve the decision of the high commissioner of Palestine not to impose income taxation, and a statement was issued to the effect that an income tax would not be introduced until a change in local circumstances "suggest[ed] that a more favourable time [had] arrived."[38] This decision was seen by Arab observers to be the result of Jewish influence in England.[39] Following the Arab Rebellion of 1936, the Peel Commission, a British royal commission of inquiry, was established to examine conditions in Palestine. One of the issues raised in the evidence given before the Commission was the incidence of taxation. Once again, Arab witnesses before the Commission called for the introduction of the income tax, and again this idea was rejected.[40]

The attempt to introduce income taxation to Palestine in the 1930s, one can conclude, was far from a straightforward process of colonial imposition.[41] In the initial phase of the process, British legislative drafters in the Colonial Office and in Palestine had created a draft that was largely oblivious to local conditions. However, these conditions did have an impact on the legislative process at later stages, leading to a decision not to impose the tax. Unlike other British-colonial territories, in Palestine there was no legislative council on which representatives of the local population sat and were able to comment on proposed legislation. Nevertheless, British rulers were not free to enact whatever tax law they wanted. The British were sensitive to local sentiments and, when they encountered opposition from local taxpayers, they abandoned the idea of imposing income taxation.

---

[37] TNA: CO 733/261, Minutes, Bushe, July 18, 1934.

[38] TNA: CO 733/261, Draft Communiqué, September 20, 1934.

[39] "Jamal Bey's Evidence," *PP*, January 15, 1937, at 16.

[40] Palestine Royal Commission, *Minutes of Evidence Heard at Public Sessions* (London: HMSO, 1937), secs. 4978, 5006–12, 5083–112; Palestine Royal Commission, *Report* (London: HMSO, 1937), 208; TNA: CO 733/346, Note by Acting Treasurer of the Government of Palestine, 8. On the incidence of taxation in the 1930s, see also TNA: CO 733/346/2.

[41] For a general discussion of the process of legislative transplantation in Palestine, see Likhovski, *Law and Identity in Mandate Palestine*, 24–45.

Behind the British stance of nonimposition of income taxation was the premise that local consent to the tax was essential. Income taxation, unlike older forms of direct taxation, requires widespread taxpayer consent. It is based on accurate bookkeeping (which requires the taxpayer's active participation), and can therefore only operate effectively where there are enough citizens committed to it – not where there are imperial or colonial subjects whose allegiance to the government is weak. Such committed citizens did not exist in 1930s Palestine. As Wauchope noted in 1934, both Arabs and Jews "[felt] no sense of moral obligation" to pay the tax.[42]

A second major reason used to justify the nonimposition of income taxation in Palestine was concerned with the relationship of income taxation to law and its professional agents (in this case, accountants). When taxpayer consent is absent, a government can rely on professional intermediaries such as accountants to ensure tax compliance. However, this was not the case in Palestine at that time. As we shall see in Chapter 5, in the 1930s there were very few accountants operating in Palestine, and even these few were perceived by British officials to be unreliable. Lack of taxpayer consent, together with the absence of a sizeable body of professional mediators on which the British could rely in lieu of the loyalty of individual taxpayers, meant that introducing the income tax would, indeed, be impracticable.

1939–1941: Enactment

In April 1936 Palestine's Arab population began a revolt against British rule and Jewish immigration and settlement in Palestine.[43] The revolt began with a civil disobedience campaign whose main manifestation was a long general strike, but it also involved a tax strike based on the principle of "no taxation without representation."[44] After a transitional period between the autumn of 1936 and the autumn of 1937, the revolt morphed into a guerrilla war against the British

---

[42] TNA: CO 733/261, Wauchope to Cunliffe-Lister, June 14, 1934.

[43] See, e.g., Yehoshua Porath, The Palestinian Arab National Movement, 1929–1939: From Riots to Rebellion (London: Frank Cass, 1977).

[44] Ibid., 168–70. See also "Arabs' Tax Strike in Palestine," The Times, May 16, 1936, at 13.

and the Jews, ultimately turning into a civil war between various factions within the Arab community in Palestine. The instability caused by the revolt was augmented by increasingly brutal measures taken during the British counterinsurgency campaign: emergency regulations, military courts, collective punishment, the demolition of houses (and indeed entire neighborhoods), looting, revenge killings, and the like. Ultimately, the revolt and British counterinsurgency tactics led to anarchy in the Arab areas of the country. Assassinations and robberies carried out by bands of peasants were accompanied by a breakdown in government services and public order, as the British lost control of parts of the country.[45] It is not surprising, therefore, that the British suffered a breakdown in their ability to collect taxes, leading to a significant decline in tax revenues on both the national and the local level.[46]

Another drop in government revenues occurred at the beginning of the Second World War. Revenues declined from a total of P£5.6 million in the fiscal year 1935/36 to P£4.6 million in 1939/40, with an additional decline of P£500,000 in the fiscal year 1940/41. The British attempted to deal with diminishing revenues by increasing import and excise duties, stamp duties, and rates on postage, telephone calls, and transportation.[47] However, the drop in revenue also served as an excellent excuse to finally introduce income taxation.

Several external developments also created a more favorable climate for the full implementation of income taxation in Palestine. This type of tax had been introduced in Egypt in 1938. When the war broke out, a number of British colonies such as Hong Kong and Cyprus also began

---

[45] See, generally, Yuval Arnon-Ohanna, *Herev mi-Bayit: Ha-Ma'avak ha-Pnimi ba-Tnu'ah ha-Falastinit, 1929–1939* (Tel Aviv: Yariv-Hadar, 1981), 285–7; Jacob Norris, "Repression and Rebellion: Britain's Response to the Arab Revolt in Palestine of 1936–39," *Journal of Imperial and Commonwealth History* 36 (2008): 25–45; Matthew Hughes, "The Banality of Brutality: British Armed Forces and the Repression of the Arab Revolt in Palestine, 1936–39," *English Historical Review* 124 (2009): 313–54.

[46] See, e.g., "Government Report on Finances: The Effect of Strike and Disturbances," *PP*, September 21, 1937, at 2; "Notes of the Week," *PP*, April 8, 1938, at 6; "Riots and Revenue," *PP*, December 30, 1938, at 11; "Safad Hard Pressed for Municipal Funds," *PP*, September 22, 1936, at 2; Porath, *The Palestinian Arab National Movement*, 170.

[47] "Increased Taxation in Palestine," *The Times*, May 2, 1940, at 5.

contemplating introducing it.[48] In October 1939 the government of Palestine announced that it was reconsidering the imposition of income taxation due to the expected decline in the revenues from customs duties, and the fact that the burden of taxation in Palestine fell heaviest on the poor and middle classes.[49] David Norman Strathie, an income

[48] "New Tax Law in Egypt," *PP*, July 26, 1938, at 5; "Egypt's Double Peace-War Programme: King Farouk Officiates at State Opening of Parliament," *PP*, November 20, 1938, at 1. Two additional countries bordering on Palestine – Syria and Lebanon – introduced income taxation only after it was introduced in Palestine. See "Income Tax Announced in Syria," *PP*, June 18, 1942, at 3; "Income Tax in Lebanon," *PP*, November 24, 1944, at 3; "Income Tax in Lebanon: Provisions May Affect Palestinians," *PP*, March 14, 1945, at 2. In British-ruled Hong Kong the tax was introduced in April 1940. See "News in Brief," *PP*, October 13, 1939, at 7; Littlewood, *Taxation without Representation*, 39. In Cyprus the tax was introduced in early 1941. See "Economic Position of Cyprus: Governor's Review of Budget," *PP*, January 24, 1941, at 5; "Cyprus Income Tax and Commerce: A Possible Model for Palestine," *PP*, April 19, 1941, at 5; Peter Clarke and Andrekos Varnava, "Accounting in Cyprus during the Last Four Decades of British Rule: Post–World War I to Independence (1918–1960)," *Accounting History* 18 (2013): 293–315, 303–6. The explicit policy of the Colonial Office at the time was to introduce the tax to all parts of the Empire. See "Income Tax Levy for Palestine: 50 Mils in the Pound and Up," *PP*, May 26, 1941, at 1; "H.M. Government's Colonial Policy During and After the War: Lord Moyn Sets-Out Principles of Far-Reaching Plans Throughout the Empire," *PP*, August 20, 1941, at 4. By 1948 almost all British territories, with the exception of Malta, the Seychelles, and the Turks and Caicos Islands, had introduced income taxation. See Eichelgrün, "Income-Tax in British Colonies," 129.

[49] "Income Tax Again Being Considered: Government Measure to Reach All Classes in Palestine," *PP*, October 8, 1939, at 1. The decision to introduce the tax (as an experimental measure) was actually taken by the Executive Council of the Government of Palestine in early 1940. See TNA: CO 814/36, Minutes of the 723rd Meeting of the Executive Council of the Government of Palestine, February 2, 1940, 2. See also TNA: CO 814/36, Minutes of the 746th Meeting of the Executive Council of the Government of Palestine, September 14, 1940, 3. In 1941 the Executive Council of the Government of Palestine discussed the imposition of income taxation in Palestine. In this discussion, one official noted that "it was not the basic intention of Government to introduce income tax as a war emergency measure and that the yield is not regarded at this stage as being of essential importance ... the tax was in fact being introduced as a desirable adjustment of the permanent fiscal structure of the country and in order to ensure that companies and wealthy persons who escape direct contribution to revenue under the existing law should make an adequate contribution." TNA: CO 814/37, Minutes of the 854th Meeting of the Executive Council of the Government of Palestine, March 8, 1941, 1.

tax adviser seconded to Palestine from Madras, arrived in Palestine in February 1941 and held consultations with relevant interest groups. A preliminary communiqué about the intention to introduce an income tax was published in March 1941. A draft bill was published in May, and comments were solicited from the Jewish Agency, the body representing the Zionist movement in Palestine, and serving in some senses as the government of the Jewish community there. The Jewish Agency, in turn, solicited comments from Jewish merchants and manufacturers.[50] In late May it was announced that the tax would be introduced as of September 1, 1941.[51] The Ordinance itself was enacted in August 1941 and duly came into force the following month.[52]

This time around, the idea of a tax on income was received far more favorably than in the mid-1930s. Some Jewish organizations were still opposed to the tax, but the general tone in the Jewish community now shifted in a more favorable direction, perhaps because the Jews and the British were now on the same side of a world conflict that threatened the very existence of the Jewish community in Palestine, and the Jews were therefore less reluctant to cooperate with their British rulers.[53] In addition, the Jewish community in Palestine had already imposed on

[50] TNA: CO 733/444, MacMichael to Moyne, May 30, 1941; "Jewish Agency Proposals on Income Tax: Suggestions Invited," *PP*, June 16, 1941, at 3.

[51] "All About the Income Tax: Government Adviser's Broadcast," *PP*, May 26, 1941, at 4.

[52] Income Tax Ordinance, 1941, PG Supp. I, 51; "Income Tax Law Published: In Force from September 1," *PP*, August 24, 1941, at 1. The Ordinance was amended several times during the 1940s, and it was also accompanied by additional wartime tax measures. The first amendment was passed in March 1942. There were additional amendments every year until 1948. A list is found in Abraham Fellman, *The Palestine Income Tax: Law and Practice* (Tel Aviv: Lapid, 1946), 28–34. See also S. Moses, *The Income Tax Ordinance of Palestine: The Income Tax (Amendment) Ordinance, 1942* (Jerusalem: Tarshish Books, 1942). In addition, there were related wartime measures, such as the War Revenue (Income Tax) (Amendment) Ordinance, 1944, and the War Revenue (Company Profits Tax) Ordinance, 1945. These expired in 1947 and 1946, respectively. See S. Moses, *The Income Tax Ordinance of Palestine: The Text as Valid Since 1st April, 1944, with Explanations of the 1944 Amendments* (Jerusalem: Tarshish Books, 1944), 71; S. Moses, *Company Profits Tax* (Jerusalem: Tarshish, 1945); S. Moses with Walter Schwarz, *The 1947 Income Tax Amendments* (Tel Aviv: Bitaon, [1947]).

[53] "Notes of the Week," *PP*, October 13, 1939, at 6; "Me-'Inyeney ha-Sha'ah," *Davar: Ha-Meshek ha-Shitufi*, February 13, 1940, at 2; "Readers' Letters: The Urban

itself a voluntary system of taxation that included a voluntary income tax (which will be discussed in detail in Chapter 3), thus weakening opposition to the government income tax.[54] The more positive attitude in the Jewish community in this regard was reflected in a *Palestine Post* article that said the new tax "[could not] be regarded as an unjustifiable burden on the population since it is modest in its demands and apparently equitable in incidence."[55] Another newspaper, *Ha-Boker*, said that the new income tax commissioner was not to be seen as an enemy of the people, and noted enthusiastically that the new Income Tax Ordinance was in "the latest European fashion."[56]

A positive attitude toward the tax was also found among Jewish lawyers, accountants, and bookkeepers, who saw the new tax as an opportunity rather than a threat. Immediately after the official announcement in March 1941 about the introduction of the tax, advertisements began to appear in the newspapers for bookkeeping and other tax-related services.[57] One such advertisement, published by the British Institute of Commerce and Accountancy in April 1941, announced that "Income Tax [is a] Chance for All," and stated that, in view of the intention to introduce an income tax, "there [were] now excellent opportunities for ambitious men and women with modern knowledge" in bookkeeping and accounting.[58] An article published in

Property Tax," *PP*, March 26, 1941, at 4; "Income Tax as Substitute," *PP*, April 2, 1941, at 2; "Arab Chambers Consider Income Tax," *PP*, April 7, 1941, at 2; "Our Treasury," *PP*, April 22, 1941, at 4; "Income Tax Favoured," *PP*, April 22, 1941, at 3. On opposition to the tax see Metzer, "Ha-Politikah," 307–15; "Mas Hakhnasah be-Erets Yisrael," *Davar*, November 6, 1939, at 2; "Opposition to Income Tax in Palestine," *PP*, January 26, 1940, at 5; "Objections to Income Tax: Jerusalem Chamber of Commerce Activities," *PP*, April 21, 1940, at 2; "Income Tax Again to the Fore: Hebrew Daily Says Move Is Premature," *PP*, March 17, 1941, at 3; "House-Owners Protest Against Income Tax," *PP*, April 2, 1941, at 2; "Jewish Merchants in Conference: Retail Turnover of LP. 12.000.000," *PP*, April 16, 1941, at 3.

54 See "Jewish 'Income Tax' Announced," *PP*, October 3, 1939, at 1; "The Week in Comment," *Palestine Review* 4 (October 1939): 341, 342; TNA: CO 733/427/12, MacMichael to Colonial Secretary, February 23, 1940.

55 "The New Income Tax," *PP*, June 2, 1941, at 4.

56 "Mutsag ba-Muze'on le-Misim: 50 Shanah le-Hanhagato shel Mas Hakhnasah be-Erets Yisrael 1941–1991," *RYM* 19 (1991): 292.

57 "Cheap Prepaids," *PP*, April 11, 1941, at 2.

58 "Income Tax: A Chance for All," *PP*, April 13, 1941, at 6.

April 1941 noted that "whatever other results may follow from its introduction, income tax legislation is going to bring much work to accountants and probably lawyers."[59] Indeed, the files of the Palestine income tax commissioner's office contain a large number of applications for positions in the new income tax department. Many of these applications were from overqualified middle-aged lawyers, judges, and accountants from central Europe who had fled to Palestine in the 1930s and were now desperately seeking employment.[60]

The new income tax bill was based on the draft prepared during the 1930s, but it also included many additions. Some of these additions drew on the recently enacted income tax laws of Kenya and Cyprus, as well as some additional provisions taken from India (from where Strathie, the Palestine income tax adviser, came).[61] Other additions were original and were meant to adapt the Ordinance to local conditions. Thus, a section dealing with family deductions, which initially allowed a deduction only for the maintenance of old or infirm family members, was redrafted to allow a deduction in any case in which taxpayers could prove they maintained a "person incapable of maintaining himself." The alteration, it was explained, was made to meet a request from Muslim taxpayers who claimed that "they [were] bound by custom to maintain relatives whether or not they [were] old or infirm."[62]

A related issue was the tax treatment of families. Strathie, the income tax adviser, at first recommended that no allowances be given for wife or children because of the difficulties involved in ascertaining the taxpayer's true family status. However, in its discussion of this

---

[59] "Reflections," *PP*, April 25, 1941, at 6.
[60] See, e.g., ISA, Record Group 16, M 1378/1.
[61] TNA: CO 733/444, MacMichael to Moyne, May 30, 1941. See also ISA, M 724/15, Income Tax Adviser Memo, March 25, 1941; ISA, M 724/15, Income Tax Adviser Memo, May 15, 1941; Eichelgrün, *Palestine Income Tax Guide*, 2–3; Fellman, *The Palestine Income Tax*, 27–8; Likhovski, "Is Tax Law Culturally Specific?," 748–9.
[62] TNA: CO 733/444, Untitled table, sec. 16 of the Ordinance; ISA, M 724/15, Income Tax Adviser Memo, May 15, 1941. See also "Government Adviser's Broadcast," *PP*, May 26, 1941, at 4 (comparing the use of allowances in European countries and Palestine); "Income Tax Law Published: In Force from September 1," *PP*, August 24, 1941, at 1; "Income Tax," *PP*, August 27, 1941, at 4; Fellman, *The Palestine Income Tax*, 27.

recommendation, the Executive Council of the government of Palestine came to the conclusion that giving a family allowance was "a common-sense principle which has been widely embodied in income tax law elsewhere," and that a reasonable solution would be to give a lump sum family allowance to married men (irrespective of whether or not they had children).[63] When explaining the solution to the public, Strathie said that this approach had been taken because in Palestine, unlike European countries, most people had relatives to support, and a more accurate differentiation between numbers and types of dependents would have required vast amounts of clerical work.[64] This provision was criticized by some taxpayers, because, it was claimed, "the State is interested in larger families, especially in the upper levels of society," and therefore should allow varying family deductions depending on the number of children.[65] The first amendment of the Ordinance, published in March 1942, lowered the level of exemptions, but (perhaps to prevent too much criticism) amended the family allowance provision by replacing the lump sum allowance with one that took into account the number of children for whom the taxpayer was responsible.[66]

To what extent did law have a role in the application of the Income Tax Ordinance? When the introduction of income taxation was contemplated in 1934, the view was that ordinary courts of law would have little to do with its administration. In his notes on the organization of income tax administration in Palestine, the Board of Inland Revenue expert, Huntington, suggested that the assessment and collection of the tax would be handled locally by the district officers and their staff, following the English model, rather than by special income tax officers, and that tax appeals would be decided by an institution "in the nature of a pie powder court [that is, the merchant courts that resolved disputes in medieval English fairs and did so informally and

---

[63] TNA: CO 814/37, Minutes of the 854th Meeting of the Executive Council of the Government of Palestine, March 18, 1941, 2.

[64] "Government Adviser's Broadcast," *PP*, May 26, 1941, at 4; "Income Tax Law Published: In Force from September 1," *PP*, August 24, 1941, at 1.

[65] "Reflections," *PP*, May 28, 1941, at 4. See also "Reflections," *PP*, August 25, 1941, at 4.

[66] "Income Tax Exemption Lowered: More Tax in Higher Brackets," *PP*, March 19, 1942, at 3. See also Abraham Fellman, "Zikhronot me-Hanhagat Mas-Hakhnasah be-Erets Yisrael," *RH* 31 (1981): 143, 144.

quickly]," rather than by ordinary courts of law. Appeals from such a court to ordinary courts of law, said Huntington, would only be permitted on legal points and only with the permission of the court of appeal.[67]

The second tax expert sent to Palestine, Strathie, was also keen to minimize the impact of courts and lawyers on the new tax, and indeed was even skeptical about the desirability of introducing the income tax at all. In a letter written in January 1941, a month before he left the United Kingdom for his new position as the income tax adviser to the government of Palestine, Strathie suggested that the Palestine Income Tax Bill be amended in line with Indian tax law. This law, which had been in effect until 1939, granted no right of appeal to taxpayers who either did not file a return or failed to produce accounts and then were assessed independently by a tax officer. This, said Strathie, was the "chief weapon [in India] in forcing the production of accounts." Such a provision "may appear retrograde," but "Orientals will certainly avoid giving returns and producing accounts (I am sure they all have them)." In addition, said Strathie, the Palestinian Ordinance was faulty because it was based "too much on English practice," and the major example he gave here was that it allowed appeals to ordinary civil courts. "In India," said Strathie, "we would never allow a District Court to touch an income tax matter." Finally, he doubted whether the income tax would yield much revenue, and he therefore suggested that it be replaced by a sales tax, to be modeled on the sales tax that he had been involved in introducing when he served in Madras.[68]

In his public speeches, however, Strathie was more sanguine about the new tax and optimistic about the possibility of preventing tax evasion. Thus, in a radio talk he gave in May 1941, he noted that one of the fears he had heard was that salary earners would be taxed, but merchants and moneylenders would be able to evade taxation. Such fears, he assured his listeners, were unfounded. In India, where he had served for twenty-nine years, the British successfully taxed the "subtle and nimble" merchants and moneylenders of the Bania caste, and he

[67] TNA: CO 733/427/12, Appendix II to Mr. Huntington's Report, 1934, at 4 (attached to a letter from MacMichael to Colonial Secretary, February 23, 1940).

[68] TNA: CO 733/444, Strathie to Downie, January 5, 1941. See also V. K. R. V. Rao, *Taxation of Income in India* (Calcutta: Longmans, 1931), 65–6.

therefore saw no reason why the British would not be as successful in taxing potential evaders in Palestine.[69]

The outbreak of the Second World War, then, essentially allowed the British to introduce income taxation in Palestine. The main obstacle that the British had encountered in the 1930s – the opposition of the Jewish community to the tax – no longer existed in the early 1940s when the Jews of Palestine found themselves on the same side as the British in the global fight against Nazism. However, the taxpayers of Palestine were still perceived by British officials to be different from British taxpayers. One can see this most clearly in Strathie's suggestion to water down the new enactment by preventing tax appeals in some cases, and in his argument that a sales tax rather than an income tax would be more appropriate as a revenue-generation tool in Palestine.

1941–1948: Applying the Income Tax

Collection of the new income tax proved to be easier than expected, and initial revenues exceeded expectations. Thus, in its first year it was estimated that the income tax would yield P£50,000, but the actual yield was almost four times as much, reaching P£193,000.[70] However, it turned out that Jewish fears about the relative burden of taxation between the two major ethnic communities in Palestine were justified. Of the P£193,000 collected, P£120,000 (or approximately 60 percent) came from Jews, P£30,000 (or approximately 15 percent) from Arabs, and the rest from others (British, Greeks, Armenians, and so forth).[71]

---

[69] "All about the Income Tax: Government Adviser's Broadcast," *PP*, May 26, 1941, at 4. On British public relations efforts during and after the Second World War, see, e.g., Sherene Seikaly, "Meatless Days: Consumption and Capitalism in Wartime Palestine 1939–1948" (Ph.D. diss., New York University, 2007), 386–94.

[70] ISA, Record Group 16, M-1379/24, Annual Progress Reports 1942–1945, "Supplement to Annual Report," April 15, 1942. The actual number of taxpayers, however, was lower than expected (5,000 instead of 7,000). Compare, "6,000 out of 7,000 Taxpayers in Towns," *PP*, June 5, 1941, at 3; "Income Tax Receipts Satisfactory: Over Five Thousand Assessees," *PP*, April 26, 1942, at 3.

[71] TNA: CO 733/444, Minutes, June 11, 1942; ISA, Record Group 16, M-1379/24, Annual Progress Reports 1942–1945, "Supplement to Annual Report," April 15, 1942. There is a slight discrepancy between the Colonial Office minutes and the report of the income tax commissioner regarding the amount collected from Arab taxpayers.

Despite having accurate data on the ethnic incidence of the tax, which, as expected, fell heavily on the Jews, the government of Palestine was anxious not to reveal this information, and therefore took active measures to conceal it by publishing the data broken down by districts, which were ethnically mixed, instead of municipalities, which often were not ethnically mixed.[72] Nonetheless, Jews claimed that they were paying 70–80 percent of the tax.[73] When the government was asked to provide information about the ethnic make-up of the income tax, it argued publicly that it was not "usual to break down the [information about the] revenue on a geographic, regional or racial basis." The Jews responded that this might be the case in Britain, "where the population was homogenous," but not in Palestine, where many major issues (including education, immigration, and land purchases) were based on ethnic distinctions, and that it was necessary to provide such information in order to dispel the feeling that the Jews were paying a disproportionate share of the tax.[74] In response, the government provided an ethnically based analysis of income tax revenues, revealing that, despite the fact that the Jews comprised only 30 percent of the population at the time, they comprised more than 75 percent of income tax payers (with 17,500 Jewish taxpayers in 1942/43 compared to 5,000 Arab taxpayers), and that Jewish income taxpayers paid five times as much per capita as Arab taxpayers.[75]

[72] ISA, Record Group 16, M-1379/24, Annual Progress Reports 1942–1945, "Supplement to Annual Report," April 15, 1942.

[73] "Needs and Means," *PP*, June 13, 1944, at 4; "System that Cries for Revision: Maximum Tax for Minimum Service," *PP*, August 17, 1944, at 4. See also Amotz Morag, *Mimun ha-Memshalah be-Yisrael: Hitpathut u-Ve'ayot* (Jerusalem: Magnes, 1967), 6.

[74] "Income Tax Revenue Yields Over Two Million Pounds: O.A.G. Discusses Economic Problems," *PP*, September 7, 1944, at 3; "Income Tax Evasion," *PP*, September 8, 1944, at 4; "Reflections," *PP*, September 23, 1946, at 4. During the period of British rule in Palestine, the Zionist community established its own independent education system, while Arabs were educated in government schools. As to Jewish immigration and Jewish land purchases in Palestine, both were heavily restricted following the publication of the White Paper of 1939.

[75] "Income Tax Statistics in February: Chief Secretary Replies to Pressmen," *PP*, February 8, 1945, at 3; "Reflections," *PP*, February 15, 1945, at 4; "1942/3 Income Tax Details Revealed," *PP*, March 8, 1945, at 3; "Taxation and Evasion," *PP*, May 4, 1945, at 4. The figures for subsequent years were similar. For the 1944/45 tax year, 62% of the taxpayers were Jewish, 14% were Arabs, and the rest were defined as "others." "Income Tax in 1944/45: 44,114 Payers," *PP*, June 23, 1946, at 2. See also

While the tax was mainly imposed on Jews, wealthy Arabs did join the Jews in opposing unfavorable changes to the tax. In January 1943, when it was learned that the government intended to raise income tax rates and also planned to introduce a new property tax, Jewish and Arab landlords joined ranks in opposition to the plan.[76] The opposition of wealthy Arabs to taxation was also manifested when the British attempted to introduce an estate duty in early 1943.[77] When this move became known, at a meeting of Arab landlords and delegates the tax was attacked as "contrary to the laws of Islam," and as being designed to "displace the Arabs from the land," and it was claimed that it would be shouldered by the Arab community alone, since Jewish property was "usually owned by holding cooperatives."[78] The opposition proved successful and the idea was abandoned, though there was another, albeit equally unsuccessful, attempt to introduce an inheritance tax in 1945.[79] The perceived unfairness of the income tax led some Jewish commentators to propose the imposition of additional taxes aimed at achieving a fairer balance between Jews and Arabs in direct taxation. Thus, in a letter written in 1946, Gabriel Eichelgrün, a Jewish tax expert, proposed that the British impose a poll tax modeled on section 25 of the West African Income Tax Ordinance (Nigeria and the Gold Coast) to tax Arab peasants and the nomadic Bedouin population of Palestine (a proposal that was not adopted by the British).[80]

Eichelgrün, *Palestine Income Tax Guide*, 204–5; "Five to One: How Jewish Taxpayers Outnumber Arab," *PP*, March 23, 1948, at 3.

[76] "Landlords Meet: Arabs and Jews Hold Joint Discussion," *PP*, January 25, 1943, at 3. On Arab opposition to British fiscal policy in 1943, see also Sherene Seikaly, *Men of Capital: Scarcity and Economy in Mandate Palestine* (Stanford: Stanford University Press, 2016), 112–13.

[77] "Palestine Pays Its Way," *PP*, February 18, 1943, at 4; "New Taxes on Incomes and Profits," *PP*, February 18, 1943, at 1.

[78] "All-Palestine Arab Conference Rejects Tax Proposals," *PP*, March 12, 1943, at 3.

[79] "New Income Tax in Force Tomorrow: Estate Duty Not Enacted; Excess Profit Tax Lower," *PP*, March 31, 1943, at 1; "Landlords' Opposition," *PP*, March 11, 1945, at 2; "War Tax on Companies Enacted: Succession Duties, Poll Tax Dropped," *PP*, July 29, 1945, at 3. On estate taxation, see also TNA: CO 733/464/7, Government of Palestine, *Report of the Revenue Committee* (Jerusalem: Government Printer, 1944), 43–6.

[80] "Income Tax and Poll Tax," *PP*, September 3, 1946, at 4. See generally Ewout Frankema, "Raising Revenue in the British Empire, 1870–1940: How 'Extractive' Were Colonial Taxes?" *Journal of Global History* 5 (2010): 447–77, 467.

Collection of the income tax proved to be quite successful, despite the fact that, as one early report noted, "in Palestine where almost none of the merchants keep correct books it is obvious that we lay ourselves open to cheating right and left," and also despite the observation that the Ordinance proved to be "unsophisticated" and thus unsuited to the "extraordinary complications of business life" in Palestine. The Palestine income tax commissioner, who noted this point, also said that while he did not propose radical changes because "in dealing with the Colonial Office departures from the Model Ordinance should be avoided if possible," one day the Ordinance would have to be redrafted completely to make it more suitable to the conditions of Palestine.[81]

One reason for the relative success of the tax may have been that in Palestine, like other British territories, a pay-as-you-earn system was put in place, and the tax was withheld at source for a number of types of income. Provisions for withholding the tax at source were especially important in the case of salaries. In most modern income tax systems, much of the revenue comes from employees, and withholding provisions create an automatic mechanism for the collection of revenue while reducing the friction between taxpayers and the state.[82]

By the fiscal year 1945/46, there were 62,000 income tax payers in Palestine, and revenues from the tax accounted for about 20 percent of total government revenues.[83] The number of government officials dealing with income taxation increased accordingly. When income taxation was first contemplated in the 1930s, Huntington envisioned an income tax department that would include only a handful of officials, and indeed when income taxation was finally introduced in 1941, the

---

[81] ISA, Record Group 16, M-1379/24, Annual Progress Reports 1942–1945, "Jerusalem District: Revenue Report for the Financial Year ended 31st March, 1942," 6; ISA, Record Group 16, M-1379/24, Annual Progress Reports 1942–1945, "Supplement to Annual Report," April 15, 1942, 3; ISA, Record Group 16, M-1379/21, Colonial Office to MacMichael, June 30, 1942; TNA: CO 733/444, Minutes, June 20, 1942.

[82] Income Tax Ordinance, 1941, sec. 41. See generally Harold C. Wilkenfeld, *Taxes and People in Israel* (Cambridge, MA: Harvard University Press, 1973), 76–7. On withholding provisions in the United Kingdom, see Ann Mumford, *Taxing Culture: Towards a Theory of Tax Collection Law* (Aldershot: Ashgate, 2002), 74–7.

[83] "How Jewish Tax-payers Outnumber Arab," *PP*, March 23, 1948, at 3; Morag, *Mimun*, 10.

FIGURE 2.1 Staff at the Tel Aviv income tax office in 1941.

number of officials administering it was rather small. However, by the
end of 1945 there were 255 permanent and temporary workers in the
income tax department. The rapid rise in the number of income tax
workers can be seen in Figures 2.1 and 2.2.[84]

   The increase in the number of taxpayers, however, was not spread
evenly. According to British reports, taxpayers belonging to certain
social groups – Arabs and "Old *Yishuv*" (that is, non-Zionist) Jews –
tended to evade income taxation more frequently than other taxpayers.[85] At least in the case of Arab taxpayers, the disappointing revenues
may have been the result of social structures rather than of active evasion. The income tax commissioner observed in 1942 that "in early
discussions the district commissioners had anticipated large sums

[84] TNA: CO 733/427/12, Appendix II to Mr. Huntington's Report, 1934 (attached
   to a letter from MacMichael to Colonial Secretary, February 23, 1940); Reuveny,
   Mimshal ha-Mandat, 87.
[85] ISA, Record Group 16, M-1379/24, Annual Progress Reports 1942–1945, "Income
   Tax: General Report for 1942/3," 2.

FIGURE 2.2 Staff at the Tel Aviv income tax office in 1946.

from rich Arab property owners. There has been no such case. Certain Arab families do own large extents of agricultural land but the income is divided up between various members of the family and has rarely proved taxable."[86]

While most Jewish taxpayers, so it seems, were willing to have their income taxed (or were at least resigned to the fact), attitudes to the tax were not static. One factor that may have led to changing attitudes was the inevitable waning of the initial spirit of civic engagement and financial sacrifice, especially once the immediate Nazi threat to Palestine had receded with the defeat of Rommel's army in the Western Desert in 1943.[87] Another factor was the growing tension between the British and the Jews as the decade progressed. During the war, the mainstream Jewish organizations in Palestine supported the British

[86] ISA, Record Group 16, M-1379/24, Annual Progress Reports 1942–1945, "Supplement to Annual Report," April 15, 1942, 2.

[87] See also Steven A. Bank, Kirk J. Stark, and Joseph J. Thorndike, *War and Taxes* (Washington, DC: Urban Institute Press, 2008), 103–4 (on the decline in the spirit of sacrifice in the United States once the Second World War began to turn in favor of the allies).

war effort, but the two Jewish right-wing factions, the Stern Gang and (beginning in 1944) the Irgun, continued their terror campaign against the British government in the hope of driving the British out of Palestine and establishing an independent Jewish state. Later, when the war ended, the mainstream Jewish militia, the Haganah, joined the fight against the British, ultimately leading to British withdrawal from the country in 1948.

One major target of the Stern Gang's campaign against the British was the tax collection machinery. Tax offices became important symbolic targets. In February 1944 the Stern Gang attacked income tax offices in the three major cities of Palestine, leading the income tax commissioner to comment later that year that:

> the public continues to respond to our demands in a manner which in the circumstances is satisfactory. The attempt of the Stern Gang to blow up the [tax] offices in Jerusalem, Tel Aviv and Haifa in February 1944 was not typical, although doubtless certain large tax payers belonging to other communities would have derived a certain satisfaction had the attempt been more successful.[88]

Perhaps out of a desire to placate the Jewish public, who continued to complain that they were paying more than their fair share in taxes and receiving less than their fair share in government services, the British decided to channel a portion of the revenue raised by the income tax back to the largest Jewish municipality in Palestine, Tel Aviv, in the form of a grant-in-aid.[89] In subsequent years, Jewish resistance to the income tax sometimes took the milder form of business strikes, but there were also additional terrorist attacks on income tax offices in 1946 and 1947.[90] In September 1947, six months before the end of the British mandate, members of the Stern Gang visited Jewish income tax officials in their homes, ordering them to resign

---

[88] "4 Explosions in Tel Aviv," *PP*, February 27, 1944, at 1; "Bombs in Income Tax Offices in Three Cities," *PP*, February 28, 1944, at 1; ISA, Record Group 16, M-1379/24, Annual Progress Reports 1942–1945, Annual Report 1943/44, 3.

[89] "Grant-in-Aid and Income Tax," *PP*, March 28, 1944, at 3.

[90] "From Dan to Beersheba: Today's Post Bag," *PP*, March 13, 1945, at 3; "One Dead, Ten Injured: J'lem Income Tax Office Blown Up," *PP*, November 21, 1946, at 1; "Shooting Breaks Up Tel Aviv Funeral," *PP*, August 3, 1947, at 1; "Charge Exploded in Income Tax Office," *PP*, August 11, 1947, at 3.

(none did).[91] When the British government gradually retreated from Palestine in the first months of 1948, the Jews were ready to take over the mandatory tax system.[92]

Informalism in the Application of the Income Tax Ordinance

One of the most striking aspects of the period between the enactment of the Income Tax Ordinance in 1941 and the end of British rule in Palestine in 1948 was the disjuncture between the way in which different actors involved in the implementation of the Ordinance – administrators, judges, lawyers, and accountants – viewed the relationship between income taxation and its law.

British tax administrators in Palestine often attempted to ignore the letter of the law in order to create a better fit between tax law and local conditions, thus reducing the friction between the state and taxpayers. One way to administratively reshape tax law was to relegate discretion to the public.[93] A concrete example of such a method was the British officials' approach to tax avoidance. A popular method of tax avoidance in Palestine was the formation of corporations and the retention of profits by these corporations (the maximum initial tax rate on the income of individuals was 30 percent, while the rate for corporations was initially set at just 10 percent).[94] One method to fight the use of corporations as a tax avoidance device was by taxing

---

[91] "Officials 'Ordered' to Resign," *PP*, September 7, 1947, at 3; "Threats Ignored by Officials," *PP*, September 8, 1947, at 3.

[92] "Income Tax for Jewish State," *PP*, April 19, 1948, at 3; "Income Tax to Jewish State," *PP*, May 4, 1948, at 1; "Income Tax in Jewish Jerusalem," *PP*, May 7, 1948, at 3; "Income-Tax," *PP*, May 9, 1948, at 3; "Income Tax to Be Doubled: 10P.C. Basic, 5P.C. War Tax," *PP*, September 3, 1948, at 1.

[93] The use of lay experts to assess and collect income, thus reducing friction between the state and taxpayers, was a well-known device. It was used, as we saw in the previous chapter, in Ottoman times, and in British-ruled Palestine in the 1920s and 1930s. It was also used in Britain. See, e.g., Martin Daunton, *Trusting Leviathan: The Politics of Taxation in Britain, 1799–1914* (New York: Cambridge University Press, 2001), 186, 188, 190; Margaret Lamb, "'Horrid Appealing': Accounting for Taxable Profits in Mid-Nineteenth Century England," *Accounting, Organizations and Society* 26 (2001): 271–98, 288.

[94] ISA, Record Group 16, M-1379/24, Annual Progress Reports 1942–1945, "Jerusalem District: Revenue Report for the Financial Year ended 31st March, 1942," 7; ISA, Record Group 16, M-1379/24, Annual Progress Reports 1942–1945, Annual Report

undistributed profits. Section 22(1) of the Income Tax Ordinance, which contained a general antiavoidance provision, was expanded in April 1943 to include specific provisions taxing undistributed profits. The authority to decide on the definition of what constituted "undistributed profits" was not given to tax administrators or the courts. Instead, it was relegated to the public. A committee was created where the majority of the members were nonofficial (two officials and three members of the public with special commercial experience). The task of the committee was to advise the income tax commissioner on the exercising of his power under this section. This attempt to "introduce responsible members of the public as advisers," noted the commissioner, proved "a conspicuous success."[95]

The use of lay advisers was legally sanctioned by the tax statute itself. This was not the case with other means used by British administrators to adapt the Income Tax Ordinance to local conditions. Sometimes administrators simply ignored the letter of the law in the application of the Ordinance.[96] For example, requests for relief in respect of Empire income tax were accepted, despite the fact that there was no formal reciprocal mechanism of the kind envisioned by section 63(3) of the Ordinance. In his 1942 Report, the income tax commissioner noted that "I gave relief in some cases in which it was not strictly speaking due, as reciprocating arrangements have not yet been made with the colonies," explaining that "in war conditions I considered it undesirable to delay relief till reciprocating arrangements were completed."[97]

Another example of the discretion used was in the treatment of evasion. In the report for the fiscal year 1942/43, the income tax

<hr />

1943/44, 3; "800 New Firms in Six Months: Income Tax and Company Life," *PP*, July 1, 1942, at 2. See also Morag, *Mimun*, 97.

[95] ISA, Record Group 16, M-1379/24, Annual Progress Reports 1942–1945, Annual Report 1943/44, 3. See also "Income Tax Panel," *PP*, March 28, 1944, at 2; Moses, *Income Tax Ordinance of Palestine: The Text as Valid Since 1st April, 1944*, 77.

[96] The use of extensive discretion also characterized tax administration in England in the nineteenth century. See Margaret Lamb, "Defining 'Profits' for British Income Tax Purposes: A Contextual Study of the Depreciation Cases, 1875–1897," *Accounting Historians Journal* 29 (2002): 105–72, 121, 123.

[97] ISA, Record Group 16, M-1379/24, Annual Progress Reports 1942–1945, "Supplement to Annual Report," April 15, 1942, 2.

commissioner noted that evasion was fairly widespread, but "having regard to the fact that income tax has been but recently introduced in Palestine, it was decided, as a matter of policy, not to take any action under sections 66 and 67 of the Ordinance that provide for penalties for the making of incorrect returns and fraudulent acts."[98]

Finally, ignoring the letter of the law was not only the result of conscious policy. It may also have been a result of the fact that British administrators were often inexperienced. This was a problem noted by Colonial Office officials when they first contemplated the introduction of a uniform income tax law in the colonies. Thus, one official, when discussing existing colonial income tax legislation in 1921, noted that in those colonies that already had income taxation, income tax acts "have to be administered by officials who necessarily lack experience and have no knowledge of the accumulated store of precedent and practice which guide the Inland Revenue here [in Britain]."[99]

While British tax administrators sometimes used discretion to ignore the letter of the law, British judges manning the courts of Palestine were less flexible. The Model Income Tax Ordinance of 1922 did not create a detailed tax appeals mechanism. Section 44 of the Model Ordinance stated that "any person who, being aggrieved by an assessment made upon him ... may appeal against the assessment to a Judge." It added that "the Chief Justice may make rules governing such appeals and providing for the method of tendering evidence and appointing places for the hearing of such appeals and prescribing the procedure to be followed on a case being stated."[100] The 1941 Palestine Ordinance provided more detail. It declared that tax appeals would be made to a "British puisne judge in chambers." The decision of this judge was final, unless he decided to "state a case on a question

---

[98] ISA, Record Group 16, M-1379/24, Annual Progress Reports 1942–1945, Income Tax – General Report for 1942/43, 2. Deviations from the letter of the law were not always in favor of taxpayers. For example, it seems that while the Ordinance required assessing officers to refund any amount that was withheld at the source in excess of the amount of tax due, the practice was instead not to refund these amounts but to carry them over to future years, in direct contravention of section 61 of the Ordinance. ISA, Record Group 16, M-151/38, Berinson to Commissioner of Income Tax, July 21, 1946.

[99] TNA: CO 323/875, Minutes, Sir G. Grindle, December 7, 1921.

[100] See *Report of the Inter-Departmental Committee on Income Tax*, 30–1.

of law, for the opinion of the Supreme Court sitting as a Court of Civil Appeal."[101]

Initially, the judges of Palestine strove to prevent what might be called the "legalization" of income taxation and the importation of English tax doctrines. However, the attempt to prevent the importation of English doctrines failed, due to the pressure exerted by lawyers presenting legal arguments that relied on English precedents. The number of income tax cases decided by the courts of Palestine was relatively high. For example, in July 1944 the income tax commissioner reported that thirty income tax appeals had been lodged in the fiscal year 1943/44. He also noted that he had met his Cypriot counterpart and suggested closer contact between the income tax administrations of all colonial territories. In that event, Palestine's contribution, he said, "would probably consist mainly in the interpretation of the provisions of the Model Ordinance given by the courts," because "the number of appeals to the courts in Palestine is far greater than that in any other territory" in which the Model Income Tax Ordinance was in force. Therefore, the legal decisions of the courts of Palestine could serve as a guide to the courts of other British territories.[102]

Unlike other mandatory ordinances, the Palestine Income Tax Ordinance did not contain a specific provision requiring judges to interpret it on the basis of English law. Thus, in their early decisions British judges declared that they were free to not follow English precedents. In one of the early Palestine tax cases, Judge David Edwards of the Supreme Court of Palestine said he would not pay attention to the English cases or literature cited by the parties because "it would be a pity if in Palestine a huge mass of case law on this ordinance is allowed to grow up in the manner and to the extent in which [it did] in England."[103]

In another case, Judge Edwards referred to an English newspaper article that said that "income tax law in England was now a 'tangled morass'." The obvious conclusion, said Edwards, was that "one should

[101] Palestine Income Tax Ordinance, 1941, sec. 53.
[102] ISA, Record Group 16, M-1379/24, Annual Progress Reports 1942–1945, Annual Report 1943/44, at 4.
[103] ITA 8/42 *Ideal Motion Pictures* v. *AO*, Tel Aviv (1942), PLR, 9:481, 9:482. See also ITA 7/42 *Warner Bros.* v. *AO Lydda District* (1942), PLR, 9:488. For a general discussion, see S. Moses, *Income Tax Ordinance of Palestine*, 2nd edn (Tel Aviv: Bitaon, 1946), 16–17.

try to interpret the Palestine Income Tax Ordinance as far as possible untrammeled by authority."[104] The same sentiment was expressed by Judge Alan Rose of the Supreme Court of Palestine. It was unlikely, Rose said, that the Palestinian legislator "desired" to introduce into Palestine "[t]he niceties and complexities of the British income tax law, which in itself is a highly specialized and fruitful branch of professional activity in England and the decisions in respect of which are conflicting and in many instances obscure."[105]

In a similar way, Chief Justice Frederic Gordon Smith commented in 1943 that it would be a "Herculean if not impossible task to give a concise and lucid explanation of the principles and system of the law of Income Tax in England, nor would any such attempt ... be profitable or, in my opinion, serve any useful purpose in being of any local legal value." He then noted that "it is significant that our Ordinance has not adopted [the English] system of schedules, cases and rules" and that "in so many respects the principles and scheme of the English Acts are so different to those contained in our Ordinance." He concluded his opinion by stating that "I do not say that decided cases in England cannot be referred to as affording some possible help and guidance in attempting to ascertain what [the] intention [of the Ordinance] is, but I do say that they cannot be regarded as authoritative and binding on this Court, in view of the differences there are in the respective principles and schemes and of the confusion which exists in England."[106]

However, despite the declared reluctance of some British judges in Palestine to turn to English tax law, they soon referred to English decisions, even if they were not formally obliged to do so.[107] Thus, in a 1943 case Judge Edwards said:

> I realize that too much reliance should not be placed upon cases decided in the United Kingdom; nevertheless no-one can doubt that the Income

[104] ITA 9/42, *An Advocate* v. *AO Jerusalem District* (1942), in Arnold M. Apelbom and B. Braude, eds., *Palestine Income Tax Cases* (Tel Aviv: Palestine Law Publishing Co., 1945), 21, 22; ITA 2/44 *Gesundheit* v. *AO Tel Aviv* (1944), PLR, 11:265, 11:269.
[105] ITA 18/42 *Assad Halaby* v. *AO, Lydda District* (1943), PLR, 10:342, 10:346.
[106] ITA 9/42 *Horowitz* v. *AO Jerusalem District* (1943), PLR, 10:255, 10:259–61. See also CA 310/44, *Gesundheit* v. *AO Tel Aviv* (1945), PLR, 12:168.
[107] See e.g., ITA 3/44 *Leather Centre, Ltd.* v. *AO Jerusalem* (1944), PLR, 11:462; ITA 25/43 *Consolidated Near East Co., Ltd.* v. *AO Haifa* (1944), PLR, 11:229. On the relationship of the case law of Palestine to English law in the 1940s, see generally Likhovski, *Law and Identity in Mandate Palestine*, 74–80.

Tax Ordinance, 1941, whether based on an Indian Income Tax Act or Statute or on the statute or ordinance in force in some Crown Colony or whether it is a result of special draftsmanship in another place, is still based on the same principles as English Income Tax Law. Guidance is therefore clearly to be found from cases decided in various courts in the United Kingdom."[108]

Thus, even if the judges were rhetorically committed to departing from English income tax law, the need to decide actual cases (as well as the attitude of the Privy Council that held in a 1943 decision that the courts of Palestine had to follow English law in the absence of local legislation), ultimately forced them to turn to English precedents.[109]

Unlike British tax administrators and (to a lesser extent) British judges, local lawyers and accountants in Palestine generally sought to eliminate the differences between Palestinian and English (and British-colonial) income tax law. Textbooks and case law were both used to achieve this goal. The Income Tax Ordinance spawned an impressive number of textbooks and commentaries during the seven final years of British rule in Palestine.[110] Indeed, one of the commentators on the Palestine Income Tax Ordinance, Gabriel Eichelgrün, created a cottage industry out of tax commentaries. His publishing firm, Paltax, published commentaries on the Income Tax Ordinance of Palestine in English and German, commentaries on other Palestinian tax enactments, and even a book in French on the new income tax law of Lebanon.[111]

Many of these books contained systematic discussions of the Ordinance based on English legislation and case law.[112] For example,

---

[108] ITA 19/43, *Trachtengott v. AO Lydda District* (1943), PLR, 10:487; Apelbom and Braude, *Palestine Income Tax Cases*, 79, 85.

[109] See PCA 1/42 *Syndic of Khoury Bankruptcy v. Khayat* (1943), PLR, 10:271.

[110] The catalog of the National Library of Israel includes about twenty books and booklets on the Palestine Income Tax Ordinance published between 1941 and 1948.

[111] Eichelgrün, *Palestine Income Tax Guide*; G[abriel] Eichelgrün, *Palästinensischer Einkommensteuerführer, abgeschlossen zum 9. April 1944* (Haifa: G. Eichelgrün, 1944); G. Eichelgrün, *Palestine Company Profits Tax 1945* (Haifa: Paltax, 1945); A. B. Plopul and André Tuéni, *L'impot sur le revenu au Liban: Commentaire théorique et pratique de la loi libanaise du 4 décembre 1944* (Beirut: 1945 [label mounted on title-page: Haifa: Paltax Publishers]).

[112] See, e.g., Fritz Hermann Strauss, *The ABC of Income Tax in Palestine* (Jerusalem: Achiasaf, 1941), preface; Moses, *Income Tax (Amendment) Ordinance,*

Eichelgrün's *Palestine Income Tax Guide* was described as "an exhaustive collection of U.K. and Empire authorities" (whose purpose was to "enable the taxpayer to find out how to reduce the tax to its legal minimum"). A review of Eichelgrün's book in an English journal noted approvingly that "the author appears to have omitted no relevant British tax case in his comments on the Ordinance."[113]

Lawyers and accountants were also busy comparing the law of Palestine to English and colonial income tax law in newspaper articles.[114] Typically, professional commentators called for greater similarity between Palestinian and English law. For example, an early attempt by the courts to ignore English tax law because of its complexity was criticized in 1944 by one lawyer, Ernst Werner Klimowsky, who argued that the complexity of tax law was due not to reliance on English law, but to "the complexity of social and commercial conditions in modern times," and to high rates of taxation that led to tax avoidance and therefore to an increasing need for legislation to combat avoidance.[115] Similarly, in 1945 Eichelgrün criticized the courts of Palestine and an earlier commentator (Moses) for their opinion that English law should merely serve as a guide for Palestinian courts, arguing that the application of English law to Palestine's income tax law was obligatory

1942, 3–8; "Guide to Income Tax," *PP*, July 2, 1942, at 4; Fellman, *The Palestine Income Tax*, preface, 23–6; David Rosolio and Ernst Werner Klimowsky, *Mas Hakhnasah be-Erets Yisrael* (Jerusalem: Kiryat Sefer, 1944).

[113] Eichelgrün, "Introduction" to *Palestine Income Tax Guide*; [Book Review], *Law Quarterly Review* 62 (1946), 190; [Ad.], "Palestine Income Tax Guide by G. Eichelgruen, Tax Consultant," *PP*, August 28, 1945, at 4; [Ad.], "Palestine Income Tax Guide by G. Eichelgruen," *PP*, June 3, 1946, at 4.

[114] See e.g., E. W. Klimowsky, "Cyprus Income Tax and Commerce: A Possible Model for Palestine," *PP*, April 19, 1941, at 5; Dr. S. Moses, "Tax on Undistributed Profits: A New Decision of the House of Lords," *PP*, October 27, 1942, at 2; "Readers' Letters: Tax on Bonus Shares," *PP*, March 24, 1943, at 4; Dr. S. Moses, "Reform Tendencies in England: The Future of Income Tax," *PP*, January 10, 1944, at 4.

[115] "'Readers' Letters: Income Tax," *PP*, November 23, 1944, at 4. Just like Sheringham's biography discussed in n. 2, Klimowsky's biography illustrates the multiple talents of some of the people involved in income taxation in Palestine in the 1940s. Klimowsky was not only an accomplished tax professional, but also an important contributor to the science of sexology. See, Volkmar Sigusch, "Ernst W. Klimowsky," in *Personenlexikon der Sexualforschung*, eds. Volkmar Sigusch and Günter Grau (Frankfurt: Campus, 2009), 366–8.

"unless a case can be distinguished from existing English decisions on account of its special circumstances."[116]

However, it should be noted that lawyers, too, were aware of the impact of local conditions on the application of the Ordinance. Thus, local tax law was heavily criticized for not taking into account local conditions, for example with critiques pointing out the anomaly "that a man who uses a motorcar for his business may depreciate it, whereas his colleague who is confined to a donkey or a camel has no such facilities."[117] Even Eichelgrün, who supported the wholesale application of English tax law in Palestine, noted the complex social and economic context that made this application difficult in practice. In a brief comparative article on income tax legislation in the British Empire published in 1948, no doubt based on his experience in Palestine, Eichelgrün noted some of the major problems that plagued British-colonial income tax systems: the fact that income taxation was too complex "for the needs of almost illiterate Indian peasants or Palestinian *fellaheen*"; the absence of reliable bookkeeping requirements; and the lack of loyalty of colonial taxpayers to the colonial state, resulting in tax evasion often being "turned into a political weapon."[118]

Eichelgrün was a German–Jewish immigrant to Palestine, and as such, he may have been influenced by notions of legal formalism typical of mainstream German legal thought at the time.[119] It is therefore not surprising that he ultimately came to the conclusion that another major difficulty of British-colonial income tax law had to do with the deeper and more basic problem of English law: its lack of formalism. British-colonial tax statutes, Eichelgrün complained, were "as little outspoken as the English taxing Acts." They only provided "general principles" and not detailed rules. Taxpayers were therefore forced to

---

[116] Eichelgrün, *Palestine Income Tax Guide*, 3.

[117] "Income Tax," PP, January 12, 1945, at 7 (citing the discussion of depreciation in Rosolio and Klimowsky, *Mas Hakhnasah be-Erets Yisrael*, 149 that actually mentioned "horses, mules and camels").

[118] Eichelgrün, "Income-Tax in British Colonies," 129–30.

[119] On early twentieth-century German legal formalism and its influence on German-Jewish immigrants to Palestine, see Fania Oz-Salzberger and Eli Salzberger, "The Secret German Sources of the Israeli Supreme Court," *Israel Studies* 3 (1998): 159–92, 168–71.

rely on three different systems of norms: statutory law; British and British-colonial case law; and administrative law. However, he noted, "no guidance whatsoever as to the applicability of these three systems of law is given by the local administration; there is no official handbook, no guide ... [and usually taxpayers find that both the] United Kingdom and the colonial law are silent as to the solution of any question." The lack of clear formal rules found in tax statutes, or in case law developed by the courts, meant that the "whole system [led] by necessity to the assessment 'by estimate,' usually agreed upon between the trader and the assessor. It [was] a state foreseen by Adam Smith in which the assessor's humour [was] usually of greater importance for the ultimate assessment than the real profits made by a trader."[120]

Conclusion

While the introduction of income taxation signified an important stage in the transformation of the tax system of Palestine, opening a large arena for the legalization and professionalization of taxation, it seems this process was neither smooth nor free of conflict between different actors pulling taxation and its law in different directions. When the new tax was imposed in 1941, British administrators (and, to a lesser extent, British judges) actively sought to prevent the convergence of the tax law of Palestine with English tax law and its complex system of rules, while local tax professionals involved in litigating tax disputes and interpreting the Ordinance in textbooks sought to increase the similarity of the Ordinance to English tax law. The ultimate result was that 1940s Palestine had an income tax regime anchored in legislation and supported by a nascent professional community devoted to legal formalism. However, the social conditions of the country, as well as the attitudes of British administrators applying this new tax, led to the creation of a system that relied to a large extent on administrative discretion, and on assessment "by estimate," rather than on the letter of the law. In this sense, it was similar to another system of taxation that appeared in Palestine during the last decade of British rule – a Jewish voluntary tax system. It is to the history of this Jewish system to which we now turn.

[120] Eichelgrün, "Income-Tax in British Colonies," 129–30.

PART II

THE ASCENDANCY OF SOCIAL NORMS

3

Taxation without Law: The Jewish Voluntary Tax System

Emanuel Harussi was a prominent Jewish writer in mandatory Palestine. He was one of the founders of a satirical theater and wrote many skits, poems, and children's songs, including one of the most popular Hebrew lullabies. Harussi also worked as the propaganda director of the voluntary Jewish tax system, the community tax (*kofer ha-yishuv*), established by the Jewish community in Palestine in 1938.[1] In 1940 Harussi wrote a pamphlet entitled "What is the Community Tax? A Call to the Young," which was illustrated by a leading artist, Nahum Gutman.[2] It urged children to pressurize their parents to become loyal taxpaying Zionists:

> Ask [your father] if he too was diligent and paid his share
> And require an answer to every little clause
> Did the father pay transportation tax?

---

[1] *Kofer* means poll tax or ransom, and *yishuv* (community) referred to the Jewish community in Palestine. In newspaper articles and British documents *kofer ha-yishuv* was sometimes called "national redemption fund," "redemption fund," or "community redemption fund." See "'Zionist Budget Must Reach One Million Pounds': Colonisation, Security, Labour and Industry Estimates before Zionist General Council," *PP*, November 16, 1938, at 2; TNA: CO 733/413/10, Shaw to Luke, March 2, 1939; TNA: CO 733/413/11, Note on the Kofer Hayishuv, March 2, 1939.

[2] Emanuel Harussi and Nahum Gutman, *Ma-Ze Kofer ha-Yishuv? Kol Kore li-Vney ha-Ne'urim* (Tel Aviv: Dfus ha-Po'el ha-Mizrahi, 1940) (a copy of this pamphlet can be found in the Nahum Gutman Museum of Art, Tel Aviv). See also "Ram Keysam le-Kofer ha-Yishuv," *Davar li-Yeladim*, November 3, 1938, at 16.

Did he put the excise stamp on the bottle of wine?
Did he buy only Jewish cigarettes?
And did he ask for a security certificate in the restaurant?
Do not forget your mother, son
Ask and be not ashamed ...
When she bought a bouquet of flowers
Did she receive a [sales tax] certificate?[3]

Harussi's 1940 pamphlet was written to bolster the voluntary tax system that the Jewish community had established during the last decade of British rule in Palestine, as part of its efforts to create the institutions of the future Jewish state.[4] The Jewish system was a hybrid one, combining certain attributes of government taxation with community charitable contributions. The payments it received were viewed by payers and collectors alike as taxes, yet they were raised by a bureaucracy that had no clear rules of assessment, no courts using formal

---

[3] Harussi and Gutman, *Ma-Ze Kofer ha-Yishuv?*, 12–14. The poem was addressed to a "boy," but for some reason the accompanying illustration (see Figure 3.1) showed a girl. On the Zionist cult of youth and the mobilization of children before and after Israeli independence, see generally Anita Shapira, *Israel: A History*, trans. Anthony Berris (Waltham, MA: Brandeis University Press, 2012), 133–7; Paula Kabalo, "Pioneering Discourse and the Shaping of an Israeli Citizen in the 1950s," *Jewish Social Studies: History, Culture, Society* 15:2 (2009): 82–110; Talia Diskin, Mishpat mi-Shelanu: Hok u-Musar be-'Itonut ha-Yeladim veha-No'ar bi-Medinat Yisrael, 1948–1958 (Ph.D. diss. draft, Tel Aviv University, submitted 2016). For similar examples of the fiscal mobilzation of children in the United States, see James T. Sparrow, *Warfare State: World War II Americans and the Age of Big Government* (New York: Oxford University Press, 2011), 137–40.

[4] The term "voluntary tax" may seem like an oxymoron, because some definitions of the term "tax" include a compulsory or coercive element. See, e.g., *Oxford English Dictionary*, s.v. "Tax," defining the term as "a compulsory contribution to the support of government ..." However, as the vast social science literature on tax compliance has shown, criminal sanctions are often not the only, or the major, factor motivating taxpayers to comply. See, e.g., Benno Torgler, *Tax Compliance and Tax Morale: A Theoretical and Empirical Analysis* (Cheltenham: Edward Elgar, 2007); Marjorie E. Kornhauser, "A Tax Morale Approach to Compliance: Recommendations for the IRS," *Florida Tax Review* 8 (2007): 599–640. For a historical discussion of the blurry line between voluntarism and compulsion in taxation, see, e.g., Carolyn C. Jones, "Bonds, Voluntarism and Taxation," in *Studies in the History of Tax Law*, ed. John Tiley (Oxford: Hart, 2007), 2:427–42, 2:429, 2:431; Bruce Bartlett, "Is Voluntary Taxation a Viable Option?" *Tax Notes* 135 (June 11, 2012): 1403–6.

FIGURE 3.1 Propaganda pamphlet, 1940. A girl asking her mother whether she paid the sales tax.

procedures to adjudicate disputes, and no central collection mechanisms able to enforce payments using criminal sanctions. Despite these characteristics, the system managed to raise relatively large amounts of money over an extended period of time.[5]

[5] The history of this system has received little scholarly attention. There are a few works written by former officials of the system, and one master's thesis that explores some aspects of its political and administrative history. See Emanuel Harussi, *Sefer ha-Magbit: Magbit ha-Hitgaysut veha-Hatsalah* (Tel Aviv: Magbit ha-Hitgaysut veha-Hatsalah, 1949/50); Emanuel Harussi, "Bi-Yemey Kofer ha-Yishuv u-Magbit ha-Hitgaysut," *Hed ha-Haganah* 13 (October 1961): 13–14; Yehuda Slutsky, *Me-Haganah le-Ma'avak*, vol. 2, part 2 of *Sefer Toldot ha-Haganah* (Tel Aviv: Dfus A. Strud, 1964), 1003–13; Mordekhai Berger, ed., *Kofer ha-Yishuv* (Jerusalem: Muze'on le-Misim, 1964); Mordekhai Berger, *Magbit ha-Hitgayshut veha-Hatsalah* (Jerusalem: Muze'on le-Misim, 1970); Michael Landau, "Ha-Yishuv bi-Tkufat ha-Sa'ar: 'Al Kofer ha-Yishuv

The history of the Jewish tax system provides an interesting counterpoint to the history of the British governmental tax system described in the previous chapters. British taxation in Palestine, especially the income tax introduced in 1941, was a top-down construct. It was based on a direct relationship between the individual taxpayer and the state. This relationship was invisible to the rest of society, and information about the payment of the taxes was considered private and secret, hidden from public view.[6] Assessment was based, at least in theory, on legal norms, and indeed on one specific sort of legal norm: clear-cut unambiguous rules. Compliance was based on the threat of criminal sanctions in cases of evasion. The individual taxpayer's willingness to pay played no role in the way the system was supposed to operate.

Jewish fund-raising in mandatory Palestine was very different, as the system was communal in nature. It was based on a bottom-up structure and relied on semivoluntary payments – that is, payments that were partly voluntary and partly based on coercion of various sorts. The relationship between the payer and the community was often mediated by social networks and organizations (such as family, friends, clients, business associates, and civil society organizations to which the taxpayer belonged). Payments were often visible and public. Social sanctions (such as shaming), rather than criminal ones (such as incarceration), were used to extract money from taxpayers.

The Jewish system reflected both the practices common in Jewish communities in the Diaspora, and also the nature of Zionist society established in Palestine beginning in the late nineteenth century. This society was based on a civic republican ideology. Zionist Jews were, in theory at least, committed to a pioneering ethos – the building of a new Jewish society based on physical labor, agricultural settlement, and self-defense. Republican duty rather than individual self-interest animated this society, and sacrifice of individual interests for the good

u-Magbit ha-Hitgaysut veha-Hatsalah," *Masu'ah: Kovets Shanti le-Toda'at ha-Sho'ah veha-Gvurah* 5 (1977): 179–98; Dina Porat, *Hanhagah be-Milkud: Ha-Yishuv Nokhah ha-Sho'ah, 1942–1945* (Tel Aviv: 'Am 'Oved, 1986), 117–20; Tali Shavit, "Magbit ha-Hitgaysut veha-Hatsalah" (master's thesis, Tel Aviv University, 1988).

6 On tax privacy, see generally Assaf Likhovski, "Chasing Ghosts: On Writing Cultural Histories of Tax Law," *UC Irvine Law Review* 1 (2011): 843–92.

of the national collective was its ultimate virtue.[7] This ethos obviously had an impact on the tax system that the Zionists were able to establish in Palestine.

A History of the Voluntary Tax System

The voluntary tax system in 1940s Palestine, a time during which the Jews of Palestine numbered about half a million (about 30 percent of the country's population), had roots in a number of different traditions and practices: Jewish communal taxation in the Diaspora, Zionist fund-raising practices in the late nineteenth and early twentieth centuries, and the taxation systems created by local Jewish communities and municipalities in 1920s and 1930s Palestine.

As we saw in Chapter 1, there was a long tradition of internal Jewish taxation (and charity) that developed in Jewish communities in the Diaspora. The specific tools used by Jewish communities in the Diaspora to assess and collect taxes were not transplanted wholesale to Palestine, nor were the Jewish law norms that developed over time in the Diaspora to deal with tax matters adopted by the (mostly secular) Zionist settlers of Palestine. However, in sources from the 1940s one can find a number of explicit traces of the influence of the communal tax systems of the Jewish Diaspora on two levels. First, the communal tax systems of the Diaspora provided the Jews of Palestine with a model of a tax system perceived externally as voluntary but viewed internally, by the community, as coercive. Second, these systems also provided the Jews of Palestine with an example of the use of social norms rather than legal norms as a tool to induce compliance.

For example, one can find reference to Jewish communal taxation in the Diaspora as a model for the voluntary–compulsory tax system of Palestine in the works of Emanuel Harussi, the aforementioned

---

[7] See, e.g., Dan Horowitz and Moshe Lissak, *Origins of the Israeli Polity: Palestine Under the Mandate*, trans. Charles Hoffman (Chicago: University of Chicago Press, 1978); Gershon Shafir and Yoav Peled, *Being Israeli: The Dynamics of Multiple Citizenship* (New York: Cambridge University Press, 2002), 42–4; Avi Bareli and Nir Kedar, *Mamlakhtiyut Yisre'elit* (Jerusalem: IDI Press, 2011), 32–47; Yoav Peled, *The Challenge of Ethnic Democracy: The State and Minority Groups in Israel, Poland and Northern Ireland* (New York: Routledge, 2014), 94; Shapira, *Israel: A History*, 137–42.

propaganda director of the voluntary tax system. According to Harussi, the origins of the voluntary tax system of Palestine were to be found in the internal autonomy that characterized Jewish communities in the Diaspora, an autonomy that was not limited to religious matters but rather extended to the fiscal sphere, creating community dues that were compulsory despite their supposed designation as charitable contributions.[8] The specific methods of Jewish taxation in the Diaspora also influenced the voluntary system of Palestine. Just as Diaspora taxation had relied on social ostracism to elicit compliance, so did the voluntary tax system in Palestine. Indeed, sometimes the old rituals associated with such methods of social ostracism in the Diaspora were evoked in the context of 1940s Palestine.[9]

Jewish communal fund-raising practices also influenced the Zionist movement in Europe. Zionism – that is, Jewish nationalism – emerged in late nineteenth-century Europe. Zionist fund-raising took different forms, including: annual membership fees (*ha-shekel ha-tsiyoni*) paid to the Zionist Organization, established in 1897, entitling its payers to vote in the biannual elections for the Zionist Congresses; contributions to the Jewish National Fund (*Ha-Keren ha-Kayemet le-Yisrael*), established in 1901; or contributions to the Palestine Foundation Fund (*Keren ha-Yesod*) established in 1920.[10]

During the period of the mandate, the Jews of Palestine created a Jewish state-in-the-making, with its own institutions that provided many of the services that the British colonial government could not, or

---

[8] See Harussi, *Sefer ha-Magbit*, 13.

[9] See text to nn. 141–142.

[10] See Robert R. Nathan, Oscar Gass, and Daniel Creamer, *Palestine: Problem and Promise* (Washington, DC: Public Affairs Press, 1946), 355–63; Nachum T. Gross and Jacob Metzer, "Public Finance in the Jewish Community in Interwar Palestine," *Research in Economic History* 3 (1978): 87–159; Jacob Metzer, *Hon Leumi le-Vayit Leumi: 1919–1921* (Jerusalem: Yad Izhak Ben-Zvi, 1979); Ernest Stock, *Partners and Pursestrings: A History of the United Israel Appeal* (Lanham, MD: University Press of America, 1987), 70–1. The influence could even be found in material aspects of the fund-raising process. For example, one of the major Zionist fund-raising bodies, the Jewish National Fund, collected money using a domestic contribution box that mimicked domestic charity boxes used to raise money in Jewish communities in Europe in the early nineteenth century, prior to the appearance of Zionism. See Shaul Stampfer, "Ha-'Pushka' ve-Gilguleyhah: Kupot Erets Yisrael ke-Tofa'ah Hevratit," *Katedrah* 21 (1981): 89–102.

did not want to, provide. In this sense, the development of Palestine's Jewish community during the period of the British mandate ran contrary to the general historical trajectory of modern Jewish history. The general trend outside Palestine was a waning of autonomous power among Jewish communities, and a gradual absorption of Jewish individuals into gentile society. In Palestine, however, the power of the (national) Jewish community gradually increased and ultimately resulted in the establishment of a Jewish state on some of the territory of British-ruled Palestine. This process is attributed to the fact that the mandatory state was a temporary entity, and British colonial rulers were seen as temporary trustees, whose mission, according to the League of Nations mandate of 1922, was to assist the Jews to establish a "national home for the Jewish people" in Palestine.

Beginning in 1920, the majority of the Jews of Palestine (excluding some anti-Zionist ultraorthodox Jews) elected a national body to represent them – the Elected Assembly (Asefat ha-Nivharim). This assembly, in turn, elected a governing body called the National Council (Ha-Va'ad ha-Leumi). The National Council was responsible for some of the internal activities of the Jewish community in Palestine such as education, health, religious services, social work, and culture, uneasily sharing political power with the body representing the Zionist movement in Palestine, the Jewish Agency. The National Council raised money using voluntary contributions. It also relied on the revenues raised by local Jewish communities.[11]

Local Jewish communities collected fees on products such as kosher meat, and on the provision of religious services. They also imposed a voluntary property tax (*mas ha-ha'arakhah*) on wealthy institutions and individuals. This tax was collected by special collectors who received a fee, as well as a fixed percentage (up to 30 percent) of the money they raised.[12] In 1928 the British government authorized local

[11] Yehoshua Porath and Yaacov Shavit, eds., *Ha-Historyah shel Erets Yisrael*, vol. 9, *Ha-Mandat ve-Habayit ha-Leumi (1917–1947)* (Jerusalem: Keter, 1982), 174–80; Avraham Mandel, ed., *Ha-Misim ve-Ata: Ma'arekhet ha-Misim be-Erets Yisrael be-'Avar uva-Hoveh* (Jerusalem: Misrad ha-Hinukh veha-Tarbut and Misrad ha-Otsar, 1985), chapter 14; Dov Weinrib, "Letikun Shitat ha-Misim ba-Kehilot," *Davar*, May 29, 1938, at 2; Dov Genachowski, *Sipurim Yerushalmiyim* (Jerusalem: Karta, 1989), 32–6, 372–6.

[12] ISA, Pe 656/27, Ha-Kehilot Yerushalayim, Tel Aviv, Heyfah, Tveria u-Tsfat, at 1; "Heyfah: 'Al Pe'ulot Va'ad ha-Kehilah," *Ha-Tzofeh*, December 22, 1938, at 3.

Jewish communities to impose "rates and fees" on their members.[13]
A new local property tax, the congregation tax (*mas ha-kehilah*), was
imposed. It was compulsory, and local Jewish communities could
resort to the British government to enforce compliance.[14]

The use of a local property tax to finance the activities of Jewish
communities fitted well with the general municipal taxation policy
of the British in Palestine. This policy viewed local property taxes
as the main source of municipal revenues. During Ottoman times, a
major source of municipal revenue had been the national property tax
(*werko*), part of which was transferred by the Ottoman government
to municipalities. When the British occupied Palestine, municipalities
were given the power to collect a municipal property tax, the amount
of which was based on a certain percentage (up to 10 percent) of the
annual rental value of properties. The local property tax had a flat
rather than a progressive rate.[15]

In addition to local communal taxation, Jewish communities in
Palestine in the 1920s and 1930s also generated income via fund-
raising campaigns designed to finance security-related expenses. The
militia of the Jewish community in Palestine, the Haganah, was initially financed by local fund-raising bodies (*sherutey gviyah* – collection services), which existed in the major Jewish towns of Palestine.[16]
Because the money was raised and used locally, the needs of the specific local community were often given precedence over those of the
entire Jewish community in Palestine. However, the Arab Revolt
of 1936–39 created a pressing need for more money, especially for
the defense of rural Jewish settlements, whose fund-raising capabilities were smaller than those of the Jewish urban centers. At a meeting of the national command of the Haganah in December 1937,
David Ben-Gurion, the chairman of the executive committee of one
of the two main political bodies of the Zionist Jews of Palestine,

[13] Regulations for the Organization of the Jewish Community, sec. 13(3), *PG*, January
1, 1928.
[14] Anat Kidron, *Beyn Le'om le-Makom: Ha-Kehilah ha-'Ivrit be-Heyfah ha-Mandatorit*
(Jerusalem: Yad Izhak Ben-Zvi, 2012), 29–34.
[15] A. Granovsky, *The Fiscal System of Palestine* (Jerusalem: Palestine and Near East
Publications, 1935), 252–3; Avraham Mandel, ed., *Hitpat'hut ha-Misim be-Erets
Yisrael: Skirah Historit* (Jerusalem: Muze'on le-Misim, 1968), 289–91.
[16] See HA, Oral History Project, M. Landau, Kofer ha-Yishuv, at 1.

the Jewish Agency, called for a "mass national tax" that would replace local Haganah fund-raising efforts. However, the national tax system envisioned by Ben-Gurion was created only in July 1938, when the community tax was imposed by the other major political body representing the Jews of Palestine, the National Council.[17]

Security-related voluntary taxation was not a unique phenomenon. Indeed, it was quite common in other communities faced by a sudden security threat. For example, at the beginning of the Second World War, British citizens in Argentina initiated a self-imposed income tax to contribute to the British war effort. British civil servants in colonial territories, such as Nigeria, also voluntarily contributed part of their salaries to the British war effort. As the war progressed, calls for similar contributions by British residents of Palestine were also made.[18] Around the same time, in the United States the war effort was partly financed by "voluntary" bond sales in which quotas and informal sanction methods were sometimes used. Similar practices appeared in the Soviet Union. Another example of security-related "voluntary" communal contributions can be found in the fund-raising efforts of the Front de Libération Nationale (FLN) among Algerian immigrants in France in the 1950s and 1960s.[19]

The Arabs in Palestine were also engaged in fund-raising efforts during the Arab Revolt of 1936–39. During this period, fund-raising campaigns were organized, using house-to-house collection of money and jewelry, lump sum contributions, and levies on the salaries of government officials, with rates ranging from 10 percent to 50 percent.[20]

[17] Berger, *Kofer ha-Yishuv*, 11–12; Harussi, *Sefer ha-Magbit*, 21–9; Slutsky, *Me-Haganah le-Ma'avak*, 1003–4; Landau, "Ha-Yishuv," 181, 183.

[18] "Men and Things," *PP*, May 7, 1940, at 3; "Readers' Letters: In Lieu of Income Tax," *PP*, August 1, 1940, at 6.

[19] See Jones, "Bonds, Voluntarism and Taxation"; Lawrence R. Samuel, *Pledging Allegiance: American Identity and the Bond Drive of World War II* (Washington, DC: Smithsonian Institution Press, 1997); Steven A. Bank, Kirk J. Stark, and Joseph J. Thorndike, *War and Taxes* (Washington, DC: Urban Institute Press, 2008), 83–108; Sparrow, *Warfare State*, 121, 129–31; Kristy Ironside, "Rubles for Victory: The Social Dynamics of State Fundraising on the Soviet Home Front," *Kritika: Explorations in Russian and Eurasian History* 15 (2014): 799–828; Alistair Horne, *A Savage War of Peace: Algeria, 1954–1962*, rev. edn (New York: Penguin Books, 1987), 236–7.

[20] Yehoshua Porath, *The Palestinian Arab National Movement 1929–1939: From Riots to Rebellion* (London: Frank Cass, 1977), 170, 173.

Local committees and individuals associated with the Arab Revolt collected monetary gifts and contributions, sometimes based on assessment lists. Rural guerrilla bands often financed their activities by demanding food, arms, and other supplies from rural and urban communities.[21] In addition, entire towns were required by these bands to pay lump sum contributions.[22] Such payments were sometimes voluntary, but there were also "fines" or "taxes" that were often collected using threats and violence. The leadership of the Arab Revolt and some local bands tried to regulate the assessment and collection process to prevent abuses, levying fixed rates from the salaries of government officials and fixed amounts from different kinds of property.[23] However, the line between voluntary or even coerced contributions and outright robbery of the civilian population was sometimes crossed.[24] Ultimately, the willingness of the Arab population to support the Revolt was undermined. The abuses and violence associated with the extraction of money and goods from the civilian population, together with the fragmentation of the Revolt into hundreds of small local peasant bands (each loyal to its own leader rather than to any national leadership) and the internal threats that accompanied this process of fragmentation, were factors that contributed to the demise of the Revolt.[25]

The community tax system established by the Jews of Palestine in 1938 used a variety of taxes. It included an income tax, whose rate was 1 percent on annual incomes of between P£60 and P£90 and between 2 percent and 7 percent on higher incomes (the 7 percent was levied on

[21] See, e.g., Ezra Danin and Ya'acov Shimoni, eds., *Te'udot u-Dmuyot mi-Ginzey ha-Knufiyot ha-'Arviyot bi-Me'ora'ot 1936–1939*, 2nd edn (Jerusalem: Magnes, 1981), 6–7, 25, 31, 125–8; Yuval Arnon-Ohanna, "Hebetim Hevratiyim u-Politiyim bi-Tnu'at ha-Mered ha-'Aravi, 1936–1939," in Danin and Shimoni, *Te'udot*, 29–30, 67–8; Yuval Arnon-Ohanna, *Herev mi-Bayit: Ha-Ma'avak ha-Pnimi ba-Tnu'ah ha-Falastinit 1929–1939* (Tel Aviv: Yariv-Hadar, 1981), 285–7.

[22] Danin and Shimoni, *Te'udot*, 9, 11–12.

[23] See, generally, Yuval Arnon, "Falahim ba-Mered ha-'Arvi be-Erets Yisrael 1936–1939" (master's thesis, Hebrew University, 1971), 72–3; Porath, *The Palestinian Arab National Movement*, 170; Danin and Shimoni, *Te'udot*, 58, 92, 127–8.

[24] See, e.g., Danin and Shimoni, *Te'udot*, 66–7, 70, 95, 96, 97–8, 103, 107, 119–20; Arnon, "Falahim," 83.

[25] Danin and Shimoni, *Te'udot*, 18–20, 22, 125, 138; Arnon-Ohanna, "Hebetim," 29–30; Arnon-Ohanna, *Herev mi-Bayit*, 279–88; Arnon, "Falahim," 61, 63, 70.

incomes above P£1,200).[26] Assessment of the taxpayer's income was undertaken in consultation with representatives of the trade or business to which the taxpayer belonged. The system also included a series of taxes on luxury items (for example cigarettes, flowers, and cinema, concert, and theater tickets), goods and services (butter, margarine, oil, cement, clothing, insurance policies, banking services, public transportation, and so forth), property (on citrus groves and vineyards), and import duties. In addition to these taxes, people were asked to donate luxury items such as wedding rings, watches, diamonds, rare books, and silverware.[27]

It is interesting to note that the British rulers of Palestine were aware of the existence of the Jewish tax system but decided to ignore it, and to make no interventions that would prevent it from functioning. While some British officials saw the existence of the system as an indication that the Jews were creating "a government within a government," others noted: "it seems likely that no effective legal action is possible because no evidence will be ever forthcoming either from members of the Jewish community or against members of the Jewish community."[28] The Executive Council of the Government of Palestine discussed the topic in March 1939. The Attorney General of Palestine advised members of the Council that "the scheme was not illegal if it was not accompanied by intimidation, false pretenses, or fraudulent misrepresentations," and the Council therefore decided

---

[26] How did the voluntary income tax rate compare to that of the governmental income tax? Comparison to the official rate is a bit difficult because the levels of exemptions and deductions for family members were different, and also because the rates of both systems changed over time. However, some comparison is still possible. For example, during the first year in which governmental income tax was levied (1941), the governmental rate ranged from 5% (on income up to P£400) to 30% (the marginal rate on income above P£3,100). The highest marginal rate later rose to 75%. It should be noted that because of personal deductions, single men whose annual income was less than P£277.8 were exempt and those earning between P£277.9 and P£722.2 per year paid 4.5% on income above P£277.8. A married taxpayer with two children earning less than P£444.4 was also exempt. For detailed tables of governmental income tax rates on various types of taxpayers in the 1940s, see Mandel, *Hitpat'hut ha-Misim*, 37–9, 52–3.

[27] Landau, "Ha-Yishuv," 184–5; Berger, *Kofer ha-Yishuv*, 22–30.

[28] TNA: CO 733/413/11, Minutes June 4, 1939; TNA: CO 733/413/11, Note on the Kofer Hayishuv, March 2, 1939, 3.

that "no action should be taken against the organization," unless it
was discovered that it used intimidation or that it misled the public to think that the contribution was levied with government sanction.[29] However, the British refused to recognize the taxes paid to the
Jewish system as deductible charitable contributions. The issue of
deductions of the voluntary Jewish taxes from the income of Jewish
taxpayers thus became a major grievance for many Jewish taxpayers
and commentators, who pointed out that the British government did
not fund healthcare, education, or social services in the Jewish sector
in Palestine, and that in the United Kingdom charitable contributions
were deductible.[30]

The community tax administration was based on local fund-
raising bodies that had existed prior to 1938 in major Jewish towns
in Palestine, but these bodies were now augmented by a national
bureaucracy headed by a presidium of five members appointed by
the National Council, representing some of the major political factions in the Jewish community: the General Federation of Jewish
Labor (Histadrut), the centrist General Zionists Party, and the religious Mizrahi movement. The right-wing Revisionist movement
and ultraorthodox Jews were not represented. The presidium was
responsible for general policy decisions. Several advisory committees
were appointed to assist the presidium, including a central auditing
committee. The daily activities of the community tax administration
were supervised by a national secretariat and local committees.[31]
The collection of custom duties was entrusted to an autonomous

[29] See TNA: CO 814/35, Palestine Sessional Papers: Executive Council Meetings 678–
684, Minutes of the 682 Meeting of the Executive Council, March 9, 1939, sec. 11
(available as part of the Gale Digital Collection "The Middle East Online: Series
1: Arab–Israeli Relations, 1917–1970"). See also CZA S53/152, Hahlatot mi-
Yeshivat Nesi'ut Kofer ha-Yishuv, February 22, 1939 (mentioning a meeting with the
head of the Palestine police to ensure that the British police would not obstruct the
collection of the travel tax imposed by the community tax administration); HA, Oral
History Project, Moshe Svirsky, at 2.

[30] See, e.g., "Reflections," *PP*, March 3, 1947, at 2. It should also be noted that, in the
1940s, British officials did try to discourage fund-raising activities among Jewish
government workers. See "Memshelet Erets Yisrael Mafri'ah Gam le-Magbit ha-
Hitgaysut," *Eshnav* 39 (February 5, 1942): 1 (a copy of this periodical can be found
in the Haganah Historical Archives, Tel Aviv).

[31] Berger, *Kofer ha-Yishuv*, 18–19.

department that included representatives of the Jewish chambers of commerce in Palestine.[32]

The actual assessment and collection process was carried out by thousands of volunteers, many of whom were Haganah members. Money was often collected using pairs of volunteer collectors belonging to the same branch of trade as the payer.[33] In the case of salaried employees, money was automatically withheld from their salary.[34] There was even a new community tax token, worth half a mil (a mil being one thousandth of a Palestine pound). This token, minted by the community tax administration, was widely distributed and used for payments within the Jewish community in Palestine.[35]

The money collected by the community tax administration was used for security-related expenditure such as the fortification of existing Jewish settlements, creating new settlements, roadbuilding between Jewish settlements, the building of a fence in the north of the country to prevent the infiltration of Arab guerrillas, funding Jewish servicemen in the British police and army, procuring armaments for the main Jewish militia, the Haganah, and in support of Jewish victims injured or killed during the Arab Revolt and their families.[36]

When the Second World War broke out in 1939, the community tax administration was separated into two different funds, covering direct and indirect taxes, respectively. The direct tax (ranging from 1 percent to 10 percent of taxpayers' income, also taking into account their family and dependents) was now called "emergency tax" (*mas herum*). This tax was used for paying unemployment benefits and social assistance payments to people suffering from the economic crisis that the war had created. The tax also funded public works such as

[32] Ibid., 46–7.

[33] Ibid., 63; Slutsky, *Me-Haganah le-Ma'avak*, 1005. Some collectors were later paid small salaries. See Shim'on Kalir, "Kofer ha-Yishuv u-Magbit ha-Hitgaysut," in *Dor ha-Haganah be-Herzliyah*, ed. B. Z. Michaeli (Tel Aviv: Irgun Havrey ha-Haganah, 1979), 118–20, 119.

[34] Slutsky, *Me-Haganah le-Ma'avak*, 1007. See also CZA J8/1902, Din ve-Heshbon 'al Pe'ulot Va'adat Kofer ha-Yishuv she'al-Yad Lishkat ha-Mis'har be-Tel Aviv ve-Yafo, at 1–2; CZA J8/875, Mahleket ha-Ta'asiyah to Va'ad Po'aley Beyt Haroshet 'Sussman ve-Shut.', May 13, 1946.

[35] See CZA J8/1892, Mordekhai Yafe, Ha-Asimon Hatsi ha-Mil shel Kofer ha-Yishuv.

[36] Berger, *Kofer ha-Yishuv*, 59–62, 73.

the building of air-raid shelters and the creation of depots for food and
health supplies. Some of the money collected was also used to assist
Jews abroad. For example, in 1941 P£1,000 was given to the Jews of
Baghdad, following the anti-Jewish riots there.[37]

At first the emergency tax system was headed by a national committee composed of a president and two members. Later, a ten-member
national administration was established. The bureaucratic apparatus
of the emergency tax was based on the existing local offices of the
community tax and its officials. The accounts and auditing process
for the money collected and spent by the emergency tax administration was, however, separated from the accounts of the community tax
administration. Unlike the community tax system, which had no court
system, the emergency tax system created honor courts to deal with
tax evaders.[38]

In the summer of 1942, when the Nazi army fighting in the Western
Desert approached Palestine, a third fund called the "mobilization
fund" (*magbit ha-hitgaysut*) was established jointly by the Jewish
Agency and the National Council. It was headed by a presidium con-
sisting of five members: two representatives from the private sector
(one representing merchants and the other industrialists), two representatives from the General Federation of Jewish Labor, and a president (Aron Barth, a banker). A four-member general secretariat was
responsible for the daily activities of the new fund, which relied on
the use of civil society organizations such as trade unions, chambers
of commerce, and merchants' and industrialists' associations. Jews in
Palestine were often heavily dependent on the services provided by
such organizations, which included services such as education, health,
and social insurance. The fund therefore used these organizations as
agents in the assessment and collection process, rather than relying on
direct contact with individuals. Each of these civil society organizations established its own fund-raising committee.

The national administration of the mobilization fund was located
in the same building that housed the community tax bureaucracy,
and used the same officials that worked for the community tax

---

[37] CZA A155/39, Mif'al Mas ha-Herum, October 1940–June 1941, at 2; Berger, *Kofer
ha-Yishuv*, 40, 43, 44.

[38] Berger, *Kofer ha-Yishuv*, 41–3. See also text to nn. 92–96.

system.[39] Initially, the money raised by the new fund was used to pay the families of thirty thousand Jewish soldiers and policemen who had volunteered to serve in the British army (within and outside Palestine), and for social welfare payments to sick and disabled Jewish soldiers. A further important goal was to raise money in preparation for the expected Nazi invasion of Palestine by Rommel's army. From 1943 the money was also used for rescue operations for Jews in Nazi-ruled Europe, and the name of the fund was accordingly changed to the "mobilization and rescue fund" (*magbit ha-hitgaysut veha-hatsalah*). After the end of the war in 1945, the role of the fund expanded yet again. New goals included assistance to demobilized soldiers, housing for new immigrants, support for Jewish refugees in Europe and their immigration to Palestine, and also for the support of prisoners belonging to the Haganah in Palestine. Money was also used to supplement payments to Jewish civil servants working for the British government, and even to fund social work targeting juvenile delinquents in Jewish urban centers in Palestine.[40]

Since there were multiple fund-raising campaigns within the Jewish community of Palestine, institutional turf wars soon arose. For example, in 1939 the leaders of the community tax administration decided to raise money by collecting a contribution linked to the sale of reserved seats in synagogues during the high holidays. The Jewish National Fund, responsible for Zionist land purchase in Palestine, raised money in the same way, and a battle between the two organizations ensued.[41] Some individuals, of course, used this battle as a pretext not to pay either organization.[42]

When the mobilization fund was established in 1942, competition arose with the emergency tax system. Both fund-raising entities relied

---

[39] CZA J1/6270, Kofer ha-Yishuv u-Mas Herum; Harussi, *Sefer ha-Magbit*, 34, 43–9, 56; Landau, "Ha-Yishuv," 186; Berger, *Magbit ha-Hitgayshut*, 21–33; Shavit, "Magbit ha-Hitgaysut," 1–7.

[40] Harussi, *Sefer ha-Magbit*, 53–4, 72, 83–6, 142–3, 160–3; Shavit, "Magbit ha-Hitgaysut," 13, 30, 47, 158–60.

[41] CZA J8/1167, Ha-Va'ad ha-Artsi le-Keren Kayemet le-Yisrael to ha-Mazkirut ha-Artsit shel Kofer ha-Yishuv, July 10, 1939, Ha-Mazkirut ha-Artsit shel Kofer ha-Yishuv to ha-Va'ad ha-Artsi le-Keren Kayemet le-Yisrael, July 14, 1939.

[42] CZA J8/1167, Va'ad Beyt ha-Kneset be-Kiryat Bialik to Hanhalat Kofer ha-Yishuv, Heyfah, November 14, 1940.

on income taxation and both sought (among other things) to assist soldiers' families. At first, the division between the two systems was justified by a difference in collection mechanisms – the emergency tax was based on individual collection, while the mobilization fund was based on the collection of money using the assistance of civil society organizations. However, this distinction proved insufficient to maintain organizational boundaries, and conflict erupted. Ultimately, the mobilization fund won, and the emergency tax was abolished in late 1942.[43]

Another turf war was fought by the mobilization and rescue fund to prevent competition from other funds assisting Jews in Nazi-ruled Europe. Indeed, one of the reasons that the name of the fund was changed from the "mobilization fund" to the "mobilization and rescue fund" was to monopolize the fund-raising efforts devoted to the rescue of Jews from the Nazis, a cause that was more popular among ordinary Jews in Palestine than the other goals of the fund.[44]

The money paid to the mobilization and rescue fund was based on a fixed rate. Salaried workers paid 4.5 percent of their salary (with the first P£60 being exempt).[45] Employers were required to match this sum. The rate paid by business owners was adjusted according to the specific type of business in question (merchants, importers, artisans, and so forth), based on decisions taken by special assessment committees. Wealthy persons who did not belong to any defined economic organization were assessed by a "Wealthy Persons Committee."[46]

How much money was raised? One estimate put the total amount raised during the decade between 1938 and 1948 at more than P£8 million. Another estimate put the sum at P£9 million.[47] For the sake of comparison, the total annual revenue of the Government of Palestine (excluding grants from the British government) in the fiscal year 1938/ 39, the year in which the community tax was imposed, was approximately P£4 million.[48]

---

[43] Harussi, *Sefer ha-Magbit*, 48; Shavit, "Magbit ha-Hitgaysut," 47–67; Berger, *Kofer ha-Yishuv*, 44–5.

[44] Shavit, "Magbit ha-Hitgaysut," 170–80, 221.

[45] Later the first P£84 and an additional P£36 per dependent family member were exempted from the tax. See Harussi, *Sefer ha-Magbit*, 49–50.

[46] Ibid., 159.

[47] Ibid., 184–5, 195, 204; Landau, "Ha-Yishuv," 189, 191.

[48] Great Britain, *Report ... on the Administration of Palestine and Trans-Jordan for the Year 1938* (London: HMSO, 1939), sec. 59. See also Gross and Metzer, "Public

It is unclear what the administrative costs of the system were. Early estimates made reference to 2–3 percent of the sums raised.[49] A later assessment mentioned "less than 10 percent."[50] Generally speaking, it seems that the system, or parts of it, was rather inefficient administratively. For example, in late 1940 and early 1941 the emergency tax raised about P£47,000, but its administrative costs for the same period amounted to P£15,000, or about 30 percent of the total tax revenue.[51]

As we saw, the system was viewed by the British government of Palestine as a voluntary one, but in fact it was a hybrid, voluntary–compulsory, system. David Ben-Gurion, the first prime minister of Israel, called the community tax a "tool of free compulsory voluntarism," while Eliezer Kaplan, the first Israeli minister of finance, called the mobilization and rescue fund a "compulsory voluntary tax" (*mas hovah voluntari*).[52] Many other contemporary observers described money collection by the community tax administration and by the mobilization and rescue fund as taxes, rather than voluntary contributions.[53] For example, in a memo dealing with possible "means of pressure" on evaders of the community tax in 1939, Hans Kaufman, a German-Jewish lawyer, described the tax "not as a charitable contribution but a defense tax, a governmental tax of our 'state in the making'."[54] A pamphlet published during the same period clarified that the community tax was not "a donation or charity, but a compulsory tax levied on every person." A related propaganda slogan said: "We don't ask for your donation, [we ask you to] fulfill your duty!"[55] Mobilization and rescue fund officials described their tax in 1947 as "a general community-wide tax (based on an agreed rate) that closely

Finance in the Jewish Community," 101. This comparison, of course, ignores the impact of inflation during the 1940s.

[49] CZA J8/790, Magbit ha-Hitgaysut Koret le-'Askanim Mitnadvim; "Magbit ha-Hitgaysut 'Alta 'al 100,000 Lira," *Davar*, October 16, 1942, at 1.

[50] Landau, "Ha-Yishuv," 189. This sum included compensation paid to the employees of the system who were dismissed when their work was terminated in the summer of 1948.

[51] CZA A155/39, Mifa'al Mas ha-Herum, October 1940–June 1941, at 3.

[52] Harussi, *Sefer ha-Magbit*, 194; Moshe Naor, *Be-Hazit ha-'Oref: Tel Aviv ve-Hitgaysut ha-Yishuv be-Milhemet ha-'Atsma'ut* (Jerusalem: Yad Izhak Ben-Zvi, 2009), 128.

[53] Harussi, *Sefer ha-Magbit*, 49–50.

[54] CZA J8/1249, Kaufman, Hatsa'ot le-Tipul be-Mishtamtim, June 22, 1939.

[55] CZA KH4/12739, Mi-Pe'ulot Kofer ha-Yishuv mi-Yom 1 be-Ogust 1938 'ad 31 be-Yanu'ar 1939, at 10.

resembles a government income tax."[56] Harussi described the community tax in similar terms: "outwardly it was seen as a donation, but inwardly these were really taxes, taxes that one *must* pay."[57] Michael Landau, the general secretary of the community tax administration, noted that, even at its inception, the idea was "not to ask for donations but to levy taxes."[58]

The term "compulsory–voluntary tax" actually reflected a bigger paradox: that of the state generally that is often conceived both as an entity based on free choice (social contract) yet simultaneously as a body from which one cannot freely exit. The founders of Israel were well aware of the complex relationship between compulsion and voluntariness. For example, David Ben-Gurion, in discussing the end of the activities of the mobilization and rescue fund, observed:

> this end reveals the great, historical transformation of our situation: We have become a sovereign nation ... [but] this does not mean that from now on we will do everything by the power of compulsion. On the contrary, in the state too we will need volunteers, no less than we did before the state, and without the good will, the devotion, the trust and the pioneering response of the people, we will not go far using the power of governmental compulsion. Even the payment of taxes, which can be raised by the force of policemen and judges, requires the will of the people, and not only in the tax sphere, but in every aspect of state life. We will succeed only if law and the forces of the government will rely on the willingness of the people, and discipline will not be a forced, coerced [discipline], but one that stems from the trust, understanding and devotion of the masses.[59]

The compulsory aspects of the tax naturally engendered opposition. Not all the members of the Jewish community in Palestine were willing to contribute to the voluntary tax system, given the fact that the Jewish community was not homogenous but split along ideological lines. The system had two major opponents: right-wing Revisionist Zionists and ultraorthodox Jews. An organization called Opponents of the Community Tax, which was a front for the Revisionists, was

---

[56] Harussi, *Sefer ha-Magbit*, 158.
[57] Harussi, "Bi-Yemey Kofer ha-Yishuv," 13, 14 (original emphasis).
[58] Landau, "Ha-Yishuv," 184.
[59] Quoted in Naor, *Be-Hazit*, 128–9.

established in 1940. The organization asked manufacturers not to pay the community tax, and sometimes asked them to set aside 25 percent of the amount of tax they collected and give it to the Revisionists (effectively paying only 75 percent of their liability to the community tax administration, rather than the full amount).[60]

In 1942 the Revisionists established their own, competing, fund-raising system – the "vanguard of Israel tax" (*mas hazit yisrael*).[61] It, too, relied on propaganda and on volunteers visiting potential contributors to collect contributions. Its main activities were carried out in Tel Aviv, where it employed about twenty salaried workers. There were two other "districts" located in the two other major Jewish population centers in Palestine, namely Jerusalem and Haifa.[62]

There were negotiations to incorporate the Revisionist system in the larger tax system, which resulted in an agreement in August 1942 to share revenues and employ Revisionists in the mobilization and rescue fund administration. However, soon after signing the agreement, tensions appeared, since the Revisionists kept their own taxes, and the two tax systems began to compete for the same revenues. Attempts were again made to resolve the conflicts between these systems – for example, by requiring the "vanguard of Israel" tax system to scale down its fund-raising campaign. Another agreement was reached in October 1943, but by the beginning of 1944 the conflict had reignited and the compromise agreement was abolished.[63] In addition to setting up its own tax system, the Revisionist militia, the Irgun, later financed its activities using robbery.[64]

The small ultraorthodox community in Palestine also opposed the taxes imposed by the secular Zionist majority. In 1938, when

---

[60] CZA J8/1251, letter by Irgun Mitnagdey Kofer ha-Yishuv, April 8, 1940; CZA J1/6262, Ha-Mazkirut ha-Artsit shel Kofer ha-Yishuv to Berlin, April 10, 1940; CZA J1/7788/2, Mishtamtim u-Makhshilim, April 10, 1940. The tax these manufacturers collected was probably a sales tax collected from consumers.

[61] Mandel, *Ha-Misim ve-Ata*, chapter 14. See also Berger, *Kofer ha-Yishuv*, 21–2.

[62] A description of the system can be found in the JIA, File G 6–15/3, Ha-Misrad ha-Mehozi bi-Yerushalayim, Mas Hazit Yisrael – Dokh li-Shnat 5702/3 [1942/3] ve-Hozer.

[63] Shavit, "Magbit ha-Hitgaysut," 68–138.

[64] See, e.g., "Brazen Robbery in Tel Aviv: Large Band Steals Utility Textiles," *PP*, October 8, 1944, at 3.

tax collectors visited the heart of the ultraorthodox community in Jerusalem, the neighborhood of Me'ah She'arim, a scuffle broke out with a group of ultraorthodox youths opposed to the tax. The main ultraorthodox anti-Zionist opposition group, Neturei Karta, crystallized from this clash.[65]

While Revisionist and ultraorthodox Jews were ideologically opposed to the community tax, nonideological noncompliance was also widespread. In Jerusalem, for example, collectors reported low compliance rates among Sephardi Jews.[66] Indeed, the records of the community tax bureaucracy sometimes read like a litany of complaints about noncompliance, negligence, and indifference involving every kind of taxpayer: butter and margarine producers, flour mill owners, wine and oil manufacturers and sellers, cigarette smokers, waiters and café-goers, transportation providers, hotel owners, and so forth.[67]

As the 1948 War approached, fund-raising activities in the Jewish community increased.[68] In November 1947 it was decided to raise

[65] Menachem Friedman, "*Haredim* and Palestinians in Jerusalem," in *Jerusalem: A City and its Future*, eds. Marshall J. Berger and Ora Ahimeir (Syracuse, NY: Syracuse University Press, 2002), 235–55, 235–7. See also Kimmy Caplan, "Hitpat'hutam shel Ma'agaley Hibadlut be-Kerev Haredim Kana'im: 'Amram Blau ke-Mikre Mivhan," *Zion* 76 (2011): 179–218, 185. Opposition to the tax continued later. For example, in 1940 a newspaper belonging to the ultraorthodox community complained about the community tax, asking rhetorically what the collectors' source of authority for taxing Jews was, and whether the [British] government was aware of the fact that such taxes were imposed, taxes that suggested that "there is a government within a government" in Palestine. CZA J1/6262, "Misim?" *Kol Yisrael: Organ ha-Yahadut ha-Haredit ba-Arets*, February 13, 1940.

[66] Gershon Svat, "Pinkas Yerushalmi," *Haaretz*, March 23, 1939, at 3.

[67] CZA J1/7788/1, Ha-Mazkirut ha-Artsit shel Kofer ha-Yishuv to Nesi'ut Kofer ha-Yishuv, September 11, 1940; CZA J1/7788/1, Ha-Mazkirut ha-Artsit shel Kofer ha-Yishuv to Hanhalat ha-Va'ad ha-Leumi, November 4, 1940; CZA J1/7788/2, M. Landau, Hatsa'ah 'al Hagbarat Hakhnasot Kofer ha-Yishuv; CZA J1/7788/2, Yediot ha-Mazkirut ha-Artsit shel Kofer ha-Yishuv, January 25, 1940; CZA J1/7788/2, Va'ad ha-Kehilah be-Heyfah to Dubek, April 30, 1940; CZA J1/7788/2, Ha-Merkaz lema'an Totseret ha-Arets to Mazkirut Kofer ha-Yishuv, May 27, 1940; CZA J1/7788/2, Mishtamtim u-Makhshilim, April 10, 1940; CZA J1/7788/2, Ha-Mazkirut ha-Artsit shel Kofer ha-Yishuv to Havrey Nesi'ut Kofer ha-Yisuv, April 12, 1940.

[68] Harussi, *Sefer ha-Magbit*, 173; Arye Halfin, ed., *Vatikey Mas Hakhnasah Mesaprim* (Jerusalem: Government Printer, 1971), 17, 21.

P£500,000 in a one-time fund-raising campaign called "For the security of the people" (*le-vit'hon ha-'am*). Wealthy Jews, whose rate of tax was determined by professional and economic organizations in the private sector, were taxed individually. Poorer Jews were asked to contribute by volunteers, most of whom were young people who collected contributions (in amounts ranging from P£2 to P£6) by going door-to-door. By the first two weeks of December 1947 about P£600,000 had been raised. Once this collection drive was over, a new campaign, entitled "a tax for our defense" (*mas le-haganatenu*), designed to raise P£2 million, was initiated.[69] This time, the campaign failed to raise the required amount, so in May 1948 a national loan program was initiated. By July of that year the new government had sold bonds to the value of P£5 million. However, by August 1948 the financial crisis faced by the Israeli government forced it to increase its reliance on coercive taxation, abolish the voluntary tax system, impose a war tax, and raise the maximum income tax rate to 75 percent. This decision was ratified by the Provisional State Council (Israel's first parliament) on September 16, 1948. The voluntary tax system of the Jewish community in Palestine was formally disbanded at a conference held in Tel Aviv on October 20, 1948. At this conference, Ben-Gurion, the Israeli Prime Minister, said the abolition of the voluntary tax system signified:

> a historical revolution, our becoming a nation governing itself and supplying its own needs in a state-like way – taxes and governmental loans. The mobilization and rescue fund ended when we rose to a higher level in our national existence, the level of Israeli independence and the ingathering of exiles. The state is now the main tool for fulfilling the task ... and it has tools that the Jewish community in Palestine did not have ... what [we can do with] a government budget, no fund [or tax], neither the community tax nor the mobilization and rescue fund, [would have enabled us to] do, but one important asset was created in the defense and illegal immigration [campaigns] by the community tax and the mobilization and rescue fund that we must preserve at all cost – the spirit of pioneering voluntarism.[70]

[69] The Revisionists established a parallel funding campaign, called "the iron fund" (*keren ha-barzel*). See Naor, *Be-Hazit*, 121.

[70] ISA, Pratey-kol Yeshivat ha-Memshalah ha-Zmanit, August 25, 1948, at 36; Harussi, *Sefer ha-Magbit*, 168–80, 195–6; CZA J8/1892, Michael Landau, Keytsad Giyasnu Ksafim Lema'an Milhemet ha-Shihrur; Naor, *Be-Hazit*, 117–32.

After Israeli independence in 1948, the new state employed mass voluntary campaigns several times in an attempt to raise money, in addition to the money generated by the governmental tax system. For example, in late 1955 and early 1956 money was raised in this way to buy weapons for the Israeli army through a "defense fund" (*keren ha-magen*).[71] Following the Six Day War in 1967, the government embarked on a campaign to finance the costs of that war and its aftermath using a series of voluntary security loans, again selling bonds to the public in addition to raising money using taxation.[72] In 1971 a voluntary payment campaign, "the immigration tax" (*kofer ʿaliyah*), was established jointly by the Ministry of Finance and the Manufacturers Association of Israel. It solicited donations of 5 percent of the income of companies and wealthy individuals.[73]

The Role of Law in the Voluntary Tax System

Soon after the community tax was imposed in 1938, pressure was put on the officials of the community tax system to create formal, law-like norms and courts to deal with assessment and collection disputes. The establishment of such courts was called for mainly by the Kartell Jüdischer Verbindungen (KJV), an organization of German-Zionist academics living in Palestine.[74]

It is not surprising that German-born Jews were interested in formalizing the tax assessment and collection process, because these Jews were famous for their positive attitude to law. Many of the Jews

---

[71] Mordekhai   Berger,   *Neshek   le-Yisrael: Keren   ha-Magen,   ha-Homah* (Jerusalem: Muzeʾon le-Misim, 1968); Moshe Naor, "The Israeli Volunteering Movement Preceding the 1956 War," *Israeli Affairs* 16 (2010): 434–54.

[72] See, e.g., "Igrot Milve Bitahon be-150 Milyon Lirot Yimakhru la-Tsibur he-Rahav le-Mimun ha-Maʾamats ha-Milhamti," *Davar*, June 8, 1967, at 6; David Lipkin, "Ha-Memshalah ʿOmedet Legayes 300 Milyon meha-Tsibur be-Milve Bitahon me-Ratson," *Davar*, April 24, 1968, at 2; M. D. "Milve Bitahon," *Davar*, April 1, 1969, at 2.

[73] "Hevrot u-Vaʿaley Emtsaim Yutremu le-Kofer ʿAliyah," *Davar*, December 30, 1971, at 3. See also Lital Levin, "Ha-Yom Lifney 39 Shanah: Ha-Memshalah Megayeset Kesef meha-Tsibur le-Mifʿal ha-ʿAliyah," *Haaretz*, December 28, 2010, part b, at 4.

[74] CZA J8/1249, Ha-Mazkirut ha-Artsit to Nesiʾut KYP, June 4, 1939. On the KJV (in Hebrew KYP – *Kvutsat Yedidim Peʿilim*), see generally Walter Gross, "The Zionist Students' Movement," *Leo Baeck Institute Yearbook* 4 (1959): 143–64, 149, 163.

of Palestine, both before and after the establishment of the State of Israel, did not have a deep commitment to universal formal norms and institutions, or to the notion of the rule of law (this cultural attitude may have had its roots in the experience of Jewish communities in the Diaspora with the discriminatory law of gentile states, in the encounter of these Jews with the late-nineteenth-century Ottoman bureaucracy and legal system in which corruption was rife, or in the socialist traditions rejecting the bourgeois notion of the rule of law that many of the new Zionist immigrants to Palestine brought with them).[75] However, German-born Jews did not share this general disdain for the notion of the rule of law. These Jews, often derogatorily called *yekkes* by their fellow Jews – a reference, perhaps, to the business jacket (*jacke*) that was their typical dress – were often portrayed as law-obeying fools who, among other things, never evaded taxation.[76] For example, in a speech given in 1957, after the establishment of the State of Israel, Attorney General Haim Cohn, a German-born Jew, complained about the low tax morale of Israeli taxpayers: "Anyone who manages to contravene provisions of the Income Tax Ordinance and pay a little less than he has to pay," said Cohn, "is not considered to have committed a crime but [to have done] a good deed, and public opinion views him positively; [indeed], far more positively than public opinion views those who pay their income tax to the last penny. These are considered '*yekkes*'."[77]

---

[75] There is an argument about the degree of legalism in the Jewish population of pre-1948 Palestine and post-1948 Israel. For the two competing views, see Ehud Sprinzak, *Ish ha-Yashar be-'Yenav: Illegalizm ba-Hevra ha-Yisre'elit* (Tel Aviv: Sifriyat Po'alim, 1986), 27–53; Nir Kedar, "Ha-Mishpat u-Mekomo ha-Merkazi ba-Historyah ha-Yisre'elit: 'Al ha-Historiografyah shel ha-Mishpat ha-Yisre'eli u-Trumatah le-Heker Yisrael," *Katedrah* 150 (2013): 155–80, 166–80. See also Alfred Witkon, "Ha-Mishpat be-Erets Mitpatahat," in *Sefer Yovel le-Pinhas Rosen*, ed. Haim Cohn (Jerusalem: Mif'al ha-Shikhpul, 1962), 66–85, 70–4 (discussing illegalism in mandatory Palestine and Israel).

[76] See generally, Yoav Gelber, *Moledet Hadashah* (Jerusalem: Leo Baeck Institute, 1990), 233. See also Fania Oz-Salzberger and Eli Salzberger, "The Secret German Sources of the Israeli Supreme Court," *Israel Studies* 3 (1998): 159–92; Rakefet Sela-Sheffy, "Ha-'Yekim' bi-Sdeh ha-Mishpat u-Dfusim shel Tarbut Burganit bi-Tkufat ha-Mandat," *'Iyunim bi-Tkumat Yisrael* 13 (2003): 295–322.

[77] Haim Cohn, "[Symposium]: Shiput ve-Hamarat Mishpat be-Kofer Kesef," *Sherut* 5 (1957): 3, 5.

German Jews tried several times to move the voluntary tax system in a more legal direction. Their efforts show both the constant desire on the part of some Jews in Palestine to use lawlike norms and institutions in the assessment and collection processes of the voluntary taxes of the 1940s, as well as the strong resistance to this impulse on the part of many officials of the voluntary tax administration.

In August 1938 the KJV informed the community tax administration they had established an honor court that would expel any member of the organization who did not pay the tax.[78] A month later, in September 1938, the presidium of the KJV submitted a memo in which it suggested a series of means to pressurize evaders, such as establishing a "court composed of respectable nonpartisan persons," publishing blacklists of evaders, "humiliating" evaders in synagogues by preventing them from participating in prayers, and, in extremely grave cases, shaming evaders by using groups of people who would "stand in front of the [evader's] store informing customers that the owner was not paying his taxes."[79]

The suggestions made in the September 1938 KJV memo were not implemented, so in March 1939 the presidium of the KJV made another attempt. The KJV sent another memo in which it proudly claimed to be the only "organization in the Jewish community that not only asked its members to pay the community tax, but also monitored this duty by [establishing] a court of honor," complaining that the community tax administration did not "take measures to motivate other organizations to take similar steps." Specifically, it complained about the fact that there were no uniform tax rates and that collectors accepted whatever amount the payers were willing to contribute. There was a kind of courtlike body, called the "oversight committee" (*va'adat bikoret*) but its members were not "well-known people" trusted by the public, and no pressure was put on evaders by this body to pay their dues, for example by publicizing their names. New taxes were created frequently, and without consulting

[78] CZA A155/11a, Mitokh Hilufe Mikhtavim Beyn Nesi'ut ha-KYP ve-Kofer ha-Yishuv (Mas Herum).

[79] CZA J8/1251, Tazkir be-'Inyeney Kofer ha-Yishuv Mehubar 'al-Yedey Nesi'ut KYP, September 1938, at 3–4.

with economic experts – and generally the administration of tax was "dilettantish."[80]

In late May 1939, in response to these critiques, it was decided to establish a committee to "formulate plans for pressure on evaders," and to form appeal courts manned "by distinguished people."[81] This new committee convened in the middle of June. It included Hans Kaufman, a lawyer and representative of the KJV. Kaufman requested that "a general legal framework for the compulsory regime of the community tax" be established. Evaders would be given the opportunity to appeal their assessment before a special committee and, if not satisfied, go to a court manned by "people who [were] trusted by the public." The suggestion of creating a court system was greeted with some skepticism by members of the committee, but Kaufman was instructed to draft a detailed plan within a week.[82]

Kaufman submitted a memo in which he discussed four "means of pressure" – moral, social, organizational, and economic – taking care to note that these means were to be used only after the question of tax liability had been decided by a court, because using these means without such a decision could be considered "internal terror."[83] Kaufman's proposal encountered opposition from the representatives of the local branches of the community tax administration, who argued that if courts or appeal committees were to be established, they should only be local, because only the local branches were familiar with local affairs, and a centralized body giving instructions to the different branches

---

[80] CZA J8/1251, Tazkir be-'Inyeney Kofer ha-Yishuv Mugash 'al-Yedey Nesi'ut ha-KYP, March 1939. Somewhat similar complaints could be found in a letter written by accountant Eliezer Bawly and published in the professional journal of the Jewish Accountants' Association in Palestine. See E. Bawly, "Mihtavim la-Ma'arekhet," *Ro'eh ha-Heshbon ha-Musmakh* (December 1939): 15. It is unclear what the scope of jusridiction of this "oversight committee" was. It should also be noted that one of the sources describing the community tax system also mentioned the existence of "appeal committees." See Berger, *Kofer ha-Yishuv*, 18–19.

[81] CZA J8/1249, Ha-Mazkirut ha-Artsit to ha-Ve'adim ha-Mekomiyim, June 8, 1939; CZA J8/1249, Ve'adat ha-Bitahon Kofer ha-Yishuv bi-Yerushlayim to ha-Mazkirut ha-Artsit, June 18, 1939.

[82] CZA J8/1249, Pratey-kol mi-Yeshivat ha-Mazkirut ha-Artsit 'im Shlihey ha-Ve'adim ha-Mekomiyim bi-Dvar She'elat ha-Mishtamtim, June 15, 1939.

[83] CZA J8/1249, Kaufman, Hatsa'ot le-Tipul be-Mishtamtim, June 22, 1939.

would create "undesirable tension." The decision was therefore taken to establish local appeal committees that would be free to use Kaufman's suggested methods of pressure to encourage evaders to pay (except publicity, the legality of which Kaufman was unsure).[84]

When the national secretariat of the community tax administration instructed the local branches to establish courts that would deal with evaders, the response of the local branches was that they needed instructions on the number of judges and the political criteria that would guide the appointment of these judges, as well as the exact function of the courts (whether they would decide questions of assessment, for instance, or whether they would discuss cases dealing with compliance).[85]

In addition, it was decided that a central court of appeal would be created and that Kaufman should be appointed as the prosecutor of the system.[86] By August 1939 he still had not been appointed, despite the fact that he had prepared a formal set of regulations governing the procedure of the proposed courts.[87] These regulations were quite elaborate. They envisioned a system of courts (local courts and a court of appeal), each with its own prosecutor. There were evidentiary provisions dealing with oaths and expert witnesses, time limits for appeals, and other procedural details.[88]

KJV members were not only keen to have appeals regulated, they also sought to regulate the assessment process. In August 1939 a meeting was held between representatives of the KJV and local and national representatives of the community tax administration. At the meeting, KJV members asked that the matter be forwarded to economists who would "deal with it in a thorough and principled way, establishing a

[84] CZA J8/1249, Pratey-kol Yeshivat ha-Mazkirut ha-Artsit 'im Shlihey ha-Ve'adim ha-Mekomiyim bi-Dvar She'elat ha-Mishtamtim, June 22, 1939.

[85] CZA J1/1309, Hahalatot mi-Yeshivat Nesi'ut Kofer ha-Yishuv, July 11, 1939; CZA J8/1249, Ha-Mazkirut ha-Artsit to ha-Ve'adim ha-Mekomiyim, July 17, 1939; CZA J8/1249, Ve'adat ha-Bitahon Heyfah, Kofer ha-Yishuv to ha-Mazkirut ha-Artsit le-Kofer ha-Yishuv, July 24, 1939.

[86] CZA J8/1249, Pratey-kol Yeshivat ha-Mazkirut ha-Artsit 'im Shlihey ha-Ve'adim ha-Mekomiyim bi-Dvar She'elat ha-Mishtamtim, June 22, 1939.

[87] CZA J8/1249, Kaufman to Kofer ha-Yishuv, August 17, 1939.

[88] CZA J8/1249, Hatsa'ah Rishonah le-Takanon le-Batey ha-Din she-Leyad Kofer ha-Yishuv.

system of levying and collecting the tax ... It is imperative to abolish the randomness of levying taxation." The response of the secretary of community tax administration was that "expertise is not necessary right now, because we have not reached a stage in which taxation is so heavy that one cannot pay it. We are still very far from the taxes paid in Europe."[89]

This response did not satisfy the members of the KJV, who, following the meeting, wrote an angry letter to the presidium of community tax administration, lamenting the unsystematic nature of the debate and of the taxes. This letter also protested the fact that Kaufman, the KJV member, was supposed to be appointed as prosecutor, but no files had been sent to him, and no courts had been established despite the fact that Kaufman had sent a draft of the court regulations "about three weeks ago."[90]

While the KJV was pressing the community tax bureaucracy to establish the courts, the local branches expressed their opposition. One letter sent from the Jerusalem branch noted that in Jerusalem there was widespread disobedience and many people who were asked to appear before community tax officials failed to do so. How could a court judge evaders when they were not even present, the letter asked. Another letter sent from Jerusalem (where tax morale was apparently quite low) stated its opposition to the establishment of the courts, based on the argument that the actual rate of payment was much lower than the formal rate, given the willingness of the collection officials to compromise. This letter warned that no one would be willing to sit as a judge in a court dealing with evaders to defend excessive demands for payments that no one actually paid.[91]

After August 1939 attempts to establish courts to deal with evaders of the community tax stopped, perhaps because of the outbreak of the

---

[89] CZA J8/1249, Pratey-kol mi-Yeshivat ha-Ve'adah ha-Metsumtsemet le-'Ibud Hatsa'ot be-Kesher 'im ha-Trumah ha-Yeshirah, August 16, 1939.

[90] CZA J8/1249, Nesi'ut ha-KYP le-Nesi'ut Kofer ha-Yishuv, August 28, 1939.

[91] CZA J8/1249, Ha-Mazkirut ha-Artsit to ha-Ve'adim ha-Mekomiyim, August 23, 1939; CZA J8/1249, Kofer ha-Yishuv: Ha-Ve'adah ha-Mekomit Petah Tikvah to ha-Mazkirut ha-Artsit shel Kofer ha-Yishuv, August 25, 1939; CZA J8/1249, Kofer ha-Yishuv: Ha-Ve'adah ha-Mekomit Yerushalayim to ha-Mazkirut ha-Artsit shel Kofer ha-Yishuv, August 28, 1939; CZA J8/1249, Walstein to ha-Mazkirut ha-Artsit shel Kofer ha-Yishuv, August 13, 1939.

Second World War. However, a more formal system of dealing with evaders did appear with the creation of the emergency tax. A "Supreme Court of Honor" for the emergency tax system was already functioning by early 1940.[92] In December 1940 it was announced that the emergency tax system had a "secret weapon" against evaders – the establishment of honor courts that would operate according to formal procedures and would use a whole range of sanctions. These sanctions included: the publication of the decisions of the honor courts; an appeal to economic, professional, religious, political, social, and cultural organizations to which the evader belonged; an appeal to the evader's clients and friends, urging them to put pressure on the evader to comply with the decision of the courts (and if he refused, to boycott him); and finally the denial of employment opportunities and of assistance by the political organizations of the Jewish community in Palestine. The plan was also to use positive means, such as the publication of the names of organizations complying with the tax, as well as the creation of a monthly list of payers open to inspection by the public.[93] Regulations of the procedures of the honor courts were issued in January 1941.[94] The appeals committee (which dealt with appeals against assessments) and the honor court (which dealt with evaders) met and decided cases. A report from late 1941 stated that a legal department had been established in the emergency tax central office, and appeals committees and honor courts had been created in the local branches in Tel Aviv, Haifa, and Jerusalem.[95] Kaufman was

[92] ISA GL 7413/10, Mas ha-Herum shel ha-Yishuv: Ha-Va'ad ha-Mekomi bi-Yerushalayim to Beyt ha-Din ha-'Elyon shel Kavod le-Mas ha-Herum, March 14, 1940.

[93] CZA J1/6275, "Ha-Neshek ha-Sodi shel Mas Herum: Mi-Tvi'a le-Beyt Din Kavod ve'ad Herem Tsiburi," *Ha-Boker*, January 2, 1941. See also ISA P 892/8.

[94] CZA A155/11a, Takanon le-Vet ha-Din shel Kavod.

[95] CZA A155/39, Mifa'al Mas ha-Herum, October 1940–June 1941. On the courts established by the emergency tax system, see also Landau, "Ha-Yishuv," 186; CZA J8/1423, Va'adat ha-Mishmaat veha-Sanktsyot. The actual results were less than satisfactory. According to one report, in Tel Aviv the appeals committee and the honor court held forty-eight meetings during the relevant period (October 1940–June 1941) and heard ninety-two cases, resulting in the collection of P£531. In Haifa there were ten meetings, resulting in the collection of P£247. The Jerusalem appeals committee heard thirty-one people and the honor courts six people, leading to the collection of "more than 300 pounds."

now finally appointed prosecutor for the emergency tax honor court.[96] This system, however, was short-lived because of the takeover of the emergency tax system in 1942 by the mobilization and rescue fund, mentioned earlier.

The mobilization and rescue fund, like the community tax, did not have a formal system of courts. During the spring and summer of 1944, there was an attempt to create a court system to deal with evaders. A disciplinary committee (va'adah le-hatalat ha-mishma'at ha-yishuvit) sought to establish honor courts, whose procedure would follow that of the rabbinical courts, to deal with evaders. Decisions would be publicized in daily newspapers to increase their impact. A draft set of regulations was created, this time by a German-Jewish official, Hans Moller, who was active in the local branch of the fund in Haifa.[97]

However, this attempt to move the mobilization and rescue fund in a legal direction failed as a result of both legal and organizational opposition. The legal opposition came from a lawyer, Franz Steif, who was asked to comment on the proposals for disciplining evaders. In his comments, Steif mentioned that some of the measures envisioned by the proposals could be considered libel and extortion according to the criminal law of Palestine.[98] Fears that such disciplinary measures would be illegal, and would thus lead the British authorities to intervene in the work of the mobilization and rescue fund, prevented their adoption.[99]

Opposition to the use of sanctions also came from civil society organizations. The opposition focused on the demand that evaders be dismissed from the economic organizations to which they belonged. For example,

---

[96] CZA A155/11, Hans Kaufman to Agudat 'Orkhey ha-Din ha-Yehudiyim, May 13, 1942 (discussing decisions given by the emergency tax honor court against Jewish lawyers who did not pay the tax).

[97] CZA J8/1869, Ha-Ve'adah le-Hatalat ha-Mishma'at ha-Yishuvit to Hanhalat ha-Va'ad ha-Leumi le-Knesset Yisrael, August 3, 1944; CZA J8/1869, 'Ezra Ichilov to Hans Moller, July 13, 1944; CZA J8/1423, Protokol shel Yeshivat Ve'adat ha-Mishma'at, July 3, 1944; CZA J8/1423, Moller to Landau, July 14, 1944; CZA J8/1423, Pratey-kol mi-Yeshivat ha-Va'adah le-Hatalat Mishma'at Yishuvit she-Hitkaymah be-Misradey Mahleket ha-Import, November 15, 1944. See also Berger, Magbit ha-Hitgayshut, 79.

[98] CZA J8/1423, F. Steif – He'arot, August 2, 1944.

[99] Berger, Magbit ha-Hitgayshut, 79.

Arye Shenkar, the head of the Manufacturers' Association of Palestine, rejected the proposal that evaders be expelled, because this would undermine the autonomy of his association.[100] Other bodies such as the Importers and Wholesalers Association of Palestine and the Merchant Council of Tel Aviv also voiced their opposition.[101] Another issue that concerned civil society organizations was the exact composition of the courts; the organizations asked that the courts be manned by representatives of the economic association to which the evader belonged.[102]

In November 1944 a meeting of the discipline committee of the mobilization and rescue fund was held, at which representatives of the civil society organizations opposing the courts presented their case. They claimed that formal sanctions would be counterproductive, given that the fund was successful and encompassed about 70 percent of the Jewish community of Palestine. Sanctions such as publicity would only create opposition, and publishing the names of evaders in newspapers would not deter them. Instead of creating the impression that there were few evaders, evaders would realize that they were actually part of a large group. If the names of evaders were published, they argued, the relevant economic organization to which the evader belonged would react by asserting that the member in question was an honest person. It might also lead to the lynching of people accused of evasion.[103] Unlike the emergency tax, which was collected directly from individuals, the mobilization and rescue fund relied on civil society organizations to collect the tax, and when these organizations opposed the proposed measures, the fate of these measures was sealed.[104]

Another explanation for the failure to establish courts imposing formal sanctions was given by Harussi, who observed:

> The power of the mobilization and rescue fund was that the Jewish person obeyed its orders based on [a sense] of internal duty. Sanctions

---

[100] CZA J8/1423, Shenkar to Barth, August 1, 1944; CZA J8/1423, Pratey-kol shel Yeshivat Ve'adat ha-Mishma'at, November 14, 1944.

[101] CZA J8/1423, Ha-Va'ad ha-Po'el [shel] Hitahadut ha-Importerim veha-Soharim ha-Sitona'im be-Erets Yisrael to ha-Nesi'ut shel-Magbit ha-Hitgaysut veha-Hatsalah, October 19, 1944.

[102] See CZA J8/1423, Han Moller to Aron Barth, September 22, 1944.

[103] CZA J8/1423, Protokol shel Yeshivat Ve'adat ha-Mishma'at, November 14, 1944.

[104] See, e.g., CZA J8/1423, Shenkar to Barth, August 1, 1944.

would have achieved the opposite of the desired result. They would have led to instinctive resistance and would ultimately damage the fund raising process. Declaring sanctions would have been like defaming the name of the Jewish community and a statement of mistrust in its volunteering power ... The power of the mobilization and rescue fund was in strengthening positive [behavior] and not in preventing negative [behavior].[105]

One interesting aspect of the story of the failed attempts by the KJV to create a more formal tax assessment and collection process relates to the cultural difference between the German Jews belonging to the KJV and the East European Jews who dominated the work of the voluntary tax system. The German Jewish members of the KJV (who described themselves as "a unified body of educated and disciplined Zionists") were keen to use lawyers and economic experts to create an orderly tax system based on the rule of law. Indeed, while they were pressurizing the community tax officials, they were also involved in a far more ambitious project seeking to create "A Zionist legal regime" in Palestine. Such a regime would include a code of "national discipline" for the Jews of Palestine, which would focus not on rights but on national duties. Such duties would include a demand for "assisting in the creation of a Jewish national home in Palestine," but also more trivial things such as a demand "that everyone would strive in their social circles to create a level of politeness that befits a civilized nation." The envisioned regime also included a system of education and mass instruction to instill these duties, as well as the creation of "Zionist courts" to enforce them.[106]

While both the community tax administration and the mobilization and rescue fund failed to establish courts of their own, they did successfully use, on occasion, another Jewish court system that existed in Palestine at the time – that of the government-backed rabbinical

[105] Harussi, *Sefer ha-Magbit*, 67–8.
[106] CZA J8/1251, Nesi'ut ha-KYP to Nesi'ut Kofer ha-Yishuv, May 1939; CZA J8/1251, Mishtar Tsiyoni [May 1939]. It seems that another factor motivating the KJV was its desire to replace the "party regime" (*mishtar ha-miflagtiyut*) that dominated the political life of the Jewish community of Palestine with a regime based on loyalty to the representative body of the Jews of Palestine, the National Council. CZA A155/11a, Mitokh Hilufe Mikhtavim Beyn Nesi'ut ha-KYP ve-Kofer ha-Yishuv, at 9.

courts.[107] According to the Palestine Order in Council, 1922, which regulated the work of these courts, they had exclusive jurisdiction in matters of marriage and divorce, alimony, confirmation of wills, and the constitution or internal administration of religious endowments. They also had jurisdiction in any other matter of personal status, where all the parties to the action consented.[108] While the Palestine Order in Council did not give these courts formal jurisdiction in monetary disputes, it was customary for Jews in the Diaspora to bring such disputes before rabbinical courts, and this custom continued in Palestine. Here, too, the government-backed rabbinical courts served as arbitration tribunals in monetary disputes (including disputes related to the voluntary tax system) when both parties consented to their jurisdiction.[109]

In 1939, when community tax officials tried to levy a contribution on the sale of seats in synagogues during the high holidays, the administration committee of the great synagogue of Tel Aviv refused to collect the money on behalf of the community tax administration. It was therefore sued by community tax officials in the rabbinical court of Tel Aviv, with the officials asking for the sum of P£37. Ultimately, the rabbinical court decided that the synagogue committee should pay the sum of P£3 and provide the community tax administration with a list of ticket holders, from whom the administration would attempt to collect money.[110] Another example of the use of the rabbinical courts occurred in 1940 when the community tax administration sued a commercial firm that failed to transfer monies it had collected on behalf of the community tax administration.[111] Occasionally, attempts to use

---

[107] The rabbinical courts were just one (semi) autonomous court system that existed in the Jewish community in mandatory Palestine. Two other autonomous systems were the Hebrew Courts of Arbitration and the socialist-inspired Comrades Courts. On these systems, see Ronen Shamir, *The Colonies of Law: Colonialism, Zionism and Law in Early Mandate Palestine* (Cambridge: Cambridge University Press, 2000); Assaf Likhovski, *Law and Identity in Mandate Palestine* (Chapel Hill: University of North Carolina Press, 2006), 35–7.

[108] Palestine Order in Council, 1922, sec. 53; M. Chigier, "The Rabbinical Courts in the State of Israel," *Israel Law Review* 2 (1967): 147–81, 151–2.

[109] See generally, Chigier, "The Rabbinical Courts," 170–1.

[110] CZA J8/1167, Ha-Mazkirut ha-Artsit to Misrad ha-Rabanut [Tel Aviv], January 3, 1940; CZA J8/1167, Psak Din, ha-Rabanut ha-Rashit li-Mehoz Yafo ve-Tel Aviv, February 27, 1940.

[111] CZA S53/1527, 'Alon Pnimi Mispar 9, October 10, 1940.

the rabbinical courts failed because the defendants refused to appear in these courts.[112]

The judges of the rabbinical courts were also sometimes utilized by the voluntary tax system. For example, in early 1940 the supreme court of honor of the emergency tax administration, manned by the two chief rabbis and a lay member, David Yellin (who was the president of the local emergency tax committee in Jerusalem), convened in Jerusalem. The court was asked to deal with the cases of five wealthy individuals who refused to contribute their fair share to the emergency tax system, despite a long process of negotiations with them. Only one of these individuals appeared before the court. The court instructed him to pay, but he ignored the decision.[113] This, perhaps, was to be expected, because even one of the two chief rabbis was sometimes reluctant to pay the amount asked of him by the emergency tax administration.[114]

Use was also made of arbitration procedures. One example of such a procedure, from 1941, was an arbitration process between some major margarine manufacturers and the national secretariat of the community tax administration. This process was meant to determine such questions as the rate of tax that would be levied on margarine, the amount of taxes due from each specific manufacturer, and the collection method of the tax. The parties appointed a four-member arbitration panel composed of two members of the National Council, and two margarine manufacturers. The panel lowered the amounts asked of the producers, decided that some of the money levied would

---

[112] CZA J1/7788/1, Hahlatot Yeshivat Nesi'ut Kofer ha Yishuv, November 24, 1940.

[113] ISA GL 7413/10, Psak Din, March 21, 1940; ISA GL 7413/10, Mas ha-Herum shel ha-Yishuv: Ha-Va'ad ha-Mekomi bi-Yerushalayim to Beyt ha-Din ha-'Elyon shel Kavod le-Mas ha-Herum, May 12, 1940.

[114] See ISA P 892/8, Mas ha-Herum shel ha-Yishuv: Ha-Va'ad ha-Mekomi to Uziel, March 30, 1941 (complaining that Chief Rabbi Uziel only paid P£0.5 of the P£4.5 asked of him in 1940, and asking him to pay P£4 for 1941. Chief Rabbi Uziel responded that "I cannot pay [the amount due for] last year because most of [last year's] income was spent on [government] taxes and repairs. As for this year, the collector should contact me, and I shall determine the amount and times of payment with him." ISA P 892/8, Uziel to Hanhalat Mas ha-Herum shel ha-Yishuv: Ha-Va'ad ha-Mekomi, April 14, 1941. He later paid the amount requested. See ISA P892/8, Uziel to Hanhalat Mas ha-Herum shel ha-Yishuv: Ha-Va'ad ha-Mekomi, May 5, 1941.

be held in a special fund that would be used to provide credit to the manufacturers, and even decided that, to prevent unfair competition, further action should be taken to ensure that small margarine producers would also be required to pay the tax, and that the tax applicable to coconut manufacturers (as well as butter and chocolate producers) would be raised to the level of the tax on margarine.[115]

Another example of the use of arbitration procedures can be found in the work of the "well-to-do" department of the mobilization and rescue fund. Several arbitration processes were carried out by this department. Arbitrators were usually lawyers. The head of the Fund, Aron Barth, also served as an arbitrator, often assisted by two "observers."[116]

The Use of Non-legal Means to Induce Compliance

Rather than relying primarily on law-like norms and institutions, the Jewish tax system used a wide range of means, all ultimately based on the civic republican Zionist ethos, to encourage compliance. I will now describe various nonlegal means used by the voluntary tax system administration in the decade between its creation in 1938 and its abolition in 1948, discussing these means analytically (rather than chronologically).

One method of inducing compliance was to appeal directly to potential taxpayers using daily and week-long fund-raising campaigns, public meetings and lectures, special columns in newspapers, pamphlets, exhibitions, and posters (see Figure 3.2).

Such appeals were directed at the general public, but also targeted specific groups such as youth organizations and new immigrants, and specific institutions such as schools and synagogues, which were deemed highly effective targets for such propaganda. Women were also described as especially effective "trustees and supervisors" who

---

[115] CZA J1/1035, Shtar Borerut, November 6, 1941; CZA J1/1035, Ha-She'elot ha-'Omdot le-Berur, November 20, 1941; CZA J1/1035, Psak Din; CZA J1/1035, Yoman Pe'ulah, November 30, 1941, at 3.

[116] See, e.g., CZA J8/906, Letter of Mahleket be'aley ha-Yekholet, March 19, 1948; CZA J8/906, Mahleket be'aley ha-Yekholet to Friedberg, March 21, 1948; CZA J8/906, Ket'a mi-Pratey-kol [shel] Yeshivat ha-Nesi'ut shel Magbit ha-Hitgaysut veha-Hatsalah, April 12, 1948.

FIGURE 3.2 Propaganda poster, 1944. The caption reads: "Lend a hand to rescuing [Jewish refugees from Nazi Europe]! The mobilization and rescue fund."

would ensure that the taxes were paid "in the market and store, in the street and at home."[117]

One specific method that was intensively discussed by officials of the voluntary tax system was the use of social pressure and shaming.[118] In his memo submitted in June 1939 to the committee created to "formulate pressure plans on evaders" of the community tax, Hans Kaufman suggested that the basic means of pressure on evaders should be a boycott, "just as our forefathers used this weapon to guard the people's unity in the Diaspora." Four types of boycott were suggested: moral (by friends and relatives, for example); social (shunning evaders in public places and family celebrations); organizational – applied by civil society organizations to which the evader belonged (denying evaders any active role on the boards or committees of such organizations, or using the disciplinary court system within these organizations to judge them); and economic (denying evaders credit or licenses, and pressurizing their clients and suppliers to boycott them).[119]

Based on Kaufman's scheme, one can distinguish between different networks that were used to apply pressure on evaders. The first network included the friends and family of evaders, who were asked to intervene to convince them to pay their taxes.[120] Reliance on the family to play this coercive role is also evident in the pamphlet written by Harussi that opened this chapter. Another example of the use of evaders' families to pressurize them can be found in a plan to send a letter urging compliance to the wives of Central European immigrants, the assumption probably being that the wife would put pressure on the husband to comply with the tax.[121]

---

[117] See, e.g., CZA J1/7788/2, Tokhnit ha-Ta'amulah le-Kofer ha-Yishuv le-Hodesh May-Yuni.

[118] On the use of shaming and other means of social pressure in other voluntary fiscal contexts, see, e.g., Jones, "Bonds, Voluntarism and Taxation." On the use of shaming in intellectual property disputes in mandatory Palestine, see Michael D. Birnhack, *Colonial Copyright: Intellectual Property in Mandate Palestine* (Oxford: Oxford University Press, 2012), 150–6.

[119] CZA J8/1249, Kaufman, Hatsa'ot le-Tipul be-Mishtamtim, June 22, 1939.

[120] CZA J8/875, S. N. to Zalman Yerushalmi, May 8, 1946.

[121] CZA J1/7788/2, Tokhnit ha-Ta'amulah le-Kofer ha-Yishuv le-Hodesh May-Yuni. It is unclear whether such letters were indeed sent or not, and also why Central European families were targeted, but the very idea is another indication of the desire to use family members to pressurize evaders.

A second type of network used to pressurize evaders involved the economic, social, and political organizations to which taxpayers belonged. Taxpayers were invited to propaganda lectures organized by economic organizations such as chambers of commerce.[122] Peer pressure at such gatherings sometimes turned physical. Michael Landau, the general secretary of community tax and mobilization and rescue fund administration, recalled a party to which a number of industrialists had been invited. The director general of the major chocolate manufacturing company, Abba Frumchenko, asked one of the invitees to contribute a large sum of money, and when this person refused, Frumchenko slapped him twice in the face.[123] The use of such violence is another indication, I believe, of the semicoercive nature of the 1940s Jewish voluntary tax system.

This network of civil society organizations was also used to deny various benefits to evaders. These organizations had been involved in levying the community tax since its inception, with many of them seeking to have their members recruited as salaried workers of the community tax administration.[124] They were therefore sometimes asked to cut their contacts and business dealings with known evaders, although it is unclear whether such contacts were indeed cut in practice.[125] In 1946 a special department was created to discipline evaders using civil society organizations. More than two hundred organizations including the Jewish Agency, the National Council, municipal councils, the Manufacturers' Association, the General Federation of Jewish Labor, and the Women's International Zionist Organization (WIZO) committed themselves to disciplining evaders. Their commitments included

[122] CZA J8/1902, Din ve-Heshbon 'al Peulot Va'adat Kofer ha-Yishuv she'al-Yad Lishkat ha-Mis'har be-Tel Aviv ve-Yafo. See also CZA J1/6262, Yediot ha-Mazkirut ha-Artsit shel Kofer ha-Yishuv no. 4, March 3, 1940.

[123] Landau, "Ha-Yishuv," 188, 189–90.

[124] See, e.g., CZA J8/1251 (containing letters from the Yemenite Organization in Palestine, the Jewish Doctors Association, the General Zionist Party, and the Agudath Israel Workers Organization); CZA J8/548, Histadrut Po'aley Agudat Yisrael be-Erets Yisrael to Magbit ha-Hitgaysut, ha-Nesi'ut, November 10, 1942.

[125] CZA KH4/12739, Mano'ah to Keren ha-Yesod, May 26, 1939; CZA S5/2623, Kofer ha-Yishuv to Hanhalat ha-Histadrut ha-Tsiyonit, September 18, 1939; CZA S6/2427, Kofer ha-Yishuv to Mahleket ha-'Aliyah shel ha-Sokhnut ha-Yehudit, December 26, 1938.

the promise not to provide services to, or request services from, evaders, and to expel them from their organization.[126]

When families of evaders or civil society organizations to which evaders belonged could not be used, publicity was resorted to. For example, the leading newspaper of the Jewish Labor movement, *Davar*, published advertisements informing its readers about transportation companies that had refused to participate in the collection of transportation taxes.[127] It also published the names of prominent individual evaders.[128] The names of firms that refused to litigate in the rabbinical courts were also published.[129]

However, the use of publicity often encountered opposition from within the community tax administration. In May 1939 the presidium of community tax administration decided to increase pressure on evaders by using publicity. Local branches were instructed to pass the names of evaders to the General Secretariat for publication.[130] The list provided by the local Ramat-Gan branch included the name of the head of the local council, Abraham Krinitzi, as well as the name of one the members of the local community tax committee.[131] Problems immediately arose. A note attached to the list instructed the director of propaganda, Harussi, not to publish Krinitzi's name without the approval of the presidium. Meanwhile, the Jerusalem branch informed

[126] Harussi, *Sefer ha-Magbit*, 149. For concrete examples, see, e.g., CZA J8/857, M. Sheflan to Hit'ahdut ha-Ta'asiyanim, May 8, 1946; CZA J8/875, S. N. to Kaplan, May 12, 1946.

[127] CZA J8/790, Haverim, De'u: Hevrot ha-Taxi Tsiyon, 'Atid ve-'Atid Mugrabi Mitnakrot le-Kofer ha-Yishuv.

[128] CZA J8/790, "[Haifa]: ...Haver Va'ad Ha-Kehilah ve-Yor Hitahadut Ba'aley ha-Batim Beyn ha-Mishtamtim mi-Mas ha-Hitgaysut," *Davar*, December 20, 1942, at 3 (reporting that a prominent Haifa merchant, who was also member of the Jewish community council and the chairman of the homeowners' association in Haifa, was evading payment to the mobilization fund).

[129] CZA J1/7788/1, Hahlatot Yeshivat Nesi'ut Kofer ha-Yishuv, November 24, 1940.

[130] CZA J8/1249, Ha-Mazkirut ha-Artsit to ha-Ve'adim ha-Mekomiyim Heyfah, Yerushalayim, Ramat-Gan veha-Svivah, May 15, 1939.

[131] CZA J8/1249, Kofer ha-Yishuv, Ve'adat ha-Gush: Ha-Mazkirut to ha-Mazkirut ha-Artsit, August 1, 1939, Rshimat ha-Mishtamtim mi-Mahzor Alef, Reshima Mispar 1. The reason that Krinitzi did not contribute may have been his opposition to centralized collection of the tax. See Mordechai Naor, *Trumat Ramat-Gan le-Vitahon Yisrael: Yarok-Haki-Adom* (Ramat-Gan: Beyt Avraham Krinitzi, 2009), 26.

the Secretariat that several members believed that publicity would result in people refusing to pay their dues. Finally, in late August 1939, after a meeting of the presidium, it was decided not to publish the names of any evaders for the time being.[132]

Because of the resistance to negative publicity, other types of publicity were used. The community tax administration issued small doorpost signs and badges, which were displayed by taxpayers to distinguish themselves from evaders.[133] In 1943 a proposal for the creation of personal loyalty certificates was submitted. The certificates were to be given to loyal payers or posted on storefront windows of businesses that paid the tax. In addition to personal certificates, it was later proposed that a "central registry" or "book of honor" or "book of loyal [taxpayers]" (*sefer ha-ne'emanim*) be created, and the names of those paying the tax would be published there.[134] Concerns were immediately raised regarding the right of people who only paid part of their dues to obtain these loyalty certificates.[135] It was only in 1947 that these loyalty certificates were finally created. A Community Tax Order of 1947 announced the distribution of "loyalty certificates" and "loyalty booklets" that would enable Jewish organizations to deny services to nonpayers.[136]

Newspapers and advertisements were also used to praise conscientious payers and condemn evaders. Newspaper reports often contained uplifting stories of people who paid their taxes. For example, *Davar* published a story of a worker in a diamond-cutting factory who, because of "special family circumstances," received a partial exemption from the payment of the tax. When this worker learned about the exemption given to him, he rebuked the workers' committee in his factory for not charging him the full amount.[137]

[132] CZA J8/1249, notes dated August 2, 1939 and August 20, 1939; CZA J8/1249, Ve'adat ha-Bitahon Kofer ha-Yishuv bi-Yerushalayim to ha-Mazkirut ha-Artsit, August 3, 1939.

[133] HA, Oral History Project, M. Landau, Kofer ha-Yishuv, at 1.

[134] CZA J8/1869, Shatner to Havrey ha-Mazkirut veha-Nesi'ut: Hatsa'ot le-Irgun Pe'ulat ha-Magbit bi-Shnat 1946, December 14, 1945.

[135] CZA J8/1869, [Poster] El Kol Ba'aley ha-'Asakim, June 1946; CZA J8/1869, Harussi to Havrey ve'adat ha-Ta'amulah, October 25, 1944; CZA J8/1869, Te'udat Miluy Hovah, undated.

[136] Harussi, *Sefer ha-Magbit*, 158.

[137] "Tove'a et Kabalat Mihsato ha-Mele'ah," *Davar*, December 13, 1942, at 1.

The use of publicity was often accompanied by religious overtones that (consciously or not) made use of rhetoric and practices typical of Jewish taxation in the Diaspora. For example, evaders were condemned using biblical-like terminology. When the community tax administration planned its first publicity campaign in 1939, advertisements containing the names of evaders were to be preceded by the following heading:

> And these are the names of the complacent of Zion, well-known people and owners of property ... for whose peace and the peace of their children the youth of Israel will sacrifice their lives, who have not committed themselves to the people when the blood of saints and martyrs is poured on the ground of the homeland ... may their name be odious forever, and may the sons be ashamed of their fathers ... may they be like lepers, until they regret their evil deeds, and purify their souls, and return to the camp to share its burden and pain, [to participate in] its building and defense.[138]

Other religious-like terms such as "purifying the ranks"[139] or the "sacred burden" (of the mobilization and rescue fund) were sometimes used.[140]

One extreme example of the use of religious symbolism in dealing with evaders can be found in a memo written by Alexander Eliash, a Jerusalem banker, sent in August 1944 to the discipline committee of the mobilization and rescue fund. In his memo, Eliash suggested that evaders be condemned at an "impressive" public ceremony, modeled after the ban (*herem*) ceremonies of Jewish communities in the Diaspora. The ceremony would be organized by the Chief Rabbinate of Palestine and "would make the heart of a man tremble." The rabbis would cover themselves in prayer shawls and light candles on a table while the evaders were tried. An indictment would be read, telling the story of the extermination of the Jews in Europe. The rabbis would scold the evaders and issue their decision while standing (the public would also be required to stand). The decision would be in the name of God and it would state that since the evader had not heeded the call to assist his brethren in the Diaspora, he would not be buried in a Jewish

138 CZA J8/1249, undated page.
139 "Po'aley Petah Tikvah le-Hagbarat ha-Giyus," *Davar*, November 3, 1942, at 2.
140 CZA J8/875, Letter to Pugacz, May 2, 1946.

cemetery, and his sin would not be forgiven. The decision would be communicated to burial societies, hospitals, and the Jewish Doctors' Association, and published in the newspapers.[141]

Eliash also suggested that, as a practical matter, the first evader chosen to undergo this ceremony would not be a "strongman," but someone who has "a despairing and frightened heart," a man with "a family which includes women: an old mother, a nervous wife, daughters, and so forth," so that when they heard about the trial, the "women of the household would come in tears to beg for mercy," and therefore "there would be very few trials." However, he continued, for many this process would be "a grave threat that would remind them of their day of death, and in many hearts, there would be repentance, and they would search their souls asking whether they had fulfilled their duty to their brethren."[142] It is unclear whether this was a serious or a sarcastic proposal.[143] However, regardless of the seriousness of the proposal, it is interesting because of the use made by Eliash of elements taken from the premodern Jewish ban ceremony, thus indicating the link that existed – in the minds of at least some observers – between the 1940s voluntary system and the tax systems of Jewish communities in the Diaspora.

Pressure sometimes led to a backlash from those opposed to the tax for ideological reasons, especially the Revisionists. For example,

---

[141] CZA J8/1423, Alexander Eliash, Hatsa'ah le-Fitron Be'ayat Kshey ha-Lev, August 3, 1944.

[142] Ibid. See also CZA J1/6275, "Ha-Neshek ha-Sodi shel Mas Herum: Mi-Tvi'ah le-Beyt Din Kavod ve'ad Herem Tsiburi," *Ha-Boker*, January 2, 1941. It is interesting to note that, at about the same time, Jewish communities in Nazi-ruled Europe, facing demands for money from their Nazi rulers, also returned to the use of the *herem* ceremony. See Aharon Weiss, "Le-Darkam shel ha-Yudenratim bi-Drom Mizrah Polin," *Yalkut Moreshet le-Heker ha-Sho'ah veha-Antishemiyut* 15 (1972): 59–122, 73; Yehuda Bauer, *The Death of the Shtetl* (New Haven: Yale University Press, 2010), 82. A somewhat similar ceremony, modeled after traditional Jewish ban ceremonies, which may have inspired Eliash, is found in a famous play, *Ha-Dybbuk* (the ceremony there was part of an exorcism ritual).

[143] On the one hand, Eliash was active in the work of the discipline committee of the mobilization and rescue fund. On the other hand, his name appeared on a 1939 blacklist of merchants "who contributed to the community tax administration, but not according to the quota required of them," so he may not have been fully committed to the system. See CZA J8/1423, Pratey-kol shel Yeshivat Ve'adat ha-Mishma'at, November 14, 1944; CZA KH4/12739, Mano'ah to Keren ha-Yesod, May 26, 1939.

in January 1939 there was an attempt to burn down the community tax office in Haifa.[144] Another attack took place in the community tax office in Jerusalem.[145] At around the same time, buses belonging to several transportation cooperatives that levied the community tax from passengers were damaged by acts of vandalism, and bombs were placed in their offices.[146] Following the attacks, negotiations were entered into by the Revisionists and community tax officials, but attacks by Revisionists on transportation cooperatives continued.[147]

Physical violence was also used, on occasion, in the collection process. The British authorities reported they had received about fifty complaints regarding acts of violence associated with the collection process.[148] The most notable events occurred in the winter and summer of 1940. One such violent incident happened in January 1940 when, according to the newspaper of the Revisionist Party, *Ha-Mashkif*, collectors of the community tax had poured oil on the fruit and vegetable produce of merchants in Tel Aviv who had refused to pay the tax, and physically assaulted a Jewish peddler who had refused to pay.[149] Another incident occurred in August 1940 at the Café Ditza, located on Tel Aviv's most fashionable street. The café owner, who

---

[144] CZA J8/855, Ve'adat ha-Matsav Heyfah to ha-Mazkirut ha-Artsit shel Kofer ha-Yishuv, January 24, 1939.

[145] "Meshalhim Esh be-Kofer ha-Yishuv!" *Davar*, January 26, 1939, at 3.

[146] CZA J8/855, undated anonymous threatening letter; CZA J8/855, Meir Shapira to Hanhalat Kofer ha-Yishuv Yerushalayim, February 8, 1939; CZA J8/914, "Yehudim Mehablim bi-Rekhush Yehudi," *Haaretz*, January 31, 1939, at 3; CZA J8/914, "Veha-Biryonim Mosifim La'akor ve-Laharos," *Haaretz*, February 6, 1939.

[147] CZA J8/914, "Masa u-Matan beyn Ba'ey Ko'ah ha-Yishuv la-Revizyonistim," *Haaretz*, February 23, 1939, at 6; CZA J8/914, "Hitnaplut Revizyonistim 'al Misrad Egged be-Tel Aviv," *Haaretz*, March 15, 1939, at 8. See also CZA J8/914, "Mi-Ta'aluleyhem ha-Hadashim shel 'ha-Almonim'," *Haaretz*, March 24, 1939, at 8 (certificates indicating payment of the community tax were stolen from the doorposts of houses of people who paid).

[148] CZA J1/6262, Ben-Zvi to Havrey Nesi'ut Kofer ha-Yishuv, February 23, 1940. See also HA, CID files 42/823, Intelligence Summary, February 29, 1940 (reporting several incidents in which Haganah members burnt cars and beat up Revisionist activists).

[149] CZA J1/6262, Shitat Kofer ha-Yishuv be-Ko'ah Nimshekhet, January 26, 1940; CZA J1/6262, "Yehdal na ha-Shod," *Ha-Mashkif*, January 28, 1940. The Revisionists were accused by their opponents of kidnapping wealthy Jews to extort money from them. See HA, Oral History Project, M. Landau, Kofer ha-Yishuv, at 5.

was opposed to the tax, expelled a tax collector from his establishment. In response, "youth committed to the community tax" (*no'ar kana'i le-kofer ha-yishuv*) staged a sit-in at the café. British policemen were called and arrested the protestors. The next day, windows, tables, dishes, and chairs belonging to the café were smashed. Fearing further violence, Michael Landau, the secretary of the community tax administration, immediately wrote a letter stating (falsely) that the café owner always paid his dues, and that the attack on the café was "a provocation ... carried out by irresponsible children."[150]

Taxation and Civic Identity-formation

Despite the occasional use of coercive violence, it seems that most of the Zionist Jews of mandatory Palestine viewed the voluntary tax system positively, and considered it a democratic system open to public involvement. The community tax administration archive contains files in which members of the public often suggested new taxes – for example, a tax on such items as knitting wool or on New Year's greeting cards.[151] Public participation was also a main feature of the assessment and collection process, whether through the use of volunteer assessment committees or volunteer collectors.

Such participation undermined uniformity and centralized control, and allowed civil society organizations to lower the tax burden on their members. For example, when the community tax was imposed in 1938, an assessment committee was formed by the chamber of commerce in Tel Aviv. The committee's first decision was that the 8 percent income tax rate decided on by the community tax administration was too high, and that the rate should be lowered to 5 percent. The collectors appointed by the chamber of commerce were instructed that this rate was final, and that they had no authority to lower it further, but that the property tax they were also supposed to collect was negotiable. The second decision of the assessment committee was to keep merchants' assessments secret, and the third decision was to report directly to the

---

[150] CZA J1/7788/2, Shneurson to ha-Va'adah ha-Mekomit shel Kofer ha-Yishuv, August 4, 1940; CZA J1/7788/2, Unsigned letter, August 6, 1940; CZA J1/7788/2, D. P., Note, August 7, 1940.
[151] See CZA J8/693 [untitled file].

chamber of commerce. Community tax personnel would not be allowed access to any written documentation on Tel Aviv chamber of commerce members, and an internal appeals committee was established.[152] The participatory collection process obviously had negative implications on the revenue raised, but these were, perhaps, at least partly offset by the fact that taxpayers' involvement created greater willingness to see the system as their own, creating a sort of "DIY tax" that consequently led to greater willingness to contribute to the system.[153]

Another aspect of the participatory nature of the tax was its impact on community creation, since giving is, among other things, a way of creating community and shared identity.[154] In a pamphlet published in 1936 entitled *The Shekel: Zionist Citizenship*, Yitzhak Gruenbaum, one of the directors of the World Zionist Organization, discussed the connection between taxes and citizenship. The topic of the pamphlet was the membership fee (the *shekel*) paid for becoming a member of the Zionist Organization. The first Zionist Congress, said Gruenbaum, declared the existence of the Jewish people, calling into life "the Jewish citizen," whose membership in the collective was determined by the purchase of the Zionist *shekel* each year. The *shekel* thus created Jewish citizenship and, because of its low cost, allowed masses of people to join the Zionist Organization and to vote.[155] The *shekel* thus constituted a citizenship certificate, and its use deepened notions of national unity.[156]

---

[152] CZA J8/1902, Din ve-Heshbon 'al Peulot Va'adat Kofer ha-Yishuv she'al-Yad Lishkat ha-Mis'har be-Tel Aviv ve-Yafo, 2, 4.

[153] On this type of behavioral effect, see generally Nikolaus Franke, Martin Schreier, and Ulrike Kaiser, "The 'I Designed It Myself' Effect in Mass Customization," *Management Science* 56 (2010): 125–40; Michael I. Norton, Daniel Mochon, and Dan Ariely, "The 'IKEA Effect': When Labor Leads to Love," *Journal of Consumer Psychology* 22 (2012): 453–60.

[154] On archaic societies, see Marcel Mauss, *The Gift: The Form and Reason for Exchange in Archaic Societies*, trans. W. D. Halls (New York: W. W. Norton, 2000). On modern societies, see generally Yanni Kotsonis, *States of Obligation: Taxes and Citizenship in the Russian Empire and Early Soviet Republic* (Toronto: University of Toronto Press, 2014).

[155] Y. Gruenbaum, *Ha-Shekel: Ezrahut Tsiyonit* (Jerusalem: Hanhalat ha-Histadrut ha-Tsiyonit, 1936), 5–7.

[156] Ibid., 6–8. Nationalist leaders in the Arab community were aware of this function of the *shekel*. In a 1936 speech Haj Amin al-Husseini, the leader of the Palestinian Arab

A similar view of taxation appeared in discussions of the voluntary taxes of the 1940s. These taxes were described by Harussi as educational tools designed to teach the Jews of Palestine "endurance, fulfilling every role and duty, freedom, pride and Israeli statism."[157] The community tax and the mobilization and rescue fund were not merely fiscal tools, said Harussi, "but a school for educating the masses, teaching them a feeling of mutual responsibility and common destiny, loyal citizenship and Hebrew sovereignty."[158]

A memo discussing the planned establishment of an "Evaders' Department," by the Jerusalem branch of the community tax in the summer of 1939, affirmed that the department had an important educational role: "to teach the Jewish community to pay taxes even before we have governmental powers that can force [taxpayers] to pay based on [the force of] law."[159] A pamphlet from the same period said that the contribution of the tax was not merely in the revenue it raised, but in its political and educational roles, creating contributions that were "state-like," and joining all the members of the Jewish community together.[160]

An editorial on the community tax, published in 1939 in the bulletin of the Council of Teachers for the Jewish National Fund, clarified that the aim of the tax was not merely to collect contributions. "Our aim [instead] is purely national-educational," part of the "cultivation of the civic consciousness of the Hebrew pupil."[161] Another pamphlet called the community tax "the bolt that joins together all sections of the Hebrew community."[162] When the new Israeli government sought to finance the 1948 War of Independence using a national loan, the

community, criticized the lack of a "spirit of voluntarism" in the Muslim community and mentioned the Zionist *shekel* as an example of such a spirit. See "'Ase ve-Lo Ta'ase," *Davar*, February 20, 1936, at 2.

[157] Harussi, *Sefer ha-Magbit*, 18.

[158] Harussi, "Bi-Yemey Kofer ha-Yishuv," 13, 14.

[159] CZA J8/1249, Ha-Makhlakah le-Mesarvim, July 3, 1939.

[160] CZA KH4/12739, Mi-Pe'ulot Kofer ha-Yishuv mi-Yom 1 be-Ogust 1938 'ad 31 be-Yanu'ar 1939, at 13.

[161] [L. I. Riklis], "Ba-Ma'arakhah: Kofer ha-Yishuv," *Shorashim: Bamah le-Mo'etset ha-Morim le-Ma'an ha-KKL* 3:1 (December 1938): 6 (a copy of this periodical can be found in the Central Zionist Archives, Jerusalem).

[162] CZA KH4/12739, Mi-Pe'ulot Kofer ha-Yishuv mi-Yom 1 be-Ogust 1938 'ad 31 be-Yanu'ar 1939, at 5–6.

loan was described not merely as a method for raising revenue but also as a "vote of confidence in the government and state" by the Jewish community in Palestine.[163]

Apart from instilling notions of civic duty and citizenship, the collection of the tax was used to unify the Jewish community in Palestine. The community tax was welcomed by organizations like the KJV because they viewed it as "a great opportunity to educate the Jewish community [and to instill in it] a civic worldview [*havanah mamlakhtit*]," its goal being "to unify the whole community using a great defense tax."[164] Aron Barth, chairman of the presidium of the mobilization and rescue fund, said in a 1946 speech that one of the results of the tax was that it created unity in the Jewish community in Palestine.[165] Even earlier, the community tax had had an indirect role in transforming the Haganah from a federation of local militias into a powerful centralized national organization.[166] A pamphlet summarizing the work of the mobilization and rescue fund in Haifa stated that the tax was one of the most clear expressions of the fact that the Jewish Community in Palestine had changed from a collection of tribes into a unified whole.[167] Of course, just as the tax was used to create a shared sense of identity and unity, opposition to it created oppositional identities. Thus the Jewish voluntary taxes were an important trigger in the construction of the oppositional identities of ultraorthodox and Revisionist Jews.[168]

Another aspect of the relationship between taxation and community formation is found in the use of the tax as a signal of the maturity of the Jewish community in Palestine and its readiness to establish a state.[169] As Aron Barth said in 1946:

> the mobilization and rescue fund has created a whole series of taxes for each economic branch, and has managed to levy these taxes like a

---

[163] Quoted in Naor, *Be-Hazit*, 125.
[164] CZA J8/1251, Tazkir be-'Inyeney Kofer-ha-Yishuv Mugash 'al-Yedey Nesi'ut ha-KYP, March 1939.
[165] Harussi, *Sefer ha-Magbit*, 141.
[166] Slutsky, *Me-Haganah le-Ma'avak*, 1012–13.
[167] CZA S115/92, Hamesh Shanim le-Magbit ha-Hitgaysut veha-Hatsalah be-Heyfah.
[168] Friedman, "*Haredim* and Palestinians in Jerusalem," 235–7.
[169] Harussi, *Sefer ha-Magbit*, 138–9. On taxation and political signaling after 1948, see Michael N. Barnett, *Confronting the Costs of War: Military Power, State and Society in Egypt and Israel* (Princeton: Princeton University Press, 1992), 161.

government does from its population, its various branches and types. We managed to gain the understanding of the Jewish community in such a way that anyone who evaded these taxes was considered a traitor ... and this thing – the imposition of a system of taxes based on the goodwill of the population – is a sign of important progress toward independence.[170]

In 1950 Barth repeated this argument by noting that:

the most conspicuous sign of an independent government is its power to impose taxes, and collect them based on objective quotas ... The Jewish community succeeded ... in creating a network of indirect taxes and collecting them over a period of several years from the entire population. The discipline that the population imposed on itself ... was the [sort of discipline] that created the state, even before it was announced. The confidence with which the People's Administration [the first Israeli government] and later the Provisional Government took upon themselves the power to rule was based on the experience of the time in which the community accepted the government of its leaders before the outside conditions necessary for the existence of independence existed.[171]

Conclusion

Formal, lawlike norms – and the courts and lawyers to enforce them – were mostly absent from the Jewish voluntary tax system. This was partly the result of necessity – the fact that the tax was levied by a community rather than by a state, albeit a community that saw itself as a state-in-the-making. However, it was also the result of choice, of an attitude to taxation that favored governance using social norms, engineered by bureaucrats but applied by civil society intermediaries, rather than governance by formal norms. That this was indeed the case is clear, both from the resistance of the community tax administration to the pleas of the KJV to move the system in a more formal direction, as well as from the numerous statements made by community tax officials about the voluntary tax system as a tool for the formation of civic identity and commitment, and not merely as a revenue-generation mechanism.

[170] Harussi, *Sefer ha-Magbit*, 140–1.
[171] Ibid., 198–9.

The use of social norms for the assessment and collection of taxation, as well as the use of the tax system as a means of constructing national unity and proving communal political maturity, distinguished the Jewish tax system of the 1940s from the British-colonial one. Once the British left Palestine in 1948, the two strands of taxation merged: the system established by the State of Israel in the first years after its independence in 1948 fused together the British and Jewish systems. The year 1948 thus marked a time of both rupture and continuity.[172] The history of this post-1948 tax system is discussed in the following chapter.

---

[172] See generally Assaf Likhovski, "Between Mandate and State: Re-thinking the Periodization of Israeli Legal History," *Journal of Israeli History* 19:2 (1998): 39–68.

4

Law and Social Norms in Early Israeli Taxation

In 1955 American advisers to the Israeli Tax Authority convinced Israeli officials to produce an income tax movie.[1] After initial fears that the initiative would become "the subject of ridicule" were overcome, the Government Information Administration commissioned a local studio to produce a 12-minute film entitled *The Tsippori Affair*. It told the "amusing and enlightening" tale of a tax resister, Shimshon Tsippori, who organizes protests against the income tax, only to discover that all government services had been shut down due to lack of funding. As the story unfolds, he visits a hospital and a welfare office and finds them closed because of the nonpayment of taxes. He goes to a primary school and sees children sitting outside the front door, playing cards, drinking wine, and smoking cigarettes. A young girl applies lipstick (see Figure 4.1).

---

[1] The government agency responsible for administering the Israeli tax system is now called the Israel Tax Authority (Rashut ha-Misim be-Yisrael). I will use the term "tax authority" as a shorthand for the various governmental bodies that have been responsible for the administration of the Israeli tax system, including the assessment and collection of income taxation, from 1948 to the present. For a detailed institutional history of these bodies until the 1970s, see Harold C. Wilkenfeld, *Taxes and People in Israel* (Cambridge, MA: Harvard University Press, 1973), 43–81. Another body that will be mentioned here is the State Revenue Administration Division in the Israeli Ministry of Finance, which is responsible for formulating tax policy rather than for the actual administration of the tax system.

FIGURE 4.1 A scene from *The Tsippori Affair*, 1955. The primary school is closed. A young girl applies lipstick.

Tsippori sees a half-finished road and bridge. Workers are sitting idly next to their earth-moving equipment. Two thieves attack him and take all his money, but he has nowhere to turn as the police station and the courts are closed. Finally, he is pursued by three individuals dressed as Arab Legion soldiers. He flees to an army base, but discovers that it, too, is closed. Reviews of the film were enthusiastic. It was described as "among the best [civic education films] so far produced in Israel and certainly the most entertaining." One report stated that "audience response was favorable everywhere, and the movie even drew applause at many showings."[2]

---

[2] *The Tsippori Affair* (a copy of this movie can be found in the Israel Film Service, Jerusalem). See also Wayne F. Anderson, *Income Tax Administration in the State of Israel: Report to the Government of Israel* (Tel Aviv: United States of America, Operations Mission to Israel, 1956), 7, 24–5 (a copy this report can be found in the National Library of Israel (NLI), Jerusalem) (describing how the income tax movie was

The Tsippori Affair epitomized a new stage in the tax history of Israel, one that combined the two legacies that Israel had inherited from Palestine of the 1940s: the British-colonial and the Jewish. It also epitomized the new challenges that appeared with the birth of the Israeli nation-state. When the State of Israel was established in May 1948, it retained the mandatory legal system, including the mandatory Income Tax Ordinance. The Israeli Income Tax Ordinance is still, even today, based on the Income Tax Ordinance of mandatory Palestine, although, of course, it has been thoroughly amended in the six decades since Israel was established.[3] The new state had endeavored to guarantee a smooth transition from the tax system of mandatory Palestine to that of Israel.[4] However, while the basic features of the British-colonial system were retained, the fiscal needs of the new state were far greater than those of the British-colonial system. The new state had to pay for the cost of the Israeli War of Independence of 1948; it had to absorb large waves of Jewish refugees from Europe and the Middle East, more than doubling its population in a short space of time; and it sought to create a welfare state. All these endeavors required far more resources than those required by the British mandatory state.

The new state attempted to meet these requirements by increasing tax rates and by raising money through a series of domestic and foreign loans. For example, in April 1948 a national loan was declared,

made based on sample movies sent to Israel by the Kentucky Department of Revenue). Government officials were closely involved in the production of the movie. The script was vetted by the minister of education and culture, Zalman Aran, who asked the producers to revise or delete some of the scenes. One of the scenes revised was the school scene. Initially, this scene showed the idle children sitting outside the front door of the school playing cards, smoking cigarettes, and drinking vodka. The vodka was replaced by wine, perhaps because vodka was considered too shocking. See Israel Film Service, Tsippori Affair File, Efrati to Rosh Minhal ha-Hasbarah, June 30, 1955. It should be noted that the movie was silent, perhaps because many of the expected viewers were new immigrants, whose command of Hebrew would have been weak.

[3] See generally, Tsilly Dagan, Assaf Likhovski, and Yoram Margalioth, "The Legacy of UK Tax Law in Israel," *British Tax Review*, 2008, 271–84. In 1961 an official Hebrew translation of the Ordinance was promulgated: the Income Tax Ordinance (New Version), 1961.

[4] Jacob Reuveny, *Mimshal ha-Mandat be-Erets Yisrael, 1920–1948: Nitu'ah Histori Medini* (Ramat-Gan: Bar-Ilan University Press, 1993), 84, 222–5.

followed by a war loan declared in December of the same year.[5] The new Israeli state also created new taxes. In 1949 it imposed an estate tax, a luxury tax, and a "land betterment tax," which taxed capital gains from the sale of real estate. In addition, income tax rates were raised, reaching a marginal rate of 90 percent in 1949, and new types of surtaxes, a war tax (*mas milhamti*), and an absorption tax (*mas klitah*) to finance the integration of new immigrants, were created.[6] These changes greatly increased the state's reliance on direct taxation, shifting the balance between indirect and direct taxes, so that while in the fiscal year 1947/48, the last year of British rule in Palestine, only 16 percent of government revenues came from income taxation, by the fiscal year 1955/56, 40 percent of the revenue came from this tax.[7]

However, merely raising tax rates and imposing new taxes was not enough. Compliance was also required. The state sought to address the problem of compliance by resorting to social norms. Compliance would now be based on the socialist ideology that was championed by the rulers of the new state, as well as on a spirit of civic commitment and voluntarism similar to that which had characterized the prestate Jewish community in Palestine. This spirit would be produced in a top-down fashion by the organs of the new state, which used a mix of education and propaganda to engender compliance.

The ideology that underpinned this effort was *mamlakhtiyut*, an Israeli version of statism, sometimes translated as "republicanism" or "civic-mindedness." *Mamlakhtiyut* was a concept advocated in the

---

[5] Yitzhak Greenberg, "Financing the War of Independence," *Studies in Zionism* 9 (1988): 63–80; Moshe Naor, "From Voluntary Funds to National Loans: The Financing of Israel's 1948 War Effort," *Israel Studies* 11 (2006): 62–82; Moshe Naor, "Israel's 1948 War of Independence as a Total War," *Journal of Contemporary History* 43 (2008): 241–57; Moshe Naor, *Social Mobilization in the Arab-Israeli War of 1948: On the Israeli Home Front* (London: Routledge, 2013), 104–14.

[6] See, generally, Avraham Mandel, ed., *Hitpat'hut ha-Misim be-Erets Yisrael: Skirah Historit* (Jerusalem: Muze'on le-Misim, 1968), 4, 39–77. The land betterment tax of 1949 was replaced in 1963 by a very similar tax, the land appreciation tax. See Land Betterment Tax Law, 5109/1949, LSI, 3:86; Land Appreciation Tax Law, 5723/1963, LSI, 17:193. On the history of the estate tax see Daphna Hacker, "Intergenerational Wealth Transfer and the Need to Revive and Metamorphose the Israeli Estate Tax," *Law and Ethics of Human Rights* 8 (2014): 59–101.

[7] See Edwin Samuel, *Problems of Government in the State of Israel* (Jerusalem: R. Mass, 1956), 80. See also Mandel, *Hitpat'hut ha-Misim*, 16.

1950s by the leading Israeli politician of the time, David Ben-Gurion, Israel's first prime minister. It meant a commitment to the rule of law. It also meant giving precedence to the authority of the central government over that of various political parties and their sectarian institutions – institutions that dominated the life of the Jewish community in mandatory Palestine. In the specific Israeli context of the 1950s, *mamlakhtiyut* also included a call for "regimented voluntarism," or "statist pioneering," managed by the new state – that is, an approach that sought mass voluntary civic participation in addition to coercion in efforts to achieve the goals of the state.[8]

Creating a spirit of civic commitment in the 1950s was a challenge, and not merely because such a spirit is hard to generate and sustain over time. The challenge was deepened by the fact that, in that period, the 650,000 Jews living in Palestine at the time of Israeli independence in 1948 had to absorb almost a million Jewish refugees from Europe and the Middle East. Many of the refugees had little ideological allegiance to the Zionist ethos, and did not share the civic republican notions of solidarity that characterized the prestate Jewish community.[9] Ben-Gurion described these refugees in 1950 in the following way:

> [T]he overwhelming majority of [the Jewish refugees] are destitute in every way. Their property was taken from them, and they lack education

[8] On "regimented voluntarism" in 1950s Israel, see Dan Horowitz and Moshe Lissak, *Trouble in Utopia: The Overburdened Polity of Israel* (Albany: SUNY Press, 1989), 109. On varieties of statism versus voluntarism, and bureaucracy versus pioneering ethos, in 1950s Israel, see, e.g., Yaacov Shavit, "Meshihiyut, Utopiyah u-Pesimiyut bi-Shnot ha-Hamishim: 'Iyun ba-Bikoret 'al ha-Medinah ha-Ben-Guryonit," *'Iyunim bi-Tkumat Yisrael* 2 (1992): 56–78; Alan Dowty, "Israel's First Decade: Building a Civic State," in *Israel: The First Decade of Independence*, eds. S. Ilan Troen and Noah Lucas (Albany: SUNY Press, 1995), 31–50, 36–7; Avi Bareli, "Ha-Mamlakhtiyut ve-Tnu'at ha-'Avodah be-Reshit Shnot ha-Hamishim: Hanahot Mivniyot," in *Etgar ha-Ribonut: Yetsirah ve-Hagut ba-'Asor ha-Rishon la-Medinah*, ed. Mordechai Bar-On (Jerusalem: Yad Izhak Ben-Zvi, 1999), 23–44; Nir Kedar, "Ben-Gurion's *Mamlakhtiyut*: Etymological and Theoretical Roots," *Israel Studies* 7 (2002): 117–33; Avi Bareli, "*Mamlakhtiyut*, Capitalism and Socialism during the 1950s in Israel," *Journal of Israeli History* 26 (2007): 201–27; Nir Kedar, *Mamlakhtiyut: Ha-Tfisah ha-Ezrahit shel David Ben-Gurion* (Jerusalem: Yad Izhak Ben-Zvi, 2009); Avi Bareli and Nir Kedar, *Mamlakhtiyut Yisre'elit* (Jerusalem: IDI Press, 2011), 48–99.

[9] On changing attitudes to voluntarism after the establishment of the state, see, e.g., Paula Kabalo, "Halutsiyut u-Mekhuyavut Ezrahit 'al-pi David Ben-Gurion,

and culture ... The diasporic Jewish communities that are now disappearing and gathering in Israel do not constitute a nation yet, but are rather a mob [*'erev rav*] and human dust [*avak adam*] without a language, without education, without roots ... Transforming this human dust into a civilized, creative independent nation ... is no mean task. It requires a huge moral and educational effort, accompanied by deep and pure love.[10]

To achieve this transformation, the new Israeli state made heavy use of public relations tools of the kind exemplified by *The Tsippori Affair*. When the British-colonial state imposed income taxation in the 1940s, it made very little use of such techniques to persuade taxpayers to comply with the new tax.[11] In marked contrast, the Israeli state of the 1950s used such tools extensively, seeking to augment legal compulsion with social norms. This chapter tells the story of the transition between the tax system of 1940s mandatory Palestine and that of post-1948 Israel, focusing mostly on income taxation in the first decade after Israeli independence. It also examines the various means, legal and nonlegal, by which the new state attempted to encourage tax compliance.

1948–1955," in *Hevrah ve-Kalkalah be-Yisrael: Mabat Histori 'Akhshavi*, eds. Avi Bareli, Daniel Gutwein, and Tuvia Friling (Sde Boker: Ben-Gurion Institute Press, 2005), 773–802, 792; Anita Shapira, "Ben Yishuv le-Medinah: Ha-Markivim shelo 'Avru," in *Leumiyut u-Politikah Yehudit: Perspektivot Hadashot*, eds. Jehuda Reinharz, Yosef Salmon, and Gideon Shimoni (Jerusalem: Merkaz Shazar, 1996), 253–71; Orit Rozin, *The Rise of the Individual in 1950s Israel: A Challenge to Collectivism*, trans. Haim Watzman (Waltham, MA: Brandeis University Press, 2011); Anita Shapira, *Israel: A History*, trans. Anthony Berris (Waltham, MA: Brandeis University Press, 2012), 200–5; Yoav Peled, *The Challenge of Ethnic Democracy: The State and Minority Groups in Israel, Poland and Northern Ireland* (New York: Routledge, 2014), 95–118; Orit Rozin, *A Home for All Jews: Citizenship, Rights, and National Identity in the New Israeli State*, trans. Haim Watzman (Waltham, MA: Brandeis University Press, 2016), 3–4. For a concrete example of the way bottom-up voluntarism was blended with the top-down use of the power of the state in revenue-raising matters in the 1950s, see Moshe Naor, "The Israeli Volunteering Movement Preceding the 1956 War," *Israel Affairs* 16 (2010): 434–54. For the social and economic history of 1950s Israel, see, generally, Amir Ben-Porat, *Keytsad Na'astah Yisrael Kapitalistit* (Haifa: Pardes, 2011).

[10] David Ben-Gurion, *Yihud vi-Ye'ud* (Jerusalem: Misrad Rosh ha-Memshalah, 1950), 41–2.

[11] As we saw in Chapter 2, D. N. Strathie, the British income tax adviser, did make use of a radio talk to introduce the tax in May 1941. Films as a tool for education on

Tax Compliance in 1950s Israel

In the first months after the establishment of the state of Israel in 1948, there was some expectation that the new Israelis would eagerly pay their taxes, especially given the precarious security situation and the threat they faced during the Israeli War of Independence. David Z. Penkas, the chairman of the Israeli Parliament (Knesset) Finance Committee, somewhat naively declared in a 1950 speech that "every person in Israel should feel joy because he gained the right to pay taxes to the State of Israel. These taxes are used to ensure its existence and development. We [Jews] who paid taxes to many foreign nations during our long years of Exile have now finally won the right to pay taxes to ourselves."[12]

During the first months after independence, the desire to pay taxes to the new state may indeed have been strong. One tax official recalled that:

> even though the citizens of the new state knew that after independence they would have to pay higher taxes than those they paid until then to the [British] government of the mandate, they enthusiastically came to pay their taxes. Two well-known citizens of Haifa argue even today [in 1958] who was the first of them to pay income tax to the provisional government.[13]

Whether taxpayers gladly paid the taxes to the new state or not, it is clear that their enthusiasm soon waned. The change may have been due to the improvement in the security situation after the signing of armistice agreements with neighboring Arab states in 1949. Additional factors contributing to a decline in compliance were government-imposed austerity measures that eroded the population's standard of

---

taxation were sometimes used in other British territories. See, e.g., Rosaleen Smyth, "The Genesis of Public Relations in British Colonial Practice," *Public Relations Review* 27 (2001): 149–62, 153.

[12] DK, 5:1778 (June 20, 1950). See also Michael N. Barnett, *Confronting the Costs of War: Military Power, State, and Society in Egypt and Israel* (Princeton: Princeton University Press, 1992), 161–2.

[13] See H. Cohen, "Mas Hakhnasah bi-Yemey ha-Mandat veha-Ma'avar uve-Yamehah ha-Rishonim shel ha-Medinah," *Sherut* 8–9 (1958): 5, 9. On the other hand, in the Jerusalem area, which originally was not supposed to be part of the new Jewish state, some Jewish taxpayers refused to pay taxes that they owed to the government

living, and a series of compulsory loans that wrung more and more money from the new citizens.[14]

The decline in compliance was also the result of a change in the demographic composition of the country, as large waves of Jewish refugees flooded Israel in the 1950s. Israeli tax officials believed that absorbing these waves of refugees and turning them into compliant citizens (and taxpayers) was the major challenge they faced. In 1953, for example, one official wrote in the newsletter of the tax authority that there were differences in the "civic maturity" of various immigrants. Those who came from "enlightened" countries were apparently willing to pay taxes; those who came from "primitive" and "backward" countries tried to evade them; and those who came from countries where Jews were legally persecuted had turned their habit of not paying taxes to the government into second nature. In conclusion, this official urged colleagues to remember "that we are not merely building a homeland, we are also building a people, and we have a duty to educate the citizen [that taxation is a necessity]."[15]

A 1956 report written by Wayne Anderson, an American adviser to the Israeli government, argued that one of the major reasons for problems in tax collection in Israel was the heterogeneity of the population – a "new and divergent population that represented a tremendous education challenge." This population, said Anderson, came from countries where the tax authorities were seen as corrupt or were

of mandatory Palestine to the new Israeli state. See ISA, Gimel 275/33, Stein, Pkid Shumah Yerushalayim to ha-Moshel ha-Tsva'i Yerushalayim, October 24, 1948.

[14] Wilkenfeld, *Taxes and People in Israel*, 4–5, 54, 213–14. The austerity regime existed between 1949 and 1959, although its impact was mainly felt in the first two years of its existence. For a general description of this regime, see Tom Segev, *1949–Ha-Yisre'elim ha-Rishonim* (Jerusalem: Domino, 1984), 280–305; Rozin, *The Rise of the Individual*; Shapira, *Israel: A History*, 208–21. Compulsory loans are taxes. However, unlike taxes, the money levied is ultimately returned to the taxpayer, usually with no or little interest. The first compulsory loan was part of the new economic policy of 1952. It was followed by a series of loans and defense duties throughout the 1950s and 1960s. See Wilkenfeld, *Taxes and People in Israel*, 275–82; Mandel, *Hitpat'hut ha-Misim*, 78–103. The last such loan was imposed during the 1982 Lebanon war. See MT, file 787–806, Milvot Hovah; MT, file 807–19, Keren ha-Magen.

[15] A. Shtark, "'Od 'al Yahasey Tsibur," *YP* (October–November 1953): 50, 51. See also H. Viliamovski, "De'ot ve-Hasagot: Yahasey Tsibur," *YP* (April-May 1953): 20–1; M. Y., "'Al Saf ha-Shanah," *YP* (April 1954): 3–4.

nonexistent, and it represented the widest possible range of taxpayer attitudes:

> It had, and has, everything from the German-Jew or English-Jew, who came to Israel as a disciplined taxpayer, through the Romanian-Jew, who had only known an ineffective and corrupt tax system, to the Oriental-Jew, who had never been exposed to income taxation at all ... Immigrants, for the most part, had little or no knowledge of the national language, and the vast majority ... brought with them a deeply ingrained attitude to the effect that "the Government is our enemy".[16]

Another American adviser, Harold Wilkenfeld, also noted that evasion was an acute problem in Israel "because of the cultural diversity of its population. The adult population is still largely non-native born with diverse and frequently negative attitudes toward taxation."[17] Because the immigrants of the 1950s "came almost entirely from the concentration camps of Europe or from the developing societies of

[16] Anderson, *Income Tax Administration*, 2–3. An Israeli tax official, Arye Lapidoth, who quoted this passage thirteen years later, noted uneasily that "the statement contains a correct description of the differences in the attitudes to tax of the various groups ... [but] the generalization concerning the influence of the country of origin on the different types of behavior cannot, of course, be more accurate than any generalization of that kind." See Arye Lapidoth, *Evasion and Avoidance of Income Tax: A Comparative Study of English Law and Israeli Law* (Jerusalem: Museum of Taxes, 1966), 42. It seems, however, that some of the stereotypes persisted even later. I could not find statistical data from the 1950s or 1960s on differences in compliance between various subgroups within the Jewish population of Israel. Public opinion surveys conducted in the middle of the 1970s found slight differences in beliefs about compliance between native-born Israelis and Israelis who were born in Middle Eastern countries. See David Bar-Haim, "Sikery Da'at Kahal be-Nosei ha-Misim," *RYM* 9 (1974): 77, 79. For a general discussion of the link between compliance and ethnic heterogeneity, see Jeffrey A. Roth, John T. Scholz, and Ann D. Witte, eds., *Taxpayer Compliance*, vol. 1, *An Agenda for Research* (Philadelphia: University of Pennsylvania Press, 1989), 136–7; Kurt J. Beron, Helen V. Tauchen, and Ann Dryden Witte, "The Effects of Audits and Socioeconomic Variables on Compliance," in *Why People Pay Taxes: Tax Compliance and Enforcement*, ed. Joel Slemrod (Ann Arbor: University of Michigan Press, 1992), 67–90, 81–2; Natalie Taylor, "Understanding Taxpayer Attitudes through Understanding Taxpayer Identities," in *Taxing Democracy: Understanding Tax Avoidance and Evasion*, ed. Valerie A. Braithwaite (Aldershot: Ashgate, 2003), 71–92.

[17] Wilkenfeld, *Taxes and People in Israel*, 250.

the Middle East, few of them had had any experience of living as free citizens in a democratic society, and the sophisticated concepts of an income tax were a mystery to them."[18] Israel, he observed, was a country with a "developing citizenry."[19]

Sometimes tax evasion was identified as the mark of Diaspora Jews, the "other" of Zionist Israelis. Unwillingness to pay taxes, argued one official, "is so developed among us Jews ... that we cannot change this using the English gentlemanly approach ... we must find a specifically Jewish method to fight the Jewish evasion and avoidance [practices] that are the legacy of [the Jewish] Diaspora."[20] Another official observed that "as we know [in Israel] there is a tradition whose sources are found in the Diaspora of a hostile attitude toward any government and there are some parts of the Israeli population that do not have even the most elementary notions about the nature of government, and its role, and the rights and duties of citizens."[21] A satirical dialogue published in the newsletter of the tax authority in 1955 quoted a tax official telling a tax evader:

> Sir, you must understand,
> This is the law of the land,
> By the way even in Romania and Poland,
> You would not have evaded your taxes.[22]

In 1956 an Israeli tax official commented that "the [Israeli] citizen of today was until yesterday a wandering Jew, who did not see tax evasion as an immoral thing."[23] Haim Cohn, the Israeli Attorney General, said that Israelis still have a "diasporic" mentality and therefore do

[18] Ibid., 5–6.

[19] Ibid., preface. See also A. Sela, "Yakhasey Tsibur be-Minhal ha-Hakhnasot," *Sherut* 4 (1957): 21, 29; P. Rosen, "Hokhahah Muhashit le-Shilton Demokrati," *Sherut* 13 (1960): 10–11. For comparative insights see, e.g., Benno Torgler, "Tax Morale in Transition Countries," *Post-Communist Economies* 15 (2003): 357–81; Evan S. Lieberman, "How South African Citizens Evaluate Their Economic Obligations to the State," *Journal of Development Studies* 38 (2002): 37–62.

[20] Dov Ben-Amitai, "'Al ha-Ezrah Lemale Hovato," *YP* (April 1954): 65, 66.

[21] Gila Uriel, "Yahasey Tsibur," *YP* (December 1955): 5. A similar argument about the influence of the Diaspora, and a general discussion of Israeli attitudes to legal compliance, can be found in Ehud Sprinzak, *Ish ha-Yashar be-'Yenav: Illegalizm ba-Hevra ha-Yisre'elit* (Tel Aviv: Sifriyat Po'alim, 1986), 77–92.

[22] Aharon Moravchik, "Du-Siyah bi-Sha'at Bikoret," *YP* (December 1955): 23, 24.

[23] S. Josephsberg, "Ha-Ezrah veha-Mefake'ah," *Sherut* 3 (1956): 17.

not view tax evasion negatively.[24] Sometimes the taxpaying public was referred to as the "generation of the desert," a term often used in the 1950s to describe the new Jewish immigrants to Israel who, like their forefathers who had wandered in the Sinai desert for forty years, were not yet suited to a life of political independence.[25]

Whether evasion was indeed more prevalent among new immigrants from Europe and the Middle East or not, it became a major subject of parliamentary debates and newspaper articles.[26] In late 1953, an article published in the workers' daily *Davar* stated that of 560,000 breadwinners in Israel, only 300,000 were registered by the tax authority; 250,000 of those registered were employees and only 50,000 were self-employed. The article asserted that, out of the non-registered taxpayers, there were 150,000 self-employed individuals evading the income tax.[27] Another estimate published in 1956 claimed

---

[24] Haim Cohn, "[Symposium]: Shiput ve-Hamarat Mishpat be-Kofer Kesef," *Sherut* 5 (1957): 3, 5.

[25] H. L. M, "Be-Shuley ha-Psikah: 'Iru'urey Mas-Hakhnasah: Tafkid Beyt ha-Mishpat," *Ha-Praklit* 14 (1958): 97–9. See, generally, Assaf Likhovski, "'The Time Has Not Yet Come to Repair the World in the Kingdom of God': Israeli Lawyers and the Failed Jewish Legal Revolution of 1948," in *Jews and the Law*, eds. Marc Galanter et al. (New Orleans: Quid Pro Books, 2014), 359–83. Another aspect of noncompliance may have been lack of knowledge of Hebrew on the part of many taxpayers. The tax authority tried to deal with this problem by issuing tax information in the many foreign-language newspapers published in Israel at the time. For example, it published tax advice in Arabic, English, French, German, Hungarian, Romanian, and Polish newspapers. See MT, file entitled "Kir 33."

[26] See, e.g., DK, 2:1367 (August 24, 1949) (Knesset Finance Committee chairman Penkas declaring that there were 122,000 income tax payers but "tens of thousands of eligible payers do not pay the tax"); DK, 5:1803 (June 21, 1950) (Minister of Finance Kaplan complaining that tax evasion is a "national sport"); DK, 15:1527 (April 5, 1954) (Minister of Finance Eshkol stating that tax evasion is widespread); Shtark, "'Od 'al Yahasey Tsibur," 50, 52 ("the plague of tax evasion has engulfed all classes of the public"); "Leket min ha-'Itonut," YP (December 1955): 8, 9 (quoting an article in *Haaretz* that stated that "the general impression is very bad, both because [it seems] that the morality of the taxpayers is low, and [because] the efficiency of the tax authority [is also low]"); T. Brosh, "Be'ayat Bitsu'a Hok Mas Hakhnasah," *Sherut* 1 (1956): 3–4. There were isolated remarks to the contrary. See "Leket min ha-'Itonut," YP (December 1953): 57, 58 (the income tax commissioner stating that the number of tax evaders is not large).

[27] "Ha-Tafkid ha-Rishon: Tosefet 150,000 Meshalmey Mas-Hakhnasah," *Davar*, October 30, 1953, 10 reprinted in YP (December 1953): 60–1. See also Dov Ben-Amitai, "'Al ha-Ezrah Lemale Hovato," YP (April 1954): 65–6.

that, while employees were paying approximately 90 percent of the tax they owed, the self-employed were paying roughly 50–65 percent of the tax they owed.[28] The ability of the self-employed to evade taxation was a result of the fact that the tax on salaries was withheld at source by employers, while the self-employed were required to actively report their income by submitting tax returns, a feature many took advantage of by failing to do so.[29]

The period between 1951 and 1954 was thus one in which tax evasion was growing rapidly, a "wild west" era as far as tax compliance was concerned.[30] Initially, the government reacted to the problem by resorting to arbitrary assessment and collection methods. This, however, only made the crisis worse and led to a breakdown in the relationship between the public and the government.[31]

Contemporary sources are full of examples of how these arbitrary measures led to generalized mistrust of the tax authority. One example in found in an article written by the Israeli satirist, Ephraim Kishon, published in April 1954. In this article, Kishon suggested that, to balance the budget, the minister of finance should expropriate an ugly house in the middle of Tel Aviv, with artificially darkened rooms. The building would house fifty low-paid sour-faced officials. It should be crowded, with dilapidated cabinets, planned disorder, and queues that "last until tomorrow." A note should be posted on the door: "Office of Government Harassment." Then every citizen would be sent the following form:

> Notice of error according to the Errors Act 739015689/32. We are
> pleased to inform you that we examined your accounts for the current

---

[28] Anderson, *Income Tax Administration*, 5.

[29] Wilkenfeld, *Taxes and People in Israel*, 76–8. In Israel (as in the UK) most wage-earners are exempted from submitting annual returns. In 1976 a universal duty to report income was imposed, but the attempt proved to be a failure because the tax authority could not handle the number of returns submitted, and in 1977 this universal duty was abolished. See "Tfasey Divuah Yishalhu be-Yom Alef le-100,000 Hasrey Tikey Mas," *Davar*, October 14, 1976, 6; "Mas Hakhnasah Yevatel Hovat ha-Divuakh ha-Klalit," *Davar*, June 6, 1977, 8. On the relationship of a universal duty of submitting tax returns and fiscal citizenship in the United States, see generally, Lawrence Zelenak, *Learning to Love Form 1040: Two Cheers for the Return-Based Mass Income Tax* (Chicago: University of Chicago Press, 2013).

[30] Wilkenfeld, *Taxes and People in Israel*, 3; Cohn, "Shiput ve-Hamarat Mishpat," 3, 8.

[31] Wilkenfeld, *Taxes and People in Israel*, 90.

year and found an error, an unpaid debt of 9.040 pounds in our favor. If you want to dispute this unfortunate error, you will have to stand in line for a period of three days from the receipt of the notice, from eight o'clock in the morning, and submit detailed arguments. Please bring with you, when submitting your appeal, documents on your income from 1938 until the present, a certificate of good conduct from the police, and a chart of your residence signed by the municipality. On the other hand, if you would like to pay your debt, you do not need to come. You can send the amount by post, and that's it. Signed, Dr. Y. Bar-Bitsu'a, Harassment Office.[32]

A similar example of public distrust in the tax authority can be found in a letter written by the well-known literary critic Baruch Kurzweil in 1955. After his income was assessed at I£ (Israeli Pounds) 7,000, Kurzweil sent a letter to the assessing officer, in which he wrote: "I hereby appoint you as the Emperor of Japan and the Pacific Ocean. This appointment is as realistic [as your assessment of my income]."[33]

In 1954 the issue of the relative tax burden on employees and the self-employed became a major locus of political contention between the socialist-led government, on the one hand, and the right-wing Herut and centrist General Zionists parties, on the other. The political conflict resulted in numerous strikes by artisans and shopkeepers. The conflict reached a climax in October 1954 when a Jerusalem taxpayer, Israel Sinai, committed suicide, leaving a note blaming the income tax for his decision. Mr. Sinai's suicide was followed by a major tax strike and the establishment of a special government committee to study the circumstances of his death. It also served as a catalyst for a major reform of the Israeli tax administration system, although reform efforts had already begun earlier with the establishment in late 1953 of a committee, headed by Ze'ev Sharef, Secretary of the Israeli Cabinet, to examine tax assessment and collection methods (Sharef would later be appointed Director of State

---

[32] Ephraim Kishon, "Had Gadya: Le-Sar Otsari Shalom Rav," *Ma'ariv*, April 2, 1954, at 8. See also Gidi Nevo, "Ha-Satirah ha-Burganit shel Ephraim Kishon," in Bareli et al., eds., *Hevrah ve-Kalkalah*, 711–45, 732–3.

[33] TM exhibit, Kurzweil to Pkid ha-Shumah, undated letter. See also Nir Hasson, "Lamah Ka'asah Lea Goldberg 'al Pkid ha-Mas," *Haaretz*, May 18, 2012, at 1, 16.

Revenue at the Ministry of Finance, the body responsible for formulating Israeli tax policy).[34]

"Training in Citizenship": Creating Tax Compliance

The Israeli Ministry of Finance was aware of the problem of widespread tax evasion. One factor that initially inhibited change was the
fact that many officials of the Israeli Tax Authority began their careers
in the voluntary Jewish tax system of the 1940s. These officials sometimes assumed that the high compliance levels they experienced in the
1940s would not decline, an assumption that soon proved unrealis-
tic.[35] Ultimately, however, they came to realize that a major overhaul
was needed. In the process of administrative reform, the Ministry of
Finance relied on the guidance of a number of foreign advisers affiliated with the UN Technical Assistance Program, the US Agency for
International Development, and the International Monetary Fund
(IMF).[36]

An obvious method for tackling evasion was to resort to the criminal sanctions found in the tax legislation inherited from the British
rulers of Palestine. Criminal prosecution of income tax evaders began
in 1952. Initially, it proved unsuccessful because the Income Tax
Ordinance did not provide sufficient penalties for evasion,[37] but in
1954 the Income Tax Ordinance was amended to increase criminal

[34] Wilkenfeld, *Taxes and People in Israel*, 7–13. See also "Taxes, Cost of Living Led to
   Suicide," *JP*, October 4, 1954, at 3; "Hit'abed me-Hamat 'Omes ha-Misim" *Haaretz*,
   October 3, 1954, at 4; "P.M. Orders 'Tax Suicide' Inquiry," *JP*, October 20, 1954,
   at 3; "Suicide Held not Responsible for Impending Tax Strike," *JP*, October 26,
   1954, at 3; "Sinai C'ttee Clears Tax Authorities," *JP*, November 1, 1954, at 1, 2. Tax
   strikes were common in 1954. The year began with another strike by small businessmen and artisans. See "Shops to Close in Tax Protest," *JP*, January 29, 1954, at 3;
   "Artisans Call Two-Day Strike in Protest of 'Fantastic' Taxes," *JP*, February 8, 1954,
   at 3. On the reform committee, see Avraham Mandel, ed., *Sefer ha-Yovel shel Agaf
   Mas Hakhnasah u-Mas Rekhush* (Tel Aviv: Yedioth Ahronoth ve-Muze'on le-Misim,
   1992), 82, 88. See also ISA Gimel Lamed 12544/31.

[35] Wilkenfeld, *Taxes and People in Israel*, 55, 56, 117.

[36] Ibid., 7–8, 121, 123.

[37] For an extensive discussion of the history of criminal prosecutions and their effect
   on compliance in the 1950s and 1960s, see Wilkenfeld, *Taxes and People in Israel*,
   209–51. An additional reason for the lack of success was the fact that the Israeli tax

penalties for tax evasion, and a policy of more vigorous enforcement was adopted.[38] In the mid-1950s judges still tended to impose fines on tax evaders, but in 1959 the first jail sentence was imposed.[39] By 1960 the income tax commissioner was claiming that the proportion of criminal prosecutions for tax evasion in relation to the number of taxpayers in Israel was one of the highest in the world.[40]

Another legal change that occurred in the mid-1950s was increased reliance by the Israeli Tax Authority on the use of legal norms instead of administrative discretion. In early 1955 a legal adviser to the income tax department was appointed – a move that led to "a more professional attitude" toward tax assessment. Compromises and negotiation were now sometimes replaced by the use of courts to determine legal

---

administration system was still relatively unorganized, and therefore courts tended to impose light sentences on offenders, taking into consideration the fact that the system was not functioning properly. Wilkenfeld, *Taxes and People in Israel*, 209–11; Shtark, "'Od 'al Yahasey Tsibur," 50, 52. The exact date of the first case in which criminal charges for income tax evasion were filed is not clear. Compare Wilkenfeld, *Taxes and People in Israel*, 209; "School Director Freed of Tax Charges," *JP*, July 6, 1950, at 3; "First Trial in Israel on Income Tax Fraud," *JP*, March 7, 1952, at 3; "Gov't Files Criminal Suit for Non-Payment of Income Taxes," *JP*, February 3, 1953, at 3. On the 1953 campaign, see "Ha-Pe'ulah neged Ma'alimey Mas," *YP* (December 1953): 63. See also CrimC (Haifa)486/53 AG v. Z. S., reprinted in *YP* (December 1953): 67; CA 276/53 *Kahana* v. *AG*, PD, 8:404 (fining tax evaders, stating that the fact that the tax authority had not prosecuted offenders before was a mitigating factor); "Criminal Cases," *YP* (April 1954): 75 (reporting criminal cases decided by the Tel Aviv District Court in February 1954).

[38] See, e.g., DK, 15:1527 (April 5, 1954) (discussing the 1954 Income Tax Ordinance Amendment Law that sought to increase the penalties for tax evasion); Lapidoth, *Evasion and Avoidance of Income Tax*, 121. An additional set of sanctions, which relied on the "State of Emergency Regulations (Exit from the Country), 1948," allowed the minister of immigration to prevent travel abroad of people who failed to pay their taxes. See Orit Rozin, "Negotiating the Right to Exit the Country in 1950s Israel: Voice, Loyalty, and Citizenship," *Journal of Israeli History* 30 (2011): 1–22, 18 n. 41; Orit Rozin, "Israel and the Right to Travel Abroad 1948–1961," *Israel Studies* 15 (2010): 147–76, 154; Mandel, *Sefer ha-Yovel*, 68–9, 82, 86.

[39] Wilkenfeld, *Taxes and People in Israel*, 214–24; Y. Wilkenfeld, "Zkhuyot Meshalmey ha-Misim lefi Pkudat Mas Hakhnasah," *Sherut* 1 (1956): 5–6; T. Brosh, "Agaf Mas Hakhnasah bi-Shnat 1955/6" *Sherut* 1 (1956): 34, 35.

[40] "Pgishat Havrey ha-Lishkah 'Im Netsigey Shiltonot ha-Mas," *RH* 10 (1959/60): 135, 140–1. See also Wilkenfeld, *Taxes and People in Israel*, 241–2; Lapidoth, *Evasion and Avoidance of Income Tax*, 122–3.

questions arising during the assessment process. A related administrative step, taken in 1958, was to separate the assessment and collection functions of the income tax department, so that the assessment process would be free of the influence of collection considerations.[41]

However, the use of criminal sanctions and the increasing turn to legal formalism were not the only means used to fight evasion. The tax authority also experimented with various nonlegal methods for creating compliance. These methods included the improvement in data collection, the reduction of friction, individualization, and the creation of social norms that would encourage compliance. I now discuss each of these methods in turn.

Improvement in Data Collection

One major feature of mid-1950s tax administration reform was the attempt to improve and rationalize the Israeli Tax Authority's data collection machinery to better monitor the taxpaying population.[42] One example of this approach was an income tax census undertaken in 1953.[43] Another example from the same year was the establishment of an intelligence collection unit (*shin alef*) employing about thirty-five agents, whose task was to gather information from various publicly available sources that might be relevant to the assessment of specific taxpayers. This unit also conducted undercover (and illegal) investigations of individual and corporate taxpayers suspected of evasion and other economic crimes. For example, it obtained information by breaking into banks to photograph confidential documents of suspected evaders. When information about such activities of the unit was leaked to the press in 1957, public outcry led to its disbandment. It was replaced by an information collection unit that relied only on publicly available sources.[44]

---

[41] Mandel, *Sefer ha-Yovel*, 116.

[42] On taxation and information collection, see generally Yanni Kotsonis, *States of Obligation: Taxes and Citizenship in the Russian Empire and Early Soviet Republic* (Toronto: University of Toronto Press, 2014). On the relationship of information collection and state construction, see, e.g., Silvana Patriarca, *Numbers and Nationhood: Writing Statistics in Nineteenth-Century Italy* (Cambridge: Cambridge University Press, 1996).

[43] "Income Tax Census Begun," *JP*, January 22, 1953, at 1.

[44] Wilkenfeld, *Taxes and People in Israel*, 219–20. See also N. Birkenfeld, "Ha-Mahlakah le-Hakirot vele-Mishpatim Plilim," *Sherut* 10 (1959): 56–7; "Shin Alef

Extensive activities were also undertaken to encourage formal bookkeeping.[45] In the early 1950s it was estimated that about 95 percent of the self-employed did not keep any books for tax purposes.[46] The original Income Tax Ordinance did not contain any provisions regarding bookkeeping. It was only in 1952 that the act was amended and a section empowering the income tax commissioner to demand bookkeeping was enacted, with the first regulations issued in 1953.[47] Rather than imposing a universal bookkeeping requirement, these regulations only covered certain professions such as medicine, law, and engineering.[48] In 1955 the regulations extended the requirements to include artisans and traders. In conjunction with the expansion of the legal requirements, American technical advisers to the Israeli Tax Authority created model account books and developed instructions for taxpayers in bookkeeping methods.[49] Nevertheless, by the end of the 1950s only about 12 percent of the self-employed were formally required to keep books.[50]

Because many returns filed in the early 1950s were unreliable, and because bookkeeping requirements were initially imposed only on a small group of taxpayers, the tax authority had to find other means to arrive at realistic assessments. The solution it identified was to provide its officers with standard assessment guides (*tahshivim*) based on economic research conducted by the Office of the Income Tax Commissioner.[51] These guides contained rules to calculate the

---

[Ad.]," *Ma'ariv*, October 18, 1957, at 10; "Shmo shel Rosh ha-Shin Alef Yaacov Cohen Nimsar le-Va'adat ha-Ksafim shel ha-Knesset," *Ma'ariv*, November 13, 1957, at 1; Yeshaayahu Avi'am, "Hayav ha-Kfulim shel Rosh ha-Shin Alef," *Ma'ariv*, November 14, 1957, at 2; Zvi Lavi, "'Ha-Ah ha-Gadol' be-Sherut Mas Hakhnasah," *Ynet*, April 23, 2007, www.ynet.co.il/articles/0,7340,L-3391144,00.html; Zvi Lavi, "Kesheha-Shabak Hitlabesh 'al Mas Hakhnasah," *Ynet*, May 7, 2008, www.ynet.co.il/articles/0,7340,L-3540123,00.html.

[45] Anderson, *Income Tax Administration*, 7–12; Lapidoth, *Evasion and Avoidance of Income Tax*, 81–9.

[46] Anderson, *Income Tax Administration*, 3.

[47] Lapidoth, *Evasion Evasion and Avoidance of Income Tax*, 83.

[48] Wilkenfeld, *Taxes and People in Israel*, 155; Mandel, *Sefer ha-Yovel*, 82.

[49] Anderson, *Income Tax Administration*, 11.

[50] H. S. Loewenberg, "Ha-Shumah veha-Shfitah," *Sherut* 15 (1961): 6.

[51] Such techniques were, of course, not new. On their use in the UK in the nineteenth century, see Chantal Stebbings, "Popular Perceptions of Income Tax Law in the

income of a given taxpayer when the assessing officer had "reasonable grounds for believing that the return [was] not correct." In such cases, the assessing officer could "determine to the best of his judgment the amount of the person's income."[52] The guides were meant to formalize the use of official discretion by providing average measures of income for various professions. The first guides were prepared to assess the income of farmers because they were considered to be "inclined ... to be resentful of authority and very difficult to assess." Many farmers were Arabs, who were considered to be less loyal to the state and more prone to tax evasion. The guides were therefore seen as "a great help in bringing the Arab farmers into the tax network on a fair and scientific basis." After creating such guides for different agricultural occupations, subsequent guides were prepared for various types of food producers, retail establishments, craftsmen, and service providers.[53] Their content was extremely detailed. For example, the guide dealing with hairdressing provided extensive information about the prices of such services as haircuts, perming, eyelash and eyebrow tinting, manicures, and depilation.[54]

The use of these standard guides was viewed as a temporary measure until bookkeeping became more prevalent. It was also seen as a way to increase the objectivity of the tax assessment process and even to involve groups of taxpayers in it (since some of the guides were prepared with the cooperation of representatives of the businesses concerned). The guides were also considered a means to scientize tax assessments as they were prepared by social science experts using statistics.[55]

In another sense, though, one can see their use as a retrograde step in the process of developing an accurate tax system. The reliance of

Nineteenth Century: A Local Tax Rebellion," *Journal of Legal History* 22 (2001): 45–71, 50. On their use in Israel, see Aharon Yoran, "Taxation of Small Firms in Israel," *Israel Law Review* 8 (1973): 312–16, 313–14. See generally Shlomo Yitzhaki, "Cost-Benefit Analysis of Presumptive Taxation," *FinanzArchiv / Public Finance Analysis* 63 (2007): 311–26.

[52] This section is currently Income Tax Ordinance, 1961, sec. 145(a)(2)(b).

[53] Lapidoth, *Evasion and Avoidance of Income Tax*, 79–81; Wilkenfeld, *Taxes and People in Israel*, 144–5.

[54] ISA Gimel 7545/2, Tahshiv le-Ba'aley Misparot le-Gvarot, 7.

[55] Wilkenfeld, *Taxes and People in Israel*, 144–50.

the tax authority on statistical measures of income (rather than on the income declared by taxpayers) echoed previous types of taxes such as the Ottoman *temettu*, the vocation tax of the late Ottoman Empire, that was mainly based on the presumed income of various categories of taxpayers and resembled a classified poll tax (that is, a poll tax with different rates for different vocational categories) more than an income tax. Another problematic aspect of these guides was that they were often based on negotiations with relevant business groups, whose interest, of course, was to minimize their taxes. Indeed, some of these groups were created mainly to achieve a favorable, minimal, tax assessment for their members.[56] This led to scathing critiques of the guides. Their widespread use was ended in 1975, although presumptive taxation is still in use in the Israeli diamond industry.[57]

A related initiative intended to provide more data on taxpayers was the farm inventory program. Its aim was to provide information on which to base the tax assessments of farmers, who had previously been covered by agreements relieving them of the responsibility for filing individual returns. In 1955 American advisers to the Israeli Tax Authority conducted a pilot program to map farm inventories in three Israeli villages. Based on the success of this project, they devised a plan

[56] Ibid., 146–7.

[57] Baruch Nadel, *Doh Nadel: Hakol 'al Mas ha-Hakhnasah be-Yisrael* (Tel Aviv: A. L. Hotsa'ah Meyuhedet, 1975). On the change in 1975, see, e.g., Yitzhaki, "Cost-Benefit Analysis of Presumptive Taxation," 315–16. According to a 1981 tax authority circular, the reason that presumptive taxation continued to be used in the diamond industry was that this industry was exempt from the bookkeeping requirements enforced in other sectors of the economy, because most of the transactions of diamond merchants were in foreign currencies, and because these transactions were carried out as part of a "special system committed to personal trust and secrecy." See Income Tax Circular 10/1981 (1981), reprinted in Alexander Rechter, *Diney Yahalomim* (Tel Aviv: Shaham, [1984/85]), 1144. A similar system of presumptive taxation also exists in Belgium, which is another center of the global diamond industry. See Misrad Mevaker ha-Medinah, *Doh Shnati 65A* (Jerusalem, 2014), 455, 472, www.mevaker. gov.il/he/Reports/Report_266/5b38bb3e-0acd-427a-895d-d11887160ee9/209-ver-4.pdf. The reason for such secrecy, according to an internal magazine of the Israeli diamond industry, was that foreign buyers and sellers often contravened the laws of their own countries when selling or buying Israeli diamonds. See, e.g., "Tshuvah la-Mashmitsim!" *Ha-Yahalom: Ktav ha-'Et li-Ve'ayot ha-Yahalomim* 46 (May 1975): 6, 11.

for a comprehensive survey of farm inventories in all tax districts and for creating a national land map for tax purposes.[58]

An additional "scientific" tool used in the process of reform was taxpayer surveys. In 1954 the Ministry of Finance enlisted the Israel Institute for Applied Social Research to conduct a survey of approximately two thousand taxpayers to measure taxpayer attitudes. Other taxpayer surveys were carried out in subsequent years.[59] In 1962 the State Revenue Administration Division in the Israeli Ministry of Finance hired a sociologist to advise it on increasing tax compliance.[60] In 1974 the Ministry of Finance began a weekly public opinion survey. The survey attempted to determine the scope of noncompliance by asking respondents whether they believed taxpayers generally complied with the income tax laws.[61]

Minimizing Friction

One important goal of the administrative reforms of the mid-1950s was to decrease conflict between taxpayers and the state, thus assuring smoother and more efficient operation of the tax collection machinery.[62] The grip on small taxpayers, who were not providing

---

[58] Anderson, *Income Tax Administration*, 20–1. For interesting analogies, see Timothy Mitchell, *Rule of Experts: Egypt, Techno-Politics, Modernity* (Berkeley: University of California Press, 2002), 80–119.

[59] See *The Taxpayer and Income Tax: Final Report on a National Survey Conducted by the Israel Institute of Applied Social Research Jerusalem, February 1955* (Jerusalem: The Institute of Applied Social Research, 1955) (a copy of this report can be found in the NLI); Wilkenfeld, *Taxes and People in Israel*, 96; Y. Artzi, "Yahasey Tsibur be-Minhal ha-Hakhnasot," *Sherut* 4 (1957): 21, 23; Mandel, *Sefer ha-Yovel*, 100.

[60] Wilkenfeld, *Taxes and People in Israel*, 114–15. The experience proved to be a failure, and when the sociologist left the tax authority in 1964, he was not replaced by a new adviser. See Yehezkel Dror, "Public Administration: Four Cases from Israel and the Netherlands," in *The Uses of Sociology*, eds. Paul F. Lazarsfeld, William H. Sewell, and Harold L. Wilensky (New York: Basic Books, 1967), 418–26, 420–1.

[61] D. Bar-Haim, "Sikrey Da'at Kahal be-Nosei ha-Misim," *RYM* 9 (1974): 77–81. About 20 percent of the respondents replied that they believed that the majority of taxpayers did not comply.

[62] Wilkenfeld, *Taxes and People in Israel*, 15, 95–6. See also Artzi, "Yahasey Tsibur." On the public demand for a more efficient civil service in the 1950s, see generally Paula Kabalo, "Beyn Ezrahim le-Medinah Hadashah: Sipurah shel Shurat ha-Mitnadvim,"

much revenue, was relaxed to focus more on larger taxpayers. Tax officials were encouraged to communicate with most taxpayers by letter or telephone. An explicit effort was also made "to break taxpayers of the habit of dropping in to the offices [of tax officials] without appointment."[63]

Specific attention was paid to redesigning the assessing offices in which taxpayers met tax officials. In Tel Aviv, for example, one assessing office was initially housed in a bank building. The tax inspectors sat together in a large open space. "With many conversations going on simultaneously, the general noise level was very high, frequently penetrated by cries of anguish or outrage ... the general atmosphere was more like a marketplace than a government office."[64] The redesign of office space was carried out based on advice given by two special advisers sent to Israel by the American government. These advisers established a model income tax office in Netanya, a small town north of Tel Aviv. They created an office in which there was an information clerk near the entrance, seats were provided for waiting taxpayers, and the filing system was improved to eliminate delays in supplying inspectors with files for interviews.[65] Studies were also carried out to improve the flow of work in tax offices by paying attention to such features as signage, lighting, ashtrays, decoration, and furniture.[66]

Interest in the maintenance of files and in filing technology also played an important role in the effort to improve service and reduce friction between taxpayers and the state. In the anarchical period immediately before the British left Palestine, Jewish employees of the mandate government were instructed by the Jewish shadow government

'Iyunim bi-Tkumat Yisrael 13 (2003): 203–32, 210–11, 214–17; Nevo, "Ha-Satirah," 711, 731–3.

[63] Wilkenfeld, *Taxes and People in Israel*, 96, 98–9; T. Brosh, "Yahasey Tsibur be-Minhal ha-Hakhnasot" *Sherut* 4 (1957): 21, 30. See also Nevo, "Ha-Satirah," 733.

[64] Wilkenfeld, *Taxes and People in Israel*, 96.

[65] Wilkenfeld, *Taxes and People in Israel*, 95; Anderson, *Income Tax Administration*, 19. There were earlier attempts during the period of the British mandate to create private spaces for tax collectors. In Tel Aviv, for example, small rooms were created in the income tax office building in order to give tax officials some privacy when meeting taxpayers. See Mandel, *Sefer ha-Yovel*. 27. See also Ilana Feldman, *Governing Gaza: Bureaucracy, Authority, and the Work of Rule, 1917–1967* (Durham, NC: Duke University Press, 2008), 105–6.

[66] Artzi, "Yahasey Tsibur."

to protect British income tax files from destruction. In some towns, tax offices were located in areas that became battlegrounds between Jews and Arabs, and it seems that some Jewish employees even risked their lives to save the files so that income tax collection could proceed smoothly after the British left.[67]

In the mid-1950s filing technology became a major aspect of tax reform. As files were arguably the most important material object of the precomputer-age tax administration, the interest in filing technology is not surprising.[68] One "important achievement" of the American technical advisers' mission to Israel, they reported, was "the installation of file cabinets, and two types of patented files" in the model income tax office that they had helped set up. In this office, the new patented files and filing cabinets replaced the previous open-shelf filing system and the "antiquated British files ... [of] the type in which papers are fastened by a string." Filing a paper in the old British files, it was explained, was "a real chore when the paper pertains to a tax year toward the bottom of the file and scores of papers must be removed from the file and the string then must be rethreaded through all of these papers." One new kind of patented file, the advisers enthused, "even allows keeping each year's papers under a separate spring, and a new paper can be readily slipped under these springs without disturbing or moving other papers in the file."[69] Filing technology was augmented by the mechanization of routine operations, first by using adding machines and creating a central card index of taxpayers, and later, in the mid-1960s, by computerization (see Figure 4.2).[70]

Since files were a highly visible component of the tax collection machinery, they also became a physical symbol of tax protests. In one 1957 incident, a taxpayer burned 200 files in a Tel Aviv income tax office after his request to postpone payment of tax arrears was refused (unfortunately for him, his personal file escaped the fire).[71]

---

[67] ISA, Gimel 115/27, Arian to Kaplan, April 25, 1948. See also Mandel, *Sefer ha-Yovel*, 55; Wilkenfeld, *Taxes and People in Israel*, 72.

[68] See Feldman, *Governing Gaza*, 31–61.

[69] Anderson, *Income Tax Administration*, 18–19.

[70] Wilkenfeld, *Taxes and People in Israel*, 127–34.

[71] "Tax Defaulter Burns Files, But His Escapes," *JP*, October 16, 1957, at 3.

FIGURE 4.2 Adding machines used by Israeli tax clerks in the 1960s.

Individualization

Israel, like many other mid-twentieth-century states, sought to "undercut the intermediary structures between the state and the citizen and [give] the state, for the first time, direct access to its subjects."[72] In 1950s Israel, this process took on special importance. Israeli society in the 1950s preserved, to a large extent, the social structure of prestate Jewish society in Palestine, a society in which labor unions, political parties, and affiliated organizations played an important role as intermediaries between individuals and the state.[73] Specifically in tax matters, such groups often successfully negotiated special extralegal tax concessions for their members, using tax strikes to achieve their goals. The importance of breaking the power of intermediate groups operating between the state and the individual was therefore self-evident.[74]

---

[72] James C. Scott, *Seeing Like a State: How Certain Schemes to Improve the Human Condition Have Failed* (New Haven: Yale University Press, 1998), 365 n. 61.

[73] See, e.g., Paula Kabalo, *Shurat ha-Mitnadvim: Korotav shel Irgun Ezrahim* (Tel Aviv: 'Am 'Oved, 2007), 19–25.

[74] Y. Shadmi, "Madu'a Son'im Etslenu et Mas ha-Hakhnasah: 'Im Yahsanim 'Osim 'Hesder Meyuhad'," *Ma'ariv*, December 21, 1959, at 3; Wilkenfeld, *Taxes and People in Israel*, 88–9.

An instructive example of such an attempt relates to the new bookkeeping regulations enacted in 1955. Income tax officials had been negotiating with a number trade organizations (representing, for example artisans, pharmacists, and bakers) that were seeking various concessions from the drafters of the regulations. But they also tried to address taxpayers directly, bypassing these groups. When it became clear that there was serious resistance to the requirements of the regulations, letters were sent directly to taxpayers informing them of their new obligations, thus undercutting the power of trade unions and chambers of commerce that opposed the regulations.[75]

Another example of the attempt to directly interact with individual taxpayers can be found in the history of the farm inventory program mentioned earlier. Jewish farmers in Israel were incorporated in political organizations that obtained various tax concessions from the government. One such concession was that certain farmers would be exempt from the responsibility of filing individual tax returns. The farm inventory program was designed, among other things, to undermine this concession and allow the tax authority to "deal confidently with those farmers formerly covered by agreements [exempting them from reporting]."[76]

Attempts to prevent individual resistance were also present in specific physical encounters between taxpayers and tax officials. A public relations official working for the tax authority observed that:

> The waiting room in the tax official's office is the gathering ground of the citizen before the decisive battle [with tax officials], and the question is to what extent we should give him additional ammunition in the last moment before the onslaught, or whether we should weaken him. If the wall is not empty and if instead of two or three angry citizens waiting in the waiting room, one inciting the other as tension grows, if instead we give him reading materials, if something attractive is hanging on the wall, a tension-reducing caricature, a pleasing diagram – this will reduce tension.[77]

---

[75] Anderson, *Income Tax Administration*, 11–12.

[76] Ibid., 20–1.

[77] Artzi, "Yahasey Tsibur," 24.

Dealing with groups of people instead of isolating taxpayers and dealing with them individually would lead to fewer taxes being collected, observed this official, recounting a visit he had made to an office in which the tax collector's desk was located at the main entrance. The dialogue between the collector and a taxpayer was heard by all the other taxpayers present in the room. Since the tax collector often agreed to compromise with the taxpayer, the other taxpayers naturally demanded to be treated in the same way, thus causing a chain reaction. This problem could be prevented, noted the official, if the desk were placed in a different location within the office that would guarantee the privacy of dealings with individual taxpayers.[78]

Creating Social Norms: Education, Trust, and Community Pressure

A final, and major, aspect of the mid-1950s tax reform program was concerned with the creation of social norms that would encourage Israelis to voluntarily comply with the tax system. Law, remarked one Israeli official in 1953:

> usually constitutes an outside force whose influence on the soul is weak. [Law] is a gazing eye ['ayin tsofiyah] or a punishing hand, but it is an eye that cannot gaze into the distance and a hand, although it may be strong, that cannot enter nooks and crannies ... [W]illingness [to pay taxes] can only be awakened by education ... [W]e will not be able to fulfill our role as long as we do not engage in proper public relations [hasbarah]."[79]

The kind of propaganda that was typical of the voluntary tax system of the 1940s continued in the 1950s. Newspaper advertisements and articles, explanatory pamphlets, public meetings with taxpayers, and organized tours of tax offices were all employed to convince taxpayers that taxes were important and that, when they were paying taxes to the state, they were actually paying themselves.[80] Courses were

---

[78] Ibid., 25.

[79] H. Viliamovski, "Yahasey Tsibur (Hemshekh)," *YP* (June–July 1953): 15–16.

[80] Wilkenfeld, *Taxes and People in Israel*, 91, 100–1, 104; "You Pay Yourself!" [Ad.], *JP*, December 23, 1952, at 3; MT, file entitled "Musafim le-'Inyeney Misim." For similar methods elsewhere, see, e.g., Carolyn C. Jones, "Class Tax to Mass Tax: The Role

designed to familiarize secondary school students with the notion of taxation and to instill the importance of tax compliance from an early age.[81] It was also suggested that lessons in taxation would be taught in the armed forces, because, said one American observer, the army was "Israel's most important institution for training in citizenship."[82]

In 1958 Avraham Mandel, the State Revenue Administration Division spokesman, suggested the creation of a museum of taxes. Mandel was an artist and head of the Jerusalem Artists Association, but he also served as a Ministry of Finance official. In creating the museum he was inspired by similar ventures in Rotterdam and Siegburg (Germany).[83] The museum, which finally opened in 1964, was designed

of Propaganda in the Expansion of the Income Tax during World War II," *Buffalo Law Review* 37 (1988): 685–737; Carolyn C. Jones, "Mass-Based Income Taxation: Creating a Taxpaying Culture, 1940–1952," in *Funding the Modern American State, 1941–1995: The Rise and Fall of the Era of Easy Finance*, ed. W. Elliot Brownlee (Washington, DC: Woodrow Wilson Center Press, 1996), 107–47; Ajay K. Mehrotra, "Anger, Irony, and the Formal Rationality of Professionalism," *Law and History Review* 28 (2010): 241–48, 243.

[81] Anderson, *Income Tax Administration*, 22 (reporting a proposal "to assist the Ministry of Education in the development of lessons on taxation to be taught in the secondary schools"); "School Students to Study Tax System," *JP*, December 14, 1956, at 2; Artzi, "Yahasey Tsibur," 23 (reporting a seminar for history and civics teachers in high schools on tax matters). The initial attempts to create such courses were not very successful. See Wilkenfeld, *Taxes and People in Israel*, 108–9. However, they were more successful in the 1960s. See Shulamit Aloni, "'Al ha-Hinukh le-Toda'at ha-Mas ke-Korakh Tsodek," *RYM* 3 (1968): 205–7 (a member of the Knesset calling for the creation of a special course on taxation in schools); Z. Kessler, "[Book Review]: Ma'arekhet ha-Misim be-Yisrael: Homer 'Ezer la-Moreh be-Nos'e ha-Misim," *RYM* 4 (1969): 346.

[82] Anderson, *Income Tax Administration*, 22. On the use of schools and the army as tools of the state to instill notions of citizenship (and a pioneering ethos), see Kabalo, "Halutsiyut u-Mehuyavut," 781, 784–7; Paula Kabalo, "Pioneering Discourse and the Shaping of an Israeli Citizen in the 1950s," *Jewish Social Studies: History, Culture, Society* 15:2 (2009): 82–110.

[83] Avraham Mandel, *Ha-Muze'on le-Misim bi-Yerushalyim* (Jerusalem: Minhal Hakhnasot ha-Medinah: Ha-Otsar, 1989), 4. See also MT, file entitled "Muze'onim ba-'Olam." On Mandel (sometimes spelled in English Mande'el or Mandl), see Gabriel Talpir, "Avraham Mandel," *Gazit: Yarhon le-Omanut ve-Sifrut* 27:9–12 (1970/71): 79–80; *Jerusalemer Künstler, 1975* ([Bremen]: [Kunsthalle Bremen], 1975), 6; Agudat ha-Tsayarim veha-Pasalim – ha-Va'ad ha-Tsiburi: Beyt Chagall, *Hamishim Omanim* (Tel Aviv: Masada, n.d.), 32; Aharon Avramson, "Ma'asey

"to develop among the general public a better understanding of the role of the tax system and of the relationship between proper taxpaying and good citizenship." The subtext to this initiative was perhaps also the message that taxation was not invented by the Israeli government, but was an inevitable fact of nature, and that there was no reason to complain because in the past the system had been even tougher on both taxpayers and evaders. Another possible reason for the establishment of the museum may have been that it was meant "to serve as a source of inspiration and pride" for tax officials. Visitors' reactions were enthusiastic: "I did not believe that one [could] find such a subject, that is really so dry, exciting, [but] I did," wrote one visitor in the guestbook.[84]

The museum published booklets to acquaint the general public with taxation, and books celebrating the history of the Israeli Tax Authority.[85] It also published a series of academic studies on the history of taxation.[86] While some of the works dealt with modern history,

Misim," *Be-Sheva* 15 (November 13, 1987), www.inn.co.il/Besheva/Article.aspx/1089; Yivsam Azgad, "Makhnisim et Mas Hakhnasah la-Muze'on," http://azgad.com/?p=1149; Hasson, "Lamah Ka'asah Lea Goldberg"; Mira Dror (Director of the Museum of Taxes, Jerusalem), interview with author, August 2012.

[84] "Nehnakh ha-Muze'on le-Misim bi-Yerushalayim" *Sherut* 21 (1964): 16; Azgad, "Makhnisim"; Alma Yitshaki Kurtzweil, ed., *Ha-Mekhes be-Yisrael: Min he-'Avar, Derekh ha-Hoveh, 'Im ha-Panim le-'Atid 1870–2010* (Jerusalem: Keter, 2011), 170.

[85] See, e.g., Avraham Mandel, *Ma'arekhet ha-Misim be-Yisrael: Homer 'Ezer la-Moreh be-Nos'e ha-Misim* (Jerusalem, Muze'on le-Misim, 1969); David Bar-Haim, ed., *The Tax System of Israel (As of May 31, 1969)* (Jerusalem: Museum of Taxes, 1969); Mordekhai Berger, ed., *Kofer ha-Yishuv* (Jerusalem: Muze'on le-Misim, 1964); Avraham Mandel, ed., *Vatikey ha-Mekhes bi-Nemal Yafo, Mesaprim,* (Jerusalem: Muze'on le-Misim, 1967); Mordekhai Berger, *Neshek le-Yisrael: Keren ha-Magen, ha-Homah* (Jerusalem: Muze'on le-Misim, 1968); Mordekhai Berger, *Magbit ha-Hitgayshut veha-Hatsalah* (Jerusalem: Muze'on le-Misim, 1970); Avraham Mandel and Sylvia Habif, eds., *Albom ha-Mekhes: 100 Shnot Mekhes be-Erets Yisrael* (Jerusalem: Muze'on le-Misim, 1973); Mandel, *Sefer ha-Yovel.*

[86] See, e.g., Joshua Bar-Droma, *Ha-Mediniyut ha-Finansit shel Medinat-Yehudah bi-Yemey ha-Bayit ha-Rishon veha-Sheni* (Jerusalem: Muze'on le-Misim, 1967). Collections of Jewish tax regulations from Turkey and Italy were also reprinted; see *Seder ha-Ha'arakhah: Mantuva 5455/1695* (Jerusalem: Minhal ha-Hakhnasot and Ha-Otsar, 1963); Yehoshua Avraham Yehudah, *Sefer 'Avodat Masa: Saloniki 1846* (Salonika: Saadi ha-Levi Ashkenazi, 1846; repr., Jerusalem: Muze'on le-Misim, 1964); Mandel, *Hitpat'hut ha-Misim.*

much attention was devoted to ancient and medieval history. One of the books whose publication was sponsored by the museum was a study of the Jewish law of taxation written by a young magistrate, Jacob Bazak.[87] In the introduction, the director of state revenue at the Ministry of Finance, Ariel Arieli, said the book was the first in a series of academic studies designed to deepen the knowledge of "young people and the educated public" in tax matters, since "knowledge is a precondition for understanding, and understanding is a precondition for willingness and agreement to obey the law."[88] These publications were later used in creating educational materials for courses on taxation in schools, in youth movements, and in the army.[89]

Education was accompanied by attempts to foster public trust in the Israeli Tax Authority. One way achieve this was to create special positions reserved only for new immigrants or for Arab tax inspectors.[90] Another way was by encouraging public participation in the tax assessment process.[91] To this end, the tax authority set up public advisory committees. These committees dealt with cases in which assessment was based on the "best judgment" of the assessing officer, either in the case of no return having been filed or the return being inadequate.[92] Some have argued that the origins of these committees can be found in the assessment committees used by the Jewish

[87] Jacob Bazak, *Hilkhot Misim ba-Mekorot ha-'Ivriyim* (Jerusalem: Muze'on le-Misim, 1964).

[88] A. Arieli, "[Introduction]" in Bazak, *Hilkhot Misim*, [10].

[89] Rachel Rokah, ed., *Misim u-Ma'asim* (Jerusalem: Misrad ha-Hinukh ve-Misrad ha-'Otsar, 1993) (a supplement to the tax video called "Max, Misim u-Ma 'Osim"). See also Avraham Mandel, ed., *Ha-Misim ve-Atah: Ma'arekhet ha-Misim be-Erets Yisrael ba-'Avar uva-Hoveh* (Jerusalem: Misrad ha-Hinukh veha-Tarbut and Misrad ha-Otsar, 1985).

[90] "Ma Perush 'To'evah'? ... : 'Olim Hadashim Nivhanim le-Misrot Mefakhey Mas-Hakhnasah," *Ma'ariv*, February 19, 1959, at 2.

[91] See, e.g., H. Viliamowski, "Yahasey Tsibur," *YP* (April–May 1953): 15–16; Viliamovski, "Yahasey Tsibur: (Hemshekh)" *YP* (June–July 1953): 20; M. Y., "'Al Saf ha-Shanah" *YP* (April 1954): 3; Gila Uriel, "Yahasey Tsibur" *YP* (December 1955): 5–6. On trust and tax compliance, see generally Martin Daunton, *Trusting Leviathan: The Politics of Taxation in Britain, 1799–1914* (New York: Cambridge University Press, 2001).

[92] Lapidoth, *Evasion and Avoidance of Income Tax*, 90–6; Wilkenfeld, *Taxes and People in Israel*, 174–5, 182–95.

voluntary tax system of the 1940s.[93] Others have traced their origins to Scandinavia.[94] In any event, the legislative provision enabling the creation of these committees was enacted in 1952 and implemented in 1954.[95]

The committees were manned by laypersons familiar with the business activity of the taxpayer in question. Committee members were selected on an individual basis or, sometimes, based on the recommendation of professional and trade associations. Members belonged to certain types of businesses in which taxpayers were often self-employed, and in which best-judgment assessments were more prevalent (artisans, shopkeepers, farmers, the free professions, providers of transportation services, and so forth). An initial roster of about a thousand individuals was compiled, and by 1964 it had grown to include about 3,300 members. The committees, composed of two individuals, were considered nonjudicial bodies dealing with factual matters related to assessments. They served only as advisors to the assessing officers, hence their decisions were not binding. However, in practice, assessing officers typically accepted their advice, and in cases in which they did not, they had to refer the matter to the income tax commissioner.[96]

Procedures were rather informal. Taxpayers who objected to their assessments could request a hearing by an advisory committee. Such a hearing could also be requested by the assessing officer. Hearings were

---

[93] MT, file 702–14, Yisrael Shivo to Ze'ev Sharef, December 27, 1959. See also Y. Kanev, "Mas ha-Hakhnasah u-Mi Meshalem Oto," *Davar*, September 7, 1951, 2.

[94] Lapidoth, *Evasion and Avoidance of Income Tax*, 93; Wilkenfeld, *Taxes and People in Israel*, 182. The approach on which these committees were based was somewhat similar to the traditional British method of taxation, based on the assessment and collection of direct taxes by the taxpayer's local peers. See generally Chantal Stebbings, *The Victorian Taxpayer and the Law: A Study in Constitutional Conflict* (Cambridge: Cambridge University Press, 2009), 20–30, 77–110. On taxpayer participation in the early stages of income taxation in other countries, see José Antonio Sánchez Román, *Taxation and Society in Twentieth-Century Argentina* (New York: Palgrave Macmillan, 2012), 64; Kotsonis, *States of Obligation*, 119–25, 175–9. On the Polish experience, which might also have been an influence, see Bronisław Hełczyński, "The Law in the Reborn State," in *Polish Law throughout the Ages*, ed. Wenceslas J. Wagner (Stanford: Hoover Institute Press, 1970), 139, 166.

[95] Wilkenfeld, *Taxes and People in Israel*, 182; Income Tax Ordinance (New Version), 1961, sec. 146.

[96] Wilkenfeld, *Taxes and People in Israel*, 182–4, 188.

chaired by the assessing officer or one of the members of his staff. The
assessing officer presented the objection of the taxpayer to the two
members of the committee, and then the taxpayers (or their representatives), as well as the inspector responsible for the assessment, were
invited to present their arguments. The committee then decided what
its recommendation would be (if the two members did not agree they
would each state their opinions separately). The assessing officer could
accept the recommendation of the committee and amend the assessment accordingly, or reject it, in which case he would have to inform
the income tax commissioner in writing about the reasons for the dis-
agreement with the committee.[97] The committees were very active. In
the first ten years of their operation, between 1954 and 1964, they
heard about one hundred thousand cases.[98] These were mostly cases
of poorer taxpayers who did not keep books and were not represented
by lawyers or accountants.[99]

The government also sought to assure taxpayers that they were
being treated fairly. For example, in a booklet published in 1950, the
Ministry of Finance informed Israeli taxpayers that:

> just as your duty as a citizen of the state is to pay what you owe, your
> right is to protect yourself from false claims ... and it is important that
> you know the principles of income taxation ... [Y]ou yourself should
> know whether you have to pay the tax required of you or whether you
> are fully or partly exempt and [you should] check whether the amount
> [requested of you] is accurate.[100]

Another way to foster trust in the tax authority was by reforming
the behavior of tax officials. The interest in such a reform was already
apparent in the transition period between British and Israeli rule in
1948. A note written in preparation for the takeover of the tax administration machinery by the new Israeli state in 1948 suggested that, when
the takeover occurred, the new Israeli minister of finance would address

[97] Ibid., 186–8.
[98] Ibid., 188.
[99] Ibid., 189–93. On the work of these committees, see also MT, file 702–14, *Hamesh Shnot Pe'ulah shel ha-Va'adot ha-Meya'atsot le-Mas Hakhnasah* (Jerusalem, 1959/60); MT, file 702–14, Ha-Otsar, *'Eser Shnot Pe'ulah shel ha-Va'adot ha-Meya'atsot le-Mas Hakhnasah* (Jerusalem, 1964/65).
[100] ISA, Gimel 316/5, Sherutey ha-Modi'in, Hoveret 'al Mas-Hakhnasah.

the public on questions of tax morale and honesty. Simultaneously, the income tax commissioner would address all tax officials "asking for wholehearted cooperation, integrity, politeness to the public, and so forth." The note added that assessing officers should be asked to make sure that "appointments are kept punctually, [and] that the public in general be treated in a manner becoming to the dignity of the office."[101]

"The education of the official," said one tax official in 1955, "should precede the education of the public ... A progressive and intelligent government does not treat the public passively, merely forbidding certain things ... no institution can be efficient if it cannot work in an atmosphere of goodwill and honor from the public that elected it."[102] It is no wonder that the internal newsletter of the income tax officials was full of articles instructing these officials how to behave properly. Such instructions were found, for example, in a table entitled "Correct and incorrect ways of treating the public" (see Table 4.1).[103]

The tax authority went so far as to appoint a special assistant to deal with public relations, whose role was to instruct the officials in dealing fairly with taxpayers. This assistant warned tax officials that:

> The development of economic, social and cultural life means that people are no longer willing to remain passive in social and political life, they are no longer cogs in a machine. People want to know and learn, and this is the source of the demand from the citizen to explain our actions and decisions, and we must get used to this situation ... If we continue to behave properly, with patience, fairness and courtesy, the general public will also get used to treating us in a civilized way.[104]

The assessing officer, said another official in 1956, "should reach a stage in which the citizen will leave his office satisfied and will pay [his taxes]."[105]

The creation of a positive desire to comply among individual taxpayers, whether based on education or on trust, was accompanied

[101] ISA G 115/27, Notes re Administration of Income Tax, 4, 6.
[102] Uriel, "Yahasey Tsibur," 6.
[103] See also Medinat Yisrael – Agaf Mas Hakhnasah, *Yalkut le-Tipu'ah ha-Pkidut ha-Tovah* (n.p., 1956) (a copy of this booklet can be found in the NLI).
[104] Y. Vild, "Tipu'ah Yahasey Tsibur Tkinim," *Sherut* 3 (1956): 15, 16.
[105] Josephsberg, "Ha-Ezrah."

Table 4.1 "Correct and incorrect ways of treating the public"

Right	Wrong
1. [Official] present when the invitee arrives	1. Is not present
2. Says "hello"	2. Does not say "hello"
3. Sits up straight	3. Slumps over his table
4. Offers a cigarette	4. Smokes alone and does not offer a cigarette
...	...
16. Does not read the newspaper in front of the invitee	16. Obstinately continues to read the newspaper

by the attempt to use a more negative method for achieving compliance, also based on the use of social norms – the publication of an annual income taxpayers register (*reshimat ha-nishomin* or *sefer ha-nishomin*). This register was meant to provide the public with information about the tax returns of individual taxpayers in the hope that, in cases where taxpayers misreported their income, their acquaintances would inform on them.

The idea of a taxpayers register may have been derived from the voluntary tax system of the 1940s that, as we saw in Chapter 3, experimented with publicizing information on tax evaders. Alternatively, it may also have been inspired by foreign sources: the Bolsheviks published lists of taxpayers (based on precedents from a number of Western countries); Lebanese tax law provided for the publication of individual assessments; there was a tax register in Sweden; and Americans also experimented with publicizing taxpayer returns in the 1920s. In 1952 the Israeli Income Tax Ordinance was revised to allow the tax authority to publish such a register. A further amendment, in 1955, required the publication of such a register no later than two years after the end of the tax year.[106] The goal of the register was to

---

[106] Mandel, *Sefer ha-Yovel*, 67; Hok le-Tikun Pkudat Mas Hakhnasah, 5711/1951, HH, 5:44, sec. 3; Hok le-Tikun Pkudat mas Hakhnasah, 5712/1952, SH, 1951/52, 298, sec. 3; Hok le-Tikun Pkudat mas Hakhnasah, 5716/1956, SH (1955/66), 84, sec. 13. See also Wilkenfeld, *Taxes and People in Israel*, 104–5, 130–2; Lapidoth, *Evasion and Avoidance of Income Tax*, 64–5. For comparative perspectives on tax publicity, see Kotsonis, *States of Obligation*, 308 (Soviet Union); G. Eichelgrün, "Income-Tax in

"stir public indignation against taxpayers who had grossly underreported their income," and to shame them into complying.[107]

The first register, containing four volumes and pertaining to the fiscal year 1952/53, was published in 1955. It included the names and reported income of self-employed individuals, corporations, and wage-earners who earned more than 25 percent of their income from sources other than wages.[108] The register was sold to the public for a small fee.[109] It attracted a great deal of public attention, and information gathered from it was used by a prominent 1950s anticorruption group, Shurat ha-Mitnadvim, in its campaign to expose incompetence, favoritism, and corruption in the Israeli government, including within the Israeli Tax Authority.[110]

Ultimately, however, the idea of publicizing taxpayer returns proved to be a failure. One problem was that the register contained many errors. Another problem was that some of the taxpayers disputed their assessments. As the law required the tax authority to publish amendments to the original lists in those cases where the taxpayer's assessment was revised, the publication of revised assessments undermined the credibility of the initial register.[111] The second edition of the register, for the fiscal year 1953/54, was delayed. It, too, proved to be full of errors. The third and final edition was published in 1958, after which the experiment was discontinued.[112]

British Colonies," *Economic Journal* 58 (1948): 128–32, 131 (Lebanon); Wilkenfeld, *Taxes and People in Israel*, xiv (Japan and Sweden); Jones, "Class Tax to Mass Tax," 689–90 (United States); Marjorie E. Kornhauser, "Doing the Full Monty: Will Publicizing Tax Information Increase Compliance?" *Canadian Journal of Law and Jurisprudence* 18 (2005): 95–117 (United States); Ken Devos and Marcus Zackrisson, "Tax Compliance and the Public Disclosure of Tax Information: An Australia/Norway Comparison," *eJournal of Tax Research* 13 (2015): 108–29 (a global survey).

[107] "Tax Assessments Published for Self-Employed Earners," *JP*, September 15, 1955, at 1; "Leket min ha-'Itonut," *YP* (December 1955): 8; Wilkenfeld, *Taxes and People in Israel*, 104–5, 131, 132.

[108] Wilkenfeld, *Taxes and People in Israel*, 131.

[109] Lapidoth, *Evasion and Avoidance of Income Tax*, 64–5.

[110] Shurat ha-Mitnadvim, *Sakanah Orevet – mi-Bifnim!* (Jerusalem, 1956).

[111] Wilkenfeld, *Taxes and People in Israel*, 130–1.

[112] "Income Tax Register Released: Sharef Doubts its Efficacy," *JP*, August 26, 1957, at 3; Lapidoth, *Evasion and Avoidance of Income Tax*, 64–5. There were unsuccessful calls to revive the register in the early 1970s. See "Tar'omet ba-'Avodah 'al Tokhnit Kalkalit shel MAPAM," *Ma'ariv*, August 12, 1970, at 8; Josef Gross, "Haganah 'al

The failure of the register was not merely due to the technical difficulties of publishing accurate lists. It was also the result of cultural aversion to the informer role that the register encouraged. "Traditionally," said one observer, "the informer is frowned upon by the Jewish community. Informing to the tax authorities, whom many considered an adversary, went against the grain."[113] Failure was probably also the result of the fact that many taxpayers misreported their income, thus sending compliant taxpayers an unintended signal that evasion was legitimate.[114]

The public realization that evasion was widespread, and the contribution of the register to this realization, is evident in the literary responses the register provoked. In 1955 a satirical poem published by Nathan Alterman, Israel's leading poet, in *Davar* (a newspaper associated with the ruling Labor Party) made fun of the register. In this poem, the "venerable" register complains that it is made to feel like a clown. "I was told that I am a proud and grave financial document," it says, "yet the public looks at me and laughs, as if [the comedian] Danny Kaye suddenly appeared in order to please it ... since how is it after all possible to offer, in a formal, grave attire, and after much toil, a document in which the profits of import magnates are seen to be equal to the income [of the lowly] ice-dispensing boy."[115]

Another forum in which the register was mentioned was a comedy entitled *Taxes and Hats*, written by Binyamin Gal. This play tells the story of Moshe Levy, the greedy owner of an electrical appliance factory. Mr. Levy wants to marry off his incompetent son to the daughter of a wealthy American millionaire, Mr. Green, who is visiting Israel

---

Nishomim," *Haaretz*, July 31, 1972, at 11; "Ben Aharon Mahayev Hidush Pirsum Sefer ha-Nishomin," *Ma'ariv*, August 7, 1972, at 4; David Lipkin, "Muts'a Lefarsem Sefer ha-Nishomim," *Davar*, October 9, 1972, at 1. However, the proposals were flatly rejected by the Israeli Parliament and government. See Yehoshua Bitsur, "Va'adat ha-Ksafim Danah be-Tsimtsum Hotsa'ot 'Iskiyot," *Ma'ariv*, September 28, 1970, at 7; Avraham Kushnir, "Minhal ha-Hakhnasot Mitnaged le-Sefer Nishomim," *Davar*, October 12, 1972, 3; Yosef Avivi, "Pirsum Sefer Nishomim: Be'ad ve-Neged," *RYM* 7 (1973): 385, 389.

[113] Wilkenfeld, *Taxes and People in Israel*, 104–5.

[114] On such signals, see generally Joshua D. Blank, "What's Wrong with Shaming Corporate Tax Abuse," *Tax Law Review* 62 (2009): 539–90, 580–2.

[115] Nathan A[lterman], "Ha-Tur ha-Shvi'i: Ne'um Arba'at ha-Krakhim," *Davar*, September 23, 1955, at 2.

to find a match for his daughter and also to dole out charity to poor Israelis. Green uses the taxpayers register to find needy Israelis, among them Mr. Levy, who misreported his income. Levy is waiting for a visit from Mr Green to seal the match between his son and Mr. Green's daughter, but mistakes an income tax inspector for Mr. Green and declares his true income, which is fifty times greater than the income reported in the register.[116] While the comedy is rather lame, the underlying perception on which it was based was that many Israelis did, indeed, deliberately misreport their income.

Despite the eventual failure of the tax register, it seems that the reforms carried out in the mid-1950s were, overall, relatively successful, at least in the short term. Accurate data on the exact scope of noncompliance are very hard to obtain. However, there appears to have been a decline in the scale of tax evasion between the late 1950s and the 1960s. Studies of Israeli tax evasion describe the mid-1950s as a period in which it was widespread, but they mention a relatively low figure of about 5 percent of gross domestic product (GDP) (a figure similar to that of Western European countries) for the year 1968.[117]

Another indicator of the decline of evasion is the growing reach of the tax authorities during this period. When the British mandate ended in 1948, there were ninety-thousand income tax payers. In the fiscal year 1962/63 the number of taxpayers increased by a factor of seven to six-hundred thousand (while the population of Israel only doubled during the same period).[118] Perhaps another quantitative sign of the decline in the scale of evasion can be found in the growth in the

---

[116] Binyamin Gal, *Misim u-Migba'ot: Komedyah be-Shalosh Tmunot* (Tel Aviv: Merkaz Yisre'eli le-Dramah, n.d.) (a copy of this play can be found in the Haifa University Library – in the catalog the play is tentatively dated to 1960). This was not the only play on the topic of tax evasion. See ISA, Gimel 3581/20, Beyt Sefer le-Meshalmey Mas Hakhnasah (a satirical play with similar themes that was submitted to the Israeli censor by the satirical theater *Ha-Matate* in 1952). See also Zvi Lavi, "Hon Shahor: Hishtamtut ha-'Ashirim mi-Mas bi-Shnot ha-50," *Ynet*, April 3, 2010, www.ynet.co.il/articles/0,7340,L-3870791,00.html.

[117] Wilkenfeld, *Taxes and People in Israel*, 4–6; Nadel, *Doh Nadel*, 58–64; Yaakov Kondor, *Meshek be-Mahteret be-Yisrael uba-'Olam* (Tel Aviv: Tsherikover, 1993), 36, 39, 77–82.

[118] Mandel, *Hitpat'hut ha-Misim*, 21, 51. This was the Israeli equivalent of the global phenomenon of the transformation of the income tax from a class tax to a mass tax in the middle decades of the twentieth century.

Table 4.2 Israeli government revenues for the fiscal years 1949/50 and 1964/65

Fiscal year	1949/50		1964/65	
	I£ (millions)	%	I£ (millions)	%
Property taxes	1.4	4	58	3
Income[a]	9.5	27	1,006.5	46
Estate tax	0	0	4.7	0
Direct taxes (total)	10.9	31	1,069.2	49
Customs	10.2	29	349.1	16
Excise and sales tax	11.1	31	604.8[b]	28
Indirect taxes (total)	21.3	60	953.9	44
Stamp duty	0.4	1	40.2	2
Fees and licenses	2.7	8	87.1[c]	4
Additional taxes	0	0	28.9	1
Other taxes and fees (total)	3.1	9	156.2	7
Total	35.3	100	2,179.3	100

Notes:

[a] Including the revenue from the income tax, the land betterment tax/land appreciation tax, and (in 1964/65) the compulsory loan for the absorption of immigration.

[b] Including the indirect security compulsory loan.

[c] Including the transaction-related security compulsory loan.

relative contribution of direct taxes to the Israeli budget between the 1950s and the 1960s, from about 30 percent to about 50 percent of the total revenue (see Table 4.2).

There are also other, more indirect, indicators of change in compliance levels. In the late 1960s one can find claims that during the previous two decades "the tax evasion graph" had been constantly declining.[119] Social perceptions of both tax evaders and tax officials also changed, with judges now more willing to impose jail sentences on tax offenders. Thus, while judges in the 1950s imposed only light fines based on the fact that tax evasion was widespread (as a mitigating circumstance), in the early 1960s imprisonment became more

[119] See Z. Kessler, "[Book Review]: Ma'arekhet ha-Misim be-Yisrael: Homer 'Ezer la-Moreh be-Nos'e ha-Misim," *RYM* 4 (1969): 346.

common.[120] As for tax officials, while in the late 1950s one could still find letters to the press complaining about arbitrary tax assessments and harsh treatment by tax officials, by the 1960s these complaints were replaced by admiring reports. One women's magazine, describing changes in the attitude of (customs) officials, informed its readers that "six or seven years ago the customs office in the port of Haifa looked like a scene from Dante's *Inferno*: Red-faced or pale travelers trembling while they argued with the customs officers as their wives cried or screamed hysterically ... and new Parisian dresses became wrinkled rags during customs inspection. Today things are completely different. Everyone ... gets rapid and courteous treatment."[121] Another mark of the growing legitimacy of the system was the public reaction to tax-related suicides. In 1954 the suicide of the alleged tax evader Israel Sinai triggered a major political crisis. In 1966, on the other hand, a similar suicide of a factory owner (who leapt to his death leaving a note saying "pay to the order of the Angel of Death – the Income Tax: the sum of my whole life") went almost unnoticed.[122]

But while the shift in public perceptions was one factor that contributed to an increase in compliance from the mid-1950s onward, this growth was also assisted by external factors. First, there were heightened concerns for security in the mid-1950s, when massive supplies of

---

[120] Wilkenfeld, *Taxes and People in Israel*, 242. See, e.g., CrimA (Tel Aviv) 297/61 K. B. v. AG, RH 12 (1962): 216–17; CrimA 96/64 AG v. *Boneh Yotser*, RH 14 (1964): 482–3 (cases stating that imprisonment should be the proper punishment for tax evaders and that there is a need to use this punishment in order to publicly express the court's view on the matter).

[121] Quoted in S. Gafni, "Hesegenu Mehayvim Hemshekh," *Sherut* 16 (1962): 26. See also M. Talmi, "'Al Mizbe'h Mas Hakhnasah" *Sherut* 13 (1960): 13; Tamar Avidar, "Panim el Panim 'im Yo'ets Mas-Hakhnasah," *Sherut* 20 (1964): 8.

[122] See "To the Angel of Death – The Income Tax," *JP*, November 4, 1966, at 8. The fact that the system matured does not mean that evasion ceased to be a problem. See Lapidoth, *Evasion and Avoidance of Income Tax*, 189 (noting that in 1966 "in spite of the extensive measures against evasion ... [it has] remained much more common [in Israel] than it is in the United Kingdom"); 'Azriel Kaminski, "Ha'alamat Misim ve-Kalkalah Sh'horah," *RYM* 16 (1988): 359–64 (quoting an economic study published in 1986 that argued that the level of tax evasion in Israel was among the highest in the West, attributing this to the fact that "Israel is a Mediterranean country in the negative sense of the word, with a problematic, disgruntled and undisciplined population").

arms began to flow to the Egyptian army, and acts of terrorism against Israelis increased, ultimately leading to the Suez crisis and the second Arab–Israeli war of 1956.[123] As is often the case, when taxpayers' sense of security declines, they are more willing to pay taxes. Indeed, during the period leading to the 1956 war, an official system of voluntary contributions called the "defense fund" (*keren ha-magen*), reminiscent of the voluntary tax system of the 1940s, was introduced.[124] Second, the change in the level of compliance may also have been the result of Israel's "economic miracle." Between 1950 and 1972 the country enjoyed rapid economic growth and a continuous rise in the real income per person (between 1950 and 1965 real income grew by an annual average of 6 percent). Growing wealth was accompanied by the simultaneous reduction of the tax burden, which, in turn, increased the taxpayers' willingness to pay.[125]

The reforms I have described here were partly local in origin and partly inspired by the technical assistance missions to Israel organized by the United Nations, the IMF, and the United States. The most important of these technical missions was the American one, involving more than 200 experts sent to Israel under the sponsorship of the United States Operations Mission to Israel (USOM/I).[126] Following the

[123] On the causes of the 1956 war, see, e.g., Guy Laron, "The Domestic Sources of Israel's Decision to Launch the 1956 Sinai Campaign," *British Journal of Middle Eastern Studies* 43 (2015): 200–18.

[124] See Wilkenfeld, *Taxes and People in Israel*, 111, 214; Berger, *Neshek*; Naor, "The Israeli Volunteering Movement."

[125] See, e.g., David Levi-Faur, "The Developmental State: Israel, South Korea, and Taiwan Compared," *Studies in Comparative International Development* 33 (1998): 65–93, 66; Paul Rivlin, *The Israeli Economy from the Foundation of the State through the 21st Century* (New York: Cambridge University Press, 2011), 41–3; Mandel, *Hitpat'hut ha-Misim*, 6.

[126] See generally [United States Operations Mission to Israel], *Five Years of Mutual Endeavor: USOM-Israel* (Tel Aviv: Haaretz Press, 1956); [US Information Service], *Investment in Progress: Fifteen Years of Creative U.S. Assistance to Israel through Grants-in-Aid, Loans, Technical Assistance, and the Food-for-Peace Program* (Tel Aviv: U.S. Information Service and the Israel Ministry of Finance [1965]); Avner Molcho, "Kapitalizm ve-'ha-Derekh ha-Amerikanit' be-Yisrael: Pir'yon, Nihul veha-Etos ha-Kapitalisti ba-Siyu'a ha-Tekhni shel Artsot ha-Brit bi-Shnot ha-Hamishim," in Bareli et al. eds., *Hevrah ve-Kalkalah be-Yisrael*, 263–94. On American productivity expertise in Israel, see Michal Frenkel and Yehouda Shenhav, "From Americanization to Colonization: The Diffusion of Productivity Models Revisited,"

massive influx of American technical assistance, Israel came to serve in the 1960s as a minor hub in the global network for the diffusion of knowledge on tax administration.[127] In the 1960s and 1970s Israeli experts were sent to African, Asian, and Latin American countries to help them reform their tax administration methods, and conferences on fiscal problems in developing countries were convened in Israel.[128]

Taxing the Arab Population of Israel

One major difference between British taxation in the 1940s and Israeli taxation in the 1950s was the attempt to base compliance on feelings of solidarity and trust between taxpayers and the state. This is not surprising given the fact that the majority of Jewish taxpayers in 1950s Israel felt more allegiance to the new Jewish state than they did to its mandatory predecessor. However, at least one segment of the Israeli

---

Organization Studies 24 (2003): 1537–61. On the influence of the American tax model globally, see generally Michael A. Livingston, "Law, Culture and Anthropology: On the Hopes and Limits of Comparative Tax," *Canadian Journal of Law and Jurisprudence* 18 (2005): 119–34, 126.

[127] The Israeli case was only one example of the export of tax administration expertise by American advisers. Other examples are found in a booklet summarizing a symposium on tax administration held by CENTO (the Central Treaty Organization) in 1965 in Iran. See CENTO, "Symposium on Tax Administration (held in Tehran, Iran, March 6–12, 1965)," 28–30, 151 (a copy of this booklet can be found in the New York University Law School Library). On global tax expertise, see generally Miranda Stewart, "Global Trajectories of Tax Reform: The Discourse of Tax Reform in Developing and Transition Countries," *Harvard International Law Journal* 44 (2003): 139–90; Holger Nehring and Florian Schui, eds., *Global Debates about Taxation* (Basingstoke: Palgrave Macmillan, 2007); W. Elliot Brownlee, Eisaku Ide, and Yasunori Fukagai, eds., *The Political Economy of Transnational Tax Reform: The Shoup Mission to Japan in Historical Context* (Cambridge: Cambridge University Press, 2013).

[128] Assistance was provided to countries such as such as Ghana, Uganda, Ceylon, Cyprus, Korea, and Bolivia. See Eliahu Galdan, "Ve'idat Rehovot ha-Shlishit le-Be'ayot Fiscaliyot u-Monitariyot be-Aratsot Mitpat'hot," *RYM* 1 (1965/66): 71–3; Meir Lahav, "Agaf Mas Hakhnasah be-Ghana," *RYM* 2 (1966/67): 372–6; Yehuda Peleg, "Kakh Hunhag Mas ha-Kniyah be-Uganda," *RYM* 4 (1969): 104–8; "A. Arieli – Yo'ets le-Memshelet Tseylon," *Davar*, August 10, 1966, at 8; Wilkenfeld, *Taxes and People in Israel*, 87; Lapidoth, *Evasion and Avoidance of Income Tax*, 9; Mandel, *Sefer ha-Yovel*, 33, 171, 174, 221; MT, file entitled "Ksharim beyn-Le'umiyim."

population, the Arabs who remained in Israel after the Israeli War of Independence in 1948, did not share this sense of trust and allegiance to the state.[129] The Arab population of Israel, numbering approximately 150,000 in the 1950s (about 10 percent of the population), was mostly located in towns and villages in Galilee in the northern part of the country and in the Negev desert in the south. Until 1966, many of them lived under a system of military rule. They participated in elections, but some of their rights, for example the right to travel, were more restricted than those of the Jewish citizens of the state.

In recent years, several studies of the Arabs of Israel in the two decades between Israeli independence in 1948 and the watershed 1967 Six Day War have been published. These studies often tell a story of a formal concession of citizenship and suffrage rights to Israel's Arab population after 1948 that actually concealed a policy of repression, exclusion, and displacement.[130] However, even studies based on this interpretation contain evidence of a messier and more contradictory reality, one that combined inclusion with exclusion, and in which the Arabs themselves were not merely passive subjects but actively made use of the formal promise of equality to safeguard their political and legal interests.[131]

The legal history of Israel's relations with its Arab citizens reveals a similarly contradictory picture. Some studies focus on how Israeli law

---

[129] On the political aspects of the use of the term "Arab" to designate this part of the population, see Introduction, n. 47. On the relationship of ethnic diversity, trust, and tax compliance, see, e.g., Roth et al., *An Agenda for Research*, 136–7; Beron et al., "The Effects of Audits and Socioeconomic Variables," 81–2; Taylor, "Understanding Taxpayer Attitudes"; Evan S. Lieberman, *Race and Regionalism in the Politics of Taxation in Brazil and South Africa* (New York: Cambridge University Press, 2003); Sherry Xin Li, "Social Identities, Ethnic Diversity, and Tax Morale," *Public Finance Review* 38 (2010): 146–77.

[130] See Gershon Shafir and Yoav Peled, *Being Israeli: The Dynamics of Multiple Citizenship* (New York: Cambridge University Press, 2002), 110–36; Hillel Cohen, *Good Arabs: The Israeli Security Agencies and the Israeli Arabs, 1948–1967* (Berkeley: University of California Press, 2010); Shira Robinson, *Citizen Strangers: Palestinians and the Birth of Israel's Liberal Settler State* (Stanford: Stanford University Press, 2013).

[131] Robinson, *Citizen Strangers*, 8–9, 134–5. See generally Arik Rudnitzky, "The Contemporary Historiographical Debate in Israel on Government Policies on Arabs in Israel during the Military Administration Period (1948–1966)," *Israel Studies* 19 (2014): 24–47.

and Israeli judges in the 1950s actively used the law to expropriate Arab land or prevent Arab refugees from returning to the villages they left or were forced to leave in 1948.[132] Other works argue that Israeli law and Israeli courts were relatively neutral, or at least not overtly biased toward the Arab population of the country.[133]

The story of the taxation of Israeli Arabs during the first two decades after 1948 is, I believe, another example of the contradictory reality of Jewish–Arab relations in post-1948 Israel. Here, somewhat paradoxically, exclusion from the core of the Israeli citizenship project proved perhaps more of an advantage than a handicap, since the state expected less compliance from its Arab taxpayers than it did from its Jewish ones. In this sense, taxation was similar to conscription to the Israeli army. Unlike the Jewish citizens of Israel, who were (and still are) conscripted at the age of eighteen for several years of compulsory military service, the Arabs of Israel (with the exception of some groups such as the Druze and the Bedouins) are exempt from military service.[134]

---

[132] See, e.g., Ronen Shamir, "Suspended in Space: Bedouins under the Law of Israel," *Law and Society Review* 30 (1996): 231–57; Oren Bracha, "Safek Miskenim, Safek Mesukanim: Ha-Mistanenim, ha-Hok u-Veyt ha-Mishpat ha-ʻElyon 1948–1954," *'Iyuney Mishpat* 21 (1998): 333–85; Alexandre Kedar, "The Jewish State and the Arab Possessor, 1948–1967," in *The History of Law in a Multi-Cultural Society: Israel, 1917–1967*, eds. Ron Harris et al. (Aldershot: Ashgate, 2002), 311–79; Geremy Forman, "Military Rule, Political Manipulation, and Jewish Settlement: Israeli Mechanisms for Controlling Nazareth in the 1950s," *Journal of Israeli History* 25 (2006): 335–59; Geremy Forman, "Law and the Historical Geography of the Galilee: Israel's Litigatory Advantages during the Special Operation of Land Settlement," *Journal of Historical Geography* 32 (2006): 796–817.

[133] Haim Sandberg, *Mekarkeʻy Yisrael: Tsiyonut u-Post-Tsiyonut* (Jerusalem: Ha-Makhon le-Mehkarey Hakikah, 2007). See also Yifat Holzman-Gazit, *Land Expropriation in Israel: Law, Culture and Society* (Aldershot: Ashgate, 2007); Ron Harris, "State Identity, Territorial Integrity and Party Banning: The Case of a Pan-Arab Political Party in Israel," *Socio-Legal Review* 4 (2008): 19–65.

[134] See Alon Peled, *A Question of Loyalty: Military Manpower Policy in Multiethnic States* (Ithaca, NY: Cornell University Press, 1998), 130–42; Peled, *The Challenge of Ethnic Democracy*, 98. Such exemptions, while certainly beneficial to those who enjoy them, are in other senses a double-edged sword, since republican conceptions of citizenship of the type prevalent in Israel privilege those citizens who fulfill all their civic duties, including army service. On the link between "full" citizenship and civic duties, see Linda K. Kerber, *No Constitutional Right to Be Ladies: Women and*

According to newspaper reports from the early 1950s, the government was generally unable to collect taxes in the Arab sector.[135] The Sharef committee's report on tax assessment and collection methods, submitted in March 1954, noted that most Arabs were "currently outside the network of income taxpayers." The report recommended that a special adviser to deal with the Arab population be appointed, and that special tax units be established in major Arab population centers. These units, it was suggested, were to be manned by about forty Arabic-speaking officials: Arab tax specialists who had worked for the British government during the mandatory era, as well as Arabic-speaking Jewish immigrants from Middle Eastern countries. In addition, the report suggested that all the measures proposed to tackle evasion by Jewish taxpayers (such as information-collection, public relations, and educational initiatives, or the use of standard assessment guides and public advisory committees) should also be implemented in the Arab sector.[136] Following the report, tax officials sought to use tools such as education and trust to increase Arab compliance, striving to "familiarize the Arab population with the idea of income taxation," to tax Arabs "on a fair and scientific basis," and to involve them in the assessment process to induce their trust.[137]

the *Obligations of Citizenship* (New York: Hill and Wang, 1998), 95–7. See also Rozin, *A Home for all Jews*, 3–4, 45–55 (discussing the nonimplementation of the 1950s legislation dealing with child marriage in the Arab sector).

[135] "Income Tax Collection," *JP*, March 12, 1952, at 1; "Arab Tax: Collection Problems," *JP*, June 22, 1954, at 4; "Minority Duties," *JP*, June 22, 1954, at 4; MT, M.1964.702-714, Ne'umo shel 'Awad Ibrahim al-'Abdallah, January 31, 1960. The speech was later reprinted as 'Awad 'Abdallah Ibrahim al-'Abdallah, "Be-Shem Ehay Netsigey ha-Kfarim ha-'Arviyim," *Sherut* 13 (1960): 11 (note the slightly different spelling of his name in these two sources). On the other hand, government reports dealing with the early 1950s did state that the income tax was also collected in the Arab sector. See, e.g., *Din ve-Heshbon Rishon 'al Hakhnasot ha-Medinah la-Shanim 1948/9–1954/5* (Jerusalem: ha-Madpis ha-Memshalti, May 1956), 119, 131–2, 148.

[136] TM Library, Din ve-Heshbon shel ha-Va'adah li-Vhinat Shitot ha-Ha'arakhah veha-Gviyah shel Mas Hakhnasah (March 1954), 59–60.

[137] "Yom ha-'Iyun shel Pkidey ha-Shumah," *YP* (October-November 1953): 59; M. Elfandari, "Ye'ul ve-Shipur Darkhey ha-Gviyah," *Sherut* 3 (1956): 8, 9; A. Sa'ad, "Mas Hakhnasah bi-Kfarey ha-Mi'utim," *Sherut* 4 (1957): 53, 54; A. Sa'ad, "Mas Hakhnasah be-Kerev ha-Mi'utim be-'Asor le-Yisrael," *Sherut* 8–9 (1958):

In 1954 a special department in the income tax commissioner's office was established to deal with taxation of minorities.[138] Attempts by this department to reform the relationship between the government and Arab taxpayers included printing tax forms and information booklets in Arabic, and training and appointing Arab tax collectors. Another reform was the spread of the public advisory committees to Arab villages. The task of these committees, it was explained, was to assist Arab farmers, who were not used to paying income tax and who saw the state as "invading" their villages.[139] Indeed, these committees became a major vehicle for mediating between the tax authority and the Arab population. By 1959 approximately a third (about 900 people) of the members of these committees were Arabs, perhaps reflecting the prevalence of "best judgment" assessments in the Arab sector, or the greater need for public legitimacy of tax assessments in that sector.[140]

Following these administrative changes, it was reported that collection of taxes in the Arab sector improved somewhat.[141] However, tax collection in this sector remained lower than in the Jewish one.

14–15; Major Sasson Ben-Zvi, "Shivtey ha-Bedu'im be-Nafat Be'er Sheva," *Sherut* 10 (1959): 46–9; 'Awad 'Abdallah Ibrahim al-'Abdallah, "Be-Shem Ehay Netsigey ha-Kfarim ha-'Arviyim," *Sherut* 13 (1960): 11–12. See also Wilkenfeld, *Taxes and People in Israel*, 144–5, 189.

[138] The year 1954 also saw the last serious (and failed) attempt at universal conscription of Arabs into the Israeli army. See Peled, *A Question of Loyalty*, 135–7; Robinson, *Citizen Strangers*, 134.

[139] Misrad Mevaker ha-Medinah, *Din ve-Heshbon Shnati Mispar 7 shel Mevaker ha-Medinah li-Shnat ha-Ksafim 1955/6* (Jerusalem: n.p., 1956), 83; ISA, Gimel 5433/ 21, Rabotay ha-'Itonut (a radio interview with Ze'ev Sharef), at 4; ISA, Gimel 5433/ 21, Kenes Menahaley Yehidot ha-Misim (April 25, 1955), at 25; ISA, Gimel Lamed 12533/70, G. Levitzky to Netziv Mas Hakhnasah, September 14, 1956; Gideon Weigert, "Mas Hakhnasah be-Kerev ha-Mi'utim," *Haaretz*, September 14, 1960, at 4, reprinted in *Sherut* 14 (1960): 31–3; Mandel, *Sefer ha-Yovel*, 89, 97, 125, 134.

[140] The ratio of Arab/Jewish participation in these committees is taken from MT, file 702–14, T. Brosh, "Introduction," in *Hamesh Shnot Pe'ulah shel ha-Va'adot ha-Meya'atsot le-Mas Hakhnasah* (Jerusalem, 1959/60), 26. Of 2,397 members in late 1959, 867 (36 percent) were Arabs. At the time Arabs comprised less than 15 percent of the population of Israel.

[141] Gideon Weigert, "Rise in Arab Tax Collection," *JP*, March 6, 1956, at 4; "Knesset Concludes Tax Reform Debate," *JP*, December 19, 1956, at 3; M. Elfandari, "Yi'ul ve-Shipur Shitot ha-Gviyah," *Sherut* 3 (1956): 8, 9.

In 1956 Goel Levitzky, the "inspector for minorities' affairs" in the income tax commissioner's office, noted that "the Arab sector is now in a state that the Jewish sector was in a few years ago. The Arab inhabitant's unwillingness to cooperate, his lack of knowledge of the law, his [unwillingness] to file reports, his ignorance, and so forth, is well known."[142]

'Awad Ibrahim al-'Abdallah, the village headman (*mukhtar*) of the village of Sakhnin, discussed Arab tax compliance in a speech he gave at a gathering of Arab members of the public advisory committees convened in Haifa in 1960. Arabs, he said, "do not seek to rebel against the payment of tax, since every intelligent person in any country in the world ... must be a loyal citizen to his state and fulfil his civic obligations." However, problems continued to exist because "most Arab taxpayers do not understand income tax law, especially Arab villagers and Bedouins who are mostly analphabets." Another source of conflict, he said, was found in Arab extended family structures, a problem already raised during the mandatory period. For example, the law did not give tax credits to unmarried daughters, sisters, or aunts living with the taxpayer.[143]

Lower collection in the Arab sector, however, was not merely the result of ignorance or of cultural difference (or, indeed, the fact that the Arab taxpayers were poorer than Jewish ones). It was also the result of outright tax resistance. Resistance was manifested in parliamentary debates, for instance when an Arab member of the Israeli Parliament argued that "tax officials were making the lives of Arab farmers 'an intolerable hell'." It also took more concrete forms, for example in a 1958 riot involving Arab villagers in the Galilee, who stoned the house of a man suspected of being an income tax informer.[144]

A comprehensive review of taxation carried out by the Israeli State Comptroller's Office in the Arab sector (both urban and rural) in

---

[142] ISA, Gimel Lamed 12533/70, G. Levitzky to Netsiv Mas Hakhnasah, September 14, 1956.

[143] MT, M.1964.702–714, Ne'umo shel 'Awad Ibrahim al-'Abdallah, January 31, 1960. On the problem of allowances for adult family members, see also Ahmad Barhum, "Daribat al-Dakhil," *Al-Anba'*, November 10, 1968, at 4.

[144] "Arab MK's Motion Divides Coalition," *JP*, January 7, 1960, at 3; "Suspected Tax Informer Stoned," *JP*, October 26, 1958, at 3.

1956/57 provides a detailed picture of how the Arab population was taxed in the 1950s.[145] The review was based on reports on the assessment and collection of taxes in several locations in the north of the country. One report described the Arab section of the tax office in the northern city of Acre. The amount of taxes collected by the Acre office was relatively meager, and there were several reasons for this. First, the workload of the inspectors was significant (three inspectors were responsible for the files of 5,600 taxpayers). These inspectors were required to see taxpayers in the office, but also to visit distant Arab villages to conduct investigations and collect taxes on the spot. A car was available one day a week, but more often the inspectors had to use public transport, and then continue on foot or by camel or donkey. In such cases, they had to eat and sleep in the villages, which, according to the report, wasted time and "undermined the respect" the villagers ought to have for the inspectors. Second, the inspectors were poorly trained and their major qualification for being hired was their knowledge of Arabic, while the Arab population did not cooperate. Third, thousands of forms were sent to Arab taxpayers each year, but they refused to accept them at the post office and most were returned without being completed. Because self-assessment did not work, the inspectors were forced to rely on other sources of information, for example: intelligence obtained from the military governors of the Arab villages; personal investigations; information from village notables and the village headman; and data from Arab informers. All these sources provided information that often proved inaccurate or false, leading to assessments that were arbitrary. Once the office sent the assessment to the taxpayer, it was almost always challenged in response and, due to a lack of reliable information, invariably lowered.[146]

The report on the city of Acre included several examples of cases in which all these factors led to low tax payments. One such example was the case of a taxpayer from the Arab village of Shefa-'Amr. In the fiscal year 1951/52 his income was arbitrarily underassessed at I£800. However, since he was the owner of 150 goats, 5 cows, 6 acres of land, 1 camel, and 1 acre of vines, his actual income, said the report, was

---

[145] ISA, Gimel Lamed 12533/70, Mas Hakhnasah le-Mi'utim.
[146] ISA, Gimel Lamed 12533/70, Dokh 'al Bikoret be-Agaf Mas Hakhnasah, Sektor ha-Mi'utim, Ako, November 1, 1956.

far higher (the amount the report mentioned as his probable actual income was I£2,380). He was asked to pay I£181 on his income, and that amount was lowered to I£30 pounds after he challenged the assessment, based on the argument that he was entitled to deductions for his seven children (it is unclear, said the report, how many children he actually had).[147]

Another report that was part of the comprehensive review dealt with the income tax unit in the Arab city of Nazareth. Here matters were superficially better. The office had fifteen workers, all of them Arabs except the assessing officer himself, and some of them had already been working there before the establishment of the state. They were responsible for 3,500 taxpayer files, a workload that was lower than that of the Acre office. However, according to this report:

> formally the taxpayers cooperate with the office: they receive the tax form by post or from their headmen and return them filled in; they appear when they are invited to the office and pay the tax and advances that they owe, but this cooperation is merely formal, and in fact the taxpayers try to evade the payment of their fair and just tax as much as they can. Their declarations are low and unrealistic, hiding sources of income and their true value … [T]his is not something that is unique to the Arab taxpayer, because in every country taxpayers attempt to evade income taxation, but not to this extent. The fact that there is practically no cooperation is one of the most important reasons for the low revenue from income taxation in the Arab sector.

The report added:

> there is no assessment that is not challenged and the taxpayers know fully well that every challenge leads to a lower tax. The tendency of the office is to reach agreement with the taxpayer at any cost because the assessing officer and inspectors believe that their assessment would not hold up in court, and that every trial would lead to unpleasantness and loss of time and money, which is not proportionate to the amounts in dispute … [Because of these compromises] the Treasury loses 60 percent of its revenue from the income tax owed by Arab taxpayers in the Nazareth region.[148]

[147] Ibid.
[148] ISA, Gimel Lamed 12533/70, Doh 'al Totsa'at ha-Bikoret be-Misrad Mas Hakhnasah be-Natsrat, at 1.

Reports on tax collection in the Arab sector sometimes reiterated the general policy message of the Israeli Tax Authority of the time, namely about the importance of the use of education in inducing compliance. The goal of the tax authority was to "educate Arabs to become honest taxpayers." The mission, said one report, was "to convince [the Arabs] that the tax imposed on them is just and legal."[149] Another report, when discussing compromises and negotiations between the state and Arab taxpayers, stated that:

> the income tax authorities emphasize the [need] to educate the Arab population to become loyal citizens of the state [and the need to] impose a just tax on all the Arab inhabitants of the state. This approach leads to the inclusion of all possible Arab taxpayers in the tax network and ultimately to shallow and negligent treatment of all the income tax files [because it is impossible to accurately deal with all the files]. This way will not lead to the imposition of a just tax, because justice [will not be served when] every citizen pays whatever amount of tax [is imposed on him] but [only if he pays] the legal amount due from him based on his real income. Justice is not found [in a situation in which] a thousand poor Arabs pay 10 pounds of income tax each and lament the heavy tax burden. [Instead, justice will be served only] if wealthy Arabs, who attempt to avoid the payment of taxes, and seek to impose the tax on all the inhabitants of the village equally, pay the legal amount due. This will be perceived by the vast majority of the Arab population as just, and will contribute much more to the [attempt] to educate the Arab citizen to become a loyal citizen, than by imposing an equal amount of tax on all the Arabs, without taking into account differences [between them] in property and income.[150]

The picture that emerged from the review of the State Comptroller's Office on taxation in the Arab sector was therefore a mixed one. The review portrayed a system, designed to address widespread evasion, that was based (in theory) on education and trust as tools for fostering compliance, but that was (in reality) based on arbitrary assessments, negotiation, and compromises. In this sense, the Israeli system of the 1950s was similar to the Ottoman and early British methods of taxation.[151]

---

[149] Ibid., at 4.

[150] ISA, Gimel Lamed 12533/70, Dokh 'al Bikoret be-Agaf Mas Hakhnasah, Sektor ha-Mi'utim, Ako, November 1, 1956, at 6.

[151] As noted before, negotiations and compromises in the 1950s were certainly not limited to the Arab sector, but were also widely prevalent in the relationship with Jewish taxpayers.

FIGURE 4.3 Photograph, 1959. The caption accompanying the photograph reads: "The notables of the [Arab] village of Sakhnin host the director of state revenue, Ze'ev Sharef [center], and the national inspector for minorities' affairs, G. Levitzky [right], in the income tax commissioner's office. [The person] marked [with an] asterisk [is] the headman of Shakhnin, 'Awad Ibrahim al-'Abdallah (1959)."

Another feature of taxation in the Arab sector reminiscent of the older model of taxation was the use of local intermediaries by the state, as well as by individual Arab taxpayers who often relied on leading members of their village, clan, or sect as intermediaries to negotiate with the tax office (see Figure 4.3).

One such example of the use of intermediaries can be found in the case of a Druze Member of the Knesset, Sheikh Saleh Khneifes. The Druze, an Arabic-speaking sect, served in the Israeli Army and enjoyed a closer relationship with the Israeli state than did other Arabic-speaking Israeli-Arabs (as they continue to do today). Khneifes, who served as a member of the Israeli Parliament in the early 1950s, was in constant contact with the tax authority, where he appeared often to deal with the income tax matters of various taxpayers. However, when he failed to pay the taxes he himself owed, forty of his cows were seized. Khneifes then complained that such a seizure sent the wrong signal to his electorate that "the government [was] no longer with Khneifes" (and therefore he could no longer be relied on as a tax intermediary).[152]

Did tax compliance and tax administration in the Arab sector change in subsequent decades? Anecdotal evidence from the 1960s and 1970s indicates the continuation of widespread tax evasion on the part of the Arab population of Israel. A newspaper report on income taxation in Arab villages in the Galilee in the 1970s claimed that while 15 percent of the population at the time were Arabs, they only paid 1.5 percent of the income tax. The report also stated that there were whole Arab villages where nobody paid the tax except employees whose tax was withheld at the source. This difference may have been partly due to the fact that the Arab population was poorer, partly due to lower rates of employment, and partly due to lower compliance rates.[153]

The use of arbitrary collection tactics on the part of the Israeli tax system also continued. For example, in a 1966 report published in the newspaper of the Israeli Communist Party, which was, for many decades, one of the major political organizations supported by the Arab population of Israel, it was reported that the government was using an "old new method" for the expropriation of Arab lands – levying high taxes on Arab residents of the village of Taibeh, to put pressure on them to sell their lands.[154] Somewhat similar tactics continue even in the twenty-first century. In East Jerusalem, occupied and annexed by Israel after the Six Day War, tax collectors were accused in 2004 of acting like "armed gangs," using force to collect taxes.[155] A recent Israeli Supreme Court case, decided in 2010, dealt with the apparently prevalent practice among both Israeli income tax and social security tax collectors of collecting tax arrears at security roadblocks set up in Arab neighborhoods in East Jerusalem by the police or the army. Arab

---

[152] ISA, Gimel Lamed 12533/68, [newspaper clip], S. Hovav, "Ha-Memshalah Nat'shah et Khneifes," *Ma'ariv*, October 7, 1959, at 3. On the use of intermediaries by the Israeli state in its relations with the Arabs, see generally Cohen, *Good Arabs*, 11–38. On Khneifes specifically, see Cohen, *Good Arabs*, 71–3.

[153] "Mas Hakhnasah Lo Goveh Hovot shel Alfey Nishomim 'Aravim," *Haaretz*, March 16, 1976, at 10.

[154] "Daribat al-Dakhil Tastasdir Amrun li-Musadarat Aradi fi al-Taybah," *Al-Ittihad*, May 27, 1966, at 5.

[155] "As'hab al-Mahal al-Muqadasiyyun: Mustakhdamu al-Daribah al-Isra'iliyyah Yustakhdamun Uslub al-'Isabat," *Al-Hayat al-Jadidah*, February 9, 2004, at 6.

residents passing through these roadblocks were often stopped by Israeli tax collectors, who threatened to impound their cars unless they paid their tax or social security debts on the spot. The petitioners in this case argued that such methods of collection were discriminatory. The roadblocks were placed in areas in which the absolute majority of vehicles were driven by Arab residents of Jerusalem, thus branding the residents with the collective mark of criminality, and therefore constituting discrimination. The court noted that such roadblocks were sometimes set up in other parts of the country, and it therefore did not deal with the argument about discrimination; but it did rule that there was no legal authority enabling tax officials to collect taxes at such roadblocks, and that such a method infringes on the rights of dignity, privacy, freedom of movement, due process, and access to justice of the people stopped at these roadblocks.[156]

Conclusion

The Israeli state of the 1950s, in marked contrast to its British colonial predecessor, made extensive use of various nonlegal methods to "train" its citizens to pay their taxes, creating compliance where none existed before. This was the result of a crisis – the breakdown in compliance in the early 1950s – but also of a civic ideology, a new conception of the relationship between state and taxpayers. Creating compliance was part of a wider attempt by the Israeli nation-state to turn itself into a new type of community – a national community – and to turn its subjects, veteran Jewish residents of Palestine and the population of Jewish refugees who came to the country in the 1950s, into loyal, self- (and other-) policing model members of the community. This was achieved by fostering compliance using social norms rather than legal compulsion. The process of turning colonial subjects into national citizens was neither straightforward nor linear, and the tax system of Israel of the 1950s relied both on "new" and "old" methods to ensure compliance. This can be seen in the way some of the new tools used by the state to deal with widespread evasion, such as the tax register, were actually an echo of previous forms of taxation. It is also evident

---

[156] HCJ 6827/04 *Dr. Adel Manna v. Rashut ha-Misim, Misim* 25(1), E – 43.

in how the resistance to taxation (for example, among the Arabs of Israel) led the state to resort to negotiations, compromises, and the use of local intermediaries when dealing with taxpayers, in ways reminiscent of Ottoman and early British-colonial taxation. Over time, the power of these intermediaries waned, but the use of intermediaries between the state and individual taxpayers did not disappear. Instead, new types of intermediaries – tax professionals relying on legal norms – gradually took over the task of mediating between taxpayers and the state. I now describe the rise of these intermediaries.

PART III

THE TRANSFORMATION OF ISRAELI
TAXATION AND ITS LAW

5

The Rise of Tax Experts: Accountants, Lawyers, and Economists

In 1959 an advertisement appeared in Israeli bookstores: "Just published – the fourth [annual] report on state revenues for the [fiscal] year 1957/8. Available for sale in this store" (see Figure 5.1).

The creator of this ad it seems, thought readers would eagerly buy such a report.[1] This says much about how taxation was a natural part of public discourse in Israel of the 1950s – a scenario unimaginable today. The ad, of course, was not the only evidence of a special relationship between ordinary taxpayers and the tax authority during this period. Many of the measures discussed in Chapter 4, such as the establishment of the Museum of Taxes (where this ad is now exhibited), also highlight the efforts of the early Israeli state to create a direct and intimate relationship with its taxpayers.

In the process of making taxation a matter of civic concern relevant to every taxpayer, the prestate Jewish community in the 1940s,

---

[1] Ze'ev Sharef, the director of state revenue in the Ministry of Finance, explained in the introduction to the first report published in 1956 that "difficulties have arisen here and there between the young tax administration and different circles of the public," and that therefore that the goal of the reports would be to "deepen the understanding" between the government and the public. See *Din ve-Heshbon Rishon 'al Hakhnasot ha-Medinah* (Jerusalem: Ha-Madpis ha-Memshalti, 1956), 7. Somewhat similar reports were also published in the last years of the British mandate period, but I did not encounter ads publicizing them. See P. J. Loftus, *National Income of Palestine, 1944* ([Jerusalem]: Government Printer, 1946); P. J. Loftus, *National Income of Palestine, 1945* ([Jerusalem]: Government Printer, 1948).

FIGURE 5.1 Advertisement, 1959: "Just published – the fourth [annual] report on state revenues for the [fiscal] year 1957/8. Available for sale in this store."

as well as the new Israeli state in the 1950s, relied on a special kind of bureaucrat: the tax propaganda (or public relations) official.[2] Two such officials in particular should be mentioned: Emanuel Harussi, the director of the propaganda department of the community tax and of the mobilization and rescue fund, and Avraham Mandel, the spokesman for the State Revenue Administration and the founder of the Israeli Museum of Taxes. Mandel, as mentioned earlier, was an artist by profession, although his work as director of the museum turned him into a self-taught tax historian with wide-ranging knowledge of philology, history, and economics.[3] Harussi was not a professional tax expert either. He was an important literary figure in mandatory Palestine, a prolific poet whose work for the community

[2] On fiscal propaganda elsewhere, see James T. Sparrow, *Warfare State: World War II Americans and the Age of Big Government* (New York: Oxford University Press, 2011), 133–43.

[3] See, e.g., Avraham Mandel, *Ha-Misim ba-Mekorot (Ha-Tanakh, ha-Mishnah veha-Talmudim)* (Jerusalem, 1987).

tax administration in the 1940s was only one minor detail in his rich curriculum vitae.

These PR professionals were engaged in a wide range of activities. For example, the work plan of Mandel's office for the fiscal year 1964/65 included long lists of planned press conferences and the publication of fourteen books and booklets on topics ranging from mundane overviews of the structure of the Israeli tax system, written for school children and foreign investors, to extremely specialized, quasi-academic publications – for example, a reproduction of the tax regulations of the Jewish community in nineteenth-century Ottoman Salonika.[4]

Over time, the importance of artists and poets working to reshape the minds of taxpayers declined. The use of tax propaganda never completely disappeared, but it was overshadowed by other, more technical, forms of knowledge.[5] These forms were based on a new (or rather, partly revived) model of the relationship between taxpayers and the state. Instead of an intimate and direct relationship, new types of tax experts that had not existed in Palestine prior to the twentieth century – accountants, lawyers, and economists – recreated the old two-tiered structure in which intermediaries intervened in the relationship between citizens and the state. However, unlike the old intermediaries (tax farmers), the new intermediaries often came to represent the interests of taxpayers, rather than those of the state.

This chapter describes the professional history of such tax experts.[6] This history is related to broad political, economic, and cultural

---

[4] MT, booklet no. 324, Minhal ha-Hakhnasot – Ha-Otsar, Tokhnit ha-Hasbarah, ha-Informatsyah ve-Aspakat Yedah la-Tsibur be-'Inyeney Misim 1964/65 (Jerusalem: Minhal ha-Hakhnasot, April 1964), 4.

[5] The Israel Tax Authority still engages periodically in public relations campaigns to foster compliance. See, e.g., Aliza Eshed, "Mas Hakhnasah Hu Lo Rak Goveh Misim Hu Gam Mehanekh," *Beyn ha-Shumot: Bit'on 'Ovdey Agaf Mas Hakhnasah ve-Misuy Mekarke'in* 37 (April 2001): 5. However, an indication of the diminishing role of PR experts can be seen in the changes in the personnel of the Museum of Taxes in Jerusalem. The Museum still exists, but today it is a marginalized institution. When it was established in the 1960s, the staff of the Museum included Mandel and four assistants. Today the museum is run by one (part-time) employee. Mira Dror (Director of the Museum of Taxes, Jerusalem), interviews conducted by author, August 2012 and March 2014.

[6] There are some related tax professionals, such as customs agents, who will not be discussed in this chapter. On such agents, see, e.g., Alma Yitshaki Kurtzweil, ed.,

changes that occurred in Israel between the 1960s and the mid-1980s, as Israel was gradually transformed from a mobilized nation-state devoted, at least rhetorically, to a collectivist ethos into an individualist, neoliberal state. These broad changes led to a relative decline in the commitment of Israelis to their state, and to the civic duties imposed on them by this state, and triggered increased demand for the services of tax professionals to assist taxpayers in minimizing their taxes. This demand brought with it a growing supply of tax experts able to meet the new requirements of Israeli taxpayers for tax advice. Between the mandatory period and the 1980s, the number of accountants and lawyers (and also economists, providing tax policy advice to the government rather than to individuals) grew, both absolutely and per capita. This growth was accompanied by institutional changes that consolidated the autonomy and power of the three professions.[7]

Alongside this numerical and institutional growth, the professional discourse of these experts changed. During the 1950s the discourse of

---

Ha-Mekhes be-Yisrael: Min he-'Avar, Derekh ha-Hoveh, 'Im ha-Panim le-'Atid 1870–2010 (Jerusalem: Keter, 2011), 22.

[7] This chapter focuses on Jewish professionals. Jews dominated all three professions discussed here during the mandatory era and certainly after 1948, when a large segment of the Palestinian urban elite in the area that became the State of Israel fled or was expelled, and the remaining Arab population was predominantly rural. During the mandatory era there were Arab lawyers and accountants, but Jewish professionals greatly outnumbered Arab ones. For example, a list of the lawyers active in mandatory Palestine in January 1948, published in the *Palestine Gazette* in April 1948, included the names of 1,187 lawyers licensed to appear before government courts. Of these, 1,059 lawyers (90 percent) were Jews, at a time when the Jews comprised only 33 percent of the population of the country. See PG, April 22, 1948, 309–20. By the 1960s the dominance of Jews in the Israeli legal profession was even greater. See Gavriel Strasman, *'Otey ha-Glimah: Toldot 'Arikhat ha-Din be-Erets Yisrael* (Tel Aviv: Lishkat 'Orkhey ha-Din, 1984), 315–39. On the Arab commercial class during the mandatory period, see generally Sherene Seikaly, *Men of Capital: Scarcity and Economy in Mandate Palestine* (Stanford: Stanford University Press, 2016). On Arab accountants, see Itamar Levin, *Heshbon Meshutaf: Lishkat Ro'ey Heshbon, Ha-Yishuv veha-Medinah: 80 Shnot Du'ah: 1931–2011* (Tel Aviv: Lishkat Ro'ey Heshbon be-Yisrael, 2011), 15. On Arab lawyers, see Assaf Likhovski, *Law and Identity in Mandate Palestine* (Chapel Hill: University of North Carolina Press, 2006), 173–91. On the Arab sector in the economy of post-1948 Israel, see, e.g., Nachum Gross, "Kalkalat Yisrael," in *'Idan: He-'Asor ha-Rishon 1948–1958*, eds. Hanna Yablonka and Zvi Zameret (Jerusalem: Yad Izhak Ben-Zvi, 1997), 137–50, 147–9.

accountants and lawyers had been characterized by statist rhetoric. This rhetoric emphasized the role of the two groups as educators of the public, echoing the general educational approach typical of the 1950s, as discussed in Chapter 4. However, in the 1960s and 1970s accountants began to describe themselves as mainly serving their clients, not the state, and lawyers emphasized their role as guardians of their clients' civil rights in the latter's dealings with the state. A somewhat similar process can be found in economic discourse in Palestine and Israel. During the mandatory era and the early years of the state, economists and many Zionist political leaders espoused a particularist approach to economic laws, arguing that they were inapplicable to the Zionist case and that ideology and education could overcome selfish individual interests. Over time, however, this belief in Zionist exceptionalism waned. In the tax field it was replaced by an approach that no longer viewed taxpayers as citizens committed to the collective, but as rational, self-interested individuals seeking to maximize their wealth.

The professionalization of the tax arena in Israel was therefore not only a story of the growing demand for tax advice, or of the growing supply of tax intermediaries able to provide such advice.[8] These intermediaries gradually came to understand themselves and their society differently. Changing professional notions echoed (and also enabled) a changed attitude toward tax compliance among the Israeli public, reflecting the broader political and cultural transformation of Israeli state and society. Demand, supply, and changing self-understanding

[8] On the growth of tax professionals in other countries, see, e.g., Victor Thuronyi and Frans Vanistendael, "Regulation of Tax Professionals," in *Tax Law Design and Drafting*, ed. Victor Thuronyi (Washington, DC: IMF, 1996), 1:135–63; Jane Frecknall-Hughes, "Contextualising the Development of the Tax Profession: Some First Thoughts," in *Studies in the History of Tax Law*, ed. John Tiley (Oxford: Hart, 2011), 5:177–91; Jane Frecknall-Hughes and Margaret McKerchar, "The History and Development of the Taxation Profession in the UK and Australia," in *Studies in the History of Tax Law*, ed. John Tiley (Oxford: Hart, 2013), 6:421–48; Jane Frecknall-Hughes and Margaret McKerchar, "Historical Perspectives on the Emergence of the Tax Profession: Australia and the UK," *Australian Tax Forum* 28 (2013): 275–88. On professionalism generally, see, e.g., Magali Sarfatti Larson, *The Rise of Professionalism: A Sociological Analysis* (Berkeley: University of California Press, 1977); Andrew Abbott, *The System of Professions: An Essay on the Division of Expert Labor* (Chicago: University of Chicago Press, 1988).

came together to transform the nature of tax compliance in Israel in the 1960s, and this transformation ultimately led the state and its institutions – courts and the legislature – to change how they dealt with noncompliance, by changing the nature of tax law.

The Waning of Collectivism

Zionist society in mandatory Palestine was animated by a collectivist ethos – the interests of the Jewish community were given precedence, at least rhetorically, over the interests of individuals belonging to it.[9] In the 1950s the rhetoric of collectivist commitment and civic duty to the new state continued to govern the official discourse of the Israeli government. For example, David Ben-Gurion, Israel's first prime minister, believed that the "rights of the State take precedence over the rights of the individual," and he suggested that Israelis impose on themselves a bill of duties rather than a bill of rights, stressing a republican view of citizenship focused not only on rights but also on duties.[10]

However, in the 1950s this collectivism was less voluntary than it had been before the creation of the state. As we saw in Chapter 4, it was now "encouraged" in a top-down manner by organs of the new state. Social historian Orit Rozin argues that the apparent continuity in the rhetoric of collectivism before and after Israeli independence in 1948 actually masked a subtle change: after 1948 tension developed between the collectivist norms and ideals propagated by the state, and the individualist desires and tendencies of large segments of the Israeli population. These tendencies had multiple sources: changes in the composition of Israeli society following large waves of nonideological Jewish immigration that flooded the country in the 1950s; political tension between different segments in Israeli society; and fatigue following the long years of social mobilization, both before and after the war of 1948.[11]

---

[9] See, e.g., Anita Shapira, *Israel: A History*, trans. Anthony Berris (Waltham, MA: Brandeis University Press, 2012), 133–42.

[10] Yoav Peled, *The Challenge of Ethnic Democracy: The State and Minority Groups in Israel, Poland and Northern Ireland* (New York: Routledge, 2014), 96; Nir Kedar, *Ben-Gurion veha-Hukah* (Or Yehuda: Dvir, 2015), 20–1.

[11] See Orit Rozin, *The Rise of the Individual in 1950s Israel: A Challenge to Collectivism*, trans. Haim Watzman (Waltham, MA: Brandeis University Press, 2011). See also Dan Horowitz and Moshe Lissak, *Trouble in Utopia: The Overburdened Polity of Israel*

The 1960s saw additional cracks appear in the collectivist ethos of Israeli society. In the 1950s and 1960s Israeli GDP grew rapidly, accompanied by swift industrialization.[12] A new middle class of businessmen, managers, and professional experts emerged.[13] The security situation improved following the Sinai campaign of 1956, and even more so following Israel's victory in the Six Day War in 1967, which greatly expanded the territory controlled by the state.[14] What had been a small, beleaguered, and relatively cohesive society committed to a pioneering, socialist ideology, was suddenly transformed, expanding both physically and mentally. After 1967 the dour, puritan values of Israel's founding fathers came under attack by growing consumerism and openness to Western, particularly American, culture. The collectivist slogans of the Israeli government, demanding sacrifice for the good of the nation, seemed increasingly dated and divorced from the aspirations and even reality of many Israelis.

Changes further accelerated in the 1970s. The shock of the 1973 war, a series of corruption scandals in the mid-1970s involving figures connected to the ruling Labor Party (in power since 1948), and the growing political weight of underprivileged Jewish groups opposed to the dominant secular, socialist ideology of the Labor Party, especially oriental and religious Jews, all ultimately led to the rise to power of the right-wing Likud Party in 1977. The party, espousing an ideology that combined nationalism, respect for traditional values embedded in religion, and free market liberalism, accelerated changes that were already under way in Israeli society. The economy was gradually liberalized, and the Israeli welfare state of the 1950s was dismantled (these processes were inspired both by the promarket ideology of factions

(Albany: SUNY Press, 1989), 110–13; Menachem Mautner, *Law and the Culture of Israel* (Oxford: Oxford University Press, 2011), 106–19; Shapira, *Israel: A History*, 200–5, 254–6.

[12] See generally David Levi-Faur, *Ha-Yad ha-Lo Ne'elamah: Ha-Politikah shel ha-Ti'us be-Yisrael* (Jerusalem: Yad Izhak Ben-Zvi, 2001), 1–2; Paul Rivlin, *The Israeli Economy from the Foundation of the State through the 21st Century* (New York: Cambridge University Press, 2011), 41–2; Amir Ben-Porat, *Keytsad Na'astah Yisrael Kapitalistit* (Haifa: Pardes, 2011), 158–91.

[13] Ben-Porat, *Keytsad*, 171–2. See also Amir Ben-Porat, *Heykhan hem ha-Burganim ha-Hem? Toldot ha-Burganut ha-Yisre'elit* (Jerusalem: Magnes, 1999).

[14] See, e.g., Shapira, *Israel: A History*, 307, 348.

within the Likud Party, as well as by the rise of neoliberalism in the Western world generally). Some of the leading institutions of the old order such as the rural cooperative communities, the *kibbutzim*, and the industrial enterprises affiliated with the largest Israeli labor union, the General Federation of Labor (Histadrut), collapsed and were privatized due to economic mismanagement and the loss of governmental support.[15] The civic republican ideal was now mostly abandoned by the Israeli public, although a mutated, nationalist–religious, version of this ideal continued to exist among the Jewish settlers who had begun to trickle into the occupied Palestinian territories after 1967. Israeli society was never homogeneous, but after 1977 the cohesive rhetoric and ethos of the 1950s disappeared, and this society no longer understood itself as unitary. Now Israelis saw their society as riven by deep ethnic, social, and cultural schisms, and divided into various warring groups.[16] The republican notion of identity that had dominated Israeli culture in the 1950s also declined, illustrated, perhaps, by the decline in the use of the term "citizen" in books in Hebrew (see Figure 5.2).

The secular socialists affiliated with the Labor party and its institutions that had dominated Israel until 1977 continued to dominate some institutions of the Israeli state such as the media, the higher education system, and the legal system, but the hegemony they had previously enjoyed disappeared.[17] More importantly, they themselves were no longer committed to the ideology of Israel of the 1950s. Individualism replaced collectivism: the Israel of the 1950s, an "East European social-democracy" characterized by "virtuous discomfort," was gone.[18] How

---

[15] Ibid., 194–200, 211–14. On the global rise of neoliberalism in the 1970s, see generally David Harvey, *A Brief History of Neoliberalism* (Oxford: Oxford University Press, 2005). On Israeli neoliberalism, see Menachem Mautner, "Petah Davar: Liberalizm be-Yisrael – 'Ha-Adam ha-Tov,' ha-Ezrah ha-Ra'' veha-Sigsug ha-Ishi veha-Hevrati," *'Iyuney Mishpat* 36 (2013): 7–79, 38–47. See also Daphne Barak-Erez, *Ezrah-Natin-Tsarhan: Mishpat ve-Shilton be-Hevrah Mishtanah* (Or-Yehudah: Kinneret, Zmora Bitan, 2012).

[16] Gershon Shafir and Yoav Peled, *Being Israeli: The Dynamics of Multiple Citizenship* (New York: Cambridge University Press, 2002), 168; Peled, *The Challenge of Ethnic Democracy*, 93–149; Shapira, *Israel: A History*, 357–90; Mautner, *Law and the Culture of Israel*, 109–43.

[17] Shapira, *Israel: A History*, 386–7; Ben-Porat, *Keytsad*, 182.

[18] See Richard Davenport-Hines, ed., *Letters from Oxford: Hugh Trevor-Roper to Bernard Berenson* (London: Phoenix, 2007), 144.

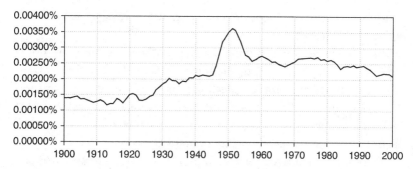

FIGURE 5.2 Use of the term "citizen" (*ezrah*) in books in Hebrew, 1900–2000.

were all these processes reflected in the tax arena? One symptom (and perhaps also a minor catalyst) of these broad social and cultural changes was the rise of tax professionals as intermediaries between tax-payers and the state.

The Growing Supply of Tax Professionals

Accountants

The history of the accounting profession in mandatory Palestine and Israel is one of continuous growth.[19] While the Ottoman state had a developed system of state accounting, private-sector accounting in the Ottoman Empire did not come into existence until the nineteenth century, when Western accounting practices first appeared in the Empire as part of the mid-nineteenth-century reforms (*tanzimat*).[20]

---

[19] An academic history of the Israeli accounting profession has not yet been written. A recently published celebratory album provides a chronology of some major landmarks in the development of the accounting profession in mandatory Palestine and Israel. See Levin, *Heshbon*. For an earlier (and briefer) English discussion, see F. S. Somekh, "Development of Public Accountancy in Israel," *The Israel C.P.A.*, 1971, 6–16. For histories of accounting in other jurisdictions, see, e.g., Anthony G. Hopwood and Peter Miller, eds., *Accounting as a Social and Institutional Practice* (Cambridge: Cambridge University Press, 1994), 1–39; John Richard Edwards and Stephen P. Walker, eds., *The Routledge Companion to Accounting History* (New York: Routledge, 2009).

[20] Mehmet Erkan and Cemal Elitaş, "Accounting Education in [the] Ottoman State," *International Journal of Business and Social Science* 2:13 (2011): 210–14; Ibrahim Mert, "A Historical Overview of Accounting in Turkey," *Internal Auditing and Risk*

It is unclear to what extent such practices were prevalent in Ottoman-ruled Palestine.

British-educated accountants arrived in Palestine after the British conquest of the country, but the initial impetus for the formation of an accounting profession in Palestine came only with the enactment of the Companies Ordinance of 1921. This ordinance required every corporation to appoint an auditor licensed by the government to report to shareholders on its accounts and annual balance sheet.[21]

During the mandatory era, accountant licenses were awarded only to persons who had passed the relevant exams and obtained a certificate from British accounting organizations.[22] In addition, accountants from a number of other Western countries were granted licenses based on their professional experience.[23] Two British firms, Russell and Co., which mainly audited Jewish corporations, and Whinney, Murray and

---

Management 31 (2013): 15–25; Peter Clarke, "Exploring the History of Accounting in Cyprus," *Global Business and Economics Review* 13 (2011): 281–95, 282–3.

[21] Companies Ordinance 1921, sec. 76, in *Legislation of Palestine 1918–1925*, comp. Norman Bentwich (Alexanderia: Whitehead Morris, 1926), 213–14. These sections were expanded in the Companies Ordinance of 1929. See Companies Ordinance 1929, secs. 106–111, Drayton, 1:256. Auditors were also mentioned in the Cooperative Societies Ordinance 1921, and the Bankruptcy Ordinance 1936. See R. D. Kesselman, "Bikoret ha-Heshbon ke-Miktso'a ba-Arets," *Ro'eh ha-Heshbon ha-Musmakh* (December 1939): 4–5; D. Rosolio, "Ro'eh ha-Heshbon veha-Lako'ah," *Ro'eh ha-Heshbon ha-Musmakh* (March 1944): 16–18; Israel Straus, "Kenes Yovel 50 Shanah le-Lishkat Ro'ey Heshbon be-Yisrael," *RH* 33 (1983): 10–11. For a similar process in Cyprus, see Peter Clarke and Andrekos Varnava, "Accounting in Cyprus during the Last Four Decades of British Rule: Post–World War I to Independence (1918–1960)," *Accounting History* 18 (2013): 293–315. It is interesting to note that in the UK, the requirement that auditors be professional accountants only appeared in 1947. See Josephine Maltby, "'A Sort of Guide, Philosopher and Friend': The Rise of the Professional Auditor in Britain," *Accounting, Business and Financial History* 9 (1999): 29–50, 42.

[22] These were the Institute of Chartered Accountants in England and Wales (ICAEW), and the London Association of Certified Accountants, which is now called the Association of Chartered Certified Accountants – ACCA. The entrance exams to these organizations were held in Palestine twice annually and supervised by the Palestine Department of Education. See Zvi E. Talmon, "Kenes Yovel 50 Shanah le-Lishkat Ro'ey Heshbon be-Yisrael: Dvar hs-Nasi," *RH* 33 (1983): 12; Levin, *Heshbon*, 38. In the UK itself there was no governmental licensing requirement. See Arnon Rojansky, "Te'udatenu be-Sha'ah Zo," *Ro'eh ha-Heshbon ha-Musmakh* (December 1939): 3.

[23] Eliezer Bawly, "Toldot Lishkat Ro'ey Heshbon be-Yisrael," *RH* 15 (1965): 354.

Co., which audited oil-related corporations (Palestine was a center for refining oil produced in Iraq), dominated the small local market in which only a few corporations operated. The first professional body of accountants in Palestine, the Association of Certified Accountants and Auditors (ACAA) (Agudat Ro'ey Heshbon Musmakhim u-Mevakrim), was established in 1931 by three Jewish accountants. At the time, there were sixteen licensed accountants in Palestine, eight of whom were in private practice. By the end of 1931, four additional Jewish account-ants had joined the three founding members of the ACAA.[24]

The enactment of the Income Tax Ordinance in 1941 represented a major boost to the development of the accounting profession in Palestine. The Ordinance did not require individual or corporate tax-payers to use professional advisors to comply with its provisions, and taxpayers could submit their own returns. It was entirely their choice whether or not to use intermediaries, and the Income Tax Ordinance did not regulate the professional qualifications of their representatives.[25]

---

[24] See Zvi Bentov, "Ha-Pe'ilut ha-Miktso'it shel Lishkat Ro'ey Heshbon be-Yisrael," *RH* 33 (1983/84): 19; "Dvar ha-Ma'arekhet: Yovel Lishkat Ro'ey ha-Heshbon be-Yisrael 1931–1981," *RH* 33 (1983): 5; Bawly, "Toldot," 468. On Russell and Co., see also "Mi-Yafo le-Tel Aviv," *Davar*, March 15, 1933, at 8; Clarke and Varnava, "Accounting in Cyprus," 303. At the time there were about 500 corporations regis-tered in Palestine, the majority of them Jewish. See Itamar Levin, "Kol 'Esek Tsarikh Heshbonaut Modernit," *RH* 27 (new series) (2011): 22. The Jewish Association was not the only professional accounting organization that existed in mandatory Palestine. A British-dominated Association of Chartered Accountants in Palestine was established in March 1940. See "Society of Chartered Accountants," *PP*, March 10, 1940, at 8; "Accountants Hosts To [sic] Australians," *PP*, May 7, 1940, at 2. A Palestine branch of the Association of International Accountants was established in 1944. See "Ro'ey ha-Heshbon le-Tipuah Miktso'am," *Davar*, January 24, 1946, at 4. On British accountants in other parts of the Empire, see, e.g., Marcia Annisette and Dean Neu, eds., "Accounting and Empire," special issue, *Critical Perspectives on Accounting* 15 (2004): 1–206.

[25] Section 45 of the Ordinance allowed anyone to represent and serve as an agent of a taxpayer. The section stated that "the assessing officer may give notice to [a taxpayer] ... requiring him within a reasonable time to complete and deliver to the assessing officer any return ... and/or to attend personally *or by representative* before him and to produce for examination any books, documents, accounts and returns." Income Tax Ordinance, 1947, sec. 45, PG Supp. I, 121 (emphasis added); Bentov, "Ha-Pe'ilut," 19; Dov Levin, "Yo'ets ha-Mas – Mekor Samkhuto ve-Ma'amado, Tkhum Tafkido ve-Akhrayuto," *Heshbona'ut u-Misim* 47 (1991): 5–21, 7.

However, in practice the Ordinance provided a "great impetus" to the growth of the accounting profession because most corporations, and some partnerships and individual taxpayers, began to employ accountants to prepare their annual tax returns and represent them before the tax authorities. Accountants therefore became important intermediaries between some taxpayers and the government.[26]

One accountant, Robert Kesselman, wrote in November 1941 that the Income Tax Ordinance was bound to make the accountant, despite himself, into an important intermediary: on the one hand, explaining to taxpayers their duties and rights, and on the other, clarifying for the tax authorities the specific circumstances of the individual business he served. Another accountant, Eliezer Bawly, noted in July 1942 that, following the enactment of the Income Tax Ordinance, the accountant's role was enhanced. From a marginal figure in the client's firm, he now became the trusted man of both the assessing officer and the business owner.[27]

A 1941 advertisement from the British Institute of Commerce in Jerusalem informed potential students that "the War is an opportunity for you ... the intention of the government to impose income taxation

---

[26] Shalom Proshan, "Be'ayot ha-Miktso'ah," *RH* 8 (1957/58): 91; Bawly, "Toldot," 354; Somekh, "Development of Public Accountancy," 7. In Cyprus, too, the introduction of income taxation in 1941 provided "an important stimulus to the development of accounting (and tax) professionals." See Clarke, "Exploring the History of Accounting in Cyprus," 286. There were additional stimuli for the growth of the profession in the 1940s, mainly the expansion of Palestine's economy during the Second World War and the concurrent growth in the number of corporations. See E. Bawly, "Ha-Miktso'a ba-Arets bi-Shnot ha-Milhamah," *Ro'eh ha-Heshbon ha-Musmakh* (January 1946): 3–5.

[27] R. D. Kesselman, "Mas Ha-Hakhnasah ve-Ro'eh ha-Heshbon," *Ro'eh ha-Heshbon ha-Musmakh* (November 1941): 4; E. Bawly, "Ha-Matsav ha-Miktso'ee shel Ro'eh ha-Heshbon ha-Musmakh ba-Shanah she-Halfah," *Ro'eh ha-Heshbon ha-Musmakh* (July 1942): 3. The growing demand was reflected in wider educational opportunities. In the 1930s, the "School of Accountancy" offered British degrees based on study by mail. See, e.g., "A Well-Paid Appointment," *PP*, July 15, 1936, at 12; "Ambitious Men," *PP*, July 23, 1936, at 3. In the 1940s this school was joined by the British Institute of Commerce and Accountancy in Jerusalem, and the Bama'aleh School of Commerce in Haifa. See "Mas ha-Hakhnasah: Hizdamnut la-Kol," *Davar*, April 10, 1941, at 3; "The Bamaaleh School of Commerce," *PP*, August 10, 1944, at 4; "Centre of Accountancy," *PP*, May 23, 1947, at 7.

will provide many opportunities for men and women who studied ... accounting, a chance to secure a decent salary in a profession that will guarantee your future."[28] In 1944 Eliezer Bawly stated that "a large part of our professional life is devoted, and will be devoted in the future, to the large amount of work produced by the introduction of income taxation," and two years later he stated that the income tax had greatly enhanced the role of accountants.[29]

After the establishment of the state of Israel in 1948, several developments solidified the professional power of the ACAA. The British firms left Palestine.[30] The new Israeli government recognized the ACAA as the sole representative body of accountants in the country.[31] In 1950 an accounting institute was established at the Tel Aviv School of Law and Economics to train new accountants, severing the link with the British accounting associations.[32] In 1955 the Israeli government enacted the Auditors' Law, regulating the profession. Following the enactment of the law, the ACAA changed its name, now calling itself the Institute of Certified Public Accountants in Israel (ICPAI) (Lishkat Ro'ey Heshbon be-Yisrael).[33] These changes were accompanied by the growing presence of corporations, both in number and economic importance. In turn, the growth in the number of corporations accelerated the demand for the services of accountants, as corporations, unlike individuals, were required to be audited annually by accountants. This turn of events was one of the factors fueling a rapid rise in the number of accountants both absolutely and per capita (see Table 5.1).[34]

---

[28] Advertisement by the British Institute of Commerce, *Davar*, April 24, 1941, at 3.

[29] E. Bawly, "'Al Be'ayot ha-Miktso'ah," *Ro'eh ha-Heshbon ha-Musmakh* (March 1944): 3; Bawly, "Ha-Miktso 'a ba-Arets," 3.

[30] Levin, *Heshbon*, 41.

[31] Ibid., 8.

[32] "Dvar ha-Ma'arekhet," *RH* 7 (1956/57): 325; Talmon, "Kenes Yovel," 13; Bawly, "Toldot," 466. On the Tel Aviv School of Law and Economics, see, generally, Likhovski, *Law and Identity*, 161–2.

[33] Auditors' Law, 5715/1955, LSI, 9:27; "Nitkabel 'Hok Ro'ey Heshbon'," *Herut*, February 1, 1955, at 1; Talmon, "Kenes Yovel," 13–14; Bawly, "Toldot," 467; Levin, *Heshbon*, 41.

[34] The share in the revenue from the income taxation of corporations rather than individuals has tripled between the early 1950s and the present. In 1951 corporations paid 10 percent of the income tax revenue collected by the state. Now they pay about

Table 5.1 Growth in the number of accountants in mandatory Palestine and Israel, 1931–1983

	Members of ACAA/ ICPAI	Population of mandatory Palestine/Israel	No. of accountants per capita
1931 (mandatory Palestine)	7	1,000,000	1/142,850
1949 (Israel)	60	900,000	1/15,000
1955	149	1,800,000	1/12,080
1965	610	2,600,000	1/4,262
1975	2,000	3,500,000	1/1,750
1983	2,826	4,100,000	1/1,450

Note: Licensed accountants are not required to become members of the ICPAI. However, almost all practicing accountants are members of the ICPAI.

The regulation of the accounting profession in the 1950s was followed in the 1960s by the regulation of tax consultancy – a field related to accountancy but lower on the professional ladder.[35] The role of tax consultants (just as in the present day) was limited to advising taxpayers and representing them before income tax officials. They usually advised relatively poor individual taxpayers and small firms that could not afford to use the services of accountants or lawyers. In mandatory Palestine of the 1940s, and Israel of the 1950s, when the economy was too small to support a large contingent of lawyers and accountants, such consultants were often the only advisers that many taxpayers could afford.[36]

As previously noted, during the period of British rule in Palestine, anyone could represent taxpayers before the assessing officer. This was in accordance with the traditional British approach that did not regulate the provision of tax advice, the preparation of returns, or

30 percent. Compare *Din ve-Heshbon Rishon 'al Hakhnasot ha-Medinah la-Shanim 1948/9–1954/5* (Jerusalem: ha-Madpis ha-Memshalti, May 1956), 113; *Minhal Hakhnasot ha-Medinah: Doh Shanti 2011–2012 no. 59* (Jerusalem, 2013), 13.

[35] The Hebrew term *Yo'ets Mas* is sometimes translated as "tax consultant" and sometimes as "tax advisor."

[36] Avraham Blinder (tax consultant), interview with author, July 2013.

the representation of taxpayers before the tax administration.[37] In the
1950s the government's intervention in the work of tax consultants
had mostly been limited to ethical matters.[38] Even then, tax consultants had to undergo an exam conducted by an assessing officer before
being allowed to practice. However, the scope of this exam was quite
limited. In any event, at that time law played little part in the work
of tax consultants, because the interaction with the assessing officer
was "bazaar-like" – that is, it was based on informal negotiations and
compromises rather than on legal norms.[39]

Beginning in the early 1960s, the state sought to regulate tax consultants by subjecting them to comprehensive exams and legal supervision.[40] This desire for regulation was the result of a series of scandals
involving tax consultants who had extorted money from taxpayers
under false pretenses, or had claimed that by using their "connections"
in the tax authority they could cancel tax debts, or had stolen taxpayers' files from tax offices, or had forged documents and bribed income
tax officials, or had obstructed justice by hiding taxpayers' files during
police searches.[41] In 1968 the right to represent taxpayers was finally

[37] Thuronyi and Vanistendael, "Regulation of Tax Professionals," 151, 163.
[38] In 1952 section 45A was added to the Income Tax Ordinance. The section empow-
ered the income tax commissioner to create rules that would prohibit any person
(other than lawyers and accountants) from appearing as a representative of the taxpayer if that person "behaved improperly in any matter regarding this Ordinance."
Income Tax Ordinance (Amendment) Law, 5712/1952, sec. 19, LSI, 6:106, 6:124,
(1951/52). See also Levin, "Yo'ets ha-Mas," 7; "Yardah Gviyat Mas Hakhnasah mi-
Skhirim bi-Shnat ha-Shumah 1963/4," *Davar*, April 14, 1964, at 13.
[39] Avraham Blinder (tax consultant), interview with author, July 2013. So widespread
was this reliance on negotiations and compromise that when, in 1956, a taxpayer
refused to compromise and insisted that his assessment be revised by the courts, his
case got widespread media attention. See Amiram Harlaff, *Mi-Yomano shel Praklit*
(Tel Aviv: Y. Golan, 1993), 55–8.
[40] "Yo'atsey Mas Hakhnasah Yehuyvu bi-Vhinot Miktso'iyot," *Ma'ariv*, April 17,
1962, at 14; "Lamah Mezayfim Hats'harot Hon," *Davar*, January 19, 1964, at 4.
[41] "Yo'ets Mas Mu'asham be-Hona'ah," *Davar*, October 11, 1962, at 5; "Yo'ets Mas-
Hakhnasah Hush'a le-Shanah," *Davar*, December 24, 1963, at 5; "Yo'ets Mas u-
Shloshah Nishomim Huzmenu le-Hakirah ba-Mishtarah," *Ma'ariv*, April 4, 1963,
at 1; "Ha-Tikim 'she-Parhu': Gilu Hats'harot Mezuyafot," *Ma'ariv*, May 8, 1963,
at 3; "Yo'atsey Mas-Hakhnasah Hashudim be-Shohad," *Davar*, June 13, 1963,
at 3; "9 Shnot Ma'asar u-Knas Kaved Hutlu al Yo'ets Mas-Hakhnasah," *Davar*,
December 13, 1963, at 20; "Ziyufey Hats'harot ha-Hon: Lema'alah mi-400 Elef

limited to four professional groups: accountants, tax consultants, persons "qualified to audit the books of a cooperative society," and lawyers.[42] The change was justified by the argument that unregulated representation had a negative impact on both the taxpayers and the tax authorities.[43]

Lawyers

Immediately before the outbreak of the First World War, about 650,000 people were living in the Ottoman territories that later became mandatory Palestine.[44] At that time there were only a handful of professional lawyers active in the country, and nonprofessional agents, rather than lawyers, served clients as petition-writers and represented them in courts.[45] This scenario was not unique to Palestine. While, in the late Ottoman period, the nature of legal representation in the Empire began to undergo a process of gradual transformation, with unlicensed agents who lacked formal legal training slowly being replaced by licensed attorneys relying on legal norms, such a transition

Lirot," *Ma'ariv*, December 29, 1963, at 1; "Ne'etsru 'Od Shney Yo'atsey Mas," *Ma'ariv*, January 7, 1964, at 2; "Yo'ets Mas: li-Shnat Ma'asar," *Ma'ariv*, May 4, 1964, at 2; "Yo'ets Mas Nidon le-Hodshayim Ma'asar," *Davar*, January 22, 1965, at 11.

[42] Income Tax Ordinance, sec. 236. For the legislative history of this section, see CA 22/71, *Yitshak Rot v. AO*, Tel Aviv 3, *Psakim* 25(2), 500; Levin, "Yo'ets ha-Mas," 8.

[43] Income Tax Ordinance (Amendment no. 13) Law, 5728/1968, LSI, 22:193 (1967/68). The new law did not totally stamp out the criminal behavior of some tax consultants, and one could still find in later years reports of tax consultants (now registered and certified) who bribed income tax officials, extorted money from their clients (leading them to believe that the money would be used to bribe income tax officials), or simply disappeared with their clients' money. "Hursh'a Yo'ets Mas Hakhnasah she-Ne'esham bi-Lekikhat Shohad," *Ma'ariv*, March 8, 1971, at 4; "2 Yo'atsey Mas Hashudim be-Tivukh le-Shohad," *Davar*, May 23, 1976, 8; "Ne'elam Yo'ets Mas me-Rishon le-Tsiyon," *Ma'ariv*, June 12, 1986, at 12.

[44] See Gad Gilbar, "Megamot be-Hitpat'hut ha-Demografit shel ha-Falastinim 1870–1948," in *Ha-Tnu'ah ha-Leumit ha-Falastinit: Me-'Imut le-Hashlamah?* eds. Moshe Ma'oz and B. Z. Kedar, 2nd edn (Tel Aviv: Misrad ha-Bitahon, 1997), 13–26, 14.

[45] For example, there were only five professional lawyers practicing in Jerusalem in August 1914. See Strasman, *'Otey*, 13–14. See also Nathan Brun, *Shoftim u-Mishpetanim be-Erets Yisrael: Beyn Kushta le-Yerushalyim 1900–1930* (Jerusalem: Magnes, 2008), 59–69.

was slow to take place in distant corners of the Ottoman Empire such as Palestine.[46]

During the first years of British rule in Palestine the number of lawyers remained small. In 1921, when the British government of Palestine began to license lawyers, only forty-nine obtained such a license. However, by the beginning of 1948 the number had grown to about 1,200 licensed lawyers.[47] This upward trend continued after Israeli independence in 1948, accompanied by growth in the institutional autonomy of the profession, epitomized by the enactment of the Israel Bar Association Act of 1961, which gave Israeli lawyers the power to regulate their profession, free of the intervention of the Israeli government.[48] By 1985 the Israeli Bar had 10,400 members (see Table 5.2).[49]

---

[46] See generally Iris Agmon, *Family and Court: Legal Culture and Modernity in Late Ottoman Palestine* (Syracuse, NY: Syracuse University Press, 2006), 168–95; Avi Rubin, "From Legal Representation to Advocacy: Attorneys and Clients in the Ottoman *Nizamiye* Courts," *International Journal of Middle East Studies* 44 (2012): 111–27.

[47] See PG, April 22, 1948, 309–20; Likhovski, *Law and Identity*, 25–6; Brun, *Shoftim*, 59–69. On the number of lawyers belonging to the Jewish Lawyers Association at the end of 1948, see "Din ve-Heshbon meha-Ve'idah ha-13 shel Histadrut 'Orkhey ha-Din be-Yisrael," *Ha-Praklit* 6 (1949): 94, 107.

[48] On the history of this act, see Neta Ziv, "Combining Professionalism, Nation Building and Public Service: The Professional Project of the Israeli Bar 1928–2002," *Fordham Law Review* 71 (2003): 1621–67, 1640–9.

[49] On the growth in the number of lawyers in Israel in recent decades, see e.g., Gad Barzilai, "The Ambivalent Language of Lawyers in Israel: Liberal Politics, Economic Liberalism, Silence, and Dissent," in *Fighting for Political Freedom: Comparative Studies of the Legal Complex and Political Liberalism*, eds. Terence C. Halliday, Lucien Karpik, and Malcolm M. Feeley (Oxford: Hart, 2007), 247–77; Limor Zer-Gutman, "Effects of the Acceleration in the Number of Lawyers in Israel," *International Journal of the Legal Profession* 19 (2012): 247–63, 247–50; Eyal Katvan, "The 'Overcrowding the Profession' Argument and the Professional Melting Pot," *International Journal of the Legal Profession* 19 (2012): 301–19. Another important process that occurred only after the period discussed in this book was the growth in the size of law firms. In the early 1990s the largest Israeli law firm employed only thirty lawyers. See Robert Budden, "The IFLR Top 40: The World's Largest Law Firms," *International Financial Law Review* 11 (1992): 13–16. An interesting process of consolidation of legal and accounting firms has recently occurred in a number of countries. In Israel, however, there is still a prohibition on partnerships or profit-sharing between lawyers and nonlawyers. See Neta Ziv, *Mi Yishmor 'al Shomrey ha-Mishpat?: 'Orkhey Din be-Yisrael beyn Medinah, Shuk ve-Hevrah Ezrahit* (Tel Aviv: Ha-Kibbutz ha-Me'uhad, 2015), 243.

Table 5.2 Growth in the number of lawyers in mandatory Palestine and Israel, 1921–1985

	Lawyers	Population of mandatory Palestine/Israel	No. of lawyers per capita
1921	49	800,000	1/16,326
1948 (mandatory Palestine)	1,187	2,000,000	1/1,684
1953 (Israel)	1,200	1,700,000	1/1,416
1962	3,744	2,300,000	1/614
1975	5,200	3,500,000	1/673
1985	10,400	4,300,000	1/413

What was the role of lawyers in the tax arena?[50] Israeli lawyers rarely assisted their clients in the preparation of tax returns, although a few provided tax advice and tax litigation services.[51] During the late Ottoman period, Shlomo Yellin, the first academically trained Jewish lawyer in the country, was professionally engaged in tax matters. Yellin, who was born in 1874, studied law at the Istanbul Law School

[50] For general discussions on the encounter of law with other professions, see Yves Dezalay and Bryant G. Garth, *The Internationalization of Palace Wars: Lawyers, Economists and the Contest to Transform Latin American States* (Chicago: University of Chicago Press, 2002); Yves Dezalay and Bryant G. Garth, *Asian Legal Revivals: Lawyers in the Shadow of Empire* (Chicago: University of Chicago Press, 2010). On developed countries, see, e.g., Christopher Tomlins, "Framing the Field of Law's Disciplinary Encounters: A Historical Narrative," *Law and Society Review* 34 (2000): 911–72. On specific aspects of the encounter between tax lawyers and other tax professionals, see, e.g., R. Cocks, "Victorian Barristers, Judges and Taxation: A Study in the Expansion of Legal Work," in *Law, Economy and Society, 1750–1914: Essays in the History of English Law*, eds. G. R. Rubin and D. Sugarman (Abingdon: Professional Books, 1984), 445–69; Michael A. Livingston, "Reinventing Tax Scholarship: Lawyers, Economists and the Role of the Legal Academy," *Cornell Law Review* 83 (1998): 365–436; Chantal Stebbings, "Bureaucratic Adjudication: The Internal Appeals of the Inland Revenue," in *Judges and Judging in the History of the Common Law and Civil Law from Antiquity to Modern Times*, eds. Paul Brand and Joshua Getzler (Cambridge: Cambridge University Press, 2012), 157–74.

[51] See, e.g., Giora Amir, *'Averot Mas ve-'Averot Halbanat Hon*, 5th edn (Tel Aviv: Sadan, 2008), sec. 12.5.1.

in the 1890s and later in Berlin. He returned to the Levant in 1901, first to Jerusalem and later to Beirut, and in 1904 he translated the Ottoman Tithe Law of 1889 into Hebrew.[52] Generally speaking, however, Yellin's tax work seems to have been a rare exception.

The first two decades of British rule in the country were also characterized by the relative absence of lawyers in tax-related matters. This was not a coincidence. In Britain too, the involvement of lawyers in tax disputes was a rare occurrence at the time. In nineteenth-century Britain, tax assessments and appeals were handled by local officials with no legal training. This was also true of the income tax. Income tax appeals to regular courts were only allowed in 1874. Before that date, income tax appeals were decided by bureaucratic adjudication – by civil servants who lacked formal legal training (although they did develop expertise in the narrow and specific field of tax law). The resolution of tax disputes by a nonjudicial body was not viewed as an anomaly. Tax appeals were perceived by the state as one stage in an administrative process – the assessment and collection of taxes. Lawyers viewed taxation as a nonlegal matter, in part because it involved questions of administration and accounting in which lawyers had no expertise.[53] This approach was not confined to litigation: it also characterized the provision of nonlitigation tax services. Nor was it confined to the nineteenth century. Well into the twentieth century, British solicitors had little interest or training in tax law (or, indeed, in other commercially related legal fields). For example, it was only in 1938 that company law and tax law were added to the final examinations of solicitors.[54]

Unlike the British administrative approach to tax appeals, the 1941 Palestine Income Tax Ordinance allowed taxpayers to appeal disputed assessments to the Supreme Court of Palestine.[55] While the ordinance

---

[52] Shlomo Yellin, trans., *Sefer ha-Hukim le-Ma'aser Pri ha-Adamah ha-Nahug be-Artsot Turkiyah* (Jerusalem: Lunz, 1904/05). On Yellin, see also Brun, *Shoftim*, 61–2, 320 n. 26.

[53] See Stebbings, "Bureaucratic Adjudication."

[54] See David Sugarman, "Who Colonized Whom? Historical Reflections on the Intersection between Law, Lawyers and Accountants," in *Professional Competition and Professional Power: Lawyers, Accountants and the Social Construction of Markets*, eds. Yves Dezalay and David Sugarman (London: Routledge, 1995), 226–37, 233.

[55] Tax appeals were heard by a British Puisne Judge of the Supreme Court in Jerusalem, sitting in Chambers. Income Tax Ordinance, 1941, sec. 53; Rules of Court (Income Tax Appeals), 1941, sec. 2, reprinted in Abraham Fellman, *The Palestine Income*

created the possibility of judicial review of tax assessments, the reality was that, during the period of the British mandate, very few cases reached the court. The high cost of hiring a lawyer and the fact that the proceedings were only heard by the Supreme Court in Jerusalem discouraged appeals. In addition, the state, represented by a private law firm, S. Horowitz and Co., often settled tax cases rather than litigated them.[56]

In 1949, after the establishment of the state of Israel, the process of tax appeal changed somewhat, allowing for greater involvement of the courts.[57] Accountants and tax consultants continued to dominate the initial stage of tax disputes, in which the taxpayer faced the assessing officer in the income tax office; lawyers appeared once an appeal was lodged with the courts.[58]

Tax: Law and Practice (Tel Aviv: Lapid, 1946), 335. The decisions of this judge were considered final, but the section added that "the Judge hearing such appeal may, if he so desires, state a case on a question of law for the opinion of the Supreme Court, sitting as a Court of Civil Appeal." Income Tax Ordinance, 1941, sec. 53. If certain conditions were met, the tax decision of the Supreme Court could even be appealed to the Privy Council in London. See Fellman, *Palestine Income Tax*, 334; G. Eichelgrün, *Palestine Income Tax Guide* (Haifa: Paltax, 1945), 202. This procedure was somewhat at variance with the procedures in both the UK and in other colonial legal systems. See Fellman, *Palestine Income Tax*, 332–3. Earlier mandatory-era taxes relied on an administrative, rather than a legal, appeal mechanism. See Tithe Commutation Ordinance, 1927, sec. 10, Drayton 2:1413; Urban Property Tax Ordinance, 1928, secs. 17, 18, Drayton 2:1520; Rural Property Tax Ordinance, 1935, secs. 13–15, PG Supp. I, 1, 13, 14; Stamp Duty Ordinance, 1927, sec. 15, Drayton 2:1334.

[56] Eichelgrün, *Palestine Income Tax*, 201. See also A. Witkowski, "Mas Hakhnasah," *Ha-Praklit* 1 (1943/44): 120–6. Alfred Witkowski (who later changed his name to Witkon) was the lawyer who represented the government in most tax cases on behalf of S. Horowitz and Co. He later became a Supreme Court justice, and the leading expert on tax law in Israel between the 1950s and the 1970s. See Harold C. Wilkenfeld, *Taxes and People in Israel* (Cambridge, MA: Harvard University Press, 1973), 197 n. 53.

[57] In cases in which the assessment was disputed, the taxpayer could ask for a review of the assessment by another tax official, and then appeal the decision to a district court. The decision of the district court could also be appealed, as a matter of right, to the Supreme Court of Palestine sitting as a court of civil appeals. See Income Tax Ordinance, 1947, sec. 60 as amended in 1949. Appeal procedures are now laid out in sections 153–158 of the Income Tax Ordinance (New Version), 1961. For a detailed description of the review processes used in disputes related to other types of Israeli taxes, see Wilkenfeld, *Taxes and People in Israel*, 177–9.

[58] A. Kost, "Ha-Praklit be-'Inyeney Mas Hakhnasah," *RH* 2 (1951/52): 94, 95; A. Polonsky, "Ro'eh ha-Heshbon ve-'Orekh ha-Din," *RH* 8 (1957/58): 189, 190.

Only a small group of lawyers developed a specialization in tax-related matters and were thus able to represent taxpayers in such disputes. A database of 1,596 tax cases decided between 1941 and 1985 illustrates the dominance of this small group of lawyers in tax litigation.[59] The database contains four categories of cases: ordinary income tax appeals, cases of income tax evasion, cases dealing with the property tax, and land betterment/appreciation tax cases (involving the taxation of capital gains from the sale of real estate). The results show that a small group of lawyers was very active in the first three categories examined. For example, there were five lawyers in particular who were very active in litigating ordinary income tax appeals. This very small group of lawyers appeared in 20 percent of the 1,102 income tax cases examined.[60]

Economists

The main role of accountants in the income tax arena was to prepare the tax returns of individuals and firms and represent their clients in

[59] The database was created using cases taken from Nevo (a general database of Israeli law: www.nevo.co.il/) and Misim (a specialized tax database: www.ronen-missim.co.il/misim/). The materials were collected in April and May 2014. Because these databases did not cover mandatory tax cases, additional cases were taken from A. M. Apelbom and B. Braude, eds., *Palestine Income Tax Cases* (Tel Aviv: Palestine Law Publishing Co., 1945). The database included all the cases appearing in the two online databases as well as in Apelbom's book. It should be noted, however, that these cases represent only a small sample of all tax appeals. In the late 1960s about 1,800 tax appeals were filed annually (although about 85 percent of the cases were settled). See Wilkenfeld, *Taxes and People in Israel*, 199, 207.

[60] These lawyers were Giora Amir, Bo'az Nahir, Ernst Klimowsky, Daniel Potchebutzky, and Moshe Druker. Two of them, Giora Amir and Bo'az Nahir, were especially dominant, each appearing in about 6 percent of the cases decided during this period. The same can be said for the tax evasion cases. The five most dominant lawyers appearing in these cases represented taxpayers in a total of 45 percent of the cases. A similar indication of specialization can be found in property tax cases, where the five most prominent lawyers appeared in a total of 22 percent of the cases. Only in land betterment/appreciation tax cases was there no similar dominance. This tax involves very common transactions in which many ordinary lawyers are involved. It is not surprising, therefore, that here there was less specialization, and the five most dominant lawyers appeared in only 11 percent of the cases. On tax specialization, see generally Paul L. Caron, "Tax Myopia, or Mamas Don't Let Your Babies Grow Up to Be Tax Lawyers," *Virginia Tax Review* 13 (1994): 517–90.

the initial stages of tax disputes. Lawyers provided tax advice and represented their clients in tax disputes, especially in the later, judicial stages of the process. Given their professional expertise, the state sometimes sought the advice of lawyers and accountants in formulating tax policy and drafting tax reforms proposals.[61] But economists were another important group of experts involved in the policy and reform stages of taxation.[62]

In mandatory Palestine and in 1950s Israel, government tax policy and tax reform proposals were the province of government administrators, not professional economists. The senior economic staff of the mandatory government at the end of the period of British rule in Palestine, for example, included only one official with formal training in economics.[63] Economic expertise, when needed, was provided by experts in London or (during the economic boom Palestine experienced during the Second World War) by the Cairo-based British Middle East Supply Centre. This lack of reliance on professional economic expertise was partly the result of the limited staff numbers of the government of Palestine, and partly the result of an ideology that preferred civil servants with a broad general education to officials with specialized professional knowledge.[64]

---

[61] See, e.g., Adam S. Hofri-Winogradow, "Professionals' Contribution to the Legislative Process: Between Self, Client, and the Public," *Law and Social Inquiry* 39 (2014): 96–126.

[62] See, e.g., Ajay K. Mehrotra and Joseph J. Thorndike, "From Programmatic Reform to Social Science Research: The National Tax Association and the Promise and Perils of Disciplinary Encounters," *Law and Society Review* 45 (2011): 593–630.

[63] See Jacob Reuveny, *Mimshal ha-Mandat be-Erets Yisrael, 1920–1948: Nitu'ah Histori Medini* (Ramat-Gan: Bar-Ilan University Press, 1993), 65 n. 3.

[64] Ephraim Kleiman, "Israel: Economists in a New State," *History of Political Economy* 13 (1981): 548–79, 548–9; Nachum Gross, "Ha-Mahlakah le-Kalkalah ba-Universitah ha-'Ivrit bi-Shnot ha-Hamishim," Morris Falk Institute for Economic Research in Israel Discussion Paper 04.06 (2004), 13–14. On the training of British colonial officials, see generally Robert Heussler, *Yesterday's Rulers: The Making of the British Colonial Service* (Syracuse, NY: Syracuse University Press, 1963), 82–129; Phiroze Vasunia, *The Classics and Colonial India* (Oxford: Oxford University Press, 2013), 193–230. On the training of government officials immediately after the British conquest of Palestine, see Bernard Wasserstein, *The British in Palestine: The Mandatory Government and Arab-Jewish Conflict, 1917–1929*, 2nd edn (Oxford: Blackwell, 1991), 19–20.

Similarly, only a few officials and politicians of the Zionist movement had any formal training in economics.[65] However, Jewish organizations in Palestine did employ some professional economists.[66] They
were mainly employed by two institutes that provided economic
advice to policy makers: the Economic Research Institute of the Jewish
Agency and the Economic Department of the Jewish Agency.[67] In addition, some economists were affiliated with two Jewish academic institutions in mandatory Palestine: the Hebrew University of Jerusalem
and the Tel Aviv School of Law and Economics. In both institutions,
economics was taught using a German-inspired, descriptive, institutionalist, historical approach focused on the unique conditions of
Jewish society in Palestine rather than on general economic theory.[68]

In 1949 Don Patinkin, a young assistant professor at the University
of Chicago, was appointed lecturer in economics at the Hebrew
University. Following Patinkin's lead, the newly established economics
department moved away from the German-inspired institutional economics approach. Instead, it adopted an American-style program based
on an analytic and mathematical approach that assumed the universal
nature of the rules of economics.[69] It was also based on what many

[65] See, e.g., Avner Molcho, "Productivization, Economics and the Transformation of
Israeli Education, 1948–1965," *Israel Studies* 16 (2011): 123–48, 128; Arie Krampf,
*Ha-Mekorot ha-Le'umiyim shel Kalkalat ha-Shuk: Pitu'ah Kalkali bi-Tkufat 'Itsuvo
shel ha-Kapitalizm ha-Yisre'eli* (Jerusalem: Magnes, 2015), 40–2.

[66] Kleiman, "Israel: Economists in a New State," 548–9; Krampf, *Ha-Mekorot*, 31–71.

[67] Krampf, *Ha-Mekorot*, 46–8.

[68] Kleiman, "Israel: Economists in a New State," 549; Nachum Gross, "Mada'ey ha-
Hevrah ba-Universitah ha-'Ivrit 'ad 1948/9: Tokhniyot ve-Hat'halot," in *Toldot ha-
Universitah ha-'Ivrit: Hitbasesut ve-Tsmihah*, ed. Hagit Lavski (Jerusalem: Magnes,
2005), 503–41, 505, 508–9, 523, 534; Micah Michaeli, "Ha-Hug le-Kalkalah ba-
Universitah ha-'Ivrit: Yemey Bereshit – Mi-Tatspit Ishit," *RK* 54 (2007): 159, 160,
176; Haim Barkai, "Don Patinkin's Contribution to Economics in Israel," in *Monetary
Theory and Thought: Essays in Honour of Don Patinkin*, eds. Haim Barkai, Stanley
Fischer, and Nissan Liviatan (Basingstoke: Macmillan, 1993), 3–14, 4. Another institution located in Tel Aviv, The Higher School for Social Sciences, was established
in the early 1950s by the General Federation of Jewish Labor, and offered courses
in economics to workers. See, e.g., David Mushiev, "Studentim Lomdim ba-Leylot,"
Davar, February 28, 1958, at 9.

[69] Kleiman, "Israel: Economists in a New State," 553; Gross, "Ha-Mahlakah," 1–2;
Michaeli, "Ha-Hug," 163, 165; Arie Krampf, "Economic Planning of the Free Market
in Israel during the First Decade: The Influence of Don Patinkin on Israeli Policy

Table 5.3 Number of economists in the Israeli civil service

	Total no. of civil servants	Professionals	No. of economists	No. of economists at the Ministry of Finance
1955	22,020	3,731	48	20
1966	29,227	8,815	217	70
1975	–	21,417	–	298

perceived as a "right-wing" perception of the relationship between individuals, markets, and the state.[70] The students who trained at the new department, the "Patinkin boys," were soon appointed to key positions in the new Israeli civil service, especially at the Ministry of Finance but also at the Ministry for Trade and Industry and the Bank of Israel. As Table 5.3 shows, in the two decades between 1955 and 1975 the number of economists (many of them graduates of the Hebrew University) at the Israeli Ministry of Finance grew by a factor of 15.

In the 1950s the Hebrew University economics department mainly influenced government policy indirectly, through its former students. Beginning in the 1960s, this influence became more direct. The members of the department became heavily involved in shaping Israeli economic policy using various channels such as meetings with leading policy makers, public symposia, petitions, op-eds, and interviews. This growing influence, in turn, shaped a new public attitude – that

Discourse," *Science in Context* 23 (2010): 507–34; Krampf, *Ha-Mekorot*, 107–10. On the similar Americanization of business administration studies in the 1950s, see Avner Molcho, "Kapitalizm ve-'ha-Derekh ha-Amerikanit' be-Yisrael: Pir'yon, Nihul veha-Etos ha-Kapitalisti ba-Siyu'a ha-Tekhni shel Artsot ha-Brit bi-Shnot ha-Hamishim," in *Hevrah ve-Kalkalah be-Yisrael: Mabat Histori ve-'Akhshavi*, eds. Avi Bareli, Daniel Gutwein, and Tuvia Friling (Sde Boker: Ben-Gurion Institute Press, 2005), 263–94. On developments in the United States at the time, see Yuval P. Yonay, *The Struggle over the Soul of Economics: Institutionalist and Neoclassical Economists in America between the Wars* (Princeton: Princeton University Press, 1998), 184–95.

[70] See David Pines, "Sipur ha-Hakamah shel ha-Hug le-Kalkalah be-Universitat Tel Aviv," *RK* 60 (2013): 11–40. On Patinkin's attitude to Keynesian ideas, see Krampf, *Ha-Mekorot*, 233.

professors of economics should be consulted in the process of developing economic (including tax) policy.[71]

What was the impact of the rise of economists on the Israeli Tax Authority? While professional economists were highly successful in taking over important positions in the Israeli Ministry of Finance, the tax authority proved more resistant to their impact. The tax authority was mostly led by people whose professional training was in accounting or law rather than economics.[72] Nevertheless, even here there was a gradual rise in the influence of professional economists. One of the first graduates of the economics department of the Hebrew University, Amotz Morag, later specialized in the study of public finance. Morag served as an adviser to the state revenue administration division in the Ministry of Finance. His advice provided tax officials with analytical tools and scientific terminology that they then used in their debates with Israeli politicians.[73]

Economists also gradually came to dominate the makeup of Israeli tax reform committees. The first major Israeli tax reform committee, the Committee for Examining the Methods of Assessment and Collection of the Income Tax (the Sharef Committee), was appointed in 1953. It was mainly staffed by Ministry of Finance officials.[74] However, by the 1970s economists had come to play a leading role in such tax reform committees. The most influential tax reform committee of the 1970s, the Ben-Shahar Committee, appointed in December 1974, had five members, none of whom were civil servants. Three were economists, one was an accountant, and one was a lawyer.[75]

[71] Michaeli, "Ha-Hug," 161–2, 168, 177–8.

[72] Kleiman, "Israel: Economists in a New State," 568.

[73] Aharon Biran, "Hatsa'ah: Mas Ahid ve-Yahid," *Ma'ariv*, July 14, 1964, at 11; Ze'ev Sharef, "Amotz Morag ZL," *RK* 13 (1967): 413–14. Gross, "Ha-Mahlakah," 1–2, 11, 22; Michaeli, "Ha-Hug," 163–6, 168; Kleiman, "Israel: Economists in a New State," 553; Krampf, "Economic Planning," 530.

[74] TM Library, Din ve-Heshbon shel ha-Va'adah le-Bhinat Shitot ha-Ha'arakhah veha-Gviyah shel Mas Hakhnasah (Jerusalem: March 1945); "R. Ipkha Mistabra, Halom Leyl-Kayits shel Mas-Hakhnasah," *Ma'ariv*, April 9, 1954, at 3. See also Avraham Mandel, ed., *Sefer ha-Yovel shel Agaf Mas Hakhnasah u-Mas Rekhush* (Tel Aviv: Yedioth Ahronoth ve-Muze'on le-Misim, 1992), 82, 84; "Ha-Va'adah le-Yi'ul Gviyat Mas ha-Hakhnasah Hegishah Maskenotehah," *'Al Ha-Mishmar*, April 7, 1954, at 1; Wilkenfeld, *Taxes and People in Israel*, 7–8.

[75] The five members were Haim Ben-Shahar, Michael Bruno, and Yoram Ben-Porat (economists), Shalom Ronel (an accountant), and Bo'az Nahir (a lawyer). Mandel,

Changing Professional Visions

Changes in the supply of professional tax services and tax reform advice between the 1930s and 1980s were accompanied by a transformation in the professional self-perception of accountants, lawyers, and economists, as well as in how they were perceived by society. During the 1950s, important subgroups within the accounting and legal professions had sought to describe themselves as actively participating in the Zionist nation-building project by serving the state and educating the public, notions that were echoed in the discourse of state officials. This self-description was gradually replaced by a noncollectivist, antistatist ideology in these two professions, as well as among economists. This change reflected a broader social and cultural change in Israeli society, and it also contributed to the formation of a new relationship between taxpayers and the state.

Accountants: From Servants of the State to Servants of Their Clients

In the 1930s, when the ACAA was established, it represented a specific notion of accounting, one that viewed the practice as neutral, universal, and technical (or "scientific"). Such a view competed with a different approach prevalent in the Jewish community at the time, which arose within the Jewish cooperative movement in Palestine. This approach linked accounting to the Zionist nation-building project, and viewed it as part of a broader ideological and educational endeavor devoted to the self-transformation of the Jews of Palestine. I will now briefly discuss the history of the cooperative movement to highlight the alternative vision of accounting it propagated.

The cooperative movement, a nineteenth-century European project, first appeared in Palestine in the late Ottoman era, but its heyday was during the period of British rule. By 1937 there were about 1,000 cooperatives in Palestine, with about 250,000 members (98 percent of them Jews, 2 percent Arab). At the time there were about 400,000 Jews in Palestine, of whom about 250,000 were adults. There were

Sefer ha-Yovel, 209; Shlomo Yitzhaki, "Reformat ha-Mas 1975," in *Reformot Mas*, ed. David Gliksberg (Jerusalem: Ha-Makhon le-Mehkarey Hakikah, 2005), 195–235. On other 1970s tax reform committees, see Mandel, *Sefer ha-Yovel*, 252–3.

agricultural, industrial, credit, housing, consumer, pension, insurance, and many other types of cooperatives.[76]

The Jewish cooperative movement was closely tied to Zionism, a project of national transformation but also of self-transformation, epitomized by an early Zionist pioneering slogan: "we came [back] to our land to build and be built by it." The rural cooperative communities, *kibbutzim* and *moshavim*, as well as the industrial cooperatives affiliated with the General Federation of Jewish Labor, were important agents in creating the "new Jews" (or "new Hebrews") of Palestine. Influenced by Russian socialism, Tolstoyan romanticism, and anarchist notions of self-management, socialist Zionists sought to transform themselves. Instead of the subservient Jews of the Diaspora, engaged in ephemeral or unproductive pursuits (including the liberal professions), they were to become hard-working, pioneering farmers and workers striving jointly to build the future Jewish state and its institutions.[77]

The bourgeois Jewish sector in Palestine also had its own thriving cooperative movement, especially large credit cooperatives that played an important role in the Jewish banking sector in Palestine. While these bourgeois cooperatives were not motivated by socialist ideology, they, too, sought to participate in the Zionist nation-building project, and they were also often animated by progressive views. In the case of bourgeois cooperatives, one major source of inspiration was the ideas of the American–Zionist US Supreme Court Justice Louis Brandeis, who saw the cooperative movement as a way to replace capitalist free competition and the pursuit of profit with economic activity based on

[76] See generally, Harry Viteles, *The Evolution of the Co-Operative Movement*, vol. 1 of *A History of the Co-Operative Movement in Israel: A Sourcebook* (London: Vallentine, Mitchell, 1966), 29–39. See also Roza I. M. El-Eini, "Rural Indebtedness and Agricultural Credit Supplies in Palestine in the 1930s," *Middle Eastern Studies* 33 (1997): 313–37, 315–24; Nahum Karlinsky, "Ha-Ko-Operatsyah ha-Pratit bi-Tkufat ha-Mandat: Ashray ve-Hisahon," in *Kalkalah ve-Hevrah bi-Yemey ha-Mandat: 1918–1948*, eds. Avi Bareli and Nahum Karlinsky (Sde Boker: Ben-Gurion Institute Press, 2003), 239–89. By 1940 there were 1,459 cooperatives compared to 1,856 corporations in Palestine. See B. C., "Ktsat Statistikah," *Ro'eh ha-Heshbon ha-Musmakh* (November 1940): 18.

[77] See, e.g., Shapira, *Israel: A History*, 133; Ephraim Kleiman, "The Waning of Israeli Etatisme," *Israel Studies* 2 (1997): 146–71, 149; Molcho, "Productivization"; Derek J. Penslar, *Shylock's Children: Economics and Jewish Identity in Modern Europe* (Berkeley: University of California Press, 2001), 223–54.

self-help, democratic self-management, and communal participation. Jewish cooperatives, whether socialist or bourgeois, thus had educational and identity-formation goals as well as economic ones.[78]

The Palestine Cooperative Societies Ordinance, enacted by the British in 1933, allowed cooperatives to be audited by a certified accountant or by associations of noncertified auditors called audit unions (*britot pikuah*).[79] Audit unions were defined as registered associations of auditors whose principal object was the audit and supervision of the cooperative societies, but the Ordinance also listed "co-operative education" as one of the tasks of such unions. They were therefore often involved in guidance and educational activities, spreading the cooperative ethos (and the ideology of nonprofit communal self-fashioning associated with it) among both members and nonmembers of the cooperative movement, through lectures, seminars, and so forth.[80] As Moshe Ossoskin, one of the leaders of the Jewish cooperative movement in Palestine, explained in 1946, the audit union did "not merely audit cooperatives from a technical and legal perspective as accountants [did]"; it also examined the activity of the cooperatives from "an ideological point of view."[81]

An article published in the workers' daily *Davar* in 1933 explained that noncertified auditing was necessary because, in addition to neutral accounting considerations, there were wider "social" aspects of the work of cooperatives that only auditors belonging to audit unions would be able to take into consideration.[82] The Accountants' Association, ACAA, was quick to respond, calling this view "bizarre."

---

[78] Viteles, *A History of the Co-Operative Movement in Israel*, 1:159; Karlinsky, "Ha-Ko-Operatsyah," 249, 266, 273, 284; Neta Ziv, "Credit Cooperatives in Early Israeli Statehood: Financial Institutions and Social Transformation," *Theoretical Inquiries in Law* 11 (2010): 209–46, 216–18, 227–8.

[79] Cooperative Societies Ordinance, 1933, sec. 20, Drayton 1:367; Viteles, *A History of the Co-Operative Movement in Israel*, 1:93, 1:129. In 1937 there were six such unions in Palestine. See Government of Palestine, *Report by the Registrar of Cooperative Societies on Developments during the Years 1921–1937* (Jerusalem: Government Printer, 1938), 22.

[80] Cooperative Societies Ordinance, 1933, sec. 2, Drayton 1:360; S. Barent, "Tafkidehen shel Britot Piku'ah," *RH* 11 (1960/61): 157–9.

[81] CZA DD1/3441, M. Ossoskin, "Brit Piku'ah," *Ko–Operatsyah*, April 1946, 12.

[82] "Le-She'elat ha-Bikoret ha-Rishmit shel ha-Ko'operativim," *Davar*, October 17, 1933, at 5.

Auditing, the ACAA stated, was a professional matter, similar to law or architecture, that should only be handled by experts. There was no such thing as "social" auditing, it argued, and therefore the practice should be left to qualified professional accountants alone.[83]

In the 1930s, therefore, two competing views of accounting existed in Palestine: a professional view espoused by members of the ACAA, linked to the Companies Ordinance, and based on an approach that viewed accounting as a universal and neutral form of knowledge and practice; and a nonprofessional notion, espoused by members of the audit unions, recognized by the Cooperative Societies Ordinance, and based on a view of accounting as part of the wider Zionist project. Indeed, the existence of the alternative vision of accounting propagated by the cooperative movement and the audit unions may have been the initial impetus for the formation of the ACAA itself.[84]

During the mandatory era, the competition between the ACAA and the audit unions did not take place in the income tax arena. The Cooperative Societies Ordinance of 1933 allowed the high commissioner to exempt cooperatives from paying the income tax (which was not even in force at the time in Palestine), and in 1942 all cooperatives were formally exempted by the high commissioner. Only after Israeli independence in 1948 was the income of cooperatives taxed.[85]

---

[83] Agudat Ro'ey Heshbon Musmahim be-Erets Yisrael, "'Emdah lo-Mutsdeket: Tshuvah," *Davar*, November 7, 1933, at 5. Complaints about the use of noncertified auditors belonging to the audit unions, instead of certified accountants, continued in later decades. See S. Barent, "Histanfut Hofshit o Hovah?" *Davar*, February 25, 1949, at 4.

[84] Arnon Rojansky, the first president of the ACAA, said that one of the reasons for the formation of the ACAA in 1931 was the fact that the Government of Palestine was drafting the Cooperative Societies Ordinance, and "it was necessary to safeguard the rights of certified accountants so they would be able to audit such cooperative societies." See Arnon Rojansky, "Me'at Zikhronot 'al Yesud ha-Lishkah," *RH* 8 (1957/58): 77, 78.

[85] Cooperative Societies Ordinance, 1933, sec. 37, Drayton 1:374. See also A. Kanne, "Ha-Ko-operativim u-Mas Hakhnasah," *RH* 17 (1967/68): 509. The exemption for industrial and transport cooperatives was abolished in 1944. On exemptions from the 1950s onwards, see "Knesset Abolishes Blanket Tax Exemption for Cooperatives," *JP*, August 26, 1949, at 2; Menachem Frend, "Mas Hakhnasah bifney Mashber Musri," *RH* 7 (1956/57): 47–9; Asher Arin and Ilana Reich, "Misuy ha-Kibbutzim veha-Agudot ha-Shitufiyot" in *'Idkunim le-Sefer Hitpatkhut ha-Misim*

While accountants did not face competition from the audit unions in the tax field, it seems that, after the establishment of the state of Israel in 1948, accountants came to adopt both the state-building and educational approaches that had characterized the audit unions in the 1930s and 1940s. During the first decade of Israeli independence, accountants attempted to legitimize themselves and their profession by forging links with the Zionist project and its rhetoric. This may have reflected a genuine belief, or may have been merely a justificatory move, paying lip-service to the dominant ideology of the time, or a combination of both. Whatever the motivation was, one can find the strong presence of statist and educational rhetoric in the periodical literature produced by accountants in the 1950s. Statist rhetoric was often present in articles published in the ACAA journal, where accountants described themselves as "trustees of the state" or "guardians of the national economy."[86] Rigorous accounting and accurate reporting, they said, "are preconditions for the success of the economy and for prosperity. Our duty as professionals and citizens of the state is to assist in the success of the [national] economy."[87]

Many officials of the Israeli government echoed this rhetoric. In Israeli parliamentary debates, government representatives stressed time and again the role of accountants as state agents.[88] For example,

be-Erets Yisrael: Legabey ha-Shanim 1964–1978, eds. Avraham Mandel and Asher Arin (Jerusalem: Muze'on le-Misim, 1982), 62–7.

[86] "Ba-Agudah," *RH* 1 (March–April 1951): 8, 9; E. Klimowsky, "Ro'eh ha-Heshebon ba-Meshek ha-Moderni," *RH* 8 (1957/58): 145, 147.

[87] "Dvar ha-Ma'arekhet: Yovel Agudat Ro'ey Heshbon be-Yisrael," *RH* 8 (December 1957): 69. See also "Ha-Yahulu Shinuyim be-Mas Hakhnasah?" *Ro'eh ha-Heshbon ha-Musmakh* (May–June 1951): 3.

[88] Already during the mandatory era accountants were viewed as possible allies of the state who would reduce the need to deal with individual taxpayers. In 1941 the British tax adviser to the government of Palestine, D. N. Strathie, held several meetings with the ACAA in which members of the Association suggested amendments to the Income Tax Ordinance. At these meetings, Strathie declared that while the government had the right to inspect the account books of merchants, in most cases a balance sheet and income statement approved by a certified accountant would suffice. "Le-'Inyan Mas ha-Hakhnasah," *Davar*, August 7, 1941, at 4. The soon to be established State of Israel also sought to rely on the services of accountants when in April 1948, immediately before the Israeli declaration of independence, the provisional government (*minhelet ha-'am*) asked the ACAA to assist the government in the organization of tax collection in the soon-to-be-born state. Levin, *Heshbon*, 8, 46.

during the first reading of the Auditors' Law in the Israeli Parliament in 1953, Pinhas Rosen, the Israeli minister of justice, stated that one of the goals of the proposed law was to give accountants both autonomy and a "statist role [or influence]" (*hashpa'ah mamlakhtit*), since they were trustees of the public, and government officials (such as assessing officers) relied on financial statements certified by them. Accountants, said Rosen, "do not audit balance sheets of corporations in order to teach companies dubious ways of paying less income tax, but, according to the right perception, they should also be public trustees," because "they are public servants no less than servants of individuals."[89] Attorney General Haim Cohn echoed Rosen's approach at a Knesset committee debate on the Auditors' Law, saying that the new law would enable the state to multiply the number of "roles and powers" given to accountants in fiscal and other matters.[90]

Theodor Brosh, the income tax commissioner, told accountants in 1957 that they had "great responsibility toward the state and the general public which demands that [tax] laws be implemented justly and equally." Taxpayers, he said, should not evade the tax imposed on them using advice provided by accountants. Brosh added that the accountant, who was trusted by both the taxpayer and the tax authority, served as a "reconciliatory and stabilizing force" between the government and the taxpayers. Indeed, the creation of a sense of trust in the Israeli tax system on the part of taxpayers was "the greatest task" of the accountants' association.[91] Public opinion also sometimes viewed accountants as agents responsible for safeguarding the interests of the state by preventing tax evasion by their clients.[92]

[89] DK, 13:448, 13:449, 13:456 (January 6, 1953). See also "Ha-Mesibah ha-Hagigit le-Regel Kabalat Hok Ro'ey Heshbon," *RH* 5 (1954/55): 137, 140.

[90] KA, Protokol mi-Yeshivat Va'adat ha-Mishne shel Va'adat ha-Hukah le-Hok Ro'ey Heshbon, February 9, 1953, 1. Member of Knesset Yohanan Bader also mentioned the assistance of accountants in the tax collection process. See ibid., 2. See also KA, Protokol mi-Yeshivat Va'adat ha-Mishne shel Va'adat ha-Hukah le-Hok Ro'ey Heshbon, June 2, 1953, at 1.

[91] T. Brosh, "Ro'eh ha-Heshbon u-Mas Hakhnasah," *RH* 8 (1957/58): 101–2. See also "Simpozyon 'al Ba'ayot Mas Hakhnasah," *Davar*, September 22, 1955, at 2.

[92] Natan Ben-Natan, "Yoman Kalkali," *Davar*, December 29, 1954, at 3.

Discussions of the educational role of accountants can also be found in the periodical literature of the 1950s. For example, in 1957 Minister of Finance Levi Eshkol noted that the role of accountants was "to improve taxpayers' morale."[93] One of the leading accountants in 1950s Israel, Efraim Kost, echoed this approach in an article entitled "The Accountant as the Client's Advocate." The accountant's duty, said Kost, was to elicit public recognition of the legality of tax assessments, thus "guarantying swift and safe collection of the amount due." The accountant, he continued, was an intermediary, whose duty was "to convince, educate and correct" the behavior of the taxpayers, assisting the individual taxpayer, the public, and the tax authority simultaneously. Without accountants, assessment would be arbitrary, "the citizens would have a sense of being abused and wronged," and such an arbitrary approach would lead to "lower production." The accountant, he stated, could minimize tax resistance, educate the taxpayer, and thus ensure regular collection more effectively than the threat of criminal law. Finally, he added, the accountant had a role in creating intimacy between the state and taxpayers: "Not only does the accountant ensure more regular tax collection, but he also assists in creating a closer relationship between the taxpaying citizen and the government, and [thus he enhances] the identification of the citizen with his state."[94]

There were also some voices that contested this statist portrayal of the role of accountants. Yitzhak Kanev, the founder of Israel's social security system and a member of the Israeli Labor Party (MAPAI), warned in a 1951 article that accountants (and lawyers) were advising taxpayers on ways to evade the income tax. This behavior, Kanev said, was a legacy of the British mandate, inappropriate for the era of Jewish independence. It was, he warned, causing "immense loss to the Ministry of Finance," and he suggested that "these saboteurs [accountants and lawyers]" be replaced by government "advice and information bureaus" that would assist taxpayers in properly paying their taxes.[95]

---

[93] Levi Eshkol, "Tafkid Ro'eh ha-Heshbon be-Yisrael," *RH* 8 (1957/58): 75.

[94] E. Kost, "Ro'eh ha-Heshbon ke-Praklit ha-Nishom," *RH* 8 (1957/58): 134, 137–8. See also "Aruhat Tsaharayim Meshutefet le-Havrey ha-Agudah," *RH* 5 (1954/55): 187, 188.

[95] Y. Kanev, "Mas ha-Hakhnasah u-Mi Meshalem Oto," *Davar*, September 7, 1951, at 2.

By the 1960s there was a palpable decline in the use of statist rhetoric. For example, in 1960 Ze'ev Sharef, the director of state revenue, likened the partnership between the state and accountants to two teams of soccer players, both committed to the rules of the game, but playing against each other.[96] In 1962 the state tried to amend the Income Tax Ordinance by inserting a provision that imposed criminal liability for corporate tax evasion not merely on the managers of corporations but also on the bookkeepers and accountants serving them, unless they could prove that they had taken "reasonable measures to ensure" the prevention of evasion. An editorial in the accountants' journal noted sarcastically that it seemed that "among certain circles in the Ministry of Finance the idea that accountants exist in order to serve the tax authorities is prevalent."[97] Such a notion of the subservience of accountants to the state was common in the 1950s, but now, apparently, it seemed out of place. Accordingly, one could now find discussions of the role of accountants that did not mention their statist role, but only their duty "to honestly provide service to the public."[98]

In the 1950s accountants, loyal to their self-portrayal as servants of the state, were careful to avoid politics.[99] By the 1960s, however, one could find a younger generation of accountants lamenting the lack of political involvement by their peers in tax reform proposals, calling on them to use their "technical knowledge" to publically take the side of taxpayers against the state and oppose "reforms by the tax authority that seek to enhance tax collection while simultaneously infringing the basic liberties of the citizen."[100] Laypersons also noted the decline of the statist ideal among accountants. In a 1963 letter to the editor of *Davar*, entitled "Professional Ethics and the Ministry of Finance," a reader complained that accountants and lawyers, some

---

[96] Ze'ev Sharef, "Hartsa'at Mar Ze'ev Sharef," *RH* 10 (1959/60): 135, 141.

[97] Hok le-Tikun Pkudat Mas Hakhnasah, 5722/1962, sec. 8, HH, 15:150–1; "Dvar ha-Ma'arekhet," *RH* 13 (1962/63): 9. See also "Ne'um Nesi Lishkat Ro'ey ha-Heshbon be-Yisra'el," *RH* 13 (1962/63): 501.

[98] Daniel Yaffe, "Ro'eh ha-Heshbon be-Yisra'el," *RH* 13 (1962/63): 354. See also "Dvar Ha-Ma'arekhet," *RH* 16 (1966): 205.

[99] "Dvar ha-Ma'arekhet," *RH* 1 (March–April 1951): 4; "Dvar ha-Ma'arekhet," *RH* 1 (May–June 1951): 1.

[100] Dan Bawly, "Ro'eh ha-Heshbon ke-Ish Tsibur," *RH* 13 (1962/63): 507–9.

of whom were former employees of the tax authority, were helping clients to evade or avoid taxation and thus were "undermining the national effort."[101]

The abandonment of the statist approach by accountants was ultimately reflected in the views of government officials. In 1967 Ya'akov Shimshon Shapira, the Israeli minister of justice, told accountants that "the government does not expect that accountants, God forbid, sacrifice the interests of their clients. We believe, sometimes gladly and sometimes less so, that you must defend your clients as much as possible." Similarly, in some quarters accountants were now saying that "we can no longer celebrate hypocritical statements claiming that in our relationship with the authorities we stand on the same side of the table."[102] By the 1970s and 1980s discussions about the statist position of accountants and their role in ensuring taxpayer compliance had all but disappeared. Such ideas were described as belonging to the past, or as being "not modern."[103] Instead, in the journal of the Institute of Certified Public Accountants in Israel one could now find discussions on topics such as "what the public [meaning corporations] expects of accountants."[104] For example, at a symposium entitled "the Image of the Institute of Certified Public Accountants," held in 1986, some of the speakers argued that the role of accountants was to assist investors, shareholders, and taxpayers by demanding tax simplification, and by "constantly fighting the bureaucratization of government systems." Accountancy professionals, said one speaker, should stress that "our role is to represent taxpayers, and taxpayers only," and that accountants serve the public and not the government.[105]

[101] M. Saba, "Etikah Miktso'it ve-Otsar ha-Medinah," *Davar*, February 20, 1963, at 3. See also Yoram Kanyuk, "Estetikah shel Hayim be-Matsav Herum," *Davar*, January 29, 1971, at 15.

[102] "Birkat Sar ha-Mishpatim," *RH* 17 (1966/67): 50; S. Gafni, "Ma'amado shel Ro'eh ha-Heshbon ve-Shiltonot ha-Mas," *RH* 19 (1968/69): 6, 8–9; D. Porat "[Tguvah]," *RH* 17 (1966/67): 93.

[103] B. Nahir, "Ha-Misim veha-Musar," *RH* 20 (June 1969/70): 493.

[104] "Mah Metsapeh he-Tsibur me-Ro'eh ha-Heshbon," *RH* 21 (1970/71): 638–56.

[105] "Tadmit Lishkat Ro'ey Heshbon," *RH* 34 (1986): 295, 296, 298, 301. A somewhat similar process of change can be found in discussions on the ethics of tax lawyers in the US between the 1950s and the 1980s. Here too one finds a move from a focus on patriotism, civic duties, and the role of tax lawyers as educators of the taxpayers (in

Lawyers: From Guardians of the Rule of Law to Defenders of the Civil Rights of Clients

Echoing the case of accountants, the relationship between lawyers and the rest of society also underwent a transformation between the mid- and late twentieth century. During the period of the British mandate and in the first three decades after Israeli independence, Jewish and later Israeli society and culture were dominated by the ideology of the Zionist Labor Movement and its image of the "new Jew" as a pioneering farmer and worker devoted to the good of the collective. Lawyers – urban, bourgeois, individualist, and liberal – were often seen as relics of the "old" Jewish Diaspora that Zionism sought to overcome.[106]

An explicit reference to this image of lawyers can be found, for example, in the writings of Alfred Witkon, a tax lawyer who was later appointed Supreme Court Justice. According to Witkon, romanticism, socialism, and the pioneering ethos of Israeli society led people "first and foremost to agricultural settlement and the redeeming of the land ... and the legal profession, along with other occupations in which the Jews excelled in the Diaspora, was considered loathsome."[107]

the 1950s, influenced partly by Cold War concerns) to a more narrow, technical, and legalistic definition of the ethical duties of tax lawyers (beginning in the mid-1960s). See Michael Hatfield, "Legal Ethics and Federal Taxes, 1945–1965: Patriotism, Duties, and Advice," *Florida Tax Review* 12 (2012): 1–57; Michael Hatfield, "Committee Opinions and Treasury Regulation: Tax Lawyer Ethics, 1965–1985," *Florida Tax Review* 15 (2014): 675–735. See also Tanina Rostain and Milton C. Regan Jr., *Confidence Games: Lawyers, Accountants and the Tax Shelter Industry* (Cambridge, MA: MIT Press, 2014), 57–73. For a discussion of the duty to clients in nineteenth-century England, see Daniel Duman, "The Creation and Diffusion of a Professional Ideology in Nineteenth Century England," *Sociological Review* 27 (1979): 113–38, 118.

[106] Ziv, "Combining Professionalism"; Rakefet Sela-Sheffy, "Integration through Distinction: German-Jewish Immigrants, the Legal Profession and Patterns of Bourgeois Culture in British-Ruled Jewish Palestine," *Journal of Historical Sociology* 19 (2006): 34–59; David De Vries, "National Construction of Occupational Identity: Jewish Clerks in British-Ruled Palestine," *Comparative Studies in Society and History* 39 (1997): 373–400. For an opposing view stressing the legalistic nature of Jewish society in mandatory Palestine, see Nir Kedar, "Ha-Mishpat u-Mekomo ha-Merkazi ba-Historyah ha-Yisre'elit: 'Al ha-Historiografyah shel ha-Mishpat ha-Yisre'eli u-Trumatah le-Heker Yisrael," *Katedrah* 150 (2013): 155–80, 169–74.

[107] Alfred Witkon, "Ha-Mishpat be-Erets Mitpatahat," in *Sefer Yovel le-Pinhas Rosen*, ed. Haim Cohn (Jerusalem: Mif'al ha-Shikhpul, 1962), 66–85, 72. See also Ziv, "Combining Professionalism," 1635.

During the mandatory period, some Jewish lawyers tried to overcome this unflattering image by serving Jewish nationalist causes. One
way to do so was to connect the work of lawyers to the Zionist cultural
revival project, specifically the idea of using religious Jewish law, the
halakhah, as the basis for the creation of a secular Jewish legal system.
In the 1920s Jewish legal revival ideas were mainly linked to systems
of autonomous Jewish courts that existed both in the bourgeois and
socialist sectors of Jewish society in Palestine. Beginning in the 1930s,
the Tel Aviv School of Law and Economics became the main vehicle
for Jewish legal revival. The school sought to "to lay the ideological
and scientific foundations of the revival of the Jewish State," creating
a new version of Jewish law and "preparing the ground for a synthesis
of ancient and modern, oriental and occidental, national and universal
principles of law and society." [108]

Another possible way to link lawyers to the Zionist national project
was by providing political–legal advice or litigation services to various Zionist organizations and movements. Examples of this approach
include the legal services provided by some leading Jewish lawyers to
the General Federation of Jewish Labor, and the work of some lawyers who represented illegal Jewish immigrants to Palestine or Jewish
militants fighting the British in the 1940s. [109] However, such avenues of
contribution to Zionist causes were not open to lawyers specializing
in tax-related matters.

Most Jewish lawyers in Palestine did not participate in nationalist
activities and instead focused on providing legal services to their clients, rather than on their Zionist collective duties (or on their duties
as subjects of the British colonial state). This was also the case with
the Jewish Bar Association, established in 1928. This association was

---

[108] CZA 212/2, School of Law and Economics Tel Aviv, "To the Friends of Hebrew
Science in the World!" For a detailed discussion, see Likhovski, *Law and Identity*,
131–2. On the autonomous Jewish court systems, see Ronen Shamir, *The
Colonies of Law: Colonialism, Zionism and Law in Early Mandate Palestine*
(Cambridge: Cambridge University Press, 2000).

[109] See Avital Margalit, "'Ha-Ye'arot asher ba-Hem Nirde et ha-Dvash': Hok, Irgun
u-Mivne Ta'agidi be-Hevrat ha-'Ovdim," *'Iyuney Mishpat* 26 (2002): 451–510;
Ziv, "Combining Professionalism," 1629; Shimon Erez-Blum, "'Ha-Mahteret ha-
Yuridit': Hishtalvutam shel 'Orkhey-Din Yehudim ba-Ma'avak ha-Tsiyoni ba-
Shanim 1938–1947 be-Palestinah," JSD diss., Tel Aviv University, 2012.

mainly concerned with promoting the interests of lawyers as a professional group against competing groups such as petition-writers. It saw itself as a neutral, apolitical body, with the nationalist aspects of its activities generally confined to issues such as promoting pleading in the Hebrew language in government courts, or lobbying for the appointment of Jewish judges to these courts. It therefore had no interest in seeking to create a Jewish "state within a state" in the legal realm (a policy that, as we saw in Chapter 3, characterized many other areas of Zionist activity in Palestine, including taxation).[110]

The problematic image and marginal position of lawyers in Zionist discourse continued after the establishment of the state of Israel in 1948. The "unproductive" nature of the calling of lawyers, their manners, dress, code of conduct, allegiance to a legal system based on foreign (English) law, bourgeois nature, formalism, and liberalism all clashed with the dominant ethos of Israeli society at the time.[111]

In the 1950s the resolution of the tension between the values dominant in Israeli society and the values associated with the legal profession was found in the idea of the rule of law. In the period after 1948, Israeli lawyers and judges sought to portray themselves as guardians of the rule of law, arguing that through their private activity (representing their clients) they were actually assisting in furthering a collective, statist, goal: to build the institutions of the new state on a solid, permanent basis.[112] During the mandatory era, especially in the 1940s, Jewish lawyers perceived the governmental legal system as arbitrary and illegitimate.[113] The legal system the lawyers were now promoting was an Israeli one, albeit based mainly on English law. Such a system, lawyers argued, had to be strengthened, as this would benefit the state.

The notion that a major task of lawyers was to advance the idea of the role of law is found, for example, in the discussions reported from the thirteenth convention of the Jewish Bar Association that took place in June 1949. In their speeches, both lawyers and government officials emphasized that the duty of lawyers was to serve as officers

---

[110] Y. Ben-David, "Ha-Mivneh ha-Hevrati shel ha-Miktso'ot ha-Hofshiyim be-Yisrael" (Ph.D. diss., Hebrew University, 1956), 255–83; Ziv, "Combining Professionalism," 1626–33; Ziv, *Mi Yishmor*, 50–8; Likhovski, *Law and Identity*, 154–61.

[111] See, e.g., Strasman, *'Otey*, 202.

[112] Ziv, "Combining Professionalism," 1637, 1649.

[113] Witkon, "Ha-Mishpat be-Erets Mitpatahat," 71.

of the court, even when this duty clashed with their clients' interests, and to educate the public to respect the state, its laws, the courts, and the police.[114]

The most explicit articulation of this statist approach was found in a speech given by David Ben-Gurion. Before the establishment of State of Israel, said Ben-Gurion, the duty of Jewish lawyers was to "confront the foreign [mandatory] state" and its oppressive laws. But now, he said, lawyers had a duty to "protect the law," secure the rule of law, and educate the public to respect the law. Ya'akov Shimshon Shapira, Israel's first Attorney General, later explained that Ben-Gurion's speech meant that lawyers could not help their clients to break the law, for example by evading taxation.[115] An article by a leading lawyer, Aharon Polonsky, published in 1962, echoed Ben-Gurion's approach, stating that "it is imperative to instill [in the public] the feeling that the intervention of the lawyer when civil rights are infringed is for the benefit of the state," and that the role of lawyers (and courts) was to educate the public in civics and "civilized" behavior.[116]

In the 1950s law and lawyers played a relatively marginal role in Israeli public life. However, beginning in the decade between 1967 and 1977, law became a dominant component of Israeli public discourse, and the Israeli public sphere began a process of legalization.[117] Legal

---

[114] "Din ve-Heshbon meha-Ve'idah ha-13 shel Histadrut 'Orkhey ha-Din be-Yisrael," *Ha-Praklit* 6 (1949): 94, 95, 99–100.

[115] Ibid., 99, 105.

[116] A. Polonsky, "Ma'amad 'Orekh-ha-Din ba-Medinah uva-Hevrah," *Ha-Praklit* 18 (1962): 168, 169, 171. Just as lawyers focused on the rule of law stressing a formalist, narrow, version of it, so did the Israeli courts. In the 1950s and 1960s these courts often emphasized the need to educate the government about the importance of the notion of the rule of law, and of judicial autonomy. See, e.g., Ziv, "Combining Professionalism," 1638; Kedar, "Ha-Mishpat u-Mekomo ha-Merkazi," 174–9.

[117] See generally Mautner, *Law and the Culture of Israel*, 54–158. On the relationship of the rise of the neoliberal state in Israel and the rise in the importance of law and the experts associated with it, see also Menachem Mautner, "Mashber ha-Republikaniyut be-Yisrael," *Mishpat ve-'Asakim* 14 (2012): 559–94, 577 n. 57; Mautner, "Petah Davar," 38–47. For a discussion and critique of the arguments made by Mautner regarding the nature of the decisions of the Israeli Supreme Court in the 1950s, see Ron Harris, *Ha-Mishpat ha-Yisre'eli – Ha-Shanim ha-Me'atsvot: 1948–1977* (Bnei Brak: Ha-Kibbutz ha-Me'uhad, 2014), 73–82. On legalism in Israeli society in the 1950s, see Kedar, "Ha-Mishpat u-Mekomo ha-Merkazi," 174–8.

historian Ron Harris has identified some important milestones in this process such as: increased litigation in the Israeli Supreme Court; the growing willingness of this court to intervene in questions that were previously considered political and therefore not prone to judicial determination; and the rising power of the Israeli Attorney General to intervene in the day-to-day work of the Israeli government. These trends, among others, all reflected a decline in the prestige and power of politics and politicians, and a concurrent rise in the power and prestige of law and lawyers. Such a decline was not a uniquely Israeli phenomenon; it echoed similar processes arising in other countries in approximately the same period.[118]

As this change occurred, a shift appeared in lawyers' own depiction of their role. Like accountants, lawyers now depicted themselves as protectors of civil rights, *in opposition* to the state.[119] The notion of the rule of law was no longer identified with the state. Instead, it came to be used as a slogan by the political rivals of successive Israeli governments, especially after the rise of the Likud Party to power in 1977.

The Rise of "Cold, Calculating" Economists

The move from statist and educational rhetoric to a client-based rhetoric in the accounting and legal professions was mirrored in a somewhat similar process among Israeli economists. Here, too, there was a discursive shift between the pre- and post-1960s period. During the first period, the vision that economists propagated was based on subordinating

---

[118] Harris, *Ha-Mishpat ha-Yisre'eli*, 201–26. On the growing visibility of the decisions of the Israeli Supreme Court from the 1970s onwards, see Bryna Bogoch and Yifat Holzman-Gazit, "Mutual Bonds: Media Frames and the Israeli High Court of Justice," *Law and Social Inquiry* 33 (2008): 53–87. On the American model of lawyer–state relationship that emerged during the first half of the twentieth century, see Daniel R. Ernst, *Tocqueville's Nightmare: The Administrative State Emerges in America, 1900–1940* (Oxford: Oxford University Press, 2014). On legalization and the growing power of courts and legal discourse globally in recent decades, see generally Lawrence M. Friedman, *Total Justice* (New York: Russell Sage Foundation, 1985), 153–6; Ran Hirschl, *Towards Juristocracy: The Origins and Consequences of the New Constitutionalism* (Cambridge, MA: Harvard University Press, 2004); Duncan Kennedy, "The Hermeneutic of Suspicion in Contemporary American Legal Thought," *Law and Critique* 25 (2014): 91–139.

[119] See, e.g., Yael Gvirtz, *Sefer ha-Yovel: 50 Shnot Lishkah 1961–2011* (n.p.: Lishkat 'Orkhey ha-Din, [2011]), 112–19.

individual desires and motivations to those of the collective, and on assuming that the universal laws of economic behavior did not apply in the case of Palestine and post-1948 Israel. Such a stance was even more evident in the thought of Zionist political leaders at the time. By the 1970s, however, particularistic notions of Israeli society and its economy were replaced by the view that in Israel, too, individual desires could not be overcome by the power of the collective, and that here, too, universal economic laws that governed individuals in other societies also applied.

During the mandatory era, professional economists served Zionist institutions in Palestine, producing arguments used in the political battles of the Jews against the British and the Arabs. These economists employed what later Israeli economists derogatorily called "apologetic economics" to further Zionist arguments (as opposed to the supposedly professional and disinterested approach of Israeli economists from the 1950s onward).[120] We have already encountered one example of such tactics in Chapter 2 – the arguments against the introduction of income taxation raised in 1932 by Arthur Ruppin, a Jewish economist and statistician who was the head the Economic Research Institute of the Jewish Agency in Palestine.[121]

A second group of professional economists was found in two Jewish academic institutions in mandatory Palestine: the Hebrew University and the Tel Aviv School of Law and Economics. At the Hebrew University, as we saw, economics was taught from a descriptive, historical, and institutionalist perspective, with little attention paid to general economic theory.[122] This was also the case at the Tel Aviv School of Law and Economics, whose creation was informed by a unique particularistic vision of law and of economics. One of the founders of the Tel Aviv School was economist Benjamin Siewe, a Russian Jew who studied in France and Germany.[123] Siewe described economics

---

[120] Michaeli, "Ha-Hug," 164. The varieties of Jewish economic discourse during the mandatory period are discussed in Arie Krampf, "Reception of the Developmental Approach in the Jewish Economic Discourse of Mandatory Palestine, 1934–1938," *Israel Studies* 15 (2010): 80–103.

[121] See Chapter 2, n. 18. On Ruppin see, e.g., Etan Bloom, "The 'Administrative Knight' – Arthur Ruppin and the Rise of Zionist Statistics," *Tel Aviver Jahrbuch für deutsche Geschichte* 35 (2007): 183–203.

[122] Michaeli, "Ha-Hug," 162.

[123] CZA 212/2, *School of Law and Economics, Tel Aviv* (July 1936), 15.

not as a universal but as a particular science, stating that "at the [Tel Aviv] school, the economic sciences would be imbued with a special Hebrew idea."[124]

This emphasis on the particular, and the general subservience of economics to the Zionist project, was even more pronounced in the economic thought of many Zionist leaders during the mandatory era. Zionist leaders rejected the view that economic motivation was merely based on selfish individual choices and the aggregation of such individual choices to maximize material benefits. Instead, many of them believed in subjugating individual preferences to the state, in government intervention in the economy, and in central planning. They rejected the notion of a free market when it was perceived as undermining the common good. Such ideas were inspired by socialist ideology, by a belief that the Zionist project was unique, and also by Keynesian notions and the experience of the planned wartime economies of the Second World War period.[125]

The most important political figure in the Zionist community in Palestine in the mandatory and early state periods, David Ben-Gurion, was perhaps the most radical in his disdain for the laws of economics. Ben-Gurion rejected the idea that economics was a "science," that the *homo economicus* existed, and that academic economic theory was useful. Instead, he believed that human will could overcome the supposedly objective and universal laws of economics.[126] As David Horowitz, the first Governor of the Bank of Israel, said of him, "the belief in economic laws, and in the autonomy of the economic mechanism, were scorned by Ben-Gurion. He never understood [these laws], he disliked them, and he saw them as a mask of mystery designed to impede human will. His desire was to overcome the laws of economics and thus demolish their dominance, and reveal their impotence." Ben-Gurion's position that human will could triumph over the laws of the economy was echoed by many other early Israeli leaders, whom

[124] CZA 212/37, Beyt ha-Sefer ha-Gavoh le-Mishpat vele-Kalkalah, *Prospekt li-Shnat ha-Limudim 1937/3*, 3. See also CZA 212/32, B. Siewe, "'Al ha-Haskalah ha-Kalkalit ba-Arets."

[125] Gross, "Kalkalat Yisrael," 139; Molcho, "Productivization," 137; Krampf, *Ha-Mekorot*, 48–51, 231–3; Kleiman, "The Waning of Israeli *Etatisme*," 155–6.

[126] Jacob Reuveny, "Hashkafato ha-Kalkalit shel Ben-Gurion," *RK* 135–136 (1988): 96, 101–4.

Horowitz described as a group motivated by "fanatical nationalism, and socialist pathos," and as "puritanical, heroical and stubborn," and therefore disdainful of "economic limitations." [127]

This disdain for economic theory influenced the composition of the Israeli civil service of the 1950s. During the first decade after Israeli independence, many high-ranking economic posts were filled by officials of the voluntary Jewish organizations of the prestate period, people who believed in the idea that individual will could be molded by the state, and self-interest could be reshaped by propaganda emphasizing the needs of the collective. According to Israeli economist Ephraim Kleiman, these officials opposed "the seemingly cold, calculating approach of the economist," and argued, like Ben-Gurion, that economic laws did not apply to Israel. [128]

Gradually, however, economists trained at the new economics department of the Hebrew University came to dominate economic discourse in Israel. By the mid-1960s the "Patinkin boys" began to have a significant impact. [129] The early particularistic and collectivist Zionist vision of the economy waned, to be replaced by an approach that saw individuals as rational maximizers of wealth, whose choices should be respected and, in any event, could not be directly reshaped by the government.

In the specific field of tax compliance, one example that epitomized this shift occurred in the early 1970s. This was a time when public finance scholars began to analyze tax noncompliance from a rational choice perspective. Inspired by University of Chicago economist Gary Becker's seminal 1968 analysis of crime as the product of rational calculation, a new model, the Allingham–Sandmo–Yitzhaki model of tax compliance, was developed. The new model suggested that the decisions of taxpayers to evade taxes were not based on moral or ideological considerations, but only on factors such as the scope of the punishment imposed on the evader, the probability of being detected, and the level of individual risk-aversion. Instead of taxation as an

---

[127] David Horowitz, *Hayim ba-Moked* (Ramat-Gan: Masadah, 1985), 27–8, 41, 57; Shapira, *Israel: A History*, 210.

[128] Kleiman, "Israel: Economists in a New State," 562–3.

[129] On the complex relationship between economists and politicians in Israel, see, e.g., Michael Keren, "Economists and Economic Policy Making in Israel: The Politics of Expertise in the Stabilization Program," *Policy Sciences* 26 (1993): 331–46.

expression of civic republican duty, economists were now analyzing tax compliance as behavior based solely on rational considerations. One of the developers of the new model was a young Israeli economist, Shlomo Yitzhaki, a student and later a professor at the Hebrew University. In 1974, the year in which he published his contribution to the Allingham–Sandmo–Yitzhaki model, Yitzhaki was appointed the head of the economic research team of the Ben-Shahar tax reform committee. The Ben-Shahar Committee's approach to the problem of tax compliance, perhaps because of Yitzhaki's input, was different from the approach prevalent in Israel in the 1950s. Instead of suggesting that the problem of noncompliance could be tackled by civic education and the use of social norms, the committee's solution was to simplify the income tax, broaden the tax base, and impose more stringent bookkeeping requirements.[130]

Conclusion

The return of tax intermediaries (now professionals relying on legal norms rather than the tax farmers of the Ottoman period) was a gradual and complex process that unfolded over many decades. It seems that the 1960s and 1970s constituted a particularly important period in the history of the rise of the power of tax experts in Israel. In the 1960s the collectivist spirit that had characterized prestate Jewish society began to wane, along with the statist rhetoric of 1950s Israel – a process that accelerated after the 1967 war and the rise of the right-wing Likud Party in 1977. As collectivism receded, taxpayers felt freer to use the services of tax professionals – accountants and lawyers – to reduce their tax burden.

The growing demand for the services of tax professionals, including tax-reduction services, met a growing supply of accountants and lawyers. This growth was driven by changes in Israeli society and its economy, but the Israeli state also assisted in the process. The state began

[130] On the Allingham–Sandmo–Yitzhaki model, see generally Joel Slemrod and Shlomo Yitzhaki, "Tax Avoidance, Evasion and Administration," in *Handbook of Public Economics*, eds. Alan J. Auerbach and Martin Feldstein (Amsterdam: Elsevier Science, 2002), 3:1423–70, 3:1429. On Yitzhaki's role on the Ben-Shahar Committee, see Shlomo Yitzhaki, "A Note on Income Tax Evasion: A Theoretical Analysis," *Journal of Public Economics* 3 (1974): 201–2; Yitzhaki, "Reformat ha-Mas," 195.

to use intermediaries who would ease friction and save time in the tax assessment and collection process, and took steps (such as regulating the accounting and legal professions) to protect the monopoly of these professions in the provision of tax-related services.

In turn, growing supply was accompanied by a transformation in the self-perception of these professions. Beginning in the 1960s, accountants and lawyers no longer described themselves as servants of the state, whose role was to educate taxpayers to fulfill their tax duties. A related professional group, economists, active in the sphere of tax reform, also underwent a process of change. Economists no longer understood and described the economy (and taxation) from a statist perspective, but rather analyzed it from an individualist stance.

As the influence of accountants and lawyers increased, and the challenges they posed to the tax system grew, the nature of the tool they relied on – tax law – also changed. Courts and the legislature reshaped tax law accordingly, adjusting it to the growing presence of tax experts. We now move to an analysis of this transformation.

6

The Transformation of Tax Law: Doctrinal and Legislative Reforms

In 1966 Arye Lapidoth, a legal adviser to the Israeli government and one of the first academic teachers of tax law in Israel, published a book entitled *Evasion and Avoidance of Income Tax*. This was a comparative study on the attitudes of English and Israeli law to tax noncompliance. The book was written from a governmental perspective, and therefore viewed avoidance negatively, a point emphasized by the illustration on the cover that showed a capitalist in a top hat deviously looking sideways, no doubt seeking some new scheme to minimize his taxes (see Figure 6.1). Given Lapidoth's professional training as a lawyer, the book naturally focused on the legal tools used to confront tax noncompliance.[1]

Lapidoth's book serves as evidence of the growing role of law in the tax arena, for both taxpayers (as a means of minimizing taxes) and for the government (as a way of ensuring tax compliance). The growing importance of law was linked to the developments described in Chapter 5 – the rise of tax professionals. These professionals relied on law to reduce their clients' taxes. In response, state institutions changed the law to meet the challenges posed by tax professionals. These changes are the topic of this chapter.[2]

---

[1] See Arye Lapidoth, *Evasion and Avoidance of Income Tax: A Comparative Study of English Law and Israeli Law* (Jerusaletm: Museum of Taxes, 1966). The book was based on Lapidoth's doctoral dissertation, supervised by a leading British tax scholar, G. S. A. Wheatcroft. A Hebrew version of the book was published simultaneously.

[2] For another discussion of the "legalization" of the tax field focusing on the 1990s, see David Gliksberg, "Ha-Mishpatizatsyah shel ha-Misim: 'Al Zikato shel ha-Siyah

FIGURE 6.1 Arye Lapidoth, *Evasion and Avoidance of Income Tax* (Jerusalem: Museum of Taxes, 1966), cover.

ha-Misi la-Siyah ha-Mishpati ha-Klali," *Misim* 23(4) (2009): A-1–A-24; David Gliksberg, "The Judicial Tax Revolution: From a Subject and Immigrant Society to a Mature Society," *British Tax Review*, 2012, 553–78.

The changes were clearly visible in judicial attitudes to tax avoidance. Beginning in the late 1960s, Israeli courts abandoned the formalist, protaxpayer attitude to tax avoidance that had characterized their decisions in the first two decades after 1948, and adopted a substantive, pro-government approach.[3] The new approach allowed courts to ask questions not only about taxpayers' behavior, but also about their "inner" state of mind: whether the *intent* of taxpayers in structuring a given transaction in a particular way was to avoid taxation. Such a shift of focus was not merely technical. It was a reflection of the changing use of different types of norms to induce compliance. In the 1950s creating inner motivation for tax compliance had mainly been the task of social norms. By the late 1960s monitoring the taxpayer's mind had become the task of legal norms. This was accompanied by a change in audience. In the 1950s the state had attempted to directly shape the mind of every taxpayer using social norms. The audience of the courts, however, was not the general public but mainly tax professionals (who are usually the only people to read judicial decisions). Instead of direct influence by social norms, the courts were now trying to influence tax compliance indirectly, through technical doctrines addressed to a professional rather than a lay audience.

As judicial doctrines were changing, parallel changes were occurring in tax legislation. Income taxation was massively reformed in 1975 following the recommendations of the Ben-Shahar Committee. The 1975 reforms abolished some aspects that had characterized the income tax system in previous decades, such as popular participation in the tax process, moving income taxation in a more professionally

---

[3] The history of the changes in Israeli tax avoidance doctrines is part of a broader story – the history of legal thought and judicial reasoning in Israel. This history is generally characterized by a move from a formalist approach to a substantive one. The leading account of this process, which argues that the "decline of formalism" occurred in Israeli case law in the 1980s, is found in Menachem Mautner, *Law and the Culture of Israel* (Oxford: Oxford University Press, 2011), 54–158. For critiques of the "Mautner thesis," including Mautner's periodization scheme, see Assaf Likhovski, "Mishpat ve-Tarbut be-Yisrael be-Fetah ha-Me'ah ha-'Esrim ve-Ahat: He'arot 'al Sifro shel Menachem Mautner," *Ha-Mishpat* 14 (2010/01): 715–23; Ron Harris, *Ha-Mishpat ha-Yisre'eli – Ha-Shanim ha-Me'atsvot: 1948–1977* (Bnei Brak: Ha-Kibbutz ha-Me'uhad, 2014), 201–23. On legal formalism, see generally Michal Alberstein, "Measuring Legal Formalism: Reading Hard Cases with Soft Frames," *Studies in Law, Politics, and Society* 57 (2012): 161–99.

oriented direction. In 1976 value-added taxation was introduced in Israel. The new tax was based on a vision of citizen–state interaction that was very different from the civic republican model on which income taxation was based in the 1950s. Finally, the adjustment of taxation to the hyperinflation that plagued Israel between the mid-1970s and early 1980s also helped to make taxation the domain of experts, and thus indirectly contributed to the demise of the old civic republican vision of taxation.

The changes evident in Israeli case law and legislation were sometimes an intentional adjustment of the law to the new conception of the citizen–state relationship that gradually emerged as the Israeli state was evolving from a mobilized nation-state to a neoliberal one during this period. Sometimes (as was the case with hyperinflation) the transformation of the relationship between the state and its taxpayers was only an unintended result of a legal measure that was meant to tackle an immediate economic problem.

The Transformation of Tax Avoidance Doctrines

Lawyers dealing with tax compliance often distinguish between two different forms of noncompliance. One form is tax evasion. Evasion is criminal behavior in clear violation of the law, for example the fabrication of accounts to reduce one's taxes. The second type of noncompliance is tax avoidance (sometimes called "aggressive tax planning"). Avoidance is similar to evasion in the sense that it is also designed to reduce or eliminate one's taxes. However, avoidance is not a criminal offense. Instead, tax avoiders achieve their goal by utilizing gaps or loopholes in the law without directly breaching specific statutory provisions.[4]

Evasion and avoidance exist along a single continuum. The actual point where evasion ends and avoidance begins is difficult to define – the boundary between the two categories is not given, nor is it static. It varies over time and is determined by political, economic, and cultural considerations. Because characterizing a certain type of behavior as "tax avoidance" is context-dependent, a history of judicial attitudes to

---

[4] See, e.g., Victor Thuronyi, ed., *Tax Law Design and Drafting* (Washington, DC: IMF, 1996), 1:44–5.

tax avoidance can provide an insight into broader trends in judicial, and also public, perceptions of tax compliance and, more generally, of taxation and citizenship.[5]

Tax Avoidance Doctrines up to the Late 1960s

The mandatory Income Tax Ordinance included several specific anti-avoidance provisions.[6] It also included a general antiavoidance provision: Section 22 of the Income Tax Ordinance, 1941 (now section 86).[7] This was a rare example of the use of a legal standard in an enactment mainly composed of legal rules.[8] It stated: "Where the Assessing Officer is of the opinion that any transaction which reduces or would reduce the amount of tax payable by any person is artificial or fictitious or that any disposition is not in fact given effect to, he may disregard any such transaction or disposition and the persons concerned shall be assessable accordingly."[9]

---

[5] See generally, Assaf Likhovski, "The Duke and the Lady: *Helvering v. Gregory* and the History of Tax Avoidance Adjudication," *Cardozo Law Review* 25 (2004): 953–1018; Assaf Likhovski, "Tax Law and Public Opinion: Explaining *IRC v Duke of Westminster*," in *Studies in the History of Tax Law*, ed. John Tiley (Oxford: Hart, 2007), 2:183–221. For an empirical approach, see Joshua D. Blank and Nancy Staudt, "Corporate Shams," *NYU Law Review* 87 (2012): 1641–712.

[6] For example, the 1946 version of the Palestine Income Tax Ordinance included section 21A, dealing with "dispositions in favour of children," section 22 dealing with undistributed profits of companies, section 28(3) disregarding agreements between a nonresident and a resident taxpayer that result in a reduction of ordinary profits, and section 45(2) disregarding nongenuine partnerships. See generally, Abraham Fellman, *The Palestine Income Tax: Law and Practice* (Tel Aviv: Lapid, 1946), 256; Lapidoth, *Evasion and Avoidance of Income Tax*, 156–64; A. Witkon with Yaakov Neeman, *Diney Misim: Misey Hakhnasah, 'Izavon ve-Shevah*, 4th edn (Jerusalem: Schocken, 1969), 56.

[7] Section 22 became section 28 in the 1947 amendment to the Income Tax Ordinance, and subsequently section 86 of the Income Tax Ordinance (New Version), 1961.

[8] On the use of standards in tax law, see generally David A. Weisbach, "Formalism in the Tax Law," *University of Chicago Law Review* 66 (1999): 860–86.

[9] The section was copied from the Kenya Income Tax Ordinance of 1940. Similar provisions also existed in the income tax legislation of other British colonies and dominions such as Cyprus, Canada, Australia, and South Africa. All these sections may have originated in the UK Excess Profits Duty legislation of 1915 that mentioned "fictitious or artificial" transactions. See Fellman, *The Palestine Income Tax*, 254–56; S. Moses, *The Income Tax Ordinance of Palestine*, 2nd edn (Tel Aviv: Bitaon,

Between 1941 and the end of the British mandate in 1948, relatively few tax cases were litigated in the courts of Palestine.[10] None of the cases that did reach the courts dealt with the antiavoidance provision of the Income Tax Ordinance. One reason for this was that the Ordinance was new and the tax authority was not keen to litigate cases whose outcome was uncertain. It therefore often settled cases instead of litigating them.[11] Perhaps another reason for the lack of use of the general antiavoidance provision was that the tax authority and lawyers of Palestine were influenced by English law and its conservative, protaxpayer stance to tax avoidance.[12]

The first case in which the general antiavoidance provision of the Income Tax Ordinance was mentioned was decided in May 1952, four years after Israeli independence and eleven years after the enactment of the Ordinance. This case, named *A. B.*, dealt with a transaction involving a building lease. The owner of a one-story building in Tel Aviv leased the roof to two builders for a period of seven years. The builders built two additional stories on the roof and sublet them, receiving substantial amounts of money from the tenants. The tax authority argued that the owner should pay income tax on the money received by the builders since he artificially diverted that sum to the builders. This argument was rejected by Judge Witkowski (Witkon), who served at

1946), 320–3; Lapidoth, *Evasion and Avoidance of Income Tax*, 164–7. See also G. S. A. Wheatcroft, "The Attitude of the Legislature and the Courts to Tax Avoidance," *Modern Law Review* 18 (1955): 209–30, 223 (discussing the UK Excess Profits Tax of 1941). Another source of such sections may have been Australia and New Zealand. See Michael Littlewood, *Taxation without Representation: The History of Hong Kong's Troublingly Successful Tax System* (Hong Kong: Hong Kong University Press, 2010), 229–30.

[10] See Fellman, *The Palestine Income Tax*, preface; Harold C. Wilkenfeld, *Taxes and People in Israel* (Cambridge, MA: Harvard University Press, 1973), 207.

[11] A. Witkowski, "Mas Hakhnasah," *Ha-Praklit* 1 (1943/44): 120–6; Fellman, *The Palestine Income Tax*, 255; Lapidoth, *Evasion and Avoidance of Income Tax*, 171.

[12] See, e.g., Fellman, *The Palestine Income Tax*, 255; Lapidoth, *Evasion and Avoidance of Income Tax*, 171–2 (quoting an opinion by the Attorney General of Palestine written in 1942 that stated that in order to use the section, "it is not sufficient to establish that a transaction is unusual or un-businesslike [since] it is a fundamental principle of the common law that a man can dispose of his property at his own sweet will.") On the formalism of English tax avoidance doctrines at the time, see Likhovski, "Tax Law and Public Opinion."

the time on the Tel Aviv District Court. In setting out what became the conventional protaxpayer interpretation of the term "artificial" until the late 1960s, Witkon stated that an artificial transaction was one that "assumes a form that is contrary to the accepted patterns of economic life, and deviates from the paths commonly adopted in order to achieve a certain economic result." Since a building lease was a common sort of transaction at the time, it was not deemed artificial.[13]

Five years later a second tax avoidance case reached the courts. In this case, *Ba'al Bayt*, decided in 1957, the court was asked to review a "fictitious" rather than an artificial transaction. Fictitious transactions (similar to "sham" transactions in English law) were defined by the court as those transactions in which the legal facts on which the taxpayer based his case were nonexistent.[14] In the *Ba'al Bayt* case, the first of many such cases, a (high-income) father leased a warehouse he owned to his (low-income) daughters, and three weeks later the daughters sublet the warehouse to a tenant, receiving five times the amount of rent they "paid" their father. Judge Shlomo Loewenberg of the Tel Aviv District Court declared that the lease to the daughters was fictitious.[15] In later years, many other fictitious

---

[13] ITA (Tel Aviv) 6/50, *A. B.* v. *AO*, PM, 7:347, 7:351. See also Lapidoth, *Evasion and Avoidance of Income Tax*, 172–3. Witkon's interpretation was protaxpayer, because if a certain kind of transaction results in a lower tax burden, it will soon become common and therefore not be considered "artificial" in Witkon's sense of the term. See Aharon Yoran, "Forty Years of Tax Law in Israel," *Israel Law Review* 24 (1990): 738–85, 748. Witkon's approach can also be called formalist because his test of "artificiality" only asked whether a given transaction assumed a "form that is contrary to the accepted patterns of economic life," instead of looking at the economic substance of the transaction. The anglophile Witkon was the leading champion of formalism in Israeli tax law. However, in some of his nonjudicial works he adopted an antiformalist approach. In these works Witkon stressed that tax law (and law generally) could not be understood without referring to its economic and social background, and declared his allegiance to a sociological-jurisprudence conception of the law. See introduction to *Diney Misim: Lefi Hartsa'otav shel A. Witkon*, ed. Michael Deu'el (Jerusalem: Akademon, 1953/54); A. Witkon, "Re'iyat Heshbon veha-Mishpat," *RH* 8 (1957): 95–6; Alfred Witkon, "Ha-Mishpat be-Erets Mitpatahat," in *Sefer Yovel le-Pinhas Rosen*, ed. Haim Cohn (Jerusalem: Mif'al ha-Shikhpul, 1962), 66–85.

[14] On sham transactions, see, e.g., John Tiley, "Judicial Anti-Avoidance Doctrines: The U.S. Alternatives," *British Tax Review*, 1987, 180–97, 195–7.

[15] ITA (Tel Aviv) 811/56 *Ba'al Bayt* v. *AO, RH* 7 (July 1957): 371 [affirmed CA 240/57 *Mikakashvili* v. *AO*, PD, 12:1485].

transactions reached the courts. Most of these cases dealt with transactions between family members.[16]

While most of the cases in the 1950s and early 1960s dealt with fictitious transactions, there were some cases in which the courts were asked to use the "artificial" clause of the general antiavoidance provision. In 1959 two such cases reached the Jerusalem and Tel Aviv District courts, both involving the supposed camouflaging of income from interest on loans. The first case was decided by the Jerusalem District Court and dealt with a corporation that loaned money. Borrowers were required to acquire a certain number of preferred shares in the corporation, in proportion to the amount of the loan. These shares were denied voting rights. They could also be denied the right to dividends and to the property of the corporation in the event of a voluntary winding-up. The tax authority asserted that the selling of preferred "shares" was an artificial transaction designed to camouflage the payment of interest that would otherwise have been taxed as income. However, the Jerusalem District Court judge who heard the case rejected this argument, asserting that the creation of such preferred shares was common practice.[17]

The second case, decided by the Tel Aviv District Court six months later, was based on similar facts. It dealt with a corporation belonging to the General Federation of Jewish Labor that loaned money to agricultural cooperatives. In addition to paying interest, the borrowers were required to purchase shares in the corporation at twice their nominal value. The tax authority claimed that the shares were worth less than their nominal value, and that the premium paid by the borrowers was, in fact, camouflaged interest that should be taxed. Judge Loewenberg accepted the tax authority's position. Loewenberg was, of course, aware of the fact that a previous decision had adopted a protaxpayer stance. He noted that Justice Witkon's definition of the term "artificial" in the 1952 *A. B.* case would limit the power of the

---

[16] For a detailed list of these cases, see Assaf Likhovski, "Formalism and Israeli Anti-Avoidance Doctrines in the 1950s and 1960s," in *Studies in the History of Tax Law*, ed. John Tiley (Oxford: Hart, 2004), 1:339–77, 349 n. 33. See also Lapidoth, *Evasion and Avoidance of Income Tax*, 179–82.

[17] ITA (Jerusalem) 25/58 *Ploni* v. AO, PM, 19:345 [affirmed CA 102/59 AO v. *"Ismar" Hevrah le-Mis'har vele-Hashka'ot*, PD, 14:2165 (October 20, 1960)]. See also Lapidoth, *Evasion and Avoidance of Income Tax*, 173–5.

courts to characterize common transactions as artificial, and suggested that the proper understanding of the term was to ask whether the legal form that the parties to the transaction chose "leads them to their economic goal in a direct, acceptable and correct way economically, or whether the form indicates that the parties chose an indirect and tortuous way that does not reflect the regular patterns of economic life."[18]

On appeal, however, Loewenberg's decision was overturned. Justice Witkon, who by then was serving on the Israeli Supreme Court, rejected Loewenberg's arguments and declared that the transaction was not artificial.[19] Following this decision, the chastised Loewenberg recanted. Soon, another, very similar, case came before him. This time Loewenberg decided against the tax authority and in favor of the taxpayer.[20]

In the early and middle 1960s, the Israeli Supreme Court adopted a protaxpayer position in a number of cases, such as the *Worok* case, decided in 1965. The issue was whether shareholders who received an interest-free loan for an unlimited period of time from the corporation they owned should be taxed. Based on English and Australian precedents, Judge Loewenberg ruled that these loans were camouflaged dividends – only to have his decision overturned again by the Supreme Court.[21]

In another such case, decided in March 1966, Justice Witkon reaffirmed his protaxpayer approach. This case involved a clause in the land appreciation tax law, taxing capital gains from the sale of real

---

[18] ITA (Tel Aviv) 713/58 *Hevrah Plonit* v. *AOLE*, PM, 21:334, 21:339–45, 21:349. Loewenberg repeated this approach in ITA (Tel Aviv) 432/60 *Merkaz* v. *AOLE*, PM, 27:135, 27:142.

[19] CA 421/59 *Nir* v. *AOLE*, PD, 15:379, 15:382. See also Lapidoth, *Evasion and Avoidance of Income Tax*, 175–6. In his decision, Justice Witkon noted that the corporation in question was a quasi-public corporation and therefore when it initiated the share-buying scheme, it (unlike ordinary corporations) took into consideration noneconomic factors, such as the desire to have as many shareholders as possible.

[20] ITA 607/61/6 (Tel Aviv) *Halva'ah ve-Hisahon Rishon le-Tsiyon* v. *AOLE*, PM, 33:410, 33:414. This was a case of a cooperative banking society that asked each borrower to pay an additional 1.5 percent of the amount of the loan as a contribution to a "building fund" to finance the building of offices for the cooperative. The tax authority argued that this amount was camouflaged interest.

[21] ITA (Tel Aviv) 1072/63 *Worok* v. *AO*, *RH* 16 (January–February 1966): 75; CA 416/65 *Worok* v. *AO*, PD, 20:351. See also CA 310/62, *AO* v. *Ron*, PD, 16:2751.

estate. The clause in question exempted apartments of less than 70 square meters (not including balconies) from the tax. The specific apartment in this case was originally larger than 70 square meters, but the taxpayers turned parts of two rooms into balconies, thereby reducing it to 69 square meters. The tax authority claimed that doing so proved the taxpayers' intention to avoid the tax. Witkon rejected this argument: "There is no point in seeking the true intentions of the respondents that led them to make the changes in their apartment." He continued:

> It is an illusion to assume that the citizen is not aware of the fiscal consequences of his acts and omissions, and to demand that he be naive. In this way we will only educate him to be a hypocrite. It is better that the fiscal legislator not use provisions that invite the citizen to change his usual habits and follow other ways that are undesirable socially. The draftsman who wrote section 49(b)(2) [of the land appreciation tax law that exempted small apartments] did not, it seems, learn the lesson of the English 'window tax' of 1695 that led to the building of airless and dark buildings ... There is no 'artificiality' in the fact that the potential taxpayer plans his actions in a way that leads to an apartment-size that the law requires, and if the law is deficient, it is the role of the legislator to correct it.[22]

Changes in the Late 1960s

Until 1966, most of the cases decided by the courts (apart from cases dealing with fictitious transactions between family members) reflected a formalist, protaxpayer position. The years 1966 and 1967 saw a shift in case law. The shift began in the summer of 1966 with two cases involving accountants who transferred their business to a corporation and became its employees. In both cases, the tax authority claimed that this was an artificial transaction, and in both cases the argument was accepted by the courts.[23]

---

[22] CA 262/65 *DLBT* v. *Tamir*, PD, 20(1):695, 20(1):700.

[23] ITA (Tel Aviv) 1065/65 *Liway* v. *AO*, PM, 52:295; ITA (Tel Aviv) 931/65 *Swirski* v. *AO*, PM, 52:365. The appeals are CA 378/66 *Liway* v. *AO*, PD, 20(4):738; CA 560/66 *Swirski* v. *AO*, PD, 21(1):533. In *Liway*, Justice Witkon accepted the tax authority's position based on the interpretation of the specific transfer agreements in question, as well as the Auditors' Law, arguing that the Auditors' Law did not permit corporations to serve as accountants, and that the transfer of the business to such a corporation made the transaction artificial in the sense that it was "contrary to the accepted patterns of economic life."

One year later, in a landmark case called *Mefi*, the definition of the term "artificial" first proposed in 1952 in the *A. B.* case was replaced by a new definition.²⁴ *Mefi* was decided in November 1967. The transaction in question involved the purchase of a loss-making corporation to offset its losses against income made by the purchasers. Justice Silberg of the Israeli Supreme Court wrote the lead opinion in the case. He argued that Witkon's definition of the term "artificial" as anything that was "uncommon" would make it impossible to disregard many transactions, because once a transaction became profitable economically, it would immediately become common. Therefore, Justice Silberg proposed a new notion of artificiality. The question that should be asked, he said, was: does the transaction have any "substance" (*tokhen*) apart from its tax consequences?

In his concurring opinion, Justice Witkon abandoned his previous, protaxpayer interpretation of the notion of artificiality. He noted that, in previous cases, he had been opposed to motivation-based tests of artificiality. In the past, he said:

> I always saw a danger in the fact that such a provision might teach the citizen to act hypocritically. If he only finds a serious reason [*ta'am*] for his action, besides the reason of tax reduction, the section would not apply to him. Often a transaction will have several underlying reasons and we cannot examine the heart and mind of the taxpayer to find out what the major one was. Here, however, the lower court found that there was no reason except for tax reduction ... One cannot therefore say that the assessing officer was mistaken when he viewed the transaction as artificial.²⁵

In this paragraph, Witkon voiced a reluctance to examine "the heart and mind" of taxpayers; yet he, too, ultimately adopted a new test – one that allowed the tax authority (and the courts) to examine the inner thoughts of the taxpayer instead of only looking at the outward, formal, shape of the transaction.²⁶

---

²⁴ CA 265/67 *Mefi* v. *AOLE*, PD, 21(2):593. For an analysis of this case, see, e.g., David Gliksberg, *Gvulot Tikhnun ha-Mas: Sivug Mehadash shel 'Iska'ot le-Tsorekh Mas* (Jerusalem: Ha-Makhon le-Mehkarey Hakikah, 1990), 177, 217–19, 227.

²⁵ *Mefi*, 603.

²⁶ For the earlier stages of the case, see ISA, Court file, CA 265/67 (a copy of the decision can be found in the Supreme Court file of the *Mefi* case in the Israel State Archives (ISA), Jerusalem). In a later case, CA 761/77 *Avna'al* v. *AOLE*, PD, 32(2):494, Witkon

Thus, 1967, the year in which the *Mefi* case was decided, marked
a shift in case law dealing with tax avoidance. In the following decades the Israeli Supreme Court decided many additional tax avoidance
cases, but the new approach first proposed in *Mefi* continued to dominate case law.[27]

The shift from a protaxpayer, formalist approach to a pro-
government, substantive one that *Mefi* epitomized occurred earlier in
the professional literature. Tax avoidance was not discussed in Israeli
newspapers or in the periodical literature of the 1950s. The first discussions on tax avoidance began to appear in the mid- and late 1960s.[28]
One of the factors boosting interest in the subject was the publication,
in 1966, of Lapidoth's book on tax avoidance, mentioned at the beginning of this chapter.[29] As was to be expected, many tax professionals
reacted to the book by defending the "right" of taxpayers to minimize
their taxes, relying on a formalist understanding of tax law.

In 1966 the Institute of Certified Public Accountants in Israel
(ICPAI) held a special symposium on tax planning.[30] In his talk,

suggested that the two tests of artificiality could be combined. A transaction that
"assumed a form that is contrary to the accepted patterns of economic life," would still
not be deemed artificial "if it had some commercial motivations." Ibid., 498–9.

[27] Examples of some 1970s and early 1980s cases are CA 11/74 *AOLE* v. *Ulpeney
Hasratah be-Yisrael*, PD, 29(1):297; CA 74/74 *Spaer* v. *Menahel Mas Rekhush*,
PD, 30(1):271; CA 761/77 *Avna'al* v. *AOLE*, PD, 32(2):494; ITA 34/78 *Adler*
v. *AO*, PDE, 10:363; ITA 23/79 *Lidor* v. *AO*, PDE, 10:254; CA 390/80 *Ta'as Mor*
v. *DLBT*, PD, 38(1):449; CA 83/81 *T.M.B.* v. *AO*, PD 40(3):402. For later discussions of the *Mefi* case, see, e.g., CA 3415/97 *AOLE* v. *Rubinstein*, PD, 57(5):915,
57(5):925–7. See also Aharon Yoran, "'Sivug Shoneh' shel 'Iskah le-Tsorekh Mas
u-Mikumah ha-Nakhon shel 'ha-'Iskah ha-Melakhutit'," *Mishpatim* 20 (1989/
90): 43–71.

[28] See, e.g., Giora Amir, "Tikhnun 'Izavon: Vari'atsyot Fiskaliot 'al Nos'e 'Atsuv," *RH*
14 (January–February 1964): 7–10; David Krivine, "The Higher the Tax, the Harder
it Is to Collect: How Businessmen Avoid Paying (Legally)," *JP*, April 30, 1964, at
3. A more technical discussion of the subject was published a year later in the journal
of the ICPAI. See E. Klimowsky, "Himan'ut mi-Mas ve-Hishtamtut mi-Mas," *RH* 15
(January–February 1965): 18–23 (a brief summary of Israeli, British, and American
law on the difference between tax avoidance and evasion).

[29] Lapidoth, *Evasion and Avoidance of Income Tax.*

[30] "Tikhnun ha-Pe'ilut ha-Kalkalit mi-Aspect ha-Misim," *RH* 17 (November–December
1966): 55–97. The Hebrew term usually used by judges and scholars in the 1960s to
describe tax avoidance was the morally neutral "himan'ut mi-mas" (tax avoidance)

Lapidoth predicted that, in the future, the courts would be more willing to intervene and nullify tax avoidance schemes devised by taxpayers.[31] Income Tax Commissioner Ya'akov Tamir also spoke at the symposium. Tamir implored his audience to restrain their clients: "I cannot here demand total abstinence from tax-planning, but it is incumbent on all of us to attempt to restrain the phenomenon [confining it] to reasonable aesthetic dimensions," he said, noting that "tax avoidance opportunities are not distributed equally, because the ability to purchase the complex advice and planning [needed] are not equally open to everyone."[32] This position annoyed many of the accountants present at the symposium, who argued that they were obliged to serve their clients and adhere to the form of the transactions they were reporting.[33] When *Mefi* was decided in 1967, it too engendered negative reactions from accountants and lawyers.[34]

By the late 1960s, tax planning had become an important (and respectable) task of Israeli accountants and lawyers. In 1969 the journal of the ICPAI inaugurated a special section devoted to tax planning,

or "hit'hamkut mi-mas" (escaping taxation). Israeli accountants in the 1960s usually used the morally positive term "tikhnun mas" (tax planning), while in the *Mefi* case and in the periodical literature of the 1960s and 1970s one finds representatives of the state using a morally negative term "ha'aramat mas" (tax fraud). See A. Lapidoth, "Nekudat Reut ha-Rashut ha-Mehokeket veha-Rashut ha-Shofetet," *RH* 17 (November–December 1966): 56; Lapidoth, *Evasion and Avoidance of Income Tax*; *Mefi*, 595; Arye Lapidoth, "'Al Nisu'ah Hukey Mas ve-'al Parshanutam," *RYM* 8 (1976): 177, 179.

[31] Lapidoth, "Nekudat Reut," 56, 63; see also Lapidoth, *Evasion and Avoidance of Income Tax*, 183, 186.

[32] Y. Tamir, "'Emdat ha-Rashut ha-Mevatsa'at: Sherutey ha-Misim," *RH* 17 (November–December 1966): 76, 83, 84.

[33] "[Symposium]: 'Al Medukhat ha--Tax Planning': Mi-Tguvot Haverim le-Divrey ha-Natsiv," *RH* 17 (November–December 1966): 86, 90–5. For additional discussions of the issue in the periodical literature of the period, see H. Loewenberg, "Perush Hukim Fiskaliyim, Tokh Simat Lev Meyuhedet la-Tsurah vela-Tokhen: Ma'amar Sheni," *RYM* 1 (1965/66): 401, 406–7; A. Witkon, "[Book Review]: 'Al Hit'hamkut ve-Himan'ut mi-Mas Hakhnasah," *RYM* 1 (1965/66): 523–7.

[34] See Amnon Rafael, "'Had Gadya Kapitalistit' – Tamrur Derekh be-Parshanut Se'if 86 li-Fkudat Mas Hakhnasah," *Ha-Praklit* 24 (1968): 160–5; Bo'az Nahir, "'Iskah Melakhutit," *RYM* 3 (1968): 211, 213; Bo'az Nahir, "Ve-'Od 'al 'Iskah Melakhutit," *RYM* 4 (1969): 31, 34.

and in 1973 the first book specifically designed to assist businessmen in tax planning was published.[35]

Post-1967 Legislative Reform

The debate in the case law and the professional literature of the late 1960s on the issue of tax avoidance also led to legislative reform. In March 1968 the government submitted a bill to the Israeli Parliament amending various sections of the Income Tax Ordinance. One of the amendments called for the addition of a new clause to the general antiavoidance provision (section 86). Until then, the provision had dealt with three types of transactions: artificial transactions; fictitious transactions; and "any disposition not in fact given effect to." The new amendment proposed to add a fourth type of transaction, one in which "one of the principal objectives of a particular transaction is improper avoidance or improper reduction of tax."[36]

The amendment was meant to clarify the power of the tax authority, following the *Mefi* decision, stressing that the authority could consider the taxpayer's personal (inner) objective, not just the (outer) form of the transaction.[37] There was some opposition to the amendment in the Israeli Parliament. Opponents, coming from right-wing opposition parties, justified their position using the rhetoric of "everybody is entitled to run his business as he deems fit." They also complained that small businessmen were already suffocating under the burden of

---

[35] See N. Fridax, "Tikhnun ha-'Izavon," *RH* 19 (1969): 400. The tax planning book was written jointly by a law professor and an accountant. See Aharon Yoran and Yehezkel Flumin, *Tikhnun Mas be-Hayey ha-'Esek* (Jerusalem: Ha-Dfus ha-Akademi, 1973).

[36] Income Tax Ordinance (Amendment no. 13) Law, 5728/1968 LSI, 22:193, 22:199 (1967/68). Such a provision was already envisioned by the British government of Palestine in the 1940s when it proposed amending the general antiavoidance provision of the Income Tax Ordinance by adding the words "or where the assessing officer is of opinion that the main purpose for which any transaction was effected was the avoidance or reduction of tax." The amendment, it was explained, was designed to make the section "more effective," since there were cases in which the tax avoidance motive was clear, but there was a problem providing evidence that the transaction was indeed fictitious or artificial. However, the proposed amendment did not appear in the final version of the law. See Lapidoth, *Evasion and Avoidance of Income Tax*, 169–70. See also Nahir, "'Iska Melakhutit."

[37] DK, 51:2017 (May 27, 1968).

taxation.[38] One member of the Knesset warned that the amendment would force middle-class taxpayers to leave Israel (a major threat in a small immigrant society surrounded by hostile neighbors).[39]

Like Lapidoth's 1966 book and the *Mefi* decision, the legislative amendment was not received kindly by tax practitioners. Bo'az Nahir, the tax lawyer who represented the taxpayer in the *Mefi* case, published an article criticizing the discretion given to the tax authority by the new amendment. It would lead, he said, to "friction between the assessing officer and the taxpayer," and to "economic uncertainty." The way to fight tax avoidance, Nahir argued, was by lowering tax rates and abolishing distinctions between various types of income (some being exempt from the tax and others not).[40] Justice Witkon, despite his conversion to a substantive approach in the *Mefi* case, published an article in 1971 questioning the wisdom of the amendment.[41] Another article, written by accountant Joseph Stern for the ICPAI journal, also criticized the new amendment for giving the assessing officer more discretion, thus leading to more litigation.[42]

The appearance of a substantive pro-government approach was not limited to the specific area of tax avoidance. It later appeared in other areas of tax law, for example in doctrines dealing with tax interpretation and the definition of income. In these areas, the courts also began to analyze the economic substance of the transaction rather than its formal legal appearance, and here, too, the appearance of a substantive approach often stemmed from the desire of courts to prevent taxpayers from abusing a formalist approach to the law to minimize their tax burden.[43]

---

[38] DK, 51:1800–1 (May 7, 1968); DK, 51:1970 (May 21, 1968); DK, 51:1974 (May 21, 1968); DK, 51:1987 (May 22, 1968).

[39] DK, 52: 2998 (July 31, 1968).

[40] Nahir, "'Iska Melakhutit," 211, 213; Nahir, "Ve-'Od," 31, 34.

[41] A. Witkon, "Be'ayat ha-Parshanut be-Diney Misim," *RYM* 6 (1971): 9, 11–3.

[42] J. Stern, "Himan'ut mi-Mas ve-Hafhatat Mas Bilti Ne'otot," *RH* 18 (1967/68): 494–503. See also E. Klimowsky, "'Iska'ot Melakhutiyot o Beduyot," *RH* 18 (1967/68): 369–77. The fears of the opponents of the amendment were unfounded. The tax authority and the courts made relatively little use of the new clause, and when they did, the courts expressed their frustration at the need to define what "improper reduction of tax" really meant. See CA 823/75 *Hertzikovich v. AOLE*, PD, 30(3):163.

[43] On changes in attitude to tax interpretation, see Likhovski, "Formalism and Israeli Anti-Avoidance Doctrines," 356–9. On changing attitudes to the definition of income,

What Caused the Doctrinal Change?

The case law, as well as the literature and legislation, of the late 1960s shows that during this period tax avoidance became a major issue. During this period the law dealing with avoidance also changed. How can one explain this change? It is, of course, notoriously difficult to "prove" that a certain factor caused a specific doctrinal change.[44] However, one can certainly point to a number of factors that may have been related to this change in some way.

One factor sometimes used to explain changes in tax doctrines is politics, and one can indeed link changes in tax avoidance doctrines to the politics of taxation in Israel in the 1950s and 1960s. Income taxation was a major political issue dividing the Left and Right in Israeli politics in the 1950s.[45] There were several aspects to the debate. One hotly contested issue was the taxation of rural cooperative communities (*kibbutzim* and *moshavim*) and the large industrial cooperatives owned by the General Federation of Jewish Labor.[46] For example, in a 1957 Knesset debate, MK Yohanan Bader of the right-wing Herut Party (a forerunner of Likud) attacked the prevailing method of taxing the *kibbutzim* that, he argued, led to their under-taxation. The *kibbutz* functioned like a large family, with members living according to the socialist slogan "to each according to his [or her] contribution." Members did not hold private property, and all the income they earned was transferred to a common fund. The tax owed by each *kibbutz* was calculated by dividing the total income of the *kibbutz* by the total number of its members, taking into account all possible individual and family credits and

---

see Tsilly Dagan, Assaf Likhovski, and Yoram Margalioth, "The Legacy of UK Tax Law in Israel," *British Tax Review*, 2008, 271–84, 277–80.

[44] For a detailed discussion, see Assaf Likhovski, "Two Horwitzian Journeys," in *Transformations in American Legal History: Essays in Honor of Professor Morton J. Horwitz*, eds. Daniel W. Hamilton and Alfred L. Brophy (Cambridge, MA: Harvard University Press, 2008), 300–18.

[45] For a comprehensive survey of the positions of various Israeli political parties on income tax matters between 1951 and 1975, see Zvi Shuldiner and Alex Radian, "'Emdotehen shel ha-Miflagot ha-Politiyot be-Yisrael be-Sugiyot Nivhharot shel Medinyut Mas Hakhnasah," *RYM* 11 (1979/80): 103–11.

[46] See, e.g., DK, 2:1368–71 (August 24, 1949); DK, 15:1542 (April 6, 1954); "Mas Hakhnasah bi-Re'i ha-'Itonut," *RH* 4 (1953/54): 56, 86, 198; Shuldiner and Radian, "Emdotehen," 104.

deductions – allowing credits, for example, for life insurance even when *kibbutz* members were not actually insured. The tax was then paid by the *kibbutz* rather than by individual members. Given the progressivity of the tax system, Bader argued, this method of calculation resulted in a lower tax on the *kibbutzim* than would otherwise have been the case had the income tax been directly imposed on individual members.[47]

Another issue, which seems mainly to have concerned the small Israeli Communist Party, was that of tax exemptions granted to foreign (largely American) investors. Such exemptions were given by the Encouragement of Capital Investments Law, enacted in 1950. This law provided subsidies and tax benefits to investors in "approved undertakings." Such entities were defined as "any undertaking in industry, agriculture, building and transport," that would assist in "developing the productive power of the State and the absorption of large-scale immigration," in the reduction of imports or the increase of exports, or in the "rational distribution of the population throughout the area of the State" and the "planned exploitation of the resources of the State." The benefits granted to investors included a relief from property taxes and various registration fees, lower income tax rates, accelerated depreciation rules, and a range of other incentives.[48]

In a 1955 Knesset debate, MK Meir Vilner of the Israeli Communist Party attacked foreign corporations exempted from the payment of income tax by the Encouragement of Capital Investments Law. Vilner suggested that these corporations, for example the Kaiser-Frazer car assembly corporation, should be taxed at a rate of 80–90 percent because they were "earning millions and smuggling them abroad." American capitalists, he added (quoting a newspaper article) "treat our country as a colony, and expect colonial rates of return," and the government was serving their interests rather than those of "the working people."[49] His suggestions were ignored by the other speakers in the debate.

---

[47] Yohanan Bader, *Netaher et Mas Hakhnasah me-'Avel ve-Aflayot: Pirkey ha-Stenogramah mi-Leyl ha-Shimurim ba-Knesset* ([Tel Aviv]: Merkaz Tnu'at ha-Herut, May 1957), 17–20 (a copy of this pamphlet can be found in the National Library of Israel (NLI), Jerusalem). See also Tsilly Dagan and Avital Margalit, "Tax, State and Utopia," *Virginia Tax Review* 33 (2014): 549–78, 562–3, 567–8.

[48] See Encouragement of Capital Investments Law, 5710/1950, LSI, 4:93.

[49] DK, 17:1459 (April 1, 1955).

The major political controversy on tax matters in the 1950s was the issue of fair allocation of the income tax burden between employees (workers) and the self-employed (businessmen). The Israeli Left argued that the tax burden was mainly shouldered by workers whose tax was withheld at the source, while some businessmen, who had to report their income to be taxed, managed to evade paying income tax by mis-reporting their income. For example, in 1950 MK Moshe Sne (a member of the socialist MAPAM Party) argued that "two thirds and more of the income taxpayers are employees who pay the income tax before they receive their salaries, because the tax is withheld at the source. The remaining third are business owners who pay in arrears one and a half years later, if they do not totally evade [the tax]. Who carries the fiscal burden? The impoverished classes!"[50] The Israeli Right rejected these arguments. Knesset members belonging to right-wing parties argued that workers were evading the income tax as well, that the burden on businessmen was unrealistically high, or that urban taxpayers were discriminated against in comparison to the agricultural sector (which was dominated by the agricultural cooperatives of the Israeli Left).[51]

Did the debate between the Left and the Right in Israeli politics influence the decisions of Israeli judges?[52] Many Israeli Supreme Court

---

[50] DK 4:1108 (March 22, 1950). See also DK 5:1779 (June 20, 1950); DK 15:1537 (April 6, 1954); "Leket min ha-'Itonut," *YP* (December 1953): 59; "Income Tax Criticism" *JP*, July 18, 1952, at 2. For the same argument more than a decade later, see Victor Shem-Tov, "Mas Emet ve-Hishtamtut mi-Mas," *RYM* 3 (1968): 311, 312.

[51] DK, 5:1428 (May 17, 1950); DK, 9:2009–10 (June 19, 1951); DK 15:1535–6, 15:1543 (April 6, 1954); "Leket min ha-'Itonut," *YP* (December 1955): 8. Wayne F. Anderson, *Income Tax Administration in the State of Israel: Report to the Government of Israel* (Tel Aviv: United States of America Operations Mission to Israel, 1956), 4 (a copy of the report can be found in the NLI) (estimating in 1954 that tax collection from employees "probably equaled 90% of their full tax liability," while the collection from the self-employed is "probably somewhere between 50% and 65%"); H. S. Loewenberg, "Ha-Shumah veha-Shfitah," *Sherut* 15 (1961): 6; Y. Lipski-Halifi, "Ha-'Atsma'i be-Mas Hakhnasah," *RH* 7 (1956/57): 87–90 (arguing that the burden imposed on the self-employed was heavier than that imposed on employees); Nachum Gross, "Kalkalat Yisrael," in *'Idan: He-'Asor ha-Rishon 1948–1958*, eds. Hanna Yablonka and Zvi Zameret (Jerusalem: Yad Izhak Ben-Zvi, 1997), 137–150, 138, 145 (arguing that tax policy, especially income tax policy, during the first decade after independence "discriminated against the self-employed").

[52] For a class-based interpretation of tax avoidance decisions in the UK, see Robert B. Stevens, *Law and Politics: The House of Lords as a Judicial Body, 1800–1976*

justices in the 1950s and 1960s came from middle-class backgrounds. Many were born or were educated in Central and Western Europe or in the United States, in contrast to the political elite of the country that was mainly East European. The ideological views of these justices, argued legal scholar Menachem Mautner, were therefore more economically liberal and individualist than the socialist views and collectivist ethos that much of the Israeli public and the Israeli government championed at the time. These justices, said Mautner, were therefore "cultural aliens," that is, liberals operating in a collectivist society.[53]

Linking judicial decisions to the political ideology of the judges that decide them is notoriously hard, because it is rare to find explicit remarks by judges justifying their decisions using ideological arguments. Judges do not often write opinions stating that they decide in favor of, or against, a certain party because they are ideologically committed to a socialist, capitalist, liberal, or conservative ideology. However, there is one indication that the conflict between the Israeli Left and Right may have had an impact on the attitude of at least one justice, Justice Witkon, toward tax avoidance.

In 1966 Witkon published a review of Lapidoth's book on evasion and avoidance. In his review, Witkon attacked the unfair distribution of the tax burden and argued that this burden fell most heavily on the "middle incomes, earned by members of the free professions, managers, and educated and skilled workers; in short, all those whose productive work is most vital to the country." He noted that only in

(Chapel Hill: University of North Carolina Press, 1978). On Stevens' arguments, see also Likhovski, "Tax Law and Public Opinion."

[53] Mautner, *Law and the Culture of Israel*, 88. There is a debate in the literature about the collectivism of Israeli state and society in the 1950s and about the liberalism of Israeli judges. For the argument that large segments of Israeli society in the 1950s rejected collectivism, see Orit Rozin, *The Rise of the Individual in 1950s Israel: A Challenge to Collectivism*, trans. Haim Watzman (Waltham, MA: Brandeis University Press, 2011). See also Zeev Sternhell, *The Founding Myths of Israel: Nationalism, Socialism, and the Making of the Jewish State*, trans. David Maisel (Princeton: Princeton University Press, 1999) (questioning the socialism of the Israeli government at the time). On the liberalism of Israeli judges at the time, see, e.g., Pnina Lahav, *Judgment in Jerusalem: Chief Justice Simon Agranat and the Zionist Century* (Berkeley: University of California Press, 1997); Fania Oz-Salzberger and Eli Salzberger, "The Secret German Sources of the Israeli Supreme Court," *Israel Studies* 3 (1998): 159–92, 176–9.

Sweden were the marginal tax rates on middle-class taxpayers higher than in Israel. He also criticized the Israeli government for succumbing to pressure from the labor unions and raising salaries in the huge government sector, on the one hand, while attempting to balance the budget by raising taxes, on the other. He rhetorically asked: "can one blame those who do not see the thin line of difference between opposition to a government salary policy that they do not like and acts of sabotage against tax collection?"[54]

More specifically, the argument that the tax burden was unfairly distributed was used by Witkon in his 1966 book review to justify the limited use of the general antiavoidance provision of the Income Tax Ordinance. He argued that it was wrong to empower judges (rather than the legislature) to decide which transactions were to be deemed artificial, because such decisions were not:

> above party and political quarrel and therefore [not] fit to be decided by the courts. In [tax law] there are many forms of discrimination between various methods of tax avoidance. For example, there are [tax] 'benefits' that certain self-employed taxpayers and employees enjoy [that] undermine fiscal morality in a far more serious way [than tax avoidance] ... but these loopholes are backed by powerful pressure groups and the authorities cannot touch them.[55]

What Witkon was implying here was that targeting middle-class tax avoiders was unfair as long as employees who were members of the large labor unions were able to enjoy legislatively or administratively sanctioned ways of reducing their tax burden.

Witkon's ire in this book review was mainly directed at the extra-legal tax concessions that proliferated in the Israeli income tax system during this period. One example of such a concession was found in the method used for calculating the income of some employees of the national airline, El Al. A part of the salaries of El Al air crews was paid in British pounds or US dollars. The income tax paid by air crews was calculated on the basis of a fictitious exchange rate agreed between the tax authority and the El Al union, in which one British pound and one US dollar equaled one Israeli pound. Because the actual exchange rate

[54] Witkon, "[Book Review]: 'Al Hit'hamkut," 525.
[55] Ibid., 527.

was far higher, this extralegal tax concession resulted in a substantial reduction in the income tax paid by air crews.[56]

Other examples of such concessions were payments to employees fictitiously characterized by their employers as the refund of expenses, rather than as salaries, with the knowledge and consent of the tax authority. For example, many employees received fictitious car expenses that were paid whether they used their cars in the service of their employers or not, and even when the employees did not actually own a car. Other types of untaxed payments came in the form of fictitious allowances for clothing, telephones, trips abroad, and so forth. In addition, part of the salaries of employees was sometimes given in the form of tax-free gifts or interest-free loans.[57]

Class sentiments may also have melded in Witkon's book review with his identification with what he perceived to be the weaker party – the taxpayer. When Witkon sought to explain his formalist approach to tax avoidance, he argued that judges often found for the taxpayer "who is considered weak and in need of the defense of the court. Based on my experience ... in many cases – too many cases – the interest of the state is not strong enough to justify the prosecution of the citizen."[58]

Class interests and identification with weak taxpayers facing a strong state may therefore explain the protaxpayer bent of Justice Witkon, who was instrumental in shaping Israeli tax doctrines in the 1950s. However, they do not explain the gradual shift from a protaxpayer to a pro-government approach in the late 1960s. Witkon's book review was published in 1966. If, at that point in time, he saw tax avoidance doctrines as

---

[56] See ISA, Ministry of Justice file GL-21324/3, Attorney General Meir Shamgar to deputy Minister of Finance Zvi Dinstein, December 20, 1972. See also Amnon E. Rafael, "Tax Reform in Israel," *Israel Law Review* 11 (1976): 187–215, 189 n. 8.

[57] On these tax concessions, see, e.g., Dan Horowitz, "Bizkhut Drakhim Slulot," *Davar*, April 26, 1963, at 2; Rafael, "Tax Reform in Israel," 189–90; Shlomo Yitzhaki, "Reformat ha-Mas 1975," in *Reformot Mas*, ed. David Gliksberg (Jerusalem: Ha-Makhon le-Mehkarey Hakikah, 2005), 195–235, 200. Extralegal tax concessions were so widespread that in 1974 they became the topic of a popular skit called "Ha-Shali'ah ba-Bank," by Israel's leading comedy group at the time, Ha-Gashash ha-Hiver.

[58] Alfred Witkon, "Darkhey ha-Parshanut bi-T'hum Diney ha-Misim," in *Sefer Loewenberg*, eds. D. Friedmann and Y. Shiloah (Tel Aviv: Bursi, 1987/88), 13–22, 14.

a way to assist middle-class taxpayers in the unfair battle between them and the socialist government of Israel, why did he change his mind only a year later, when he joined Justice Silberg in the 1967 *Mefi* decision that moved Israeli law in a progovernment, substantive direction?

A second way to explain the history of changing attitudes to tax avoidance is by reference to legal culture. One can argue that the formalist, protaxpayer attitude to tax avoidance in Israel in the 1950s was the result of the impact of English formalist approaches to tax law generally, and that the changes that began in the 1960s, and intensified later, were the result of the Americanization of Israeli law.[59]

The Income Tax Ordinance, unlike other legislative acts originally enacted by the British in Palestine, did not contain any section instructing the judges interpreting it to turn to English law to find the correct interpretation of specific provisions of the Ordinance.[60] However, as we saw in Chapter 2, judges deciding income tax cases during the British mandate period (and after Israeli independence in 1948) often did refer to English case law when interpreting the Ordinance.[61]

The English protaxpayer attitude certainly made some impact on Israeli judges. Thus in his 1966 review of Lapidoth's book, for example, Justice Witkon drew on English precedents to justify the limited use of the Israeli general antiavoidance provision.[62] However, English case law was not uniform. There were English cases that adopted an antiformalist stance, and Witkon was aware of them.[63] In

---

[59] On Americanization of Israeli law, see, e.g., Mautner, *Law and the Culture of Israel*, 37; Pnina Lahav, "American Moment[s]: When, How, and Why Did Israeli Law Faculties Come to Resemble Elite U.S. Law Schools?" *Theoretical Inquiries in Law* 10 (2009): 653–97. On formalism in English and American law, see generally P. S. Atiyah and R. S. Summers, *Form and Substance in Anglo-American Law: A Comparative Study of Legal Reasoning, Legal Theory, and Legal Institutions* (Oxford: Clarendon Press, 1987).

[60] See Wilkenfeld, *Taxes and People in Israel*, 205–6.

[61] See Chapter 2, text to nn. 100–109. See also Lapidoth, *Evasion and Avoidance of Income Tax*, 23–5; Witkon, "Darkhey ha–Parshanut," 15. For an empirical study on the use of English law by Israeli judges, see Yoram Shachar, Ron Harris, and Miron Gross, "Nohagey ha-Histamkhut shel Beyt ha-Mishpat ha-'Elyon: Nitukhim Kamutiyim," *Mishpatim* 27 (1996): 119–217.

[62] Witkon, "[Book Review]" 'Al Hit'hamkut," 526–7.

[63] See Witkowski, "Mas Hakhnasah," 121 (discussing the pro-government *Latilla* case decided by the House of Lords in 1943).

addition, when Israeli judges had no wish to use English precedents, they were quick to reject them.[64] Even Witkon, who was known to be one of the most anglophile justices on the Israeli Supreme Court, sometimes rejected English precedents in favor of American ones when he believed the occasion called for it.[65] Therefore, the fact that English tax law was formalist in the 1950s cannot entirely explain the Israeli decisions.

A third factor that may have contributed to the changes in tax law in the late 1960s was economic in nature. The period between 1954 and 1965 was one of rapid economic growth. Between 1965 and 1967, however, the Israeli economy went into a deep recession that ended only after the 1967 war.[66] In the two years of recession prior to the 1967 war, government revenues declined (in real terms) by about 10 percent, while total expenditures rose by more than 20 percent, and defense spending rose by more than 40 percent.[67] Economic hardship and budgetary deficits seem to create a less tolerant attitude to tax avoidance in many legal systems (one example being the United States

[64] ITA (Tel Aviv) 713/58 *Hevrah Plonit* v. *AOLE*, PM, 21:334, 21:339–40, 343. In this case, Judge Loewenberg of the Tel Aviv District Court stated that in tax avoidance cases it would be more appropriate to turn to American rather than to English law, and that in the United States the rule was that it was allowable to "pierce the veil of certain monetary relationships in order to see if the form of transaction chosen by the parties is not void because it is artificial, and leads first and foremost to tax avoidance." Loewenberg also noted that in English law there was no statutory provision similar to the Israeli general antiavoidance provision, and that even if there had been no such provision in Israeli law, the Income Tax Ordinance did not contain a provision obliging judges to refer to English law in order to interpret the ordinance. For a similar argument in the District Court's decision in the *Mefi* case, see ITA (Tel Aviv) 957/66 *Mefi* v. *AOLE*, 3 (a copy of the decision can be found in the Israeli Supreme Court file of the *Mefi* case in the ISA).

[65] See CA 545/59 *'Dan' Agudah Shitufit* v. *AO*, PD, 14:2088, 14:2096 (rejecting a narrow English definition of fringe benefits and adopting a broader, pro-government American test). On Witkon's anglophilia, see Oz-Salzberger and Salzberger, "The Secret German Sources," 185.

[66] See, e.g., Gross, "Kalkalat Yisrael," 30; Paul Rivlin, *The Israeli Economy from the Foundation of the State through the 21st Century* (New York: Cambridge University Press, 2011), 41.

[67] Based on tables in Avraham Mandel and Asher Arin, eds., *'Idkunim le-Sefer Hitpat'hut ha-Misim be-Erets Yisrael: Legabey ha-Shanim 1964–1978* (Jerusalem: Muze'on le-Misim, 1982), 28, 42.

during the New Deal era of the 1930s).[68] This may also have been the case in Israel.

Another event, related to the specific circumstances of the 1967 war, was the declaration of a general amnesty, including a tax amnesty, following the Israeli victory. The cut-off date for the amnesty was November 7, 1967, only twelve days before the decision in the *Mefi* case. Perhaps the justices deciding the *Mefi* case felt that tax evaders and avoiders had been given a chance to mend their ways, and that this case should signal a new, tougher stance toward noncompliance.[69]

However, while the economic recession of 1966 or the tax amnesty of 1967 may explain the specific outcome of the *Mefi* case, they cannot explain the broader trend. *Mefi* was not a unique case, but part of a long-term change in judicial attitudes to avoidance that continued for decades, long after the recession of 1966 ended and the tax amnesty of 1967 was forgotten.

A fourth way to explain the change in the *Mefi* decision can be found in the context of changing forms of noncompliance. In the 1950s there were almost no cases in which the general antiavoidance provision of the Income Tax Ordinance was mentioned, and until the mid-1960s judges were reluctant to use the provision. These facts may be connected to the history of tax evasion in Israel. When one considers that there was little criminal prosecution for tax evasion before 1955, that when cases of evasion did reach the courts in the 1950s judges were very lenient, and that the early tax administration machinery seemed to lack the required capabilities to deal with tax evasion and avoidance, one can perhaps understand why the courts were reluctant to intervene in the relatively few cases of tax avoidance that did reach

---

[68] See, e.g., John F. Witte, *The Politics and Development of the Federal Income Tax* (Madison: University of Wisconsin Press, 1985), 100–4; Likhovski, "The Duke and the Lady," 953, 1015; Joseph J. Thorndike, *Their Fair Share: Taxing the Rich in the Age of FDR* (Washington, DC: Urban Institute Press, 2013), 199–205.

[69] On the tax amnesty, see Wilkenfeld, *Taxes and People in Israel*, 245–9; "'Erev 'Iyun: Hok Mas Hakhnasah [Hats'harot Metaknot], 1967," *RH* 17 (1967): 453–68; Zvi Wechsler, "Mi-Gilyon le-Gilyon," *RYM* 3 (1968): unnumbered page; Naftali Birkenfeld, "Halbanat Hon be-Mivhan ha-Bitsu'a," *RYM* 3 (1968): 168–73; Arye Lapidoth, "'Al ha-Haninot be-T'hum ha-Misim," *RYM* 3 (1968): 173–8; David Krivine, "For Real Offenders Only," *JP*, February 1, 1968, at 5.

them.[70] The formalist approach of Israeli courts to tax avoidance in the 1950s may thus have been part of a wider phenomenon – the attempt by the courts to buttress the rule of law in a society in which there was widespread disdain for legal norms.[71] This attempt saw courts ignoring the less blatant contraventions of the law in cases of avoidance, in which the letter (if not the spirit) of the law was followed.

A related argument suggested by some commentators is that, in the 1950s, there was simply very little aggressive tax planning going on, so the issue of avoidance may not have seemed important enough to warrant the attention of Israeli judges.[72] It has also been argued that there was little incentive for tax avoidance, as most transactions in the 1950s were simply not large enough to justify the use of costly tax professionals.[73]

Was there indeed little tax planning? It is difficult to answer this question. On the one hand, it seems reasonable to assume so, given the relatively undeveloped state of both the Israeli economy and the accounting and legal professions in the 1950s. On the other hand, there

[70] See, e.g., CrimC (Haifa) 486/53 AG v. Z. S., reprinted in *YP* (December 1953): 67; CA 276/53 *Kahana* v. AG, PD, 8:404 [1954] (fining tax evaders and stating that one of the considerations for light punishment was the fact that these were the first criminal cases, or that the tax authority had not prosecuted offenders before). See also Wilkenfeld, *Taxes and People in Israel*, 215 (noting the "lack of ability on the part of the administration to prove a case against the more sophisticated tax cheaters"). A somewhat similar argument about the relationship between evasion and avoidance was used to explain the lack of interest in tax avoidance cases during the last years of British rule in Palestine. See Hanan Cohen, "25 Shanah le-Hanhagat Mas Hakhnasah ba-Arets," *RYM* 1 (1965/66): 395, 396–7.

[71] On the focus of the 1950s Supreme Court on maintaining the rule of law, see Neta Ziv, "Combining Professionalism, Nation Building and Public Service: The Professional Project of the Israeli Bar 1928–2002," *Fordham Law Review* 71 (2003): 1621–67, 1638; Oz-Salzberger and Salzberger, "The Secret German Sources," 180; Oren Bracha, "Safek Miskenim, Safek Mesukanim: Ha-Mistanenim, ha-Hok u-Veyt ha-Mishpat ha-'Elyon 1948–1954," *'Iyune Mishpat* 21 (1998): 333, 383–4. On general attitudes to the notion of the rule of law in Israel of the 1950s, see Nir Kedar, "Ha-Mishpat u-Mekomo ha-Merkazi ba-Historiyah ha-Yisre'elit: 'Al ha-Historiografyah shel ha-Mishpat ha-Yisre'eli u-Trumatah le-Heker Yisrael," *Katedrah* 150 (2013): 155, 174–9.

[72] Lapidoth, *Evasion and Avoidance of Income Tax*, 9, 13, 15, 40, 200–1; Witkon, "[Book Review]: 'Al Hithamkut," 523.

[73] Eli Nathan (judge), interview with author, December 2002.

are also indications that tax planning was common in certain areas of Israeli tax law even in the 1950s. A case in point is the land betterment tax of 1949. This tax was levied, among other things, on the sale of shares in corporations whose main business was the acquisition and occupation of land. However, land owners found easy ways to bypass the tax by issuing new shares to the buyer, thus transferring ownership in the land without the transaction constituting a "sale." This led to the incorporation of many corporations whose only purpose was to avoid the land betterment tax. This and other loopholes in the 1949 law forced the government to revise it in 1963.[74] One might also argue that what was important was not the prevalence of tax avoidance per se but the public's perception of it. In the 1950s tax avoidance was not regarded as a problem because the public was unaware of its existence. Indeed, it only became a burning topic in the months prior to the *Mefi* decision because of the publication of Lapidoth's book on the topic in 1966 and the discussion it provoked among tax professionals.[75]

A final factor that may help explain the doctrinal transformation is the changing relationship between law and social norms. It can be argued that the growing interest of courts in regulating taxpayer compliance reflected a wider process, one in which the Israeli courts gradually stepped in to intervene in shaping the relationship between taxpayers and the state, taking upon themselves the normative and educational role of maintaining social solidarity in Israeli society – a role that other state institutions had previously performed using social norms.

When discussing the educational role of courts, one can distinguish between different types of projects. In the specific context of Israel, one can distinguish between the 1950s, when the educational role of courts was narrower and mainly focused on teaching the Israeli government (rather than the Israeli people) to respect the notion of the rule of law, and later decades, in which the educational role of the courts was expanded to encompass the Israeli public and to cover other values beyond the formalist notion of the rule of law.

---

[74] See, e.g., DK, 35:177–8 (November 19, 1963) (Minister of Finance Eshkol describing some of the loopholes used by Israeli taxpayers to circumvent the 1949 law).
[75] "[Symposium]: 'Al Medukhat ha-'Tax Planning': Mi-Tguvot Haverim le-Divrey ha-Natsiv," *RH* 17 (November–December 1966): 86–97.

As I noted earlier, legal scholar Menachem Mautner argued that Israeli judges in the 1950s were "cultural aliens." According to Mautner, the liberal values of the first generation of Israeli judges clashed with the collectivist values championed by the Israeli government and Israeli society in the 1950s. Because of this clash, the Israeli Supreme Court of the 1950s was a relatively weak institution. The decisions of the Israeli courts in the 1950s were characterized by a relatively high degree of legal formalism. This formalism, argued Mautner, enabled a weak court to downplay the normative dimension of its decisions and present them as merely the result of a professional and mechanical process of narrowly applying the letter of the law.[76] Accordingly, the educational scope of the decisions of the Israeli Supreme Court in the 1950s was also narrow, concerned mostly with ensuring that governmental agencies were not overstepping the boundaries of their formal legal authority.

In later decades Israeli courts gradually expanded their educational ambitions, as a result of the growing power and prestige of the Israeli judges in relation to Israeli politicians. Judges were no longer "cultural aliens," because the values of Israeli society gradually shifted and courts were no longer weak in relation to the political sphere (due to a decline in the prestige of politicians). The expanded educational role of courts might also have been a result of a vacuum created by a decline in the use (or efficiency) of social norms as tools of civic education.

One important champion of the view that Israeli law had an educational role was Justice Witkon. In a 1962 article entitled "Law in a Developing Country," Witkon stated that in an immigrant society that was "not homogeneous in terms of its cultural level," the law should serve as "an active educational tool," used to "shape the image of society" and reform the population.[77] In this context, Witkon specifically

---

[76] Mautner, *Law and the Culture of Israel*, 88.

[77] Witkon, "Ha-Mishpat be-Arets Mitpatahat," 66, 68–9, 78–9, 80–2. Witkon was not alone in holding this view. In the political discourse and case law of the 1950s, one can find additional statements expressing the same desire to use law as a tool for educating the Israeli public. See, e.g., DK, 4:734 (February 7, 1950) (MK Yisrael Bar Yehuda stated that "we are living in a country of unique circumstances, of a gathering of the exiles, of people from many ethnic origins from all parts of the world, with different habits and ... with various unwritten constitutions ... and we want to create a single nation from this admixture. To do this, we must take all possible actions ...

stressed the educational role of law regarding "the whole system of laws that impose duties on citizens, such as army service [and the payment of] taxes ... the common denominator [of such duties] is that they address the 'sense of good citizenship' of the person."[78] He noted that in "immature societies" duty-imposing laws will sometimes be enacted with the clear understanding that they will be opposed, and that "the atmosphere needed" to apply them has not been created yet. In such a scenario, he continued, "everyone agrees that an educational and propaganda campaign will be needed," but there may be a debate about the question of whose duty it is to "educate the people to obey the law." There are "many educational institutions in our society: schools, the army, the health and welfare authorities, vocational training [institutions] ..." but the law, he stressed, should also be considered one of these educational institutions.[79]

However, in this 1962 article Witkon still believed that the educational task of the law, including its role in instilling a "sense of good citizenship," was not to be pursued by the courts. He explicitly noted that this educational role was not imposed on "the legal profession generally, and the courts specifically." Instead, it was "the [role of] the idea of law as an abstract entity ... that addresses the person and seeks to attract him, so [this person] will accept its authority and discipline."[80]

Courts, of course, often have a problem undertaking such an educational role, given the technical nature of their decisions, which are not often read by the lay public. However, this problem can be overcome. Sometimes judges speak directly with their intended audience, as was the case with early US Supreme Court justices who saw themselves as "republican schoolmasters" of the citizens of the new state.[81] Sometimes judges convey their educational messages indirectly, for example by relying on media exposure of their decisions (such exposure grew tremendously in Israel from the 1970s onward), or by

to live together ... and this tendency must also be reflected in the law – by education through a single legal system for everyone").

[78] Witkon, "Ha-Mishpat be-Arets Mitpatahat," 80–1.

[79] Ibid., 81.

[80] Ibid., 69.

[81] Ralph Lerner, "The Supreme Court as Republican Schoolmaster," *Supreme Court Review*, 1967: 127–80, 130–1.

assuming that lawyers and other professional agents will convey their views to the general public.[82]

Whatever the means of public dissemination, some observers have noted that the Israeli court system, especially the Supreme Court, gradually took upon itself the task of educating the public in proper social values ("good citizenship"), seeking to teach the Israeli government and Israeli society not just about the necessity of upholding the rule of law, but also about the importance of adhering to the values of social solidarity and altruism. This educational process, according to legal scholars Menachem Mautner and Shahar Lifshitz, happened in private law, family law, and commercial law in the 1980s and 1990s.[83] The history of the Israeli tax avoidance doctrines show that this process may have appeared even earlier in the field of tax law, as Witkon and other justices gradually expanded their conception of the educational role of courts in cases such as *Mefi*.

If this indeed was the case, it seems that the courts were acting here in a countercyclical way. In the 1950s, when the state was seemingly powerful and society was collectivist (at least according to some accounts), the courts sought to counter the power of the state by propagating a formalist notion of the rule of law, using this notion in a protaxpayer way in their tax avoidance decisions. As Israeli society became more individualistic, the power of social norms waned, and tax professionals came to use law to minimize the tax burden of their clients. In response, the courts changed their attitude and shifted the focus of their educational endeavors to the public rather than the government, and to notions of duty, solidarity, and altruism instead of merely advocating a formalist notion of the rule of law.

---

[82] On the Israeli Supreme Court and the media, see Bryna Bogoch and Yifat Holzman-Gazit, "Mutual Bonds: Media Frames and the Israeli High Court of Justice," *Law and Social Inquiry* 33 (2008): 53–87. For a detailed discussion of the various channels of communication between the courts and their audiences, see Olga Frishman, "Court–Audience Relationships in the 21st Century," *Mississippi Law Journal* (forthcoming).

[83] Menachem Mautner, *Yeridat ha-Formalizm ve-'Aliyat ha-'Arakhim be-Mishpat ha-Yisre'eli* (Tel Aviv: Ma'agaley Da'at, 1993), 101–17; Shahar Lifshitz, "Diney Zugiyut Hiloniyim ba-Yovel ha-Bah: Beyn 'Libertaryanizatsyah' u-Veyn Beyt ha-Mishpat 'ha-Mehashek'," *Mehkarey Mishpat* 17 (2001): 159–262, 240–60.

Legislative Transformations 1975–1985

In the late 1960s Israeli courts changed their attitude to tax avoidance, moving from a formalist to a substantive approach. In the following decades the substantive approach spread to other areas of income tax law. Meanwhile, legislation was also changing the nature of tax law and, indirectly, of state–citizen interaction. Three major legislative changes occurred in the period between 1975 and 1985: modifications to the nature of income tax assessment and collection following the recommendation of the Ben-Shahar Committee of 1975; the introduction of value-added taxation in 1976; and, finally, changes meant to address the impact of the hyperinflation of the early 1980s on income taxation.[84] All three developments contributed to the decline of the civic republican model of taxation.

The Ben-Shahar Committee Reforms

In December 1974 a five-member tax reform committee headed by Tel Aviv University economist Haim Ben-Shahar was appointed by the Israeli minister of finance to reform and simplify Israel's direct tax system.[85] At the time, the income tax base was greatly eroded because of the complex array of tax concessions that had been created over the previous decades, not by legislation but by negotiation between the tax authority and powerful interest groups.[86] Another characteristic of the pre-1970s Israeli income tax system was the widespread use of presumptive taxation, rather than taxation of the real income of individual taxpayers. As we saw in Chapter 4, presumptive taxation

---

[84] See, generally, Avraham Mandel, ed., *Hitpat'hut ha-Misim be-Erets Yisrael: Skirah Historit* (Jerusalem: Muze'on le-Misim, 1968); Mandel and Arin, eds., *'Idkunim le-Sefer Hitpat'hut ha-Misim*; Avraham Mandel, ed., *Sefer ha-Yovel shel Agaf Mas Hakhnasah u-Mas Rekhush* (Tel Aviv: Yedioth Ahronoth ve-Muze'on le-Misim, 1992), 243, 262; David Gliksberg, ed., *Reformot Mas* (Jerusalem: Ha-Makhon le-Mehkarey Hakikah, 2005); Amnon Rafael with Shlomi Lazar, *Mas Hakhnasah*, 4th edn (Tel Aviv: Ronen, 2009), 1:5–21.

[85] On this committee, see, e.g., Rafael, "Tax Reform in Israel"; Alex Radian, "On the Differences between the Political Economy of Introducing and Implementing a Tax Reform: Israel 1975–1978," *Journal of Public Economics* 11 (1979): 261–71; Yitzhaki, "Reformat ha-Mas 1975."

[86] Mandel and Arin, *'Idkunim le-Sefer Hitpat'hut ha-Misim*, 5, 7; Yitzhaki, "Reformat ha-Mas 1975," 200–1; Rivlin, *The Israeli Economy*, 48–9.

relied on standard assessment guides, and these guides were also partly based on negotiations and bargaining between the tax authority and taxpayers' representative bodies.

The narrowing of the income tax base meant that rates gradually rose in compensation for the erosion of the tax base, thus creating an increased incentive for tax evasion. For example, in 1964 the marginal rate on a monthly income of between I£2,500–£3,000 (adjusted to inflation) of a married taxpayer with two children was 32 percent, but by 1975 it had risen to 58 percent.[87]

While the income tax base eroded, the fiscal needs of the Israeli government grew dramatically. After the Six Day War of 1967, and the War of Attrition that followed it, Israel's defense spending increased. Defense costs peaked in the period between 1973 and 1975 when Israel had to reconstitute and enlarge its army following the 1973 war, in response to the threat posed by Arab armies. Between the early 1960s and 1975 annual defense expenditure (adjusted to inflation) grew by a factor of six. Defense spending (including military aid, financed by United States loans and grants) now reached an amount that equaled more than 30 percent of Israel's GNP.[88] This period also saw a rapid rise in oil costs following the 1973 war and the Arab oil embargo, and the beginning of a long period of high inflation. In 1974 consumer prices rose by 40 percent, triple the 1972 rate of inflation.[89]

The erosion of the tax base, combined with the pressing defense needs of the government and the other problems facing the Israeli economy, meant that the Israeli tax system had to be reformed. Such a reform was legitimized not only by these needs, but also by the political atmosphere of the post-1973 period. The near-defeat Israel suffered in the 1973 war shattered the trust that Israelis had previously had in their government, and led to widespread demand for both political and economic change.[90] The last prime minister belonging to Israel's founding fathers' generation, Golda Meir, was forced to resign

---

[87] [Ben-Shahar Committee], *Hamlatsot le-Shinuy ha-Mas ha-Yashir: Din ve-Heshbon ha-Ve'adah le-Reformah ba-Misim* (Jerusalem: Ha-Madpis ha-Memshalti, 1975), chapter 1, 1–3.

[88] Rivlin, *The Israeli Economy,* 119–20.

[89] Ibid., 48–9.

[90] Yitzhaki, "Reformat ha-Mas 1975," 197.

in April 1974, and was replaced by the inexperienced Yitzhak Rabin. Israel was rocked by political protests, and an atmosphere of gloom engulfed the country.[91]

The Ben-Shahar Committee, appointed by Rabin's government, is often seen as the most important reform committee in Israeli tax history. The committee suggested a number of major changes to the Income Tax Ordinance, including a massive expansion of the income tax base, simplification and reduction of the bracket structure, and the indexation of some tax provisions to inflation.[92] One particularly significant change initiated by the committee was the abolition of the widespread use of presumptive taxation. This change was enabled by the imposition of compulsory bookkeeping duties, which increased the demand for the services of accountants, tax consultants, and book-keepers. It thus assisted in the transformation of income taxation – from a system based on direct interaction between taxpayers and the state, to one based on reliance on professional intermediaries. Another change was the abolition of the many nontransparent tax exemptions, concessions, and deductions given to powerful pressure groups. The 1975 reforms therefore constituted an important milestone in the evolution of the Israeli income tax system, shifting away from opaque bargaining between taxpayers' groups or individual taxpayers and the tax authority, toward clear legal rules that were implemented uniformly and individually (rather than collectively), and often mediated by tax professionals.[93]

[91] Anita Shapira, *Israel: A History,* trans. Anthony Berris (Waltham, MA: Brandeis University Press, 2012), 340–2.

[92] Mandel and Arin, '*Idkunim le-Sefer Hitpat'hut ha-Misim,* 7–11; Yitzhaki, "Reformat ha-Mas 1975," 200, 210, 226–32; Mandel, *Sefer ha-Yovel,* 212, 218; David Gliksberg, "Does the Law Matter? Win Rates and Law Reforms," *Journal of Empirical Legal Studies* 11 (2014): 378–407, 390–1. One reform recommendation that was implemented, but almost immediately rescinded, was the imposition of a universal duty of filing returns. Radian, "On the Differences between the Political Economy of Introducing and Implementing a Tax Reform," 266–8.

[93] David Bar-Haim and Nachum Vermus, "Seker Tguvot ha-Ponim le-Lishkot ha-Yi'uts shel Mas Hakhnasah," *RYM* 7 (1972): 201–2; Yitzhaki, "Reformat ha-Mas 1975," 226–7, 234–5. On the impact of the reforms of the Ben-Shahar Committee on the demand for tax professionals, see Y. Ben-Porath and M. Bruno, "Reply to Dr. Radian," *Journal of Public Economics* 11 (1979): 395–6.

One result of the reforms initiated by the Ben-Shahar Committee was the disappearance of the public advisory committees, institutions which epitomized the 1950s notion of taxation as a nonprofessional civic activity. As we saw in Chapter 4, the public advisory committees, created in 1954, were designed to deal with cases in which assessment was based on the "best judgment" of the assessing officer as no return was filed (or the return was inadequate). These committees were composed of laypersons familiar with the business activity of the taxpayer in question, who heard factual objections by taxpayers to their assessments, and who could advise the assessing officer on revising the assessment in question.

The use of these committees was partly driven by necessity. Until the 1970s few taxpayers formally recorded their transactions, and presumptive taxation based on standard assessment guides was the norm.[94] This nonindividualistic and inaccurate method of assessment naturally led to a large number of objections that tax inspectors could not handle on their own. The public advisory committees were seen as a solution to the problem of a large backlog in deciding objections against "best judgment" assessments. However, the use of these committees was also related to a view of taxation as a democratic, participatory, and collective activity rather than as a battle between taxpayers (or the tax professionals serving them) and the state. The income tax commissioner in the late 1950s, Theodor Brosh, described the committees in 1959 as "one of the democratic institutions that a free people builds for itself."[95]

By the 1970s, however, these committees were coming under increasing criticism. The first major tax reform committee of the 1970s, the Asher Committee, argued that the public advisory committees were an obsolete relic of a past era. They used to be of worth, argued the Asher Committee report, at a time when tax officials were inexperienced and needed the advice of laypersons to assess

[94] Wilkenfeld, *Taxes and People in Israel*, 144, 155–66; MT Library, [Asher Committee], Ha-Ve'adah ha-Tsiburit li-Vdikat Ma'arekhet ha-Misim be-Yisrael, Dokh ha-Ve'adah be-Nos'e Yi'ul ha-Gviyah shel Mas Hakhnasah (April 1973), 13 (noting that only about 7 percent of the self-employed kept books; most of the other taxpayers who did not were exempt by law from this duty).

[95] MT, file 702–14, T. Brosh, "Introduction," in *Hamesh Shnot Pe'ulah shel ha-Va'adot ha-Meya'atsot le-Mas Hakhnasah* (Jerusalem, 1959/60), 1.

taxpayers. This, however, was no longer the case, now that the tax authority's knowledge far surpassed the personal knowledge of any individual citizen. In addition, there were many problems in the work of these committees. They were merely advisory bodies, not judicial bodies relying on legal norms. Sometimes the laypersons appointed to serve on these committees did not have the specialized knowledge required, and they were sometimes influenced by improper motives. To address these shortcomings, the Asher Committee recommended that every taxpayer be required to keep books, and that the public advisory committees be abolished. Objections to "best judgment" assessments would now be submitted to a three-member appeal committee, chaired by a lawyer. In addition, the Asher Committee report suggested the creation of "book acceptability committees" – three-person committees composed of professional accountants who would decide whether the books kept by taxpayers were adequate.[96]

The recommendations of the Asher Committee were not implemented at first, but in 1975 the Ben-Shahar Committee repeated the suggestion that the advisory committees be abolished and replaced by professional "book acceptability committees." This time the recommendation was accepted and enacted into law.[97] This meant that the lay committees, composed of nonprofessional members of the public, were now replaced by committees composed of accountants.

The use of the public advisory committees had indeed been problematic and, both from an efficiency perspective and from an individual justice perspective, it was desirable to move to an assessment process based on bookkeeping requirements. However, these committees had also played a civic role, allowing lay participation in the taxation process and creating intimate ties between the state and its

---

[96] MT Library, [Asher Committee], Ha-Ve'adah ha-Tsiburit li-Vdikat Ma'arekhet ha-Misim be-Yisrael, Dokh ha-Ve'adah be-Nos'e Yi'ul ha-Gviyah shel Mas Hakhnasah (April 1973), 13, 19, 24–6. One member of the Committee submitted a minority opinion in which he objected to these recommendations: ibid., 41–2.

[97] [Ben-Shahar Committee], *Hamlatsot le-Shinuy ha-Mas ha-Yashir: Din ve-Heshbon ha-Ve'adah le-Reformah ba-Misim* (Jerusalem: Ha-Madpis ha-Memshalti, 1975), chapter 8, 1–7; chapter 9, 6–9. Income Tax Ordinance (New Version), 1961, sec. 146. See also Moshe Gavish, "Ha-Va'adot le-Kvilut Pinkasim be-Mas Hakhnasah: Samkhuyot ve-Hahlatot," *RYM* 17 (1989): 357–64.

citizens. These ties were now severed, to be replaced by interaction of the state with tax professionals rather than the taxpayers themselves.[98]

Value-added Taxation

A second major change that occurred in mid-1970s Israel was the introduction, in 1976, of value-added taxation (VAT). Embryonic forms of VAT were first introduced in France in the late 1940s and 1950s, while the first full VAT was introduced in Denmark in 1967. It later rapidly spread to other countries, in Europe and beyond.[99] The introduction of VAT in Israel had already been proposed in an academic article published in 1964. In 1968 the State Revenue Administration Division in the Ministry of Finance established a committee to examine the possibility of introducing it in Israel. This committee, as well as the 1971 Asher Committee, recommended that the tax be introduced by 1974, although the 1973 war delayed its introduction until 1976.[100] VAT soon came to play a major role in the Israeli tax system (see Table 6.1).

The introduction of VAT was prompted by the desire to impose a simple, broad-based indirect tax that would be neutral in its impact on consumption, partly replacing a series of specific excise and sales taxes. It was also motivated by the impulse to foster closer economic ties with the countries of Western Europe, where VAT was already widely in place. However, tax compliance considerations also played a role. VAT was seen by Israeli policy makers as a way to expand bookkeeping by taxpayers, and as a means to create an "automatic" system of tax compliance. Every taxpayer in the production chain (apart from the final consumer) is allowed to deduct the VAT paid on inputs. This deduction, however, is allowable only based on the submission of invoices. VAT thus creates an incentive to demand such invoices from the previous links in the production

---

[98] For a discussion of similar dilemmas involving the use of juries in various legal systems, see Markus D. Dubber, "The Schizophrenic Jury and Other Palladia of Liberty: A Critical Historical Analysis," *Comparative Legal History* 3 (2016): 307–24.

[99] See Kathryn James, *The Rise of Value-Added Tax* (New York: Cambridge University Press, 2015), 2–3 nn. 6–7.

[100] A. Morag, "Mas 'Erekh Musaf," *RK* 41–42 (1964): 67–73; Yoram Gabai, "Mas 'Erekh Musaf ba-Shanim 1976–1978," in Mandel and Arin, *'Idkunim le-Sefer Hitpat'hut ha-Misim*, 107–15; Yosef Dinur, *Ma'am be-Yisrael be-Hit'havuto: Skirah Historit* (Jerusalem: Muze'on le-Misim, 1988), 9, 12, 21, 29, 32.

Table 6.1 Israeli government revenues for two fiscal years, 1974 and 1985

Fiscal year	1974		1985[a]	
	I£ (millions)	%	Shekels (millions)	%
Property tax	759	3	266	3
Income tax	10,400[b]	45	4,191[c]	52
Estate tax	24	0	0	0
Direct taxes (total)	11,183	48	4,457	55
Customs	5,818	25	442	5
Excise and sales tax	5,389	24	938[d]	12
VAT	0	0	1,949	24
Indirect taxes (total)	11,207	49	3,329	41
Stamp duty	368	2	30	0
Fees and licenses[e]	275	1	356	4
Other taxes and fees (total)	643	3	386	4
Total	23,033	100	8,172	100

Notes:

[a] The data is for the period April–December 1985.

[b] Including the income tax, the land appreciation tax and employers' tax.

[c] Including the income tax, employers' tax and VAT on the salaries of employees of nongovernmental organizations and financial institutions.

[d] Including sales taxes on imported products.

[e] In 1985 this category included a tax on foreign travel and the purchase of foreign currency.

chain.[101] These invoices are then submitted to the tax authority, allowing it to better monitor the economic transactions of taxpayers.[102]

Unlike income taxation, VAT was based on a different conception of the relationship between the taxpayers and the tax authority. While the payment of income tax, at least in the 1950s and 1960s, was

---

[101] Hatsa'at Hok Mas 'Erekh Musaf, 5736/1975, HH, 28:239; Dinur, *Ma'am*, 17; Value Added Tax Law, 5736/1975, sec. 38, LSI, 30:46 (1975/76). For a detailed discussion of the many economic and political factors that may explain the adoption of VAT in specific cases, see James, *The Rise of Value-Added Tax.*

[102] Dinur, *Ma'am*, 17.

based on notions of civic duty, VAT was based on a material incentive, that of a tax refund to all links in the chain of production except the end consumer. Furthermore, to encourage the use of VAT invoices, in 1979 the tax authority initiated a scheme called the "invoice prize." End consumers (who could not get the VAT they paid refunded) were invited to mail invoices they received to the tax authority and participate in a lottery, in which they could win a cash prize of I£500,000 (see Figure 6.2).[103]

This scheme was reminiscent, in some sense, of the taxpayers' register of the 1950s. In both cases, the tax authority made use of the public to gain information on tax evasion. However, the "invoice prize" scheme also represented a new view of the relationship between the state and taxpayers. Now the provision of information was not motivated by a sense of a civic duty that the taxpayer owed to the state. Instead, it was encouraged by an appeal to the desire to win a material reward.

The Impact of Inflation

A third major change that occurred from the mid-1970s was the adjustment of income taxation to inflation. In the 1960s the average annual rate of inflation was about 5 percent. In the years following the 1973 war, the rate rose to about 40 percent, and by 1984 it had reached a staggering annual rate of almost 500 percent.[104] Inflation reshaped the Israeli tax system in many ways. One example is its contribution to the abolition of one form of direct taxation, the Israeli estate tax, imposed in 1949.[105] As early as 1974, a member of the newly established Likud Party, Simha Erlich, had called for an end to estate taxation because one effect of inflation was that the revenue from the tax did not justify

---

[103] On this campaign, see Dinur, *Ma'am*, 69, 72; MT, file 612–33.

[104] See Zalman F. Shiffer, "Money and Inflation in Israel: The Transition of an Economy to High Inflation," *Federal Reserve Bank of St. Louis Review* 64:7 (1982): 28–40, 30; Rivlin, *The Israeli Economy*, 57; David Elkins, "Taxing Income under Inflationary Conditions: The Israeli Experience," *SMU Law Review* 60 (2007): 363–81, 365 n. 13. In 1985 an economic stabilization program dramatically lowered the rate of inflation, and by the late 1980s the annual rate was about 20 percent.

[105] On the history of the tax, see Daphna Hacker, "Intergenerational Wealth Transfer and the Need to Revive and Metamorphose the Israeli Estate Tax," *Law and Ethics of Human Rights* 8 (2014): 59–101, 63–76.

FIGURE 6.2 An Invoice Prize poster, circa 1979. The rhyming caption reads: "The Invoice Prize: I bought myself a record, I asked for an invoice, God willing, I will win half a million."

the amount spent on collecting it. In 1977, when the Likud Party won the elections, calls for the abolition of the tax multiplied, and in 1981 it was finally abrogated by legislation.[106] The major reason given for its abolition was the hyperinflation of the period that made the assessment of the assets and liabilities of the deceased totally arbitrary.[107] The tax raised very little revenue (on average between 0.1 and 0.2 percent of all tax revenues in the three first decades after 1948).[108] However, its abolition in 1981 was another blow to 1950s ideal of social solidarity, an ideal that at least some observers viewed as one of the goals of this tax.[109]

A second example of the impact of inflation can be found in the way it reshaped the nature of Israeli income tax law. Tax systems, including the pre-1970s Israeli system, usually ignore inflation and tax income based on nominal values. However, as inflation rates grew, such an approach created many distortions in the measurement of income. At first, a series of ad hoc measures were adopted to partially deal with some of the major distortions. For example, following the recommendations of the Ben-Shahar Committee in 1975, tax brackets were periodically adjusted to inflation, and capital gains were indexed.[110] With the beginning of hyperinflation in the late 1970s, the need for a complex treatment of the problem became more urgent, and a comprehensive system was put in place to deal with it. This was done via the Income Tax Ordinance (Taxation under Conditions of Inflation) Law, 1982 that was later amended, becoming the Income Tax (Adjustments by Reasons of Inflation) Law, 1985.[111]

---

[106] Ibid., 73–4.

[107] [Ben-Bassat Committee], Dokh ha-Va'adah ha-Tsiburit le-Reformah be-Mas Hakhnasah (Jerusalem, May 2000), http://ozar.mof.gov.il/reform/basat_report. htm, 110.

[108] Mandel, *Hitpat'hut*, 166; Mandel and Arin, *'Idkunim le-Sefer Hitpat'hut ha-Misim*, 98.

[109] Hacker, "Intergenerational Wealth Transfer," 70–1.

[110] Yishai Beer, "Taxation under Conditions of Inflation: The Israeli Experience," *Tax Notes International* 5 (1992): 299–306, 300, 302.

[111] LSI, 36:249; LSI, 39:184. See also Rafael, *Mas Hakhnasah*, 9–10. The system was based on adding a "deduction for inflation" or "an addition to inflation" to the taxpayer's income based on the question of whether the taxpayer's assets were financed by debt or equity. See Beer, "Taxation under Conditions of Inflation," 303–5; Elkins, "Taxing Income," 376–7. In 2008 the 1985 law was suspended. See Hok

The 1982 and 1985 laws gave full protection from the impact of inflation only to taxpayers using double-entry bookkeeping.[112] In addition, the laws made use of technical accounting terminology that was inaccessible to laypersons. Shlomo Meiri, an accountant writing in 1984 in the ICPAI journal, stated (somewhat triumphantly) that the legislation dealing with inflation was the least "legal" tax legislation ever enacted.[113] It is no wonder, then, that some observers have viewed this period as the heyday of accountants and of accounting discourse in tax matters.[114] The dominance of such technical discourse raised a major obstacle for the direct participation of ordinary taxpayers in their own assessment process, forcing them to use the services of tax professionals instead.

Conclusion

When discussing the 1950s, we saw that legal norms were but one tool used by the state to deal with the problem of noncompliance, along with social norms. During this period, judicial and legislative interventions in tax avoidance schemes seem to have been minimal. Beginning in the late 1960s, case law and, later, legislation were modified to better deal with tax avoidance. In the process, the law changed and became both more flexible and more intrusive, adopting a substantive approach that focused, like social norms, on the taxpayers' inner motivation rather than on their outward behavior.

Changing judicial attitudes to avoidance were accompanied by legislative changes. Tax legislation enacted between 1975 and 1985 further eroded the 1950s model of income taxation based on civic participation. The reforms of the Ben-Shahar Committee of 1975 abolished institutions such as the public advisory committees that had given lay taxpayers some say in the income tax assessment process. The 1976 introduction of VAT created a powerful competitor to

Mas Hakhnasah (Te'umim beshel Inflatsyah) (Tikun mispar 20), 5748/2008, SH, 2008, 227.

[112] Elkins, "Taxing Income," 336, 379–81.

[113] Shlomo Meiri, "Ktsarot," *RH* 33 (December 1984): 255. See also Itamar Levin, *Heshbon Meshutaf: Lishkat Ro'ey Heshbon, Ha-Yishuv veha-Medinah: 80 Shnot Du'ah: 1931–2011* (Tel Aviv: Lishkat Ro'ey Heshbon be-Yisrael, 2011), 92.

[114] Gliksberg, "The Judicial Taxation Revolution," 560–1.

income taxation and propagated a vision of the taxpayer–state relationship based on material interests rather than on civic duty. Later, the hyperinflation period of the early 1980s further strengthened the hold of tax professionals on the taxation process by introducing technical accounting terminology into tax legislation, a terminology that was inaccessible to ordinary taxpayers.

These legislative changes were the result of a mixture of causes: growing professionalization, economic need, and the impact of political ideology, before and after the rise of the economically liberal right-wing Likud Party to power in 1977. Together with the judicial transformation that occurred earlier – also the result of multiple factors – the tax system of Israel was transformed, reflecting the broader changes in Israeli society as the country gradually moved from a mobilized nation-state in the 1950s to a neoliberal one by the mid-1980s.

Epilogue

This book opened in the rolling fields of Be'er Tuvia, a small Jewish village in the southern part of Ottoman-ruled Palestine, among farmers who complained about the collection of the produce tax, the tithe. Twenty kilometers south of Be'er Tuvia, in the very same fields, now stands the production plant of the multinational semiconductor chip manufacturer, Intel. One of the reasons that Intel's plant came to these fields in 1999 was a series of tax concessions granted by the Israeli government with the aim of persuading the firm to build its plant in Israel, rather than in other suitable locations such as Ireland. The last of these concessions was given by the Israeli government in 2014. In return for a US$6 billion investment plan, Intel was granted a special tax rate of 5 percent on its income, one fifth of the standard tax rate on the income of Israeli corporations.[1]

[1] For a summary of Intel's history of investment in Israel, see, e.g., "Intel in Israel: A Fab Relationship Faces Criticism," September 29, 2014, http://knowledge.wharton. upenn.edu/article/intel-israel-old-relationship-faces-new-criticism. On tax competition between Israel and Ireland, see, e.g., Adrian Weckler, "Israel Gives Intel 5pc Corporation Tax Rate and State-Aid for Chip Facility," *Irish Independent*, September 23, 2014, www. independent.ie/business/world/israel-gives-intel-5pc-corporation-tax-rate-and-stateaid-for-chip-facility-30606777.html; Ora Coren, "Israel Grants Intel $300 Million in Investment Subsidies," *Haaretz [English Edition]*, October 1, 2014, at 7. The legal basis for the concessions to Intel is found in the Israeli Encouragement of Capital Investments Law. See Hok le-'Idud Hashka'ot Hon, 5719/1959, section 51K, as amended by Hok ha-Medinyut ha-Kalkalit la-Shanim 2011–2012 (Tikuney Hakikah), 5771/2011, SH (2010/1), 138, 174–5. This act allows the tax authority to grant concessions to

The Jewish farmers of Be'er Tuvia and Intel seem worlds apart, yet there is one similarity they share: both used foreign status in the quest to lower their tax burden. The farmers of Be'er Tuvia sought to lower their tax burden by asking a foreigner, a Hungarian Jew, to protect them from rapacious Ottoman tax collectors. Intel, too, relied on its foreign status as multinational corporation to negotiate a tax deal based on global tax competition. The use of foreign status is related, perhaps, to another similarity between the Jewish farmers and Intel: a relatively low degree of commitment to the taxing state.

The problem of creating civic commitment to taxation was the topic of this book. I have shown how, in the middle decades of the twentieth century, there were attempts to address this problem using social norms, first by the Jewish voluntary tax system of the 1940s and later by the Israeli "intimate fiscal state" of the 1950s. I have also described how, beginning in the 1960s, the reliance of the state on such norms gradually waned, to be replaced by the growing dominance of legal norms and tax professionals.

Recently, however, interest in the use of social norms has been reawakened. This renewed interest is partly the result of novel challenges that national tax systems face. Since the 1980s there has been an exponential growth in evasion and avoidance by individual and corporate taxpayers, who use national tax shelters and international tax havens to minimize their liability.[2] Governments and international

---

"special priority enterprises," defined as corporations that invest large amount of money in machinery or in research and development, or employ a sizeable number of Israeli employees, and thus contribute significantly to the Israeli economy.

[2] See generally, Reuven S. Avi-Yonah, "Globalization, Tax Competition and the Fiscal Crisis of the Welfare State," *Harvard Law Review* 113 (2000): 1573–676; Reuven S. Avi-Yonah, "Corporate Taxation and Corporate Social Responsibility," *NYU Journal of Law and Business* 11 (2014): 1–29; Ronen Palan, Richard Murphy, and Christian Chavagneux, *Tax Havens: How Globalization Really Works* (Ithaca, NY: Cornell University Press, 2010). On Israel as a tax haven for wealthy foreign Jews, see, e.g., Meirav Arlosoroff, "How Israel Became a Tax Shelter for Wealthy Foreign Jews," *Haaretz* [English Edition], November 12, 2013, at 8; Moti Bassok, "Israel Fights Against Becoming Tax Haven for Diaspora Jews," *Haaretz* [English Edition], December 4, 2013, at 8. On wealthy Israelis holding assets abroad to avoid Israeli taxation, see, e.g., Adam S. Hofri-Winogradow, "Professionals' Contribution to the Legislative Process: Between Self, Client, and the Public," *Law and Social Inquiry* 39 (2014): 96–126, 101–2.

organizations have belatedly turned their attention to the problem, and a number of major initiatives have been undertaken to deal with it.[3]

One tool for the prevention of noncompliance that has recently received much attention is the idea of including tax practices in corporate social responsibility (CSR) codes. CSR is a term used to refer to "obligations ... of corporations organized for profit, voluntarily to pursue social ends that conflict with the presumptive shareholder desire to maximize profits."[4] CSR codes are adopted as a goodwill measure by corporations eager to protect or to enhance their reputation among consumers, investors, politicians, and other constituencies. Because they are based on voluntary compliance rather than on legal obligations, CSR codes rely on social norms for their enforcement. Usually these codes deal with issues such as human rights, labor laws, and the protection of the environment. However, for more than a decade there have been calls to use CSR codes to tackle tax avoidance, and in the last few years the interest in the use of these codes has moved beyond the academic literature. Now the idea has been taken up by social activists and their organizations.[5] Such attempts have also appeared in the Israeli context.[6]

The recent rise in interest in the use of CSR codes in the tax arena serves as evidence, I believe, that the desire to use social norms has not disappeared, but has merely mutated. Now such norms are seen as a way to deal with the problem of noncompliance on a global rather than on a national scale, social norms (or "soft law") are created by

---

[3] See, e.g., Gabriel Zucman, *The Hidden Wealth of Nations: The Scourge of Tax Havens*, trans. Teresa Lavender Fagan (Chicago: University of Chicago Press, 2015).

[4] David L. Engel, "An Approach to Corporate Social Responsibility," *Stanford Law Review* 32 (1979): 1–98, 5–6. See also Jasmine M. Fisher, "Fairer Shores: Tax Havens, Tax Avoidance, and Corporate Social Responsibility," *Boston University Law Review* 94 (2014): 337–65, 350.

[5] See, e.g., John Christensen and Richard Murphy, "The Social Irresponsibility of Corporate Tax Avoidance: Taking CSR to the Bottom Line," *Development* 47:3 (2004): 37–44. See also John Hasseldine and Gregory Morris, "Corporate Social Responsibility and Tax Avoidance: A Comment and Reflection," *Accounting Forum* 37 (2013): 1–14, 8–9; Kevin Holland, Sarah Lindop, and Fatimah Zainudin, "Tax Avoidance: A Threat to Corporate Legitimacy? An Examination of Companies' Financial and CSR Reports," *British Tax Review*, 2016, 310–38.

[6] Moran Harari, "Ha-Milyardim ha-Haserim: Tikhnuney Mas Agresivim be-Yisrael ve-Ahrayut Hevratit shel Ta'agidim," www.clb.ac.il/uploads/TAAGIDIM.pdf.

nongovernmental and international organizations rather than the state, and the intention is to use consumers and investors to shame multinational corporations that avoid their taxes, rather than using fellow citizens to shame individual taxpayers.[7]

Only time will tell whether the use of social norms in dealing with global noncompliance will be more or less successful than the use that was made of such norms in nation-states such as Israel in the mid-twentieth century. Given the fact that the large, globalized communities the CSR discourse is addressing are much more diffuse than the relatively small and cohesive societies of 1940s (Jewish) Palestine or 1950s Israel, it seems doubtful that they will prove effective. In addition to issues of efficiency, the use of social norms in this context raises interesting normative questions. It is not clear that the use of such norms to shame corporate, or indeed individual, tax evaders and avoiders is something that should be applauded. Shaming is related to coercion, intimidation, and mob pressure. It undermines important values such as the rule of law. Social norms are related to social solidarity, which is often seen as a positive value, but social solidarity also has a dark side, that of collective imposition on individual freedoms.

Regardless of the normative approach that we adopt in order to evaluate the current stage in the history of the use of social norms to encourage tax compliance, I believe the story told here is interesting because of the lessons it holds about the past, rather than about the present or future. Three lessons seem to me especially pertinent. One is about the necessity of writing the history of taxation and citizenship together. Taxation may seem a dry and technical pursuit, but it is deeply embedded in political and social structures, and in the cultural values and identities of a given society.[8] Therefore, the history of taxation may be used as a lens through which one can view cultural changes. Specifically, one can use the history of taxation to gain a better understanding of how civic identity in a given society was created

---

[7] On consumers and investors as the audience of tax CSR codes see Fisher, "Fairer Shores," 359–63. For arguments against using shaming in the corporate context, see Joshua D. Blank, "What's Wrong with Shaming Corporate Tax Abuse," *Tax Law Review* 62 (2009): 539–90; Joshua D. Blank, "Reconsidering Corporate Tax Privacy," *NYU Journal of Law and Business* 11 (2014): 31–121.

[8] See, e.g., Assaf Likhovski, "Chasing Ghosts: On Writing Cultural Histories of Tax Law," *UC Irvine Law Review* 1 (2011): 843–92.

and changed over time. The history of taxation is usually seen as a subcategory of economic history, and one can certainly study taxation focusing on the revenue raised by specific taxes, or on the way these taxes impeded or advanced certain types of economic activity. But the history of taxation, especially of tax compliance, is also relevant to cultural historians interested in questions of identity-formation and transformation. Tax compliance is not determined merely by economic incentives. It is, as we have seen in this book, also shaped by the taxpayers' identities.

A second lesson is about the relative novelty of state law and its agents – lawyers and accountants – in the taxation process, at least in the context of mandatory Palestine and Israel. We tend to think that, over time (certainly in the twentieth century), state law and its agents have become more important. We live, so the argument goes, in a period in which law has gradually come to dominate our lives. The story told in this book about Israeli tax law does indeed provide some evidence of the growing importance of law and of the professionals using it in the realm of taxation. However, the book also shows that the rise in the importance of state law was not a simple linear process. Rather, it was accompanied by a rise in the use of social norms to ensure compliance, at least in the mid-twentieth century. During this period, Israel was an "intimate fiscal state," in the sense that it attempted to induce taxpayers to pay their taxes by creating familial-like ties between itself and its taxpayers, relying on social norms to establish this close relationship.

Finally, the story told here also contains a general lesson about the relationship of law to social norms. As we have seen, law is only one normative system used by the state. Other systems (religion, as well as secular moral systems based on various ideologies) can also be used by the state to govern its subjects. The history of law therefore cannot be studied without taking into account the history of these systems. Law does not replace other instruments of power, nor is it replaced by them. Law and other methods of governing, including social norms, are all present in the toolbox of the state. The choice between them changes over time, and, as a result, these instruments themselves change, but their history cannot be studied in isolation. Historians of law should therefore also be historians of social norms.

Bibliography

This bibliography contains a list of the primary and secondary sources used in the book. It does not mention specific journal and newspaper articles taken from published primary sources. The URLs cited in this work were checked in July 2016.

Archives

Central Zionist Archives, Jerusalem
Haganah Historical Archives, Tel Aviv
Israel Film Service, Jerusalem
Israel State Archives, Jerusalem
Jabotinsky Institute Archive, Tel Aviv
Knesset Archive, Jerusalem
Museum of Taxes, Jerusalem
National Archives, London
National Library of Israel, Jerusalem

Annual Government Publications, Newspapers, and Periodicals

Agaf Mas Hakhnasah: Yedi'on Pnimi. Continued by *Sherut: Divrey 'Ovdim be-Sherutey ha–Misim*
Davar
Hatsa'ot Hok

The Laws of Palestine: In Force on the 31st Day of December, 1933,
    ed. Robert Harry Drayton (London: Waterlow and Sons, 1934)
Laws of the State of Israel
Ma'ariv
Minhal Hakhansot ha-Medinah. *Din ve-Heshbon Shnati*
Misim
Misrad Mevaker ha-Medinah. *Din ve-Heshbon Shnati*
Palestine Gazette
Palestine Law Reports
Palestine Post. Continued by *Jerusalem Post*
Piskey Din
Piskey Din Ezrahiyim
Psakim Mehoziyim
Ha-Praklit
Ha-Riv'on le-Kalkalah
Ha-Riv'on ha-Yisre'eli le-Misim
Ro'eh ha-Heshbon ha-Musmakh. Continued by *Ro'eh ha-Heshbon*
Sefer ha-Hukim
The Times

Interviews

Avraham Blinder (tax consultant), July 2013
Mira Dror (Director of the Museum of Taxes, Jerusalem), August
    2012 and March 2014
Eli Nathan (judge), December 2002

Additional Primary and Secondary Sources

Abbott, Andrew. *The System of Professions: An Essay on the Division of Expert Labor.* Chicago: University of Chicago Press, 1988.
Abcarius, M. F. "The Fiscal System." In *Economic Organization of Palestine,* edited by Sa'id B. Himadeh. Beirut: American Press, 1938, 505–56.
Agmon, Iris. *Family and Court: Legal Culture and Modernity in Late Ottoman Palestine.* Syracuse, NY: Syracuse University Press, 2006.
Agudat ha-Tsayarim veha-Pasalim – ha-Va'ad ha-Tsiburi: Beyt Chagall. *Hamishim Omanim.* Tel Aviv: Masada, n.d.
"AHR Roundtable: Historians and the Question of 'Modernity'." *American Historical Review* 116 (2011): 631–751.

Alberstein, Michal. "Measuring Legal Formalism: Reading Hard Cases with Soft Frames." *Studies in Law, Politics, and Society* 57 (2012): 161–99.

Altshuler, Yehuda. "Hitpat'hutam u-Mashma'utam shel Misey ha-Kahal be-Ashkenaz me-Reshit ha-Hityashvut ve-'Ad la-Magefah ha-Sh'horah." Ph.D. diss., Bar-Ilan University, 2009.

Amir, Giora. *'Averot Mas ve-'Averot Halbanat Hon.* 5th edn. Tel Aviv: Sadan, 2008.

Anderson, Benedict. *Imagined Communities: Reflections on the Origin and Spread of Nationalism.* New edn. London: Verso, 2006.

Anderson, Wayne F. *Income Tax Administration in the State of Israel: Report to the Government of Israel.* Tel Aviv: United States of America Operations Mission to Israel, 1956.

Annisette, Marcia, and Dean Neu, eds. "Accounting and Empire." Special Issue, *Critical Perspectives on Accounting* 15 (2004): 1–206.

Apelbom, A. M., and B. Braude, eds. *Palestine Income Tax Cases.* Tel Aviv: Palestine Law Publishing Co., 1945.

Arlosoroff, Haim. "Mi-Reshimot ha-Hodesh." *Ahdut ha-'Avodah* 1 (1930): 461–73.

Arin, Asher, and Ilana Reich. "Misuy ha-Kibbutzim veha-Agudot ha-Shitufiyot." In *'Idkunim le-Sefer Hitpatkhut ha-Misim be-Erets Yisrael: Legabey ha-Shanim 1964–1978,* edited by Avraham Mandel and Asher Arin. Jerusalem: Muze'on le-Misim, 1982, 62–7.

Arnon, Yuval. "Falahim ba-Mered ha-'Arvi be-Erets Yisrael 1936–1939." Master's thesis, Hebrew University, 1971.

Arnon-Ohanna, Yuval. "Hebetim Hevratiyim u-Politiyim bi-Tnu'at ha-Mered ha-'Aravi, 1936–1939." In *Te'udot u-Dmuyot mi-Ginzey ha-Knufiyot ha-'Arviyot bi-Me'ora'ot 1936–1939,* edited by Ezra Danin and Ya'acov Shimoni, 2nd edn. Jerusalem: Magnes, 1981, 25–32.

Arnon-Ohanna, Yuval. *Herev mi-Bayit: Ha-Ma'avak ha-Pnimi ba-Tnu'ah ha-Falastinit, 1929–1939.* Tel Aviv: Yariv-Hadar, 1981.

[Asher Committee]. Ha-Ve'adah ha-Tsiburit li-Vdikat Ma'arekhet ha-Misim be-Yisrael. Dokh ha-Ve'adah be-Nos'e Yi'ul ha-Gviyah shel Mas Hakhnasah (April 1973).

Atiyah, P. S., and R. S. Summers. *Form and Substance in Anglo-American Law: A Comparative Study of Legal Reasoning, Legal Theory, and Legal Institutions.* Oxford: Clarendon Press, 1987.

Atran, Scott. "Le masha'a et la question foncière en Palestine, 1858–1948." *Annales. Économies, Sociétés, Civilisations* 42 (1987): 1361–89.

Avci, Yasemin. "The Application of *Tanzimat* in the Desert: The Bedouins and the Creation of a New Town in Southern Palestine (1860–1914)." *Middle Eastern Studies* 45 (2009): 969–83.

Avi-Yonah, Reuven S. "Corporate Taxation and Corporate Social Responsibility." *NYU Journal of Law and Business* 11 (2014): 1–29.

Avi-Yonah, Reuven S. "Globalization, Tax Competition and the Fiscal Crisis of the Welfare State." *Harvard Law Review* 113 (2000): 1573–676.

Bader, Yohanan. *Netaher et Mas Hakhnasah me-'Avel ve-Aflayot: Pirkey ha-Stenogramah mi-Leyl ha-Shimurim ba-Knesset.* [Tel Aviv]: Merkaz Tnu'at ha-Herut, May 1957.

Baer, Gabriel. *Mavo le-Toldot ha-Yahasim ha-Agrariyim ba-Mizrah ha-Tikhon, 1800–1970.* Tel Aviv: Ha-Kibbutz ha-Me'uhad, 1971/2.

Baer, Gabriel. *Ha-Mukhtar ha-Kafri be-Erets Yisrael: Toldot Ma'amado ve-Tafkidav.* Jerusalem: Magnes, 1978.

Baier, Matthias, ed. *Social and Legal Norms: Towards a Socio-legal Understanding of Normativity.* Farnham: Ashgate, 2013.

Bank, Steven A. *Anglo-American Corporate Taxation: Tracing the Common Roots of Divergent Approaches.* Cambridge: Cambridge University Press, 2011.

Bank, Steven A. *From Sword to Shield: The Transformation of the Corporate Income Tax, 1861 to Present.* New York: Oxford University Press, 2010.

Bank, Steven A., Kirk J. Stark, and Joseph J. Thorndike. *War and Taxes.* Washington, DC: Urban Institute Press, 2008.

Barak-Erez, Daphne. *Ezrah-Natin-Tsarhan: Mishpat ve-Shilton be-Hevrah Mishtanah.* Or-Yehudah: Kinneret, Zmora Bitan, 2012.

Bar-Droma, Joshua. *Ha-Mediniyut ha-Finansit shel Medinat Yehudah bi-Yemey ha-Bayit ha-Rishon veha-Sheni.* Jerusalem: Muze'on le-Misim, 1967.

Bareli, Avi. "*Mamlakhtiyut,* Capitalism and Socialism during the 1950s in Israel." *Journal of Israeli History* 26 (2007): 201–27.

Bareli, Avi. "Ha-Mamlakhtiyut ve-Tnu'at ha-'Avodah be-Reshit Shnot ha-Hamishim: Hanahot Mivniyot." In *Etgar ha-Ribonut: Yetsirah ve-Hagut ba-'Asor ha-Rishon la-Medinah,* edited by Mordechai Bar-On. Jerusalem: Yad Izhak Ben-Zvi, 1999, 23–44.

Bareli, Avi, and Nir Kedar. *Mamlakhtiyut Yisre'elit.* Jerusalem: IDI Press, 2011.

Barfoot, J. F., and G. G. Evans, "Obituaries: John Guy Tempest Sheringham." *Montgomeryshire Collections* 84 (1996): 155.

Bar-Haim, David, ed. *The Tax System of Israel (As of May 31, 1969).* Jerusalem: Museum of Taxes, 1969.

Barkai, Haim. "Don Patinkin's Contribution to Economics in Israel." In *Monetary Theory and Thought: Essays in Honour of Don Patinkin,* edited by Haim Barkai, Stanley Fischer, and Nissan Liviatan. Basingstoke: Macmillan, 1993, 3–14.

Barnai, Jacob. "Takanot Yerushalayim ba-Me'ah ha-Shmoneh-'Esreh ke-Makor le-Hakarat ha-Hevrah, ha-Kalkalah veha-Pe'ilut ha-Yom-Yomit shel ha-Kehilah ha-Yehudit." In *Prakim be-Toldot Yerushalayim be-Reshit ha-Tkufah ha-'Othmanit,* edited by Amnon Cohen. Jerusalem: Yad Izhak Ben-Zvi, 1979, 271–316.

Barnett, Michael N. *Confronting the Costs of War: Military Power, State, and Society in Egypt and Israel.* Princeton: Princeton University Press, 1992.

Bartlett, Bruce. "Is Voluntary Taxation a Viable Option?" *Tax Notes* 135 (June 11, 2012): 1403–6.

Barzilai, Gad. "The Ambivalent Language of Lawyers in Israel: Liberal Politics, Economic Liberalism, Silence, and Dissent." In *Fighting for Political Freedom: Comparative Studies of the Legal Complex and Political Liberalism*, edited by Terence C. Halliday, Lucien Karpik, and Malcolm M. Feeley. Oxford: Hart, 2007, 247–77.

Bauer, Yehuda. *The Death of the Shtetl*. New Haven: Yale University Press, 2010.

Baxendale, Sidney J. "Taxation of Income in Israel and the West Bank: A Comparative Study." *Journal of Palestine Studies* 18 (1989): 134–41.

Bayly, C. A. *The Birth of the Modern World: 1780–1914*. Oxford: Blackwell, 2004.

Bazak, Jacob. *Hilkhot Misim ba-Mekorot ha-'Ivriyim*. Jerusalem: Muze'on le-Misim, 1964.

Beer, Yishai. "Taxation under Conditions of Inflation: The Israeli Experience." *Tax Notes International* 5 (1992): 299–306.

Beito, David T. *Taxpayers in Revolt: Tax Resistance during the Great Depression*. Chapel Hill: University of North Carolina Press, 1989.

[Ben-Bassat Committee]. "Dokh ha-Va'adah ha-Tsiburit le-Reformah be-Mas Hakhnasah." Jerusalem, May 2000. http://ozar.mof.gov.il/reform/basat_report.htm.

Ben-Bassat, Yuval. "In Search of Justice: Petitions Sent from Palestine to Istanbul from the 1870's Onwards." *Turcica* 41 (2009): 89–114.

Ben-Bassat, Yuval. *Petitioning the Sultan: Protests and Justice in Late Ottoman Palestine*. London: I. B. Tauris, 2013.

Ben-Bassat, Yuval, and Fruma Zachs, "Correspondence Manuals in Nineteenth-Century Greater Syria: Between the *Arzuhalci* and the Advent of Popular Letter Writing." *Turkish Historical Review* 4 (2013): 1–25.

Ben-David, Y. "Ha-Mivneh ha-Hevrati shel ha-Miktso'ot ha-Hofshiyim be-Yisrael." Ph.D. diss., Hebrew University, 1956.

Ben-Gurion, David. *Yihud vi-Ye'ud*. Jerusalem: Misrad Rosh ha-Memshalah, 1950.

Ben-Porat, Amir. *Heykhan hem ha-Burganim ha-Hem? Toldot ha-Burganut ha-Yisre'elit*. Jerusalem: Magnes, 1999.

Ben-Porat, Amir. *Keytsad Na'astah Yisrael Kapitalistit*. Haifa: Pardes, 2011.

Ben-Porath, Y., and M. Bruno. "Reply to Dr. Radian." *Journal of Public Economics* 11 (1979): 395–6.

[Ben-Shahar Committee]. *Hamlatsot le-Shinuy ha-Mas ha-Yashir: Din ve-Heshbon ha-Ve'adah le-Reformah ba-Misim*. Jerusalem: Ha-Madpis ha-Memshalti, 1975.

Berger, Mordekhai, ed. *Kofer ha-Yishuv*. Jerusalem: Muze'on le-Misim, 1964.

Berger, Mordekhai, *Magbit ha-Hitgayshut veha-Hatsalah*. Jerusalem: Muze'on le-Misim, 1970.

Berger, Mordekhai, *Neshek le-Yisrael: Keren ha-Magen, ha-Homah*. Jerusalem: Muze'on le-Misim, 1968.

Bernstein, Deborah S. *Nashim ba-Shulayim: Migdar ve-Leumiyut be-Tel Aviv ha-Mandatorit.* Jerusalem: Yad Izhak Ben-Zvi, 2008.

Beron, K. J., Helen V. Tauchen, and Ann Dryden Witte. "The Effects of Audits and Socioeconomic Variables on Compliance." In *Why People Pay Taxes: Tax Compliance and Enforcement,* edited by Joel Slemrod. Ann Arbor: University of Michigan Press, 1992, 67–90.

Birla, Ritu. *Stages of Capital: Law, Culture, and Market Governance in Late Colonial India.* Durham, NC: Duke University Press, 2009.

Birnhack, Michael D. *Colonial Copyright: Intellectual Property in Mandate Palestine.* Oxford: Oxford University Press, 2012.

Blank, Joshua D. "Reconsidering Corporate Tax Privacy." *NYU Journal of Law and Business* 11 (2014): 31–121.

Blank, Joshua D. "What's Wrong with Shaming Corporate Tax Abuse." *Tax Law Review* 62 (2009): 539–90.

Blank, Joshua D., and Nancy Staudt. "Corporate Shams." *NYU Law Review* 87 (2012): 1641–712.

Bloom, Etan. "The 'Administrative Knight' – Arthur Ruppin and the Rise of Zionist Statistics." *Tel Aviver Jahrbuch für deutsche Geschichte* 35 (2007): 183–203.

Bogoch, Bryna, and Yifat Holzman-Gazit. "Mutual Bonds: Media Frames and the Israeli High Court of Justice." *Law and Social Inquiry* 33 (2008): 53–87.

Bonney, Richard. "Introduction" to *The Rise of the Fiscal State in Europe, c.1200–1815,* edited by Richard Bonney. Oxford: Oxford University Press, 1999, 1–17.

Bonney, Richard and W. M. Ormrod. "Introduction: Crises, Revolutions and Self-Sustained Growth: Towards a Conceptual Model of Change in Fiscal History." In *Crises, Revolutions and Self-Sustained Growth: Essays in European Fiscal History, 1130–1830,* edited by W. M. Ormrod, Margaret Bonney, and Richard Bonney. Stamford: Shaun Tyas, 1999, 1–21.

Booth, Anne. "Night Watchman, Extractive, or Developmental States? Some Evidence from Late Colonial South-East Asia." *Economic History Review* 60 (2007): 241–66.

Bracha, Oren. "Safek Miskenim, Safek Mesukanim: Ha-Mistanenim, ha-Hok u-Veyt ha-Mishpat ha-'Elyon 1948–1954." *'Iyuney Mishpat* 21 (1998): 333–85.

Braude, Benjamin, and Bernard Lewis, eds. *Christians and Jews in the Ottoman Empire.* New York: Holmes and Meier, 1982.

Brown, L. Carl. "The Setting: An Introduction." In *Imperial Legacy: The Ottoman Imprint on the Balkans and the Middle East,* edited by L. Carl Brown. New York: Columbia University Press, 1996, 1–12.

Brownlee, W. Elliot. *Federal Taxation in America: A Short History.* 2nd edn. Cambridge: Cambridge University Press, 2004.

Brownlee, W. Elliot, Eisaku Ide, and Yasunori Fukagai, eds. *The Political Economy of Transnational Tax Reform: The Shoup Mission to Japan in Historical Context*. Cambridge: Cambridge University Press, 2013.

Brun, Nathan. *Shoftim u-Mishpetanim be-Erets Yisrael: Beyn Kushta le-Yerushalyim 1900–1930*. Jerusalem: Magnes, 2008.

Budden, Robert. "The IFLR Top 40: The World's Largest Law Firms." *International Financial Law Review* 11 (1992): 13–16.

Bunton, Martin. *Colonial Land Policies in Palestine, 1917–1936*. Oxford: Oxford University Press, 2007.

Bunton, Martin. ed. *Land Legislation in Mandate Palestine*. Cambridge: Cambridge Archive Editions, 2009.

Burg, David F. *A World History of Tax Rebellions: An Encyclopedia of Tax Rebels, Revolts, and Riots from Antiquity to the Present*. New York: Routledge, 2004.

Bush, Barbara, and Josephine Maltby. "Taxation in West Africa: Transforming the Colonial Subject into the 'Governable Person'." *Critical Perspectives on Accounting* 15 (2004): 5–34.

Campos, Michelle U. "Making Citizens, Contesting Citizenship in Late Ottoman Palestine." In *Late Ottoman Palestine: The Period of Young Turk Rule*, edited by Yuval Ben-Bassat and Eyal Ginio. London: I. B. Tauris, 2011, 17–33.

Campos, Michelle U. *Ottoman Brothers: Muslims, Christians and Jews in Early Twentieth-Century Palestine*. Stanford: Stanford University Press, 2011.

Caplan, Kimmy. "Hitpat'hutam shel Ma'agaley Hibadlut be-Kerev Haredim Kana'im: 'Amram Blau ke-Mikre Mivhan." *Zion* 76 (2011): 179–218.

Capozzola, Christopher. *Uncle Sam Wants You: World War I and the Making of the Modern American Citizen*. New York: Oxford University Press, 2008.

Caron, Paul L. "Tax Myopia, or Mamas Don't Let Your Babies Grow Up to Be Tax Lawyers." *Virginia Tax Review* 13 (1994): 517–90.

Charlesworth, Neil. "The Problem of Government Finance in British India: Taxation, Borrowing and the Allocation of Resources in the Inter-war Period." *Modern Asian Studies* 19 (1985): 521–48.

Chigier, M. "The Rabbinical Courts in the State of Israel." *Israel Law Review* 2 (1967): 147–81.

Chodorow, Adam S. "Biblical Tax Systems and the Case for Progressive Taxation." *Journal of Law and Religion* 23 (2008): 51–96.

Chodorow, Adam S. "Maaser Kesafim and the Development of Tax Law." *Florida Tax Review* 8 (2007): 153–208.

Christensen, John, and Richard Murphy. "The Social Irresponsibility of Corporate Tax Avoidance: Taking CSR to the Bottom Line." *Development* 47:3 (2004): 37–44.

Clarke, Peter. "Exploring the History of Accounting in Cyprus." *Global Business and Economics Review* 13 (2011): 281–95.

Clarke, Peter, and Andrekos Varnava. "Accounting in Cyprus during the Last Four Decades of British Rule: Post-World War I to Independence (1918–1960)." *Accounting History* 18 (2013): 293–315.

Cocks, R. "Victorian Barristers, Judges and Taxation: A Study in the Expansion of Legal Work." In *Law, Economy and Society, 1750–1914: Essays in the History of English Law*, edited by G. R. Rubin and D. Sugarman. Abingdon: Professional Books, 1984, 445–69.

Cohen, Amnon. *Palestine in the 18th Century: Patterns of Government and Administration*. Jerusalem: Magnes, 1973.

Cohen, Amnon, and Bernard Lewis. *Population and Revenue in the Towns of Palestine in the Sixteenth Century*. Princeton: Princeton University Press, 1978.

Cohen, Elizabeth F. *Semi-Citizenship in Democratic Politics*. Cambridge: Cambridge University Press, 2009.

Cohen, Hillel. *Good Arabs: The Israeli Security Agencies and the Israeli Arabs, 1948–1967*. Berkeley: University of California Press, 2010.

Cohen, Julia Phillips. *Becoming Ottomans: Sephardi Jews and Imperial Citizenship in the Modern Era*. Oxford: Oxford University Press, 2014.

Cohen, Mark R. *Poverty and Charity in the Jewish Community of Medieval Egypt*. Princeton: Princeton University Press, 2005.

Cooper, Frederick. *Colonialism in Question: Theory, Knowledge, History*. Berkeley: University of California Press, 2005.

Coşgel, Metin M. "Efficiency and Continuity in Public Finance: The Ottoman System of Taxation." *International Journal of Middle East Studies* 37 (2005): 567–86.

Coşgel, Metin M. "Ottoman Tax Registers (*Tahrir Defterleri*)." *Historical Methods* 37 (2004): 87–100.

Coşgel, Metin M. "The Political Economy of Law and Economic Development in Islamic History," in *Law and Long-Term Economic Change*, edited by Jan Luiten van Zanden and Debin Ma. Stanford: Stanford University Press, 2011, 158–77.

Coşgel, Metin M. "Taxes, Efficiency, and Redistribution: Discriminatory Taxation of Villages in Ottoman Palestine, Southern Syria, and Transjordan in the Sixteenth Century." *Explorations in Economic History* 43 (2006): 332–56.

Coşgel, Metin M., and Thomas J. Miceli. "Tax Collection in History." *Public Finance Review* 37 (2009): 399–420.

Dagan, Tsilly, Rick Krever, Assaf Likhovski, and Yoram Margalioth, eds., "Comparative Tax Law and Culture." Special issue, *Theoretical Inquiries in Law* 11 (2010): 469–821.

Dagan, Tsilly, Assaf Likhovski, and Yoram Margalioth. "The Legacy of UK Tax Law in Israel." *British Tax Review,* 2008, 271–84.

Dagan, Tsilly, and Avital Margalit. "Tax, State and Utopia." *Virginia Tax Review* 33 (2014): 549–78.

Danin, Ezra, and Ya'acov Shimoni, eds. *Te'udot u-Dmuyot mi-Ginzey ha-Knufiyot ha-'Arviyot bi-Me'ora'ot 1936–1939*. 2nd edn. Jerusalem: Magnes, 1981.

Darling, Linda T. *A History of Social Justice and Political Power in the Middle East: The Circle of Justice from Mesopotamia to Globalization*. New York: Routledge, 2013.

Darling, Linda T. *Revenue-Raising and Legitimacy: Tax Collection and Finance Administration in the Ottoman Empire, 1560–1660*. Leiden: Brill, 1996.

Daunton, Martin. *Just Taxes: The Politics of Taxation in Britain, 1914–1979*. Cambridge: Cambridge University Press, 2002.

Daunton, Martin. *State and Market in Victorian Britain: War, Welfare and Capitalism*. Woodbridge: Boydell Press, 2008.

Daunton, Martin. *Trusting Leviathan: The Politics of Taxation in Britain, 1799–1914*. New York: Cambridge University Press, 2001.

Davenport-Hines, Richard, ed. *Letters from Oxford: Hugh Trevor-Roper to Bernard Berenson*. London: Phoenix, 2007.

Deu'el, Michael, ed. *Diney Misim: Lefi Hartsa'otav shel A. Witkon*. Jerusalem: Akademon, 1953/54.

Devos, Ken. *Factors Influencing Individual Taxpayer Compliance Behaviour*. Dordrecht: Springer, 2014.

Devos, Ken, and Marcus Zackrisson. "Tax Compliance and the Public Disclosure of Tax Information: An Australia/Norway Comparison." *eJournal of Tax Research* 13 (2015): 108–29.

De Vries, David. "National Construction of Occupational Identity: Jewish Clerks in British-Ruled Palestine." *Comparative Studies in Society and History* 39 (1997): 373–400.

Dezalay, Yves, and Bryant G. Garth. *Asian Legal Revivals: Lawyers in the Shadow of Empire*. Chicago: University of Chicago Press, 2010.

Dezalay, Yves, and Bryant G. Garth. *The Internationalization of Palace Wars: Lawyers, Economists and the Contest to Transform Latin American States*. Chicago: University of Chicago Press, 2002.

Dinur, Yosef. *Ma'am be-Yisrael be-Hit'havuto: Skirah Historit*. Jerusalem: Muze'on le-Misim, 1988.

Diskin, Talia. Mishpat mi-Shelanu: Hok u-Musar be-'Itonut ha-Yeladim veha-No'ar bi-Medinat Yisrael, 1948–1958. Ph.D. diss., Tel Aviv University, submitted 2016.

Doumani, Beshara. *Rediscovering Palestine: Merchants and Peasants in Jabal Nablus, 1700–1900*. Berkeley: University of California Press, 1995.

Dowty, Alan. "Israel's First Decade: Building a Civic State." In *Israel: The First Decade of Independence*, edited by S. Ilan Troen and Noah Lucas. Albany: SUNY Press, 1995, 31–50.

Dror, Yehezkel. "Public Administration: Four Cases from Israel and the Netherlands." In *The Uses of Sociology*, edited by Paul F. Lazarsfeld,

William H. Sewell, and Harold L. Wilensky. New York: Basic Books, 1967, 418–26.

Dubber, Markus D. "The Schizophrenic Jury and Other Palladia of Liberty: A Critical Historical Analysis." *Comparative Legal History* 3 (2016): 307–24.

Duman, Daniel. "The Creation and Diffusion of a Professional Ideology in Nineteenth Century England." *Sociological Review* 27 (1979): 113–38.

Edwards, John Richard, and Stephen P. Walker, eds. *The Routledge Companion to Accounting History*. New York: Routledge, 2009.

El-Eini, Roza I. M. "Government Fiscal Policy in Mandatory Palestine in the 1930s." *Middle Eastern Studies* 33 (1997): 570–96.

El-Eini, Roza I. M. "Rural Indebtedness and Agricultural Credit Supplies in Palestine in the 1930s." *Middle Eastern Studies* 33 (1997): 313–37.

Elkins, David. "Taxing Income under Inflationary Conditions: The Israeli Experience." *SMU Law Review* 60 (2007): 363–81.

Elon, Menachem. *Jewish Law: History, Sources, Principles – Ha-Mishpat ha-Ivri*. Translated by Bernard Auerbach and Melvin J. Sykes. Philadelphia: Jewish Publication Society, 1994.

Elon, Menachem. ed. *The Principles of Jewish Law*. Jerusalem: Encyclopaedia Judaica, 1975.

Eichelgrün, G[abriel]. "Income-Tax in British Colonies." *Economic Journal* 58 (1948): 128–32.

Eichelgrün, G[abriel]. *Palästinensischer Einkommensteuerführer, abgeschlossen zum 9. April 1944*. Haifa: G. Eichelgrün, 1944.

Eichelgrün, G[abriel]. *Palestine Company Profits Tax 1945*. Haifa: Paltax, 1945.

Eichelgrün, G[abriel]. *Palestine Income Tax Guide*. Haifa: Paltax, 1945.

Engel, David L. "An Approach to Corporate Social Responsibility." *Stanford Law Review* 32 (1979): 1–98.

Engelstein, Laura. "Combined Underdevelopment: Discipline and the Law in Imperial and Soviet Russia." *American Historical Review* 98 (1993): 338–53.

Erez-Blum, Shimon. "'Ha-Mahteret ha-Yuridit': Hishtalvutam shel 'Orkhey-Din Yehudim ba-Ma'avak ha-Tsiyoni ba-Shanim 1938–1947 be-Palestinah." JSD diss., Tel Aviv University, 2012.

Erkan, Mehmet, and Cemal Elitaş. "Accounting Education in [the] Ottoman State." *International Journal of Business and Social Science* 2:13 (2011): 210–14.

Ernst, Daniel R. *Tocqueville's Nightmare: The Administrative State Emerges in America, 1900–1940*. Oxford: Oxford University Press, 2014.

Eshed, Aliza. "Mas Hakhnasah Hu Lo Rak Goveh Misim Hu Gam Mehanekh." *Beyn ha-Shumot: Bit'on 'Ovdey Agaf Mas Hakhnasah ve-Misuy Mekarke'in* 37 (April 2001): 5.

'Etz-Hadar, Avraham. *Ilanot: Le-Toldot ha-Yishuv be-Erets Yisrael 1830–1920*. Tel Aviv: Dfus Niv, 1967.

Evans, Alfred B., Jr. "Civil Society in the Soviet Union?" In *Russian Civil Society: A Critical Assessment*, edited by Alfred B. Evans Jr., Laura A. Henry, and Lisa McIntosh Sundstrom. Armonk: M. E. Sharpe, 2006, 28–54.

Feldman, Arye L. "Tshuvot Hakhmey Bartselonah ve-Kataluniyah be-'Inyan Misim ve-Arnoniyot ve-Dina de-Malkhuta Dina." *Gnuzot: Kovets-'Et li-Gnuzot Rishonim* 1 (1984): 67–98.

Feldman, Ilana. *Governing Gaza: Bureaucracy, Authority, and the Work of Rule, 1917–1967.* Durham, NC: Duke University Press, 2008.

Fellman, Abraham. *The Palestine Income Tax: Law and Practice.* Tel Aviv: Lapid, 1946.

Findley, Carter Vaughn. "The Ottoman Administrative Legacy and the Modern Middle East." In *Imperial Legacy: The Ottoman Imprint on the Balkans and the Middle East*, edited by L. Carl Brown. New York: Columbia University Press, 1996, 158–73.

Fisher, Jasmine M. "Fairer Shores: Tax Havens, Tax Avoidance, and Corporate Social Responsibility." *Boston University Law Review* 94 (2014): 337–65.

Forman, Geremy. "Law and the Historical Geography of the Galilee: Israel's Litigatory Advantages during the Special Operation of Land Settlement." *Journal of Historical Geography* 32 (2006): 796–817.

Forman, Geremy. "Military Rule, Political Manipulation, and Jewish Settlement: Israeli Mechanisms for Controlling Nazareth in the 1950s." *Journal of Israeli History* 25 (2006): 335–59.

Foucault, Michel. *The Birth of Biopolitics: Lectures at the Collège de France, 1978–1979.* Edited by Michel Senellart. Translated by Graham Burchell. Basingstoke: Palgrave Macmillan, 2010.

Foucault, Michel. *Discipline and Punish: The Birth of the Prison.* 2nd edn. New York: Vintage Books, 1995.

Foucault, Michel. *Madness and Civilization: A History of Insanity in the Age of Reason.* Translated by Richard Howard. London: Routledge, 1989.

Foucault, Michel. *Security, Territory, Population: Lectures at the Collège de France, 1977–1978.* Edited by Michel Senellart. Translated by Graham Burchell. Basingstoke: Palgrave Macmillan, 2009.

Foucault, Michel. *"Society Must Be Defended": Lectures at the Collège de France, 1975–1976.* Edited by Mauro Bertani and Alessandro Fontana. Translated by David Macey. New York: Picador, 1997.

Franke, Nikolaus, Martin Schreier, and Ulrike Kaiser. "The 'I Designed It Myself' Effect in Mass Customization." *Management Science* 56 (2010): 125–40.

Frankema, Ewout. "Raising Revenue in the British Empire, 1870–1940: How 'Extractive' Were Colonial Taxes?" *Journal of Global History* 5 (2010): 447–77.

Frecknall-Hughes, Jane. "Contextualising the Development of the Tax Profession: Some First Thoughts." In vol. 5 of *Studies in the History of Tax Law*, edited by John Tiley. Oxford: Hart, 2011, 177–91.

Frecknall-Hughes, Jane, and Margaret McKerchar. "Historical Perspectives on the Emergence of the Tax Profession: Australia and the UK." *Australian Tax Forum* 28 (2013): 275–88.

Frecknall-Hughes, Jane, and Margaret McKerchar. "The History and Development of the Taxation Profession in the UK and Australia." In vol. 6 of *Studies in the History of Tax Law*, edited by John Tiley. Oxford: Hart, 2013, 421–48.

Freedman, Judith, ed. "The Legacy of UK Taxation." Special issue, *British Tax Review*, 2008, 197–306.

Frenkel, Aharon, and Yosef Rachman. "Ha-Yahas le-Ha'alamot Mas ba-Mishpat ha-'Ivri." *Magal: Hidushey Torah u-Ma'amarim* 11 (1995): 237–96.

Frenkel, Michal, and Yehouda Shenhav. "From Americanization to Colonization: The Diffusion of Productivity Models Revisited." *Organization Studies* 24 (2003): 1537–61.

Frenkel, Yehoshua. "Mavo le-Toldot ha-Yahasim ha-Agrarim be-Erets Yisrael ba-Tkufah ha-Mamlukit: Hagdarot Mishpatiyot shel Mekarke'in, Misim ve-'Ikarim." *Ofakim be-Geografiyah* 44–45 (1996): 97–113.

Friedman, Lawrence M. *Total Justice.* New York: Russell Sage Foundation, 1985.

Friedman, Menachem. "*Haredim* and Palestinians in Jerusalem." In *Jerusalem: A City and its Future*, edited by Marshall J. Berger and Ora Ahimeir. Syracuse, NY: Syracuse University Press, 2002, 235–55.

Frishman, Olga. "Court-Audience Relationships in the 21st Century." *Mississippi Law Journal* (forthcoming).

Gabai, Yoram. "Mas 'Erekh Musaf ba-Shanim 1976–1978." In *'Idkunim le-Sefer Hitpat'hut ha-Misim be-Erets Yisrael: Legabey ha-Shanim 1964–1978*, edited by Avraham Mandel and Asher Arin. Jerusalem: Muze'on le-Misim, 1982, 107–15.

Gal, Binyamin. *Misim u-Migba'ot: Komedyah be-Shalosh Tmunot.* Tel Aviv: Merkaz Yisre'eli le-Dramah, n.d.

Gardner, Leigh A. *Taxing Colonial Africa: The Political Economy of British Imperialism.* Oxford: Oxford University Press, 2012.

Gelber, Yoav. *Moledet Hadashah.* Jerusalem: Leo Baeck Institute, 1990.

Genachowski, Dov. *Sipurim Yerushalmiyim.* Jerusalem: Karta, 1989.

Gerber, Haim. "A New Look at the Tanzimat: The Case of the Province of Jerusalem." In *Palestine in the Late Ottoman Period: Political, Social, and Economic Transformation*, edited by David Kushner. Jerusalem: Yad Izhak Ben-Zvi, 1986, 30–45.

Gerber, Haim. *Ottoman Rule in Jerusalem, 1890–1914.* Berlin: Klaus Schwarz, 1985.

Ghandour, Zeina B. *A Discourse on Domination in Mandate Palestine: Imperialism, Property and Insurgency.* Abingdon: Routledge, 2010.

Gil, Moshe. "Ha-Misim be-Erets Yisrael bi-Tkufat ha-Kibush ha-Muslemi ha-Rishonah (634–1099)." *Zion* 45 (1980): 268–85.

Gilbar, Gad. "Megamot ba-Hitpat'hut ha-Demografit shel ha-Falastinim 1870–1948." In *Ha-Tnu'ah ha-Leumit ha-Falastinit: me-'Imut le-Hashlamah?*, edited by Moshe Ma'oz and B. Z. Kedar, 2nd edn. Tel Aviv: Misrad ha-Bitahon, 1997, 13–26.

Gliksberg, David. "Does the Law Matter? Win Rates and Law Reforms." *Journal of Empirical Legal Studies* 11 (2014): 378–407.

Gliksberg, David. *Gvulot Tikhnun ha-Mas: Sivug Mehadash shel 'Iska'ot le-Tsorekh Mas*. Jerusalem: Ha-Makhon le-Mehkarey Hakikah, 1990.

Gliksberg, David. "The Judicial Tax Revolution: From a Subject and Immigrant Society to a Mature Society." *British Tax Review*, 2012, 553–78.

Gliksberg, David. "Ha-Mishpatizatsyah shel ha-Misim: 'Al Zikato shel ha-Siyah ha-Misi la-Siyah ha-Mishpati ha-Klali." *Misim* 23(4) (2009): A-1–A-24.

Gliksberg, David, ed. *Reformot Mas*. Jerusalem: Ha-Makhon le-Mehkarey Hakikah, 2005.

Goadby, Frederic M., and Moses J. Doukhan. *The Land Law of Palestine*. Tel Aviv: Shoshany, 1935.

Goitein, S. D. *A Mediterranean Society: The Jewish Communities of the Arab World as Portrayed in the Documents of the Cairo Geniza*. vol. 2. *The Community*. Berkeley: University of California Press, 1971.

Golder, Ben, ed. *Re-reading Foucault: On Law, Power and Rights*. Abingdon: Routledge, 2012.

Golder, Ben, and Peter Fitzpatrick. *Foucault's Law*. New York: Routledge, 2009.

Goldin, Simha. *Ha-Yihud veha-Yahad: Hidat Hisardutan shel ha-Kvutsot ha-Yehudiyot bi-Yemey ha-Beynayim*. Tel Aviv: Ha-Kibbutz ha-Me'uhad, 1997.

Government of Palestine. *Report of a Committee on the Economic Conditions of Agriculturalists in Palestine and the Fiscal Measures of Government in Relation Thereto*. Jerusalem: Greek Conv. Press, 1930.

Government of Palestine. *Report by the Registrar of Cooperative Societies on Developments during the Years 1921–1937*. Jerusalem: Government Printer, 1938.

Granovsky, A. *The Fiscal System of Palestine*. Jerusalem: Palestine and Near East Publications, 1935.

Great Britain. *Report ... on the Administration of Palestine and Trans-Jordan for the Year 1938*. London: HMSO, 1939.

Great Britain. *Report of the Inter-Departmental Committee on Income Tax in the Colonies Not Possessing Responsible Government*. London: HMSO, 1922.

Greenberg, Yitzhak. "Financing the War of Independence." *Studies in Zionism* 9 (1988): 63–80.

Gross, Nachum. "Ha-Mahlakah le-Kalkalah ba-Universitah ha-'Ivrit bi-Shnot ha-Hamishim." Discussion Paper 04.06, Morris Falk Institute for Economic Research in Israel, 2004.

Gross, Nachum. "Ha-Medinyut ha-Kalkalit shel Memshelet Erets-Yisrael bi-Tkufat ha-Mandat." In *Lo 'Al ha-Ru'ah Levadah: 'Iyunim ba-Historiyah ha-Kalkalit shel Erets Yisrael ba-'Et ha-Hadashah.* Jerusalem: Yad Izhak Ben-Zvi, 1999, 172–227.

Gross, Nachum. "Kalkalat Yisrael." In *'Idan: He-'Asor ha-Rishon 1948–1958*, edited by Hanna Yablonka and Zvi Zameret. Jerusalem: Yad Izhak Ben-Zvi, 1997, 137–150.

Gross, Nachum. "Kalkalat Yisrael, 1954–1967." In *'Idan: He-'Asor ha-Sheni*, edited by Hanna Yablonka and Zvi Zameret. Jerusalem: Yad Izhak Ben-Zvi, 2000, 29–46.

Gross, Nachum. "Mada'ey ha-Hevrah ba-Universitah ha-'Ivrit 'ad 1948/9: Tokhniyot ve-Hat'halot." In *Toldot ha-Universitah ha-'Ivrit: Hitbasesut ve-Tsmihah*, edited by Hagit Lavski. Jerusalem: Magnes, 2005, 503–41.

Gross, Nachum T., and Jacob Metzer. "Public Finance in the Jewish Community in Interwar Palestine." *Research in Economic History* 3 (1978): 87–159.

Gross, Walter. "The Zionist Students' Movement." *Leo Baeck Institute Yearbook* 4 (1959): 143–64.

Grout, V., and B. Sabine. "The First Hundred Years of Tax Cases." *British Tax Review,* 1975, 75–83.

Gruenbaum, Y. *Ha-Shekel: Ezrahut Tsiyonit.* Jerusalem: Hanhalat ha-Histadrut ha-Tsiyonit, 1936.

Grunhaus, Nechama. "Nohal Ma'asi u-Basis Hilkhati le-Gviyat Mas ha-Kniyah bi-Kehilat Izmir." *Pe'amim* 116 (2008): 79–116.

Gvirtz, Yael. *Sefer ha-Yovel: 50 Shnot Lishkah 1961–2011.* N.p.: Lishkat 'Orkhey ha-Din, [2011].

Hacker, Daphna. "Intergenerational Wealth Transfer and the Need to Revive and Metamorphose the Israeli Estate Tax." *Law and Ethics of Human Rights* 8 (2014): 59–101.

Hadfield, Gillian K., and Barry R. Weingast. "Law without the State: Legal Attributes and the Coordination of Decentralized Collective Punishment." *Journal of Law and Courts* 1 (2013): 3–34.

Haj, Rafiq. "Ha-He'anut le-Tashlum Misim 'Ironiyim ba-Hevrah ha-'Arvit be-Yisrael ke-Mikreh Bohan shel ha-Hishtatfut bi-Fe'ulah Kolektivit." In *Ha-Shilton ha-Mekomi ba-Hevrah ha-Falastinit be-Yisrael*, edited by Yousef Jabareen and Mohanad Mustafa. Haifa: Pardes, 2013, 283–323.

Halfin, Arye, ed. *Vatikey Mas Hakhnasah Mesaprim.* Jerusalem: Government Printer, 1971.

Halperin, Israel, ed. *Pinkas Va'ad Arab'a Aratsot.* Jerusalem: Mosad Bialik, 1945.

Hanioğlu, M. Şükrü. *A Brief History of the Late Ottoman Empire.* Princeton: Princeton University Press, 2008.

Harari, Moran. "Ha-Milyardim ha-Haserim: Tikhnuney Mas Agresivim be-Yisrael ve-Ahrayut Hevratit shel Ta'agidim." www.clb.ac.il/uploads/TAAGIDIM.pdf.

Hareuveni, Imanuel. *Leksikon Erets-Yisrael*. Tel Aviv: Yedioth Ahronoth, 1999.

Harlaff, Amiram. *Mi-Yomano shel Praklit*. Tel Aviv: Y. Golan, 1993.

Harris, Peter. *Income Tax in Common Law Jurisdictions: From the Origins to 1820*. Cambridge: Cambridge University Press, 2006.

Harris, Ron. *Ha-Mishpat ha-Yisre'eli – Ha-Shanim ha-Me'atsvot: 1948–1977*. Bnei Brak: Ha-Kibbutz ha-Me'uhad, 2014.

Harris, Ron. "State Identity, Territorial Integrity and Party Banning: The Case of a Pan-Arab Political Party in Israel." *Socio-Legal Review* 4 (2008): 19–65.

Harussi, Emanuel. "Bi-Yemey Kofer ha-Yishuv u-Magbit ha-Hitgaysut." *Hed ha-Haganah* 13 (October 1961): 13–14.

Harussi, Emanuel. *Sefer ha-Magbit: Magbit ha-Hitgaysut veha-Hatsalah*. Tel Aviv: Magbit ha-Hitgaysut veha-Hatsalah, 1949/50.

Harussi, Emanuel, and Nahum Gutman. *Ma-Ze Kofer ha-Yishuv?: Kol Kore li-Vney ha-Ne'urim*. Tel Aviv: Dfus ha-Po'el ha-Mizrahi, 1940.

Harvey, David. *A Brief History of Neoliberalism*. Oxford: Oxford University Press, 2005.

Hasseldine, John, and Gregory Morris. "Corporate Social Responsibility and Tax Avoidance: A Comment and Reflection." *Accounting Forum* 37 (2013): 1–14.

Hatfield, Michael. "Committee Opinions and Treasury Regulation: Tax Lawyer Ethics, 1965–1985." *Florida Tax Review* 15 (2014): 675–735.

Hatfield, Michael. "Legal Ethics and Federal Taxes, 1945–1965: Patriotism, Duties, and Advice." *Florida Tax Review* 12 (2012): 1–57.

Hayashi, Kayoko, and Mahir Aydin, eds. *The Ottoman State and Societies in Change: A Study of the Nineteenth Century Temettuat Registers*. London: Kegan Paul, 2004.

Hełczyński, Bronisław. "The Law in the Reborn State." In *Polish Law throughout the Ages*, edited by Wenceslas J. Wagner. Stanford: Hoover Institute Press, 1970, 139–76.

Helman, Anat. *Becoming Israeli: National Ideals and Everyday Life in the 1950s*. Waltham, MA: Brandeis University Press, 2014.

Helman, Sara. "Militarism and the Construction of Community." *Journal of Political and Military Sociology* 25 (1997): 305–32.

Heussler, Robert. *Yesterday's Rulers: The Making of the British Colonial Service*. Syracuse, NY: Syracuse University Press, 1963.

Heyd, Uriel. "Yehudey Erets Yisrael be-Sof ha-Me'ah ha-17 'al-Pi Pinkasim Turkiyim shel Mas ha-Gulgolet." *Yerushalayim: Riv'on le-Heker Yerushaliyim ve-Toldotehah* 4 (1952/53): 173–84.

Higgs, Edward. *The Information State in England*. London: Palgrave Macmillan, 2004.

Hildesheimer, Meir. "Misim ve-Tashlumehem be-Yahadut Ashkenaz ba-Me'ah ha-17 'al-Pi Sifrut ha-She'elot veha-Tshuvot." *Sinai* 73 (1973): 263–83.

Hirschl, Ran. *Towards Juristocracy: The Origins and Consequences of the New Constitutionalism*. Cambridge, MA: Harvard University Press, 2004.

Hofri-Winogradow, Adam S. "Professionals' Contribution to the Legislative Process: Between Self, Client, and the Public." *Law and Social Inquiry* 39 (2014): 96–126.

Holland, Kevin, Sarah Lindop, and Fatimah Zainudin. "Tax Avoidance: A Threat to Corporate Legitimacy? An Examination of Companies' Financial and CSR Reports." *British Tax Review*, 2016, 310–38.

Holzman-Gazit, Yifat. *Land Expropriation in Israel: Law, Culture and Society*. Aldershot: Ashgate, 2007.

Hope Simpson, John. *Palestine: Report on Immigration, Land Settlement and Development*. London: HMSO, 1930.

Hopwood, Anthony G., and Peter Miller, eds. *Accounting as a Social and Institutional Practice*. Cambridge: Cambridge University Press, 1994.

Horne, Alistair. *A Savage War of Peace: Algeria, 1954–1962*. Rev. edn. New York: Penguin Books, 1987.

Horowitz, Dan, and Moshe Lissak. *Origins of the Israeli Polity: Palestine Under the Mandate*. Translated by Charles Hoffman. Chicago: University of Chicago Press, 1978.

Horowitz, Dan, and Moshe Lissak. *Trouble in Utopia: The Overburdened Polity of Israel*. Albany: SUNY Press, 1989.

Horowitz, David. *Hayim ba-Moked*. Ramat-Gan: Masadah, 1985.

Howard, Douglas A. "Historical Scholarship and the Classical Ottoman Kanunnames." *Archivum Ottomanicum* 14 (1995/96): 79–109.

Hughes, Matthew. "The Banality of Brutality: British Armed Forces and the Repression of the Arab Revolt in Palestine, 1936–39." *English Historical Review* 124 (2009): 313–54.

Hunt, Alan. *The Sociological Movement in Law*. Philadelphia: Temple University Press, 1978.

Hunt, Alan, and Gary Wickham. *Foucault and Law: Towards a Sociology of Law as Governance*. London: Pluto Press, 1994.

Ibn-Ezra, Joseph Ben Issac. *Masa Melekh: Diney Misim u-Minhagim*. Edited by Yaakov Shmuel Spiegel. Jerusalem: Yad ha-Rav Nisim, 1988/89.

Ilan, Shahar. *Haredim Ba'am: Ha-Taktsivim, ha-Hishtamtut ve-Remisat ha-Hok*. Jerusalem: Keter, 2000.

İnalcık, Halil. "Kanunname," In *Encyclopedia of Islam*. New edn. Leiden: Brill, 1978.

İnalcık, Halil with Donald Quataert. *An Economic and Social History of the Ottoman Empire, 1300–1914*. New York: Cambridge University Press, 1994.

Ironside, Kristy. "Rubles for Victory: The Social Dynamics of State Fundraising on the Soviet Home Front." *Kritika: Explorations in Russian and Eurasian History* 15 (2014): 799–828.

İslamoğlu, Huri. "Modernities Compared: State Transformations and Constitutions of Property in the Qing and Ottoman Empires." In *Shared*

Histories of Modernity: China, India and the Ottoman Empire, edited by Huri İslamoğlu and Peter C. Perdue. New Delhi: Routledge, 2009, 109–46.

İslamoğlu, Huri. "Politics of Administering Property: Law and Statistics in the Nineteenth-Century Ottoman Empire." In *Constituting Modernity: Private Property in the East and West*, edited by Huri İslamoğlu. London: I. B. Tauris, 2004, 276–319.

İslamoğlu, Huri. "Towards a Political Economy of Legal and Administrative Constitutions of Individual Property." In *Constituting Modernity: Private Property in the East and West*, edited by Huri İslamoğlu. London: I. B. Tauris, 2004, 3–34.

İslamoğlu, Huri, and Peter C. Perdue. "Introduction" to *Shared Histories of Modernity: China, India and the Ottoman Empire*, edited by Huri İslamoğlu and Peter C. Perdue. New Delhi: Routledge, 2009, 1–20.

İslamoğlu, Huri, and Peter C. Perdue. eds. *Shared Histories of Modernity: China, India and the Ottoman Empire*. New Delhi: Routledge, 2009.

James, Kathryn. *The Rise of Value-Added Tax*. New York: Cambridge University Press, 2015.

Jayal, Niraja Gopal. *Citizenship and Its Discontents: An Indian History*. Cambridge, MA: Harvard University Press, 2013.

Jenkins, C. L. "1860: India's First Income Tax." *British Tax Review*, 2012, 87–116.

Jerusalemer Künstler, 1975. [Bremen]: [Kunsthalle Bremen], 1975.

Jones, Carolyn C. "Bonds, Voluntarism and Taxation." In vol. 2 of *Studies in the History of Tax Law*, edited by John Tiley. Oxford: Hart, 2007, 427–42.

Jones, Carolyn C. "Class Tax to Mass Tax: The Role of Propaganda in the Expansion of the Income Tax during World War II." *Buffalo Law Review* 37 (1988): 685–737.

Jones, Carolyn C. "Mass-Based Income Taxation: Creating a Taxpaying Culture, 1940–1952." In *Funding the Modern American State, 1941–1995: The Rise and Fall of the Era of Easy Finance*, edited by W. Elliot Brownlee. Washington, DC: Woodrow Wilson Center Press, 1996, 107–47.

Kabalo, Paula. "Beyn Ezrahim le-Medinah Hadashah: Sipurah shel Shurat ha-Mitnadvim." *'Iyunim bi-Tkumat Yisrael* 13 (2003): 203–32.

Kabalo, Paula. "Halutsiyut u-Mekhuyavut Ezrahit 'al-pi David Ben-Gurion, 1948–1955." In *Hevrah ve-Kalkalah be-Yisrael: Mabat Histori 'Akhshavi*, edited by Avi Bareli, Daniel Gutwein, and Tuvia Friling. Sde Boker: Ben-Gurion Institute Press, 2005, 773–802.

Kabalo, Paula. "Pioneering Discourse and the Shaping of an Israeli Citizen in the 1950s." *Jewish Social Studies: History, Culture, Society* 15:2 (2009): 82–110.

Kabalo, Paula. *Shurat ha-Mitnadvim: Korotav shel Irgun Ezrahim*. Tel Aviv: 'Am 'Oved, 2007.

Kalir, Shim'on. "Kofer ha-Yishuv u-Magbit ha-Hitgaysut." In *Dor ha-Haganah be-Herzliyah*, edited by B. Z. Michaeli. Tel Aviv: Irgun Havrey ha-Haganah, 1979, 118–20.

Karlinsky, Nahum. "Ha-Ko-Operatsyah ha-Pratit bi-Tkufat ha-Mandat: Ashray ve-Hisahon." In *Kalkalah ve-Hevrah bi-Yemey ha-Mandat: 1918–1948*, edited by Avi Bareli and Nahum Karlinsky. Sde Boker: Ben-Gurion Institute Press, 2003, 239–89.

Katvan, Eyal. "The 'Overcrowding the Profession' Argument and the Professional Melting Pot." *International Journal of the Legal Profession* 19 (2012): 301–19.

Kedar, Alexandre. "The Jewish State and the Arab Possessor, 1948–1967." In *The History of Law in a Multi-Cultural Society: Israel, 1917–1967*, edited by Ron Harris et al. Ashgate: Aldershot, 2002, 311–79.

Kedar, Nir. "Ben-Gurion's *Mamlakhtiyut*: Etymological and Theoretical Roots." *Israel Studies* 7 (2002): 117–33.

Kedar, Nir. *Ben-Gurion veha-Hukah*. Or Yehuda: Dvir, 2015.

Kedar, Nir. *Mamlakhtiyut: Ha-Tfisah ha-Ezrahit shel David Ben-Gurion*. Jerusalem: Yad Izhak Ben-Zvi, 2009.

Kedar, Nir. "Ha-Mishpat u-Mekomo ha-Merkazi ba-Historyah ha-Yisre'elit: 'Al ha-Historiografyah shel ha-Mishpat ha-Yisre'eli u-Trumatah le-Heker Yisrael." *Katedrah* 150 (2013): 155–80.

Kennedy, Duncan. "The Hermeneutic of Suspicion in Contemporary American Legal Thought." *Law and Critique* 25 (2014): 91–139.

Kenny, Lawrence W., and Stanley L. Winer. "Tax Systems in the World: An Empirical Investigation into the Importance of Tax Bases, Administration Costs, Scale and Political Regime." *International Tax and Public Finance* 13 (2006): 181–215.

Kerber, Linda K. *No Constitutional Right to Be Ladies: Women and the Obligations of Citizenship*. New York: Hill and Wang, 1998.

Keren, Michael. "Economists and Economic Policy Making in Israel: The Politics of Expertise in the Stabilization Program." *Policy Sciences* 26 (1993): 331–46.

Khoury, Dina Rizk. "Administrative Practice between Religious Law and State Law on the Eastern Frontiers of the Ottoman Empire." In *Shared Histories of Modernity: China, India and the Ottoman Empire*, edited by Huri İslamoğlu and Peter C. Perdue. New Delhi: Routledge, 2009, 46–73.

Kidron, Anat. *Beyn Le'om le-Makom: Ha-Kehilah ha-'Ivrit be-Heyfah ha-Mandatorit*. Jerusalem: Yad Izhak Ben-Zvi, 2012.

Kimmerling, Baruch, and Joel S. Migdal. *The Palestinian People: A History*. Cambridge, MA: Harvard University Press, 2003.

Kleiman, Ephraim. "Israel: Economists in a New State." *History of Political Economy* 13 (1981): 548–79.

Kleiman, Ephraim. "The Waning of Israeli *Etatisme*." *Israel Studies* 2 (1997): 146–71.

Knesset. "Knesset Election Results." http://main.knesset.gov.il/mk/elections/Pages/default.aspx.

Kondor, Yaakov. *Meshek be-Mahteret be-Yisrael uba-'Olam*. Tel Aviv: Tsherikover, 1993.

Kornhauser, Marjorie E. "Doing the Full Monty: Will Publicizing Tax Information Increase Compliance?" *Canadian Journal of Law and Jurisprudence* 18 (2005): 95–117.

Kornhauser, Marjorie E. "Shaping Public Opinion and the Law in the 1930s: How a 'Common Man' Campaign Ended a Rich Man's Law." *Law and Contemporary Problems* 73 (2010): 123–47.

Kornhauser, Marjorie E. "A Tax Morale Approach to Compliance: Recommendations for the IRS." *Florida Tax Review* 8 (2007): 599–640.

Kornhauser, William. *The Politics of Mass Society*. New York: Free Press 1965.

Kotsonis, Yanni. *States of Obligation: Taxes and Citizenship in the Russian Empire and Early Soviet Republic*. Toronto: University of Toronto Press, 2014.

Krampf, Arie. "Economic Planning of the Free Market in Israel during the First Decade: The Influence of Don Patinkin on Israeli Policy Discourse." *Science in Context* 23 (2010): 507–34.

Krampf, Arie. *Ha-Mekorot ha-Le'umiyim shel Kalkalat ha-Shuk: Pitu'ah Kalkali bi-Tkufat 'Itsuvo shel ha-Kapitalizm ha-Yisre'eli*. Jerusalem: Magnes, 2015.

Krampf, Arie. "Reception of the Developmental Approach in the Jewish Economic Discourse of Mandatory Palestine, 1934–1938." *Israel Studies* 15 (2010): 80–103.

Kreitner, Roy. "The Jurisprudence of Global Money." *Theoretical Inquiries in Law* 11 (2010): 177–208.

Kronman, Antony T. *Max Weber*. Stanford: Stanford University Press, 1983.

Kushner, David. "Ha-Dor ha-Aharon le-Shilton ha-'Othmanim be-Erets Yisrael, 1882–1914." In *Toldot ha-Yishuv ha-Yehudi be-Erets Yisrael me-Az ha-'Aliyah ha-Rishonah: Ha-Tkufah ha-'Othmanit*, edited by Israel Kolatt. Jerusalem: Mosad Bialik, 1989/90, 1–74.

Kwass, Michael. *Privilege and the Politics of Taxation in Eighteenth-Century France: Liberté, Égalité, Fiscalité*. New York: Cambridge University Press, 2000.

Lahav, Pnina. "American Moment[s]: When, How, and Why Did Israeli Law Faculties Come to Resemble Elite U.S. Law Schools?" *Theoretical Inquiries in Law* 10 (2009): 653–97.

Lahav, Pnina. *Judgment in Jerusalem: Chief Justice Simon Agranat and the Zionist Century*. Berkeley: University of California Press, 1997.

Lamb, Margaret. "Defining 'Profits' for British Income Tax Purposes: A Contextual Study of the Depreciation Cases, 1875–1897." *Accounting Historians Journal* 29 (2002): 105–72.

Lamb, Margaret. "'Horrid Appealing': Accounting for Taxable Profits in Mid-Nineteenth Century England." *Accounting, Organizations and Society* 26 (2001): 271–98.

Lamb, Margaret. "Taxation." In *The Routledge Companion to Accounting History*, edited by John Richard Edwards and Stephen P. Walker. Abingdon: Routledge, 2009, 579–97.

Landau, Michael. "Ha-Yishuv bi-Tkufat ha-Sa'ar: 'Al Kofer ha-Yishuv u-Magbit ha-Hitgaysut veha-Hatsalah." *Masu'ah: Kovets Shanti le-Toda'at ha-Sho'ah veha-Gvurah* 5 (1977): 179–98.

Lapidoth, Arye. *'Ekronot Mas Hakhnasah ve-Mas Rivhey Hon.* Jerusalem: Muze'on le-Misim, 1970.

Lapidoth, Arye. *Evasion and Avoidance of Income Tax: A Comparative Study of English Law and Israeli Law.* Jerusalem: Museum of Taxes, 1966.

Lapidoth, Arye. "Trends in the Income Tax Legislation of Israel." In *Studies in Israel Legislative Problems*, edited by Gad Tedeschi and Uri Yadin. Jerusalem: Magnes Press, 1966, 325–41.

Laron, Guy. "The Domestic Sources of Israel's Decision to Launch the 1956 Sinai Campaign." *British Journal of Middle Eastern Studies* 43 (2015): 200–18.

Lazar, Hadara. *Ma'arekhet ha-Misuy ba-Gadah ha-Ma'aravit uvi-Retsu'at 'Azah ke-Makhshir le-Akhifat ha-Shilton bi-Tkufat ha-Hitkomemut.* Jerusalem: B'tselem, 1990.

Lerner, Ralph. "The Supreme Court as Republican Schoolmaster." *Supreme Court Review*, 1967: 127–80.

Levi, Margaret. *Of Rule and Revenue.* Berkeley: University of California Press, 1988.

Levi-Faur, David. "The Developmental State: Israel, South Korea, and Taiwan Compared." *Studies in Comparative International Development* 33 (1998): 65–93.

Levi-Faur, David. *Ha-Yad ha-Lo Ne'elamah: Ha-Politikah shel ha-Ti'us be-Yisrael.* Jerusalem: Yad Izhak Ben-Zvi, 2001.

Levin, Dov. *The Litvaks: A Short History of the Jews of Lithuania.* Jerusalem: Yad Vashem, 2000.

Levin, Dov. "Yo'ets ha-Mas – Mekor Samkhuto ve-Ma'amado, Tkhum Tafkido ve-Akhrayuto." *Heshbona'ut u-Misim* 47 (1991): 5–21.

Levin, Itamar. *Heshbon Meshutaf: Lishkat Ro'ey Heshbon, Ha-Yishuv veha-Medinah: 80 Shnot Du'ah: 1931–2011.* Tel Aviv: Lishkat Ro'ey Heshbon be-Yisrael, 2011.

Levitats, Isaac. *The Jewish Community in Russia, 1772–1844.* New York: Columbia University Press, 1943.

Li, Sherry Xin. "Social Identities, Ethnic Diversity, and Tax Morale." *Public Finance Review* 38 (2010): 146–77.

Lieberman, Evan S. "How South African Citizens Evaluate Their Economic Obligations to the State." *Journal of Development Studies* 38 (2002): 37–62.

Lieberman, Evan S. *Race and Regionalism in the Politics of Taxation in Brazil and South Africa.* New York: Cambridge University Press, 2003.

Lifshitz, Shahar. "Diney Zugiyut Hiloniyim ba-Yovel ha-Bah: Beyn 'Libertaryanizatsyah' u-Veyn Beyt ha-Mishpat 'ha-Mehashek'." *Mehkarey Mishpat* 17 (2001): 159–262.

Likhovski, Assaf. "Between Mandate and State: Re-thinking the Periodization of Israeli Legal History." *Journal of Israeli History* 19:2 (1998): 39–68.

Likhovski, Assaf. "Chasing Ghosts: On Writing Cultural Histories of Tax Law." *UC Irvine Law Review* 1 (2011): 843–92.

Likhovski, Assaf. "The Duke and the Lady: *Helvering v. Gregory* and the History of Tax Avoidance Adjudication." *Cardozo Law Review* 25 (2004): 953–1018.

Likhovski, Assaf. "Formalism and Israeli Anti-Avoidance Doctrines in the 1950s and 1960s." In vol. 1 of *Studies in the History of Tax Law*, edited by John Tiley. Oxford: Hart, 2004, 339–77.

Likhovski, Assaf. "Is Tax Law Culturally Specific? Lessons from the History of Income Tax Law in Mandatory Palestine." *Theoretical Inquiries in Law* 11 (2010): 725–63.

Likhovski, Assaf. *Law and Identity in Mandate Palestine.* Chapel Hill: University of North Carolina Press, 2006.

Likhovski, Assaf. "Mishpat ve-Tarbut be-Yisrael be-Fetah ha-Me'ah ha-'Esrim ve-Ahat: He'arot 'al Sifro shel Menachem Mautner." *Ha-Mishpat* 14 (2010/01): 715–23.

Likhovski, Assaf. "Protestantism and the Rationalization of English Law: A Variation on a Theme by Weber." *Law and Society Review* 33 (1999): 365–91.

Likhovski, Assaf. "Tax Law and Public Opinion: Explaining *IRC v Duke of Westminster*." In vol. 2 of *Studies in the History of Tax Law*, edited by John Tiley. Oxford: Hart, 2007, 183–221.

Likhovski, Assaf. "'The Time Has Not Yet Come to Repair the World in the Kingdom of God': Israeli Lawyers and the Failed Jewish Legal Revolution of 1948." In *Jews and the Law*, edited by Marc Galanter et al.. New Orleans: Quid Pro Books, 2014, 359–83.

Likhovski, Assaf. "'Training in Citizenship': Tax Compliance and Modernity." *Law and Social Inquiry* 32 (2007): 665–700.

Likhovski, Assaf. "Two Horwitzian Journeys." In *Transformations in American Legal History: Essays in Honor of Professor Morton J. Horwitz*, edited by Daniel W. Hamilton and Alfred L. Brophy. Cambridge, MA: Harvard University Press, 2008, 300–18.

Littlewood, Michael. *Taxation without Representation: The History of Hong Kong's Troublingly Successful Tax System.* Hong Kong: Hong Kong University Press, 2010.

Livingston, Michael A. "Law, Culture and Anthropology: On the Hopes and Limits of Comparative Tax." *Canadian Journal of Law and Jurisprudence* 18 (2005): 119–34.

Livingston, Michael A. "Reinventing Tax Scholarship: Lawyers, Economists and the Role of the Legal Academy." *Cornell Law Review* 83 (1998): 365–436.

Loftus, P. J. *National Income of Palestine, 1944.* [Jerusalem]: Government Printer, 1946.

Loftus, P. J. *National Income of Palestine, 1945.* [Jerusalem]: Government Printer, 1948.

Loo, Ern Chen, and Margaret McKerchar. "The Impact of British Colonial Rule on the Malaysian Income Tax System." *eJournal of Tax Research* 12 (2014): 238–52.

Madden, Richard Robert. *The Turkish Empire: In Its Relations with Christianity and Civilization.* London: T. Cautley Newby, 1862.

Malchi, Eliezer. *Toldot ha-Mishpat be-Erets Yisrael: Mavo Histori la-Mishpat bi-Medinat Yisrael.* Tel Aviv: Dinim, 1953.

Maltby, Josephine. "'A Sort of Guide, Philosopher and Friend': The Rise of the Professional Auditor in Britain." *Accounting, Business and Financial History* 9 (1999): 29–50.

Mandel, Avraham, ed. *Hitpat'hut ha-Misim be-Erets Yisrael: Skirah Historit.* Jerusalem: Muze'on le-Misim, 1968.

Mandel, Avraham, *Ma'arekhet ha-Misim be-Yisrael: Homer 'Ezer la-Moreh be-Nos'e ha-Misim.* Jerusalem: Muze'on le-Misim, 1969.

Mandel, Avraham, *Ha-Misim ba-Mekorot (Ha-Tanakh, ha-Mishnah veha-Talmudim).* Jerusalem, 1987.

Mandel, Avraham, ed. *Ha-Misim ve-Atah: Ma'arekhet ha-Misim be-Erets Yisrael ba-'Avar uva-Hoveh.* Jerusalem: Misrad ha-Hinukh veha-Tarbut and Misrad ha-Otsar, 1985.

Mandel, Avraham, ed. *Ha-Muze'on le-Misim bi-Yerushalyim.* Jerusalem: Minhal Hakhnasot ha-Medinah: Ha-Otsar, 1989.

Mandel, Avraham, ed. *Sefer ha-Yovel shel Agaf Mas Hakhnasah u-Mas Rekhush.* Tel Aviv: Yedioth Ahronoth ve-Muze'on le-Misim, 1992.

Mandel, Avraham, ed. *Vatikey ha-Mekhes bi-Nemal Yafo, Mesaprim.* Jerusalem: Muze'on le-Misim, 1967.

Mandel, Avraham, and Asher Arin, eds. *'Idkunim le-Sefer Hitpat'hut ha-Misim be-Erets Yisrael: Legabey ha-Shanim 1964–1978.* Jerusalem: Muze'on le-Misim, 1982.

Mandel, Avraham, and Sylvia Habif, eds. *Albom ha-Mekhes: 100 Shnot Mekhes be-Erets Yisrael.* Ramat-Gan and Jerusalem: Masadah and Muze'on le-Misim, 1973.

Ma'oz, Moshe. *Ottoman Reform in Syria and Palestine, 1840–1861: The Impact of the Tanzimat on Politics and Society.* Oxford: Clarendon Press, 1968.

Marcus, Joseph. *Social and Political History of the Jews in Poland, 1919–1939.* Berlin: Mouton Publishers, 1983.

Margalit, Avital. "'Ha-Ye'arot asher ba-Hem Nirde et ha-Dvash': Hok, Irgun u-Mivney Ta'agidi be-Hevrat ha-'Ovdim." *'Iyuney Mishpat* 26 (2002): 451–510.

Martin, Isaac William, Ajay K. Mehrotra, and Monica Prasad, eds. *The New Fiscal Sociology: Taxation in Comparative and Historical Perspective.* New York: Cambridge University Press, 2009.

Mauss, Marcel. *The Gift: The Form and Reason for Exchange in Archaic Societies.* Translated by W. D. Halls. New York: W. W. Norton, 2000.

Mautner, Menachem. *Law and the Culture of Israel.* Oxford: Oxford University Press, 2011.

Mautner, Menachem. "Mashber ha-Republikaniyut be-Yisrael." *Mishpat ve-'Asakim* 14 (2012): 559–94.

Mautner, Menachem. "Petah Davar: Liberalizm be-Yisrael – 'Ha-Adam ha-Tov,' 'ha-Ezrah ha-Ra'' veha-Sigsug ha-Ishi veha-Hevrati." *'Iyuney Mishpat* 36 (2013): 7–79.

Mautner, Menachem. *Yeridat ha-Formalizm ve-'Aliyat ha-'Arakhim ba-Mishpat ha-Yisre'eli.* Tel Aviv: Ma'agaley Da'at, 1993.

Mehrotra, Ajay K. "Anger, Irony, and the Formal Rationality of Professionalism." *Law and History Review* 28 (2010): 241–48.

Mehrotra, Ajay K. *Making the Modern American Fiscal State: Law, Politics, and the Rise of Progressive Taxation, 1877–1929.* New York: Cambridge University Press, 2013.

Mehrotra, Ajay K. "Reviving Fiscal Citizenship." *Michigan Law Review* 113 (2015): 943–72.

Mehrotra, Ajay K., and Joseph J. Thorndike. "From Programmatic Reform to Social Science Research: The National Tax Association and the Promise and Perils of Disciplinary Encounters." *Law and Society Review* 45 (2011): 593–630.

Meron, Simcha. "Mekorot ha-Mishpat le-Diney Misim etsel Hamishah mi-Poskey Ashkenaz." *Diney Yisrael* 3 (1972): 61–70.

Mert, Ibrahim. "A Historical Overview of Accounting in Turkey." *Internal Auditing and Risk Management* 31 (2013): 15–25.

Messick, Brinkley. *The Calligraphic State: Textual Domination and History in a Muslim Society.* Berkeley: University of California Press, 1996.

Metzer, Jacob. *The Divided Economy of Mandatory Palestine.* Cambridge: Cambridge University Press, 1998.

Metzer, Jacob. "Fiscal Incidence and Resource Transfer between Jews and Arabs in Mandatory Palestine." *Research in Economic History* 7 (1982): 87–132.

Metzer, Jacob. *Hon Leumi le-Vayit Leumi: 1919–1921.* Jerusalem: Yad Izhak Ben-Zvi, 1979.

Metzer, Jacob. "Jews in Mandatory Palestine and Additional Phenomena of Atypical Settler Colonization in Modern Time." In *Settler Economies in World History*, edited by Christopher Lloyd, Jacob Metzer, and Richard Sutch. Leiden: Brill, 2013, 169–202.

Metzer, Omri. "Ha-Politikah shel Hit'ahdut Ba'aley ha-Ta'asiyah bi-Shnot ha-Shloshim: Ha-Ma'amatsim li-Vlimat Mas ha-Hakhnasah vele-'Idud Totseret ha-Arets." *'Iyunim bi-Tkumat Yisrael* 22 (2012): 290–324.

Miller, Ruth. "The Legal History of the Ottoman Empire." *History Compass* 6 (2008): 286–96.

Miller, Ylana N. *Government and Society in Rural Palestine, 1920–1948.* Austin: University of Texas Press, 1985.

Mitchell, Timothy. *Rule of Experts: Egypt, Techno-Politics, Modernity.* Berkeley: University of California Press, 2002.

Molcho, Avner. "Kapitalizm ve-'ha-Derekh ha-Amerikanit' be-Yisrael: Pir'yon, Nihul veha-Etos ha-Kapitalisti ba-Siyu'a ha-Tekhni shel Artsot ha-Brit bi-Shnot ha-Hamishim." In *Hevrah ve-Kalkalah be-Yisrael: Mabat Histori 'Akhshavi,* edited by Avi Bareli, Daniel Gutwein, and Tuvia Friling. Sde Boker: Ben-Gurion Institute Press, 2005, 263–94.

Molcho, Avner. "Productivization, Economics and the Transformation of Israeli Education, 1948–1965." *Israel Studies* 16 (2011): 123–48.

Morag, Amotz. *Mimun ha-Memshalah be-Yisrael: Hitpat'huyot u-Ve'ayot.* Jerusalem: Magnes, 1967.

Morgan, Kimberly J., and Monica Prasad. "The Origins of Tax Systems: A French-American Comparison." *American Journal of Sociology* 114 (2009): 1350–94.

Moses, S., *Company Profits Tax.* Jerusalem: Tarshish, 1945.

Moses, S., *The Income Tax Ordinance of Palestine: The Income Tax (Amendment) Ordinance, 1942.* Jerusalem: Tarshish Books, 1942.

Moses, S., *The Income Tax Ordinance of Palestine.* 2nd edn. Tel Aviv: Bitaon, 1946.

Moses, S., *The Income Tax Ordinance of Palestine: The Text as Valid Since 1st April, 1944, with Explanations of the 1944 Amendments.* Jerusalem: Tarshish Books, 1944.

Moses, S., with Walter Schwarz. *The 1947 Income Tax Amendments.* Tel Aviv: Bitaon, [1947].

Mumford, Ann. *Taxing Culture: Toward a Theory of Tax Collection Law.* Aldershot: Ashgate, 2002.

Mustard and Cress [P. E. F. Cressall]. *Palestine Parodies: Being the Holy Land in Verse and Worse.* Tel Aviv: Azriel Press, printed for private circulation, 1938.

Nadan, Amos. *The Palestinian Peasant Economy under the Mandate: A Story of Colonial Bungling.* Cambridge, MA: Harvard Center for Middle Eastern Studies, 2006.

Nadel, Baruch. *Doh Nadel: Hakol 'al Mas ha-Hakhnasah be-Yisrael.* Tel Aviv: A. L. Hotsa'ah Meyuhedet, 1975.

Naor, Mordechai. *Trumat Ramat-Gan le-Vitahon Yisrael: Yarok-Haki-Adom.* Ramat-Gan: Beyt Avraham Krinitzi, 2009.

Naor, Moshe. *Be-Hazit ha-'Oref: Tel Aviv ve-Hitgaysut ha-Yishuv be-Milhemet ha-'Atsma'ut.* Jerusalem: Yad Izhak Ben-Zvi, 2009.

Naor, Moshe. "From Voluntary Funds to National Loans: The Financing of Israel's 1948 War Effort." *Israel Studies* 11 (2006): 62–82.

Naor, Moshe. "The Israeli Volunteering Movement Preceding the 1956 War." *Israeli Affairs* 16 (2010): 434–54.

Naor, Moshe. "Israel's 1948 War of Independence as a Total War." *Journal of Contemporary History* 43 (2008): 241–58.

Naor, Moshe. *Social Mobilization in the Arab–Israeli War of 1948: On the Israeli Home Front*. London: Routledge, 2013.

Nathan, Robert R., Oscar Gass, and Daniel Creamer. *Palestine: Problem and Promise*. Washington, DC: Public Affairs Press, 1946.

Nehring, Holger, and Florian Schui, eds., *Global Debates about Taxation*. Basingstoke: Palgrave Macmillan, 2007.

Nerré, Birger. "Tax Culture: A Basic Concept for Tax Politics." *Economic Analysis and Policy* 38 (2008): 153–67.

Nevo, Gidi. "Ha-Satirah ha-Burganit shel Ephraim Kishon." In *Hevrah ve-Kalkalah be-Yisrael: Mabat Histori 'Akhshavi*, edited by Avi Bareli, Daniel Gutwein, and Tuvia Friling. Sde Boker: Ben-Gurion Institute Press, 2005, 711–45.

Nirenberg, David. *Communities of Violence: Persecution of Minorities in the Middle Ages*. Princeton: Princeton University Press, 1998.

Nonhoff, Martin, and Frieder Vogelmann. "Paying for Identity: The Formation of Differentiated Collectives through Taxes." Unpublished Paper. http://ecpr.eu/Filestore/PaperProposal/52007b86-b202-4b1e-920d-fa284438dfd7.pdf.

Norris, Jacob. "Repression and Rebellion: Britain's Response to the Arab Revolt in Palestine of 1936–39." *Journal of Imperial and Commonwealth History* 36 (2008): 25–45.

Norton, Michael I., Daniel Mochon, and Dan Ariely. "The 'IKEA Effect': When Labor Leads to Love." *Journal of Consumer Psychology* 22 (2012): 453–60.

Nützenadel, Alexander, and Christoph Strupp, eds. *Taxation, State, and Civil Society in Germany and the United States from the 18th to the 20th Century*. Baden-Baden: Nomos, 2007.

Oats, Lynne, ed. *Taxation: A Fieldwork Research Handbook*. Abingdon: Routledge, 2012.

Oden, Robert A., Jr. "Taxation in Biblical Israel." *Journal of Religious Ethics* 12 (1984): 162–81.

OECD. *OECD Reviews of Labour Markets and Social Policies: Israel*. Paris: OECD Publishing, 2010.

Onu, Diana, and Lynne Oats. "The Role of Social Norms in Tax Compliance: Theoretical Overview and Practical Implications." *Journal of Tax Administration* 1 (2015): 113–37.

Orr, Robert. "Reflections on Totalitarianism, Leading to Reflections on Two Ways of Theorizing." *Political Studies* 21 (1973): 481–9.

Ottensooser, Robert David. *The Palestine Pound and the Israel Pound: Transition from a Colonial to an Independent Currency*. Geneva: E. Droz, 1955.

Owen, Roger. *The Middle East in the World Economy 1800–1914*. Rev. edn. London: I. B. Tauris, 1993.

Özbudun, Ergun. "The Continuing Ottoman Legacy and the State Tradition in the Middle East." In *Imperial Legacy: The Ottoman Imprint on the Balkans and the Middle East*, edited by L. Carl Brown. New York: Columbia University Press, 1996, 133–57.

Oz-Salzberger, Fania, and Eli Salzberger. "The Secret German Sources of the Israeli Supreme Court." *Israel Studies* 3 (1998): 159–92.

Palan, Ronen, Richard Murphy, and Christian Chavagneux. *Tax Havens: How Globalization Really Works*. Ithaca, NY: Cornell University Press, 2010.

Palestine Royal Commission. *Minutes of Evidence Heard at Public Sessions*. London: HMSO, 1937.

Palestine Royal Commission. *Report*. London: HMSO, 1937.

Pamuk, Şevket. "The Evolution of Fiscal Institutions in the Ottoman Empire." In *The Rise of Fiscal States: A Global History, 1500–1914*, edited by Bartolomé Yun-Casalilla and Patrick K. O'Brien with Francisco Comín Comín. Cambridge: Cambridge University Press, 2012, 304–31.

Pamuk, Şevket, and K. Kivanç Karaman. "Ottoman State Finances in European Perspective, 1500–1914." *Journal of Economic History* 70 (2010): 593–629.

Parrillo, Nicholas R. *Against the Profit Motive: The Salary Revolution in American Government, 1780–1940*. New Haven: Yale University Press, 2013.

Patriarca, Silvana. *Numbers and Nationhood: Writing Statistics in Nineteenth-Century Italy*. Cambridge: Cambridge University Press, 1996.

Peled, Alon. *A Question of Loyalty: Military Manpower Policy in Multiethnic States*. Ithaca, NY: Cornell University Press, 1998.

Peled, Yoav. *The Challenge of Ethnic Democracy: The State and Minority Groups in Israel, Poland and Northern Ireland*. New York: Routledge, 2014.

Peled, Yoav, and Adi Ophir, eds. *Yisrael: Mi-Hevrah Meguyeset le-Hevrah Ezrahit?* Tel Aviv: Ha-Kibbutz ha-Me'uhad, 2001.

Peleg, Ilan, and Dov Waxman. *Israel's Palestinians: The Conflict Within*. Cambridge: Cambridge University Press, 2011.

Penslar, Derek J. *Shylock's Children: Economics and Jewish Identity in Modern Europe*. Berkeley: University of California Press, 2001.

Plopul, A. B., and André Tuéni. *L'impot sur le revenu au Liban: Commentaire théorique et pratique de la loi Libanaise du 4 Décembre 1944*. Beirut: 1945 [label mounted on title-page: Haifa: Paltax Publishers].

Porat, Dina. *Hanhagah be-Milkud: Ha-Yishuv Nokhah ha-Sho'ah, 1942–1945*. Tel Aviv: 'Am 'Oved, 1986.

Porath, Yehoshua, *The Palestinian Arab National Movement 1929–1939: From Riots to Rebellion*. London: Frank Cass, 1977.

Porath, Yehoshua, and Yaacov Shavit, eds., *Ha-Historyah shel Erets Yisrael*. Vol. 9, *Ha-Mandat ve-Habayit ha-Leumi (1917–1947)*. Jerusalem: Keter, 1982.

Posner, Eric A. "Law and Social Norms: The Case of Tax Compliance." *Virginia Law Review* 86 (2000): 1781–819.

Radian, Alex. "On the Differences between the Political Economy of Introducing and Implementing a Tax Reform: Israel 1975–1978." *Journal of Public Economics* 11 (1979): 261–71.

Rafael, Amnon E. "Tax Reform in Israel." *Israel Law Review* 11 (1976): 187–215.

Rafael, Amnon, with Shlomi Lazar. Vol. 1 of *Mas Hakhnasah*. 4th edn. Tel Aviv: Ronen, 2009.

Rafael, Amnon, Vol. 2 of *Mas Hakhnasah*. 2nd edn. Tel Aviv: Ronen, 2014.

Rao, Gautham. *National Duties: Custom Houses and the Making of the American State*. Chicago: University of Chicago Press, 2016.

Rao, V. K. R. V. *Taxation of Income in India*. Calcutta: Longmans, 1931.

Rechter, Alexander. *Diney Yahalomim*. Tel Aviv: Shaham, [1984/85].

Reuveny, Jacob. *Mimshal ha-Mandat be-Erets Yisrael, 1920–1948: Nitu'ah Histori Medini*. Ramat-Gan: Bar-Ilan University Press, 1993.

Riesenberg, Peter. *Citizenship in the Western Tradition: Plato to Rousseau*. Chapel Hill: University of North Carolina Press, 1992.

[Riklis, L. I.]. "Ba-Ma'arakhah: Kofer ha-Yishuv." *Shorashim: Bamah le-Mo'etset ha-Morim le-Ma'an ha-KKL* 3:1 (December 1938): 6.

Rivlin, Paul. *The Israeli Economy from the Foundation of the State through the 21st Century*. New York: Cambridge University Press, 2011.

Robinson, Shira. *Citizen Strangers: Palestinians and the Birth of Israel's Liberal Settler State*. Stanford: Stanford University Press, 2013.

Rogan, Eugene L. *Frontiers of the State in the Late Ottoman Empire: Transjordan, 1850–1921*. Cambridge: Cambridge University Press, 2002.

Rokach, Issac. *Pardesim Mesaprim*. Ramat-Gan: Masadah, 1970.

Rokah, Rachel, ed. *Misim u-Ma'asim*. Jerusalem: Misrad ha-Hinukh ve-Misrad ha-Otsar, 1993.

Román, José Antonio Sánchez. *Taxation and Society in Twentieth-Century Argentina*. New York: Palgrave Macmillan, 2012.

Rosman, Moshe. *Polin: Prakim be-Toldot Yehudey Mizrah Eropah ve-Tarbutam*. Tel Aviv: Ha-Universitah ha-Ptuhah, 1994.

Rosolio, David, and Ernst Werner Klimowsky. *Mas Hakhnasah be-Erets Yisrael*. Jerusalem: Kiryat Sefer, 1944.

Rostain, Tanina, and Milton C. Regan, Jr. *Confidence Games: Lawyers, Accountants and the Tax Shelter Industry*. Cambridge, MA: MIT Press, 2014.

Roth, Jeffrey A., John T. Scholz, and Ann D. Witte, eds. *Taxpayer Compliance*. Vol. 1, *An Agenda for Research*. Philadelphia: University of Pennsylvania Press, 1989.

Rozen, Minna. "Litrat ha-Basar: Sahar ha-Basar veha-Ma'avakim ha-Hevratiyim be-Istanbul ha-Yehudit, 1700–1918." *Pe'amim* 105–6 (2006): 83–126.

Rozin, Orit. *A Home for All Jews: Citizenship, Rights, and National Identity in the New Israeli State*. Translated by Haim Watzman. Waltham, MA: Brandeis University Press, 2016.

Rozin, Orit. "Israel and the Right to Travel Abroad 1948–1961." *Israel Studies* 15 (2010): 147–76.

Rozin, Orit. "Negotiating the Right to Exit the Country in 1950s Israel: Voice, Loyalty, and Citizenship." *Journal of Israeli History* 30 (2011): 1–22.

Rozin, Orit. *The Rise of the Individual in 1950s Israel: A Challenge to Collectivism*. Translated by Haim Watzman. Waltham, MA: Brandeis University Press, 2011.

Rubin, Avi. "British Perceptions of Ottoman Judicial Reform in the Late Nineteenth Century: Some Preliminary Insights." *Law and Social Inquiry* 37 (2012): 991–1012.

Rubin, Avi. "From Legal Representation to Advocacy: Attorneys and Clients in the Ottoman *Nizamiye* Courts." *International Journal of Middle East Studies* 44 (2012): 111–27.

Rubin, Avi. "Ottoman Judicial Change in the Age of Modernity: A Reappraisal." *History Compass* 7 (2009): 119–40.

Rubin, Avi. *Ottoman Nizamiye Courts: Law and Modernity*. New York: Palgrave Macmillan, 2011.

Rudnitzky, Arik. "The Contemporary Historiographical Debate in Israel on Government Policies on Arabs in Israel during the Military Administration Period (1948–1966)." *Israel Studies* 19 (2014): 24–47.

Ruppin, Arthur. "Income Tax in Palestine: A Premature and Ill-Advised Project – A Serious Menace to Development." *Palestine and Near East Economic Magazine* 18–19 (1932): 443–6.

Sagy, Yair. "Le-Ma'an ha-Tsedek? 'Al Hakamato shel Beyt ha-Mishpat ha-Gavohah le-Tsedek." *'Iyune Mishpat* 28 (2004): 225–98.

Salaymeh, Lena. "Taxing Citizens: Socio-Legal Constructions of Late Antique Muslim Identity." *Islamic Law and Society* 23:4 (2016), 333–67.

Salzmann, Ariel. "Citizens in Search of a State: The Limits of Political Participation in the Late Ottoman Empire." In *Extending Citizenship, Reconfiguring States*, edited by Michael Hanagan and Charles Tilly. Lanham: Rowman and Littlefield, 1999, 37–66.

Samuel, Edwin. *A Lifetime in Jerusalem: The Memoirs of the Second Viscount Samuel*. London: Vallentine, Mitchell, 1970.

Samuel, Edwin. *Problems of Government in the State of Israel*. Jerusalem: R. Mass, 1956.

Samuel, Lawrence R. *Pledging Allegiance: American Identity and the Bond Drive of World War II*. Washington, DC: Smithsonian Institution Press, 1997.

Sandberg, Haim. *Mekarke'y Yisrael: Tsiyonut u-Post-Tsiyonut*. Jerusalem: Ha-Makhon le-Mehkarey Hakikah, 2007.

Sarfatti Larson, Magali. *The Rise of Professionalism: A Sociological Analysis*. Berkeley: University of California Press, 1977.

Schölch, Alexander. *Palestine in Transformation, 1856–1882: Studies in Social, Economic and Political Development*. Translated by William C. Young and Michael C. Gerrity. Washington, DC: Institute for Palestine Studies, 1993.

Scott, James C. *Seeing Like a State: How Certain Schemes to Improve the Human Condition Have Failed*. New Haven: Yale University Press, 1998.

Seder ha-Ha'arakhah: Mantuva 5455/1695. Jerusalem: Minhal ha-Hakhnasot and Ha-Otsar, 1963.

Segev, Tom. *1949–Ha-Yisre'elim ha-Rishonim*. Jerusalem: Domino, 1984.

Seikaly, Sherene. "Meatless Days: Consumption and Capitalism in Wartime Palestine 1939–1948." Ph.D. diss., New York University, 2007.

Seikaly, Sherene. *Men of Capital: Scarcity and Economy in Mandate Palestine*. Stanford: Stanford University Press, 2016.

Sela-Sheffy, Rakefet. "Integration through Distinction: German-Jewish Immigrants, the Legal Profession and Patterns of Bourgeois Culture in British-Ruled Jewish Palestine." *Journal of Historical Sociology* 19 (2006): 34–59.

Sela-Sheffy, Rakefet. "Ha-'Yekim' bi-Sdeh ha-Mishpat u-Dfusim shel Tarbut Burganit bi-Tkufat ha-Mandat." *'Iyunim bi-Tkumat Yisrael* 13 (2003): 295–322.

Shachar, Yoram, Ron Harris, and Miron Gross. "Nohagey ha-Histamkhut shel Beyt ha-Mishpat ha-'Elyon: Nitukhim Kamutiyim." *Mishpatim* 27 (1996): 119–217.

Shafir, Gershon, and Yoav Peled. *Being Israeli: The Dynamics of Multiple Citizenship*. New York: Cambridge University Press, 2002.

Shamir, Ronen. *The Colonies of Law: Colonialism, Zionism and Law in Early Mandate Palestine*. Cambridge: Cambridge University Press, 2000.

Shamir, Ronen. "Suspended in Space: Bedouins under the Law of Israel." *Law and Society Review* 30 (1996): 231–57.

Shapira, Anita. "Ben Yishuv le-Medinah: Ha-Markivim shelo 'Avru." In *Leumiyut u-Politikah Yehudit: Perspektivot Hadashot*, edited by Jehuda Reinharz, Yosef Salmon, and Gideon Shimoni. Jerusalem: Merkaz Shazar, 1996, 253–71.

Shapira, Anita. *Israel: A History*. Translated by Anthony Berris. Waltham, MA: Brandeis University Press, 2012.

Shavit, Tali. "Magbit ha-Hitgaysut veha-Hatsalah." Master's thesis, Tel Aviv University, 1988.

Shavit, Yaacov. "Meshihiyut, Utopiyah u-Pesimiyut bi-Shnot ha-Hamishim: 'Iyun ba-Bikoret 'al ha-Medinah ha-Ben Guryonit." *'Iyunim bi-Tkumat Yisrael* 2 (1992): 56–78.

Shaw, Stanford J. "The Nineteenth-Century Ottoman Tax Reforms and Revenue System." *International Journal of Middle East Studies* 6 (1975): 421–59.

Shiffer, Zalman F. "Money and Inflation in Israel: The Transition of an Economy to High Inflation." *Federal Reserve Bank of St. Louis Review* 64:7 (1982): 28–40.

Shilo, Shmuel, *Dina de-Malkhutah Dina*. Jerusalem: Defus Akademi, 1974.

Shmuelevitz, Aryeh. *The Jews of the Ottoman Empire in the Late Fifteenth and the Sixteenth Centuries: Administrative, Economic, Legal and Social Relations as Reflected in the Responsa*. Leiden: Brill, 1984.

Shochat, Azriel. "'Inyeney Misim ve-Hanhagot Tsibur bi-Kehilot Yavan ba-Me'ah ha-16." *Sfunot* 11 (1971–1977): 299–339.

Shurat ha-Mitnadvim. *Sakanah Orevet – mi-Bifnim! Jerusalem*, 1956.

Sigusch, Volkmar. "Ernst W. Klimowsky." In *Personenlexikon der Sexualforschung*, edited by Volkmar Sigusch and Günter Grau. Frankfurt: Campus Verlag, 2009, 366–8.

Singer, Amy. *Palestinian Peasants and Ottoman Officials: Rural Administration around Sixteenth-Century Jerusalem*. Cambridge: Cambridge University Press, 1994.

Skinner, Quentin, and Bo Stråth, eds. *States and Citizens: History, Theory, Prospects*. New York: Cambridge University Press, 2003.

Slemrod, Joel, and Shlomo Yitzhaki. "Tax Avoidance, Evasion and Administration." In vol. 3 of *Handbook of Public Economics*, edited by Alan J. Auerbach and Martin Feldstein. Amsterdam: Elsevier Science, 2002, 1423–70.

Slutsky, Yehuda. *Sefer Toldot ha-Haganah*. Vol. 2, Part 2, *Me-Haganah le-Ma'avak*. Tel Aviv: Dfus A. Strud, 1964.

Smith, Barbara J. *The Roots of Separatism in Palestine: British Economic Policy 1920–1929*. London: I. B. Tauris, 1993.

Smyth, Rosaleen. "The Genesis of Public Relations in British Colonial Practice." *Public Relations Review* 27 (2001): 149–62.

Somekh, F. S. "Development of Public Accountancy in Israel." *The Israel C.P.A.*, 1971, 6–16.

Sparrow, James T. *Warfare State: World War II Americans and the Age of Big Government*. New York: Oxford University Press, 2011.

Spierenburg, Pieter. *The Spectacle of Suffering: Executions and the Evolution of Repression*. Cambridge: Cambridge University Press, 1984.

Sprinzak, Ehud. *Ish ha-Yashar be-'Yenav: Illegalizm ba-Hevra ha-Yisre'elit*. Tel Aviv: Sifriyat Po'alim, 1986.

Stampfer, Shaul. "Ha-'Pushka' ve-Gilguleyhah: Kupot Erets Yisrael ke-Tofa'ah Hevratit." *Katedrah* 21 (1981): 89–102.

Stebbings, Chantal. "Bureaucratic Adjudication: The Internal Appeals of the Inland Revenue." In *Judges and Judging in the History of the Common Law and Civil Law from Antiquity to Modern Times*, edited by Paul Brand and Joshua Getzler. Cambridge: Cambridge University Press, 2012, 157–74.

Stebbings, Chantal. "The General Commissioners of the Income Tax: Assessors or Adjudicators?" *British Tax Review*, 1993, 52–64.

Stebbings, Chantal. "Income Tax Tribunals: Their Influence and Place in the Victorian Legal System." In *Studies in the History of Tax Law*, edited by John Tiley. Oxford: Hart, 2004, 57–79.

Stebbings, Chantal. "The Origins of the Application of *Certiorari* to the General Commissioners of Income Tax." *British Tax Review*, 1997, 119–30.

Stebbings, Chantal. "Popular Perceptions of Income Tax Law in the Nineteenth Century: A Local Tax Rebellion." *Journal of Legal History* 22 (2001): 45–71.

Stebbings, Chantal. *The Victorian Taxpayer and the Law: A Study in Constitutional Conflict*. Cambridge: Cambridge University Press, 2009.

Stein, Kenneth W. *The Land Question in Palestine, 1917–1939*. Chapel Hill: University of North Carolina Press, 1984.

Steinmo, Sven. *Taxation and Democracy: Swedish, British, and American Approaches to Financing the Modern State*. New Haven: Yale University Press, 1996.

Sterling, Joyce S., and Wilbert E. Moore. "Weber's Analysis of Legal Rationalization: A Critique and Constructive Modification." *Sociological Forum* 2 (1987): 67–89.

Stern, Yosef. *Mas Hakhnasah: Le-Halakhah ule-Ma'aseh*. Tel Aviv: Yavneh, 1949.

Sternhell, Zeev. *The Founding Myths of Israel: Nationalism, Socialism, and the Making of the Jewish State*. Translated by David Maisel. Princeton: Princeton University Press, 1999.

Stevens, Robert B. *Law and Politics: The House of Lords as a Judicial Body, 1800–1976*. Chapel Hill: University of North Carolina Press, 1978.

Stewart, Miranda. "Global Trajectories of Tax Reform: The Discourse of Tax Reform in Developing and Transition Countries." *Harvard International Law Journal* 44 (2003): 139–90.

Stock, Ernest. *Partners and Pursestrings: A History of the United Israel Appeal*. Lanham: University Press of America, 1987.

Stow, Kenneth R. *Taxation, Community and State: The Jews and the Fiscal Foundations of the Early Modern Papal State*. Stuttgart: Anton Hiersemann, 1982.

Strasman, Gavriel. *'Otey ha-Glimah: Toldot 'Arikhat ha-Din be-Erets Yisrael*. Tel Aviv: Lishkat 'Orkhey ha-Din, 1984.

Strauss, Fritz Hermann. *The ABC of Income Tax in Palestine*. Jerusalem: Achiasaf, 1941.

Sugarman, David. "Who Colonized Whom? Historical Reflections on the Intersection between Law, Lawyers and Accountants." In *Professional Competition and Professional Power: Lawyers, Accountants and the Social Construction of Markets*, edited by Yves Dezalay and David Sugarman. London: Routledge, 1995, 226–37.

Sunstein, Cass R. "Social Norms and Social Roles." *Columbia Law Review* 96 (1996): 903–68.

Talpir, Gabriel. "Avraham Mandel." *Gazit: Yarhon le-Omanut ve-Sifrut* 27:9–12 (1970/71): 79–80.

Tax Justice Network. Homepage. www.taxjustice.net/.

Taylor, Natalie. "Understanding Taxpayer Attitudes through Understanding Taxpayer Identities." In *Taxing Democracy: Understanding Tax Avoidance and Evasion*, edited by Valerie A. Braithwaite. Aldershot: Ashgate, 2003, 71–92.

Thorndike, Joseph J. *Their Fair Share: Taxing the Rich in the Age of FDR*. Washington, DC: Urban Institute Press, 2013.

Thuronyi, Victor, ed. *Tax Law Design and Drafting*. Washington, DC: IMF, 1996.

Thuronyi, Victor, and Frans Vanistendael. "Regulation of Tax Professionals." In vol. 1 of *Tax Law Design and Drafting*, edited by Victor Thuronyi. Washington, DC: IMF, 1996, 135–63.

Tidhar, David. *Entsiklopedyah le-Halutsey ha-Yishuv u-Vonav: Dmuyot u-Tmunot*. Tel Aviv: Sifriyat Rishonim, 1950.

Tiley, John. "Judicial Anti-Avoidance Doctrines: The U.S. Alternatives." *British Tax Review*, 1987, 180–97.

Tilly, Charles. *Coercion, Capital and European States, AD 990–1992*. Rev. edn. Cambridge, MA: Blackwell, 1992.

Toledano, Ehud R. "The Emergence of Ottoman-Local Elites (1700–1900): A Framework for Research." In *Middle Eastern Politics and Ideas: A History from Within*, edited by Ilan Pappé and Moshe Ma'oz. London: I. B. Tauris, 1997, 145–62.

Tomlins, Christopher. "Framing the Field of Law's Disciplinary Encounters: A Historical Narrative." *Law and Society Review* 34 (2000): 911–72.

Torgler, Benno. *Tax Compliance and Tax Morale: A Theoretical and Empirical Analysis*. Cheltenham: Edward Elgar, 2007.

Torgler, Benno. "Tax Morale in Transition Countries." *Post-Communist Economies* 15 (2003): 357–81.

[US Information Service]. *Investment in Progress: Fifteen Years of Creative U.S. Assistance to Israel through Grants-in-Aid, Loans, Technical Assistance, and the Food-for-Peace Program*. Tel Aviv: US Information Service and the Israel Ministry of Finance, [1965].

[United States Operations Mission to Israel]. *Five Years of Mutual Endeavor: USOM-Israel*. Tel Aviv: Haaretz Press, 1956.

Van den Boogert, Maurits H. *The Capitulations and the Ottoman Legal System: Qadis, Consuls and Beratlıs in the 18th Century*. Leiden: Brill, 2005.

Vasunia, Phiroze. *The Classics and Colonial India*. Oxford: Oxford University Press, 2013.

Viteles, Harry. *The Evolution of the Co-Operative Movement*. Vol. 1 of *A History of the Co-Operative Movement in Israel: A Sourcebook*. London: Vallentine, Mitchell, 1966.

Wasserstein, Bernard. *The British in Palestine: The Mandatory Government and Arab-Jewish Conflict, 1917–1929*. 2nd edn. Oxford: Blackwell, 1991.

Watenpaugh, Keith David. *Being Modern in the Middle East: Revolution, Nationalism, Colonialism, and the Arab Middle Class*. Princeton: Princeton University Press, 2006.

Webber, Carolyn, and Aaron Wildavsky. *A History of Taxation and Expenditure in the Western World*. New York: Simon and Schuster, 1986.

Weber, Max. *Economy and Society*. Edited by Guenther Roth and Claus Wittich. New York: Bedminster Press, 1968.

Wein, Avraham. "Ha-Irgun ha-Otonomi shel Yehudey Polin: Mi-Kehilah Masortit le-Va'ad Dati." In vol. 1 of *Kiyum va-Shever: Yehudey Polin le-Doroteyhem*, edited by Israel Bartal and Israel Gutman. Jerusalem: Merkaz Zalman Shazar, 1997, 49–57.

Weisbach, David A. "Formalism in the Tax Law." *University of Chicago Law Review* 66 (1999): 860–86.

Weiss, Aharon. "Le-Darkam shel ha-Yudenratim bi-Drom Mizrah Polin." *Yalkut Moreshet le-Heker ha-Sho'ah veha-Antishemiyut* 15 (1972): 59–122.

Wheatcroft, G. S. A. "The Attitude of the Legislature and the Courts to Tax Avoidance." *Modern Law Review* 18 (1955): 209–30.

Wilkenfeld, Harold C. *Taxes and People in Israel*. Cambridge, MA: Harvard University Press, 1973.

Witkon, Alfred. "Darkhey ha-Parshanut bi-T'hum Diney ha-Misim." In *Sefer Loewenberg*, edited by D. Friedmann and Y. Shiloah. Tel Aviv: Bursi, 1987/88, 13–22.

Witkon, Alfred. *Diney Misim: Misey Hakhnasah, 'Izavon ve-Shevah*. With Yaakov Neeman. 4th edn. Jerusalem: Schocken, 1969.

Witkon, Alfred. "Ha-Mishpat be-Erets Mitpatahat." In *Sefer Yovel le-Pinhas Rosen*, edited by Haim Cohn. Jerusalem: Mif'al ha-Shikhpul, 1962, 66–85.

Witte, John F. *The Politics and Development of the Federal Income Tax*. Madison: University of Wisconsin Press, 1985.

Yehudah, Yehoshua Avraham. *Sefer 'Avodat Masa: Saloniki 1846*. Salonika: Saadi ha-Levi Ashkenazi, 1846; repr., Jerusalem: Muze'on le-Misim, 1964.

Yellin, Shlomo, trans. *Sefer ha-Hukim le-Ma'aser Pri ha-Adamah ha-Nahug be-Artsot Turkiyah*. Jerusalem: Lunz, 1904/05.

Yitshaki Kurtzweil, Alma, ed. *Ha-Mekhes be-Yisrael: Min he-'Avar, Derekh ha-Hoveh, 'Im ha-Panim le-'Atid 1870–2010*. Jerusalem: Keter, 2011.

Yitzhaki, Shlomo. "Cost-Benefit Analysis of Presumptive Taxation." *FinanzArchiv / Public Finance Analysis* 63 (2007): 311–26.

Yitzhaki, Shlomo. "A Note on Income Tax Evasion: A Theoretical Analysis." *Journal of Public Economics* 3 (1974): 201–2.

Yitzhaki, Shlomo. "Reformat ha-Mas 1975." In *Reformot Mas,* edited by David Gliksberg. Jerusalem: Ha-Makhon le-Mehkarey Hakikah, 2005, 195–235.

Yonay, Yuval P. *The Struggle over the Soul of Economics: Institutionalist and Neoclassical Economists in America between the Wars.* Princeton: Princeton University Press, 1998.

Yoran, Aharon. "Forty Years of Tax Law in Israel." *Israel Law Review* 24 (1990): 738–85.

Yoran, Aharon. "'Sivug Shoneh' shel 'Iskah le-Tsorekh Mas u-Mikumah ha-Nakhon shel 'ha-'Iskah ha-Melakhutit'." *Mishpatim* 20 (1989/90): 43–71.

Yoran, Aharon. "Taxation of Small Firms in Israel." *Israel Law Review* 8 (1973): 312–16.

Yoran, Aharon, and Yehezkel Flumin. *Tikhnun Mas be-Hayey ha-'Esek.* Jerusalem: Ha-Dfus ha-Akademi, 1973.

Young, George. *Corps de Droit Ottoman.* Oxford: Clarendon Press, 1905–06.

Yun-Casalilla, Bartolomé, and Patrick K. O'Brien with Francisco Comín Comín, eds. *The Rise of Fiscal States: A Global History, 1500–1914.* Cambridge: Cambridge University Press, 2012.

Zelenak, Lawrence. "The Great American Tax Novel." *Michigan Law Review* 110 (2012): 969–84.

Zelenak, Lawrence. *Learning to Love Form 1040: Two Cheers for the Return-Based Mass Income Tax.* Chicago: University of Chicago Press, 2013.

Zer-Gutman, Limor. "Effects of the Acceleration in the Number of Lawyers in Israel." *International Journal of the Legal Profession* 19 (2012): 247–63.

Ziv, Neta. "Combining Professionalism, Nation Building and Public Service: The Professional Project of the Israeli Bar 1928–2002." *Fordham Law Review* 71 (2003): 1621–67.

Ziv, Neta. "Credit Cooperatives in Early Israeli Statehood: Financial Institutions and Social Transformation." *Theoretical Inquiries in Law* 11 (2010): 209–46.

Ziv, Neta. *Mi Yishmor 'al Shomrey ha-Mishpat?: 'Orkhey Din be-Yisrael beyn Medinah, Shuk ve-Hevrah Ezrahit.* Tel Aviv: Ha-Kibbutz ha-Me'uhad, 2015.

Zucman, Gabriel. *The Hidden Wealth of Nations: The Scourge of Tax Havens.* Translated by Teresa Lavender Fagan. Chicago: University of Chicago Press, 2015.

Index